Founding Fictions

Founding Fictions

JENNIFER R. MERCIECA

THE UNIVERSITY OF ALABAMA PRESS
Tuscaloosa

Hardcover edition published 2010.
Paperback edition published 2012.
eBook edition published 2010.

Typeface: Bembo

Cover design: Todd Lape/Lape Designs

∞

The paper on which this book is printed meets the minimum requirements of American National Standard for Information Science–Permanence of Paper for Printed Library Materials, ANSI Z39.48-1984.

Paperback ISBN: 978-0-8173-5734-4

A previous edition of this book has been catalogued by the Library of Congress as follows:

Library of Congress Cataloging-in-Publication Data
Mercieca, Jennifer R.
Founding fictions / Jennifer R. Mercieca.
p. cm. — (Rhetoric, culture, and social critique)
Includes bibliographical references and index.
ISBN 978-0-8173-1690-7 (cloth : alk. paper) — ISBN 978-0-8173-8355-8 1. United States—Politics and government—To 1775. 2. United States—Politics and government—1775–1783. 3. United States—Politics and government—1783–1865. 4. Citizenship—United States—History—18th century. 5. Citizenship—United States—History—19th century. 6. Political culture—United States—History—18th century. 7. Political culture—United States—History—19th century. 8. Political stability—United States—History. 9. Political participation—United States—History. 10. Democracy—United States—History. I. Title.
E302.1.M47 2010
973.2—dc22

2009032189

For my mother, whose unfailing love gave me the confidence to try.

Viva Lir-Rebbieħ!

(Hail to the Victor!)

Malo periculosam libertatem quam quietam servitutem [I prefer the tumult of liberty to the quiet of servitude]

—Thomas Jefferson to James Madison, January 30, 1787

Consistency, is not, I know a trait in democracy! When it suits there [*sic*] purpose—when unanswerable arguments are opposed to democrats, then our ears are stunned with the *people,* the *sovereign people* demand it—the *public* will is in its favor—& we must bow submissive. But these same men, when they pursue measures to which they conceive the *public mind* is opposed, then tell us, that the people are *uninformed*—they are a *rabble incapable of judging*—& good legislatures will not consult them.

—New Hampshire senator William Plumer, 1803

Your question is: why am I so interested in politics? But if I were to answer you very simply, I would say this: why shouldn't I be interested? That is to say, what blindness, what deafness, what density of ideology would have to weigh me down to prevent me from being interested in what is probably the most crucial subject to our existence, that is to say the society in which we live, the economic relations within which it functions, and the system of power which defines the regular forms and the regular permissions and prohibitions of our conduct. . . . So instead of asking me, you should ask someone who is not interested in politics and then your question would be well-founded, and you would have the right to say 'Why, damn it, are you not interested?'

—Michel Foucault, 1971

Contents

Acknowledgments

In the spring of 1998, I was in a graduate seminar on Political Communication at the University of Illinois taught by the late David Swanson. We had been reading essay after essay chronicling escalating voter apathy, civic disengagement, and citizen withdrawal from American politics, and I recall throwing down the pen with which I had been taking notes in frustration and blurting out, "What the hell are we doing here then?" Professor Swanson—not used to such indecorous outbursts, even from me—generously gave a thoughtful answer to allay my frustration: we are here because democracy matters; we are here because people *do* vote (sometimes, especially when there is a war or a bad economy); we are here, examining the research on apathy and disengagement, because as scholars of political communication we need to understand the rhetorical context within which our messages operate. Unsatisfied with any of these answers, I decided I needed to know more about American democracy. I was fortunate that about this time Illinois welcomed two new, extremely talented professors: Cara Finnegan and Stephen Hartnett. Professors Finnegan and Hartnett taught courses about rhetoric, the public sphere, and American history, which helped me to think more carefully about the questions of active citizenship. Professor Finnegan taught me how to find my argument, even though she was forced to write "Your argument appears to be in your head and not on the paper" on far too many of my seminar papers. Professor Hartnett taught me both how to write and to look to our shared history for answers to today's questions. It was all there, he assured us in our seminars; we just needed to know how to tell good stories about the past to make sense of where we are today. I owe a large debt of gratitude to Professors Swanson, Finnegan, and Hartnett, each of whom acted as a generous mentor, critic, scholar, and teacher. I hope that Cara and Stephen will each see what they taught me reflected back to them: I hope that Cara will find my argument right there on the page where it belongs and that Stephen will find that I've told my stories as vibrantly as I could—even though he and I both know that my prose is no match for his own eloquence. I'm sure that David Swanson would have found that this book says exactly what he had expected that it would.

Fortuna smiled upon me in the summer of 2000 when I was selected to attend the National Communication Association's Doctoral Honors Seminar at Northwestern University, which was ably and thoughtfully led by Celeste Condit, Robert Ivie, and James Arnt Aune. The conversations we had over the course of the seminar reinforced my belief that the questions of active citizenship and democracy needed to be grounded in both political theory and historical analysis. Professor Aune responded to my paper on the emergence of the norm of *eunomia* (good order) in ancient Greece with thought-provoking questions—to which I made feeble answers—giving the whole exchange the appearance of a debate rather than what it should have been, a brilliant professor giving advice to a (silent!) student. Thankfully, Jim was too generous to hold my (nervous, unintended) petulance against me and he took an interest in my work, reading every draft of every seminar paper, essay, and book chapter I've written for almost a decade. Meeting Jim that summer was a fortunate bit of academic serendipity: his unwavering support is the reason that I did not give up on this project when rejections made success seem impossible. I am constantly amazed at Jim's ability to deal patiently, gently, and generously with people and ideas. Jim is a prince among academics, and I am lucky to call him my friend, colleague, and mentor.

My colleagues in the Department of Communication at Texas A&M University—past and present—have nurtured both me and this project with their thoughtful advice, helpful criticism, and generous kindness. I know how lucky I am to work with unfailingly smart, kind, and reasonable people who care as much for ideas and research as they do for community service and good teaching. This project in particular has benefited from the helpful advice of Jim Aune, Leroy Dorsey, Rick Street, Linda Putnam, Barbara Scharf, Christopher Swift, and Antonio La Pastina, all of whom gave me their time, criticism, and wisdom. Vanessa Beasley, Jim Jasinski, John Murphy, and John Sloop deserve a special thank-you for being the best colleagues-from-a-distance that anyone has ever had. I had no reasonable expectation of your help and kindness, which makes the fact that you each gave me yours so willingly and generously all the more exceptional. Stirling Newberry, Anthony Mora, and Ted George generously took time away from their own writing projects to help me with mine, and this project owes a specific debt of gratitude to each of them. The folks at The

University of Alabama Press have been unfailingly patient as I struggled to learn how to write a book. In their hands my project received the kind of generous and thorough criticism that is rare even in academe. The anonymous reviewers' advice helped me to clarify my ideas and strengthen my argument; because of their help, *Founding Fictions* is much smarter than I could have made it on my own.

The Friday Happy Hours group at Texas A&M, especially Tracy Hammond, Jenny Irish, Miladin Radovic, Courtney Schumacher, and David Kalil, made life in Bryan–College Station significantly more fun. My Illinois grad school peeps—Ted Bailey, Jennifer Jones, Liz Perea, Jack Bratich, Donovan Conley, Trevor Potts, and Jeremy Packer—were some of my best teachers. BFFs Lisa Meid, Courtney Ballard McKay, Vanessa Cazzell, Sandy Dennington, Grace Gualco, and Michele Patton have shared their lives with me and in so doing have made mine much more pleasant. Janet Brehe Johnson was the first to notice that I might have a talent for rhetoric; her encouraging me to join her forensics team changed my life and is the reason why I ended up where I am today. My genius brother Victor Mercieca has constantly imagined that I could do grander things with my life and has always been willing to send his grateful sister much-needed gift certificates to buy books, without which this project might have never come to fruition. My amazing Auntie Carm would give me anything and everything in her power, and I know just how lucky I am to have her love. Finally, my loving thanks are due to my parents, Victor and Diane Mercieca, who gave me more love, more opportunities, and more support than anyone justly deserves. There are no words to express the immeasurable impact that their love and kindness have had on making me who I am today.

Portions of chapter 5 originally appeared in *Rhetoric and Public Affairs,* vol. 10, no. 1, and vol. 11, no. 3, published by Michigan State University Press, and appear here with their permission. I was fortunate to receive financial support for this project from the University of Illinois's Department of Speech Communication (2001 Summer Research Stipend), the Melbern G. Glasscock Center for Humanities Research (2003 Communication and 2008 American Studies Fellowships), Texas A&M University College of Liberal Arts (2006 Research Fellowship), and Texas A&M University (2007 Scholarly and Creative Activities Fellowship).

Founding Fictions

Introduction

Aristotle once said that the "good citizen must have the knowledge and the ability both to be ruled and to rule." He did not believe a citizen was a mere member of a state, but rather that the state itself was "a kind of partnership" in which citizens worked together to promote "the security of their community" and defend "the constitution." Citizen-partners acted "with absolute justice" only when they governed for "the common advantage" rather than for their personal advantage.[1] To be a citizen, then, was to be an officer of the government who was obligated and empowered to defend the community and the constitution. The defining characteristic of the citizen in Aristotle's view—often labeled republican or communitarian by citizenship scholars—is that citizens have the power to act. Citizens would act by being governed, by governing, by defending the constitution, and by promoting the common good. Aristotle's description of the active citizen-partner has much in common with the view of the republican citizen that emerged among American radicals between 1764 and 1776. However, by 1787 some Americans no longer believed that citizens were capable of acting to defend the Constitution or to promote the common good, and they would design a republican government in which citizens would govern less and be governed more. By 1828, though many still believed that citizens could not be trusted to act with absolute justice, and while there were few changes made to the Constitution, Jacksonians would call America's republican government a democracy. The power of American citizens to act is therefore ambiguous: Are they partners of the state obligated and empowered to act, or not? The history of the political discourse that invented, defined, and delimited the American citizen's ability to act and to govern has not been thoroughly understood; *Founding Fictions* tells that story.

Scholars across disciplines have carefully studied the important and complex questions of American democratic citizenship.[2] American citizenship has been studied most notably by Jacksonian-era scholars such as Alexis de Tocqueville, Progressive Era scholars such as John Dewey and Walter Lippmann, post–World War II scholars such as Hannah Arendt, and late-twentieth-century scholars such as Benjamin Barber, Carole Pateman, and Robert Putnam. If we read this scholarship as a narrative of American citizenship, we learn that America once enjoyed a vibrant and active (white, male, landed property owner) citizenry that has steadily declined into apathy and withdrawal from the political process. This "decline thesis" has been challenged most notably by Michael Schudson and Rogers Smith, both of whom argue that de Tocqueville's original analysis was too optimistic and therefore that we have not really witnessed a decline in participation, even though with an average voter turnout of 48 percent America ranks 114th out of the 140 nations in the world that hold free elections.[3] Other scholars, such as Robert Asen and Ernesto Laclau, have rejected the decline thesis by arguing that the traditional markers of citizenship—voting, participating in political parties, and membership in civic organizations, for example—are not the best criteria by which to judge citizenship; these scholars have asked us to view citizenship as "discursive action" based primarily upon how people act together outside the constitutional order. A group of rhetorical scholars such as Vanessa Beasley, Leroy Dorsey, Alisse Portnoy, and Susan Zaeske has sidestepped the question of decline by examining America's political rhetoric both for how "American" has been constructed within elite discourses and for how those excluded from traditional citizenship rights have nonetheless found ways to participate in the public sphere. Still other scholars, such as Michael Hardt, Antonio Negri, and Jacques Rancière, have asked scholars to approach the question of citizenship from a global perspective and have sought to change the focus from a scholar's lament that citizens do not consistently participate to a celebration of the carnivalesque, sporadic participations of the multitude.

Founding Fictions neither wholly embraces the Tocquevillian optimism of the rise of Jacksonian democracy nor wholly rejects Putnam's decline thesis; rather, it offers a different story of American citizenship. By retelling the stories that Americans told themselves about citizenship between 1764 and 1845, *Founding Fictions* describes how our construction of American citizenship is much more conflicted, paradoxical, and complex than either de Tocqueville's *Democracy in America* or Putnam's *Bowling Alone* would suggest.[4] Above all, *Founding Fictions* highlights an important contradiction in American political theory and practice: national stability and active citizen participation are fundamentally at odds. In making this argument, *Founding Fictions* separates the question of who counts as a citizen from how citizens are imagined to act within the institutional structures of the American political system—rather than asking who can participate, *Founding Fictions* asks what actions are possible by whoever "the people" are thought to be. This orientation allows me to develop the concept of a "political fiction," trace the development of America's republican and democratic political fictions, and analyze how these fictions positioned American citizens as romantic heroes, tragic victims, and ironic partisans. From this analysis it becomes clear that Aristotle's active citizenship is only possible when Americans are imagined as romantic heroes and that the view of Americans as tragic victims and ironic partisans all but eclipsed the view of Americans as romantic heroes in America's democratic political fiction. Quite simply, this book is a sustained discussion of how the founders' republican fiction turned into America's democratic fiction and how these fictions portrayed American citizens.[5] While much has been written about the possibilities of American citizenship, how Americans have used their republican and democratic fictions to imagine citizen participation is unclear. This is a regrettable lacuna, because the founding generation crafted our republican fiction and the second generation crafted our democratic fiction in response to specific constraints; our failure to understand the relationships between these fictions and these contexts impinges upon our ability to assess democracy today.

A Brief Note on Rhetorical History

We find attempts to influence others through symbols—that is, rhetoric—in places where we are unaccustomed to look for it (in political theory, for example), and we would do well to examine how these instances of rhetoric have informed how we understand American citizenship. Rhetorical scholars will recognize this argument from Kenneth Burke's *Rhetoric of Motives,* and indeed, *Founding Fictions*' use of the term "rhetoric" has much in common with Burke, who viewed it as "the use of words by human agents to form attitudes or to induce actions in other human agents."[6] The crucial aspect of this view of rhetoric is that it is a kind of action—we do things with rhetoric, and rhetoric, in turn, does things to us. Rhetoric helps us to constitute, position, describe, frame, and delimit political communities and the people who inhabit them in particular ways; indeed, this is one of rhetoric's most important functions.[7] *Founding Fictions* draws from and synthesizes the work of scholars such as Michel Foucault, Hayden White, and Kenneth Burke, among others, in an approach that can best be described as a meta-rhetorical history. In other words, it examines how the structural elements within texts—the arguments, tropes, and figures—contributed to building the political fictions that permeated and dominated the contexts of which they were a part.[8] Or, as Kathleen Turner has argued, whereas "rhetorical criticism seeks to understand the message in context, rhetorical history seeks to understand the context through messages that reflect and construct that context."[9] Specifically, *Founding Fictions* uses this meta-rhetorical historical approach to analyze the construction of American citizenship, and in so doing it takes our obligation to the history of ideas seriously and views criticism as ripe with the potential for political transformation.

Taking our obligations to the history of ideas and to active criticism seriously has led me to a humbly ironic and contextual approach to rhetorical history.[10] Stephen J. Hartnett has described "humble irony" as an approach to rhetorical history that "recognizes that our present is indeed indebted to the past our forebears created and lived and that this past was structured by cultural fictions that, although perhaps strange to us, must surely have been enabling in some way for them."[11] In other words, rhetorical discourse must be—in fact, can only be—understood by placing it within the complex web of dominant ideas and events in its immediate historical context. Judging any text outside its immediate context—the prevailing ideas in circulation, the material conditions of its production and dissemination, the situational constraints that motivated its purpose—has two negative consequences: first, ignoring context prevents modern scholars from understanding how, why, and to what effect historical discourses were composed and circulated; second, ignoring context robs those who came before us of their own history and attempts to remake the world in our own image—it is the epitome of academic hubris. Therefore, the recognition of our obligation to the history of ideas requires that rhetorical scholarship pay close attention to context and that it re-create historical contexts with humble irony.

In other words, *Founding Fictions*' method of rhetorical history is based upon a kind of *scholarship as caretaker:* scholars are caretakers of ideas past, present, and future, and as such we have an obligation to represent those ideas as accurately as possible and to meet the authors of those ideas on their own ground.[12] Yet, while *Founding Fictions* recognizes that scholars are caretakers of ideas, we should not accept uncritically the ideas that have come before us. The critical interrogation of political ideas is one of the most important tasks of citizenship, and as such, *Founding Fictions* hopes to practice criticism as political action.

Writing any book—Hayden White would say especially writing history—is a poetic act. I have made certain choices in the conceptualization, research, and presentation of this study of American citizenship, and I am responsible for those choices.[13] I began with a study of political theory, American history, and the biographies of the major figures and their friends and colleagues—in this phase of my research I found it illuminating to study the authors that the founders were known to have read and studied—authors as diverse as the ancient Greek democrats, Roman republicans, Renaissance humanists, British Whigs, French physiocrats, and Scottish moral philosophers. Once I had familiarized myself with the secondary literature, I examined the published and unpublished papers of the first two generations in addition to the newspapers, public and private correspondence, literature, and journals of their era. Once I had studied the archival materials I then turned my attention to the political deliberations and the resulting public pronouncements of deliberative bodies. This methodology allowed me to gauge how the first two generations' private reflections and study of political theory and history and the private negotiations and attempts to persuade friends and colleagues recorded in journals and correspondence resulted in the public discourse found in debates, pronouncements, and policies.[14] I have moved back and forth from texts to contexts and back again, from political theory to history and back again; I have always approached my study of our past with a careful eye to detail. My recovery, description, and explanation of how the first two generations of Americans understood their government culminates in an analysis of the narratives that Americans created to support those views and of how those narratives portrayed citizens. In so doing, this analysis stands apart from more traditional conceptual change histories, even as it complements those studies.[15]

I have endeavored to treat each character in my story fairly, although I must confess that the difficulties of impartiality are great. There are always favorite people and ideas, and it is nearly impossible to prevent a deep involvement with the partisanship of the eighteenth and nineteenth centuries, for we are indeed still fighting their fights. My biases—where they are apparent—are toward transparent public argument and active citizen participation, even at the expense of stability. The reader will note that many of the same characters reappear in my story in different contexts—Thomas Jefferson seems to be everywhere at once, for example; this is largely because the founding fathers were leaders in every facet of society and enjoyed extraordinarily long political careers.[16] I also want to point out that the metaphor of movement provides a subtext for this discussion of American citizenship. Sometimes the movement was linear—as with Americans rejecting the monarchical fiction and crafting the republican fiction between 1764 and 1776.[17] At other times the movement was circular—as with Americans returning to our nation's founding as we repeatedly ask ourselves how to prevent tyranny and defend liberty. I think that the metaphor of movement is apropos because the development of American political theory was both linear and circular. Sometimes the discussions of republicanism and democracy led to new ways of thinking about the relationship between the people and the government, and sometimes Americans reverted back to old truisms and did not question received wisdom. The biggest tragedy is that in the end Americans forgot that we invented our political fictions in the first place and we stopped debating their meaning all together. This forgetting, yet another form of movement, is why I believe it is imperative that we revisit our founding fictions.

Outline of the Text

Chapter 1, "'Republicanism was an indefinite term': Political Fictions as Critical Tools for Citizenship," may be of particular interest to scholars of American political theory and American political discourse. I lead the reader through an overview of my arguments in the subsequent chapters by answering seven questions: Why does *Founding Fictions* use an interdisciplinary approach to study American citizenship? Why did the founders fear democracy? How did the founders define republicanism? What were the features of republican constitutions? What are political fictions? What does it mean to say that Americans were cast as romantic heroes, tragic victims, and ironic partisans? And finally, how do we analyze political fictions? Answering these questions at the beginning of the book allows me to bracket the scholarly business of my argument from the historical narratives I tell, which I hope will make the book useful and accessible to both scholars and citizens.

Chapter 2, "'The Revolution was in the minds of the people': Citizens as Romantic Heroes, 1764–1776," demonstrates how the rhetorical situation leading up to the American Revolution led to the destruction of the monarchical fiction and the creation of the republican fiction. I focus on the rhetorical moves made in three phases of the conflict between Britain and its North American colonies: the reaffirming phase, in which Americans demanded their rights as British subjects; the challenging phase, in which Americans positioned themselves as patriot subjects; and the destroying phase, in which Americans declared themselves patriot citizens who would act to defend the rights and liberties of all. The culmination of this shift from subjects to citizens was to imagine Americans as romantic heroes who would act for the common good and protect liberty.

Chapter 3, "'The American Constitution is that little *article* of HOPE, left at the bottom of *Pandora's* box of evils': Citizens as Tragic Victims, 1783–1789," demonstrates how the rhetorical situation leading up to the ratification of the Constitution led to a major shift in the republican fiction and the portrayal of citizens as childlike or as complicit victims of corruption. I ask why the people would willingly consent to a new republican fiction that minimized their power, and find that structural issues such as who was allowed to vote, whether or not state delegates voted consistent with their constituents' wishes, and whether or not there was voter fraud and intimidation raised serious questions about the legitimacy of the 1,648 votes cast in the thirteen state conventions during the ratification process. Furthermore, James Madison's public relations campaign allowed Federalists to rely upon arguments by prestige and authority and to take over their state conventions. Yet, unlike Anti-Federalists, Federalists offered a specific plan to solve the problems of the Republic, which may have made their arguments more appealing. The effect of this change in America's republican fiction was to offer the Americans who found romantic citizenship too idealistic, chaotic, and egalitarian another legitimate interpretation of citizenship and to limit how the citizen was imagined to act within the American government.

Chapter 4, "'Who would not have been willing to have died such a death?' Citizens as Reified Patriot Heroes, July 4, 1826," demonstrates how romantic and tragic citizenship could be conflated in the public discourse of the second generation. When Americans learned of the deaths of John Adams and Thomas Jefferson on the fiftieth anniversary of the Declaration of Independence, they found that they were confronted with a hermeneutical choice: did the deaths represent a curse or a blessing? Americans of the second generation would choose to believe that the deaths of the founders were a blessing, and they would reconstitute the founders and themselves as romantic patriot heroes. Contrary to history, when Americans retold themselves the story of Adams's and Jefferson's republicanism they conflated their very different views of government into one and clothed the nation's republican political fiction in the divine-right narrative of the old monarchical fiction. The story of how Americans responded to the deaths of Adams and Jefferson highlights the transition between the founding generation and the second generation, between the republican and democratic fictions, and highlights the conflation of romantic and tragic views of citizenship. The effect of the conflation of romantic and tragic citizenship was to turn Americans into reified romantic heroes—they claimed the appearance of patriotism but not the substance—and to set the stage for the rise of the democratic fiction.

Chapter 5, "'I will not look up to the weather-cock of popularity, to see which way the gale is blowing': Citizens as Ironic Partisans, 1816–1845," demonstrates how the shift from republican to democratic representation, the shift from republican to democratic campaigning, and the shift in how Americans talked about political theory characterized the rise of America's new democratic fiction. The increase in the number of eligible voters after the War of 1812, the public's negative response to the Compensation Act of 1816, the "corrupt bargain" and the House's selection of John Quincy Adams for president in 1824, Andrew Jackson's four-year presidential campaign and triumphant victory in 1828, the people's anti-removal petition campaign of 1830, and the rise in abolitionist petitions after 1835 led to an ambiguously democratic political fiction. The people earnestly used the democratic fiction in their attempts to control the government, and the political elite ironically used the democratic fiction to retain stability and control. The effect of the rise of the democratic fiction was to turn romantic and tragic citizens into ironic partisans: the people could act to control the government, but only through the mechanisms of the party system.

In the conclusion I briefly retell *Founding Fictions*' narrative, highlighting how America's political fiction and its view of citizenship evolved between 1764 and 1845 and describing how romantic heroes, tragic victims, and ironic partisans would answer the question "What does it mean to be a good citizen?" I also argue for the benefits of the analysis of political theory as political fiction, and link *Founding Fictions*' arguments to previous and current research on American citizenship and deliberative democracy.

1

"Republicanism was an indefinite term"

Political Fictions as Critical Tools for Citizenship

Almost five years after the September 11, 2001, attacks on New York City and Washington, D.C., President George W. Bush discussed the relationship between terrorism and democracy in his weekly radio address: "Terrorists and their sponsors recognize that the Middle East is at a pivotal moment in its history. Freedom has brought hope to millions, and it's helped foster the development of young democracies from Baghdad to Beirut. Yet these young democracies are still fragile, and the forces of terror are seeking to stop liberty's advance and steer newly free nations to the path of radicalism. The terrorists fear the rise of democracy because they know what it means for the future of their hateful ideology."[1] Note the narrative explicit in the president's address: when freedom brings hope to millions, liberty will advance and democracy will rise to defeat radicalism and hateful ideology. Note also who or what has the power of action in this narrative: freedom brings hope; liberty advances; democracy rises; and terrorists recognize, seek, steer, fear, know, and hate. Meanwhile, the millions of newly hopeful citizens—those who should, according to President Bush's logic, now be capable of advancing liberty—are merely passive receivers of freedom's hope and incapable of acting to defend their own democracy. Thus rendered inactive victims of terror, the president's democratic citizens must rely upon the benevolence of powerful others or suffer the consequences of radicalism and ideology.[2]

This passage from President Bush's radio address highlights several important aspects of how we talk about the relationship between democracy and citizenship: note which words are used as "god terms"—as unquestionably good things—freedom, hope, liberty, and democracy; note also which are used as "devil terms"—as unquestionably bad things—radicalism, ideology, and terrorism.[3] The terms President Bush singles out as positive or negative take on a central role in his narrative; indeed, because they are so important, we should hazard war and death to preserve or prevent them. Once again citizens are left out, are rendered passive and inactive by the president's failure to characterize them in either god or devil terms. Though ignored and underestimated, President Bush's democratic citizens still motivate his avowed purpose: they are the reason why we need to act to protect freedom and liberty and stop terrorism. Crucial, yet negligible; at the center, but on the margins of power; the president's democratic citizens occupy a fragile liminal space somewhere between liberty and radicalism.[4]

I do not mean to suggest that there was something unique about this particular radio address; indeed, President Bush's choice of words was largely unremarkable for his era. His use of words like "democracy" and "liberty" seems so ordinary, so commonplace, so much in line with the well-known and currently accepted vocabulary of American political discourse that it is natural and uncontroversial. In fact, the United States has not had a legitimate politician argue against democracy—and for, say, aristocracy or monarchy—for generations. It therefore would have sounded rather odd for the president to have defined and defended his view of democracy at all, for whom would he be arguing with? With any memory of the once vibrant debates over its meaning lost, it simply did not occur to him or, probably, to his audience, that the merits of democracy could be debated. In current political discourse, only terrorists argue against democracy, never Americans.

Such was not always the case. In 1805, Federalist Fisher Ames believed that "in democracies the people are the depositories of political power," but that it was "impossible they should exercise it themselves." Indeed, said Ames, "we know from history . . . that every democracy, in the very infancy of its vicious and troubled life, is delivered bound hand and foot into the keeping of ambitious demagogues." And, therefore, that "our sages in the great Convention . . . intended our government should be a *republic,* which differs more widely from a democracy than a democracy from a despotism."[5] "Democracy" and the "demagogues" who flattered the people into believing they had more power than they actually did were devil terms in Ames's 1805 essay; therefore Ames would have certainly found President Bush's use of "democracy" in his 2006 radio address puzzling, if not downright treasonous. Yet, despite the manifest differences in how Bush and Ames valued the word "democracy" itself, there is a fundamental similarity between the two views: neither Bush nor Ames believed that citizens had the power to act to defend their own freedom and liberty, and both argued that benevolent and powerful others must act on citizens' behalf. Therefore, while current political discourse has embraced the term "democracy" as an unquestionable positive good that should, and must, be fought for, the way that some of America's political elite view the capability of democratic citizens to act within the government has not changed dramatically in the last two hundred years.

Yet it is striking that President Bush portrayed democratic citizens as incapable and passive victims, for what is a democracy if not a political community characterized by citizens who capably and actively defend their own freedom and liberty? Political theorists such as Aristotle, John Dewey, Benjamin Barber, Robert Dahl, and Hannah Arendt have argued that the defining characteristic of democratic citizens is that they are *active.*[6] Yet, the liminal space within which President Bush's democratic citizens reside is one in which action is impossible—quite simply, citizens are not empowered to act in this narrative of democracy. The president's radio address therefore highlights a conundrum: What do Americans mean when they call their government a democracy? As Ames argued, the founding generation believed that they had created a republic, not a democracy; does this difference in terminology have any meaning for Americans today? And, if the differences between republicanism and democracy are meaningful, what can the founders' debates over republicanism and democracy teach us about how the average citizen is able to act in the American government today? How do the narratives we tell about citizenship help to define the possibilities of democracy?

By analyzing the rise of America's republican and democratic political fictions, *Founding Fictions* critically interrogates how, why, and to what effect Americans began to think of their government as a democracy rather than as a republic. I tell the story of how American republicanism and democracy were invented and debated between 1764 and 1845 and how these debates influenced how citizens were imagined to act. This book has three major arguments. First, there are important differences between what *Founding Fictions* calls republican and democratic political fictions, that is, between political narratives based upon republican or democratic theories of government. Second, scholars and citizens can judge their political fiction based upon the degree to which it can be characterized as dialogic, authored, debated, circulated, ratified, and open, and such judgment can help us to determine whether or not the political fiction has citizen consent. Third, there are important differences between romantic and tragic views of citizenship, that is, views of citizenship that seek either to empower or suppress citizen action. This analysis of America's republican and democratic fictions results in a new perspective on a familiar story and in new critical tools for analyzing American political discourse. Further, *Found-*

ing Fictions demonstrates that if America is going to have anything like an active democratic citizenry, we need to recover and implement romantic citizenship. In other words, *Founding Fictions* is a sustained discussion of how the founders' republican fiction turned into America's democratic fiction and what that transformation teaches us about the nature of American citizenship and democracy.

Why Does *Founding Fictions* Use an Interdisciplinary Approach to Study American Citizenship?

At first it may appear odd to propose to study American citizenship through a rhetorical and historical analysis of political fictions, but I hope to make a convincing case that this interdisciplinary approach allows us to learn something about American political discourse that we otherwise would not. Scholars traditionally have made convenient, if false, distinctions between poetical, dialectical, and rhetorical language; these rigid classifications prevent us from conceiving of political theory as at least partially both poetical and rhetorical. Poetical language—drama, poetry, prose—has often been thought to be the "expression of beauty," and it has been judged based upon its degree of beauty or how well it entertains or pleases an audience, but not overtly upon how well it corresponds to "reality" or persuades; dialectical language—philosophy, science, news reports, and so forth—has often been thought to be the "expression of truth," and it has been judged based upon how well it "provides accurate information," but not explicitly upon how well it pleases or persuades; rhetorical language—epideictic, deliberative, forensic—has often been thought to be the "expression of power," and it has been judged based upon how well it adapts its form and content to specific situations and audiences to achieve its goals, but not necessarily upon how well it conforms to "reality" or pleases. In short, language has been divided into poetic, dialectic, and rhetoric based upon its purposes, and it has been judged according to how well it fulfilled those purposes.[7] Within this view of language, political theory would be classified as dialectic, and the best political theory would be one that provides the most accurate assessment of the possibilities and pitfalls associated with managing institutions, people, and power in a political community. Hence, to try to assess political theory based upon how well it adapts to audiences and contexts or to place it within the realm of language that does not seek to describe political "reality" as accurately as possible would seem to be antithetical to its form and function.

Putting aside the question of the wisdom of such rigid distinctions between poetic, dialectic, and rhetoric, the view of political theory as strictly dialectical language does not bear scrutiny. First, political theory is utopian; it literally describes "no place," and in that sense it is always a kind of fiction. For example, Plato's *Republic* is considered one of the great works of political theory, but it is also fiction—in it Plato imagined how the just state *could* be formed, but he did not describe any actually existing political regime. What is true of Plato's *Republic* is true of all political theory.[8] Indeed, what would a non-fictional, non-invented political theory look like? Such a theory would not be an act of human creation, but would have existed prior to any human invention. If this were true, all political theory would have to be considered a part of divine law or would have to be a Platonic form, which would mean that there could only be one best theory for all peoples and all political communities. The fact that people and political theorists have created and argued for various kinds of government—monarchy, aristocracy, meritocracy, democracy, and so forth—demonstrates that there is not one ideal form of government, but rather a plurality of political theories that must be adapted to the particular people and circumstances of a particular political community. Therefore political theory could be judged based upon the standards of poetics because it is always an act of human imagination and does not necessarily describe "reality."

The second reason why political theory is not strictly dialectical language is because, as James Arnt Aune has written, it "strives for advantage over its opponents," and so it is always a kind of persuasion. Because political theory is neither divine law or Platonic form—because it is always an act of human imagination—it must compete in the marketplace of ideas with other views of the best kind of government. Mostly, these debates over the best kind of government occur within the sphere of expert political theorists.[9] The highly technical language used in these debates, coupled with the need to devote years of study to examining the best and worst regimes in world political history, prohibits all but the most interested from throwing their oar into the conversation, as Kenneth Burke would have said.[10] There have been remarkable instances when the merits of a particular political theory were openly debated—the years between 1787 and 1789 when Americans debated the proposed constitution springs to mind—but these open discussions of political theory have been few and far between. Nonetheless, whether elite expert discourse communities are debating political theory or whether average citizens are included in the discussion, the fact remains that political theory *can be debated*. If something can be debated, it is inherently rhetorical, because when there is no a priori decision rule for how to judge the merits of the proposed political system, then both how to judge and the judgment itself are open to persuasion. Therefore political theory could be judged based upon the standards of rhetoric because it attempts to influence how political communities are constructed and maintained.

But, just because political theory *could* be judged based upon these standards, does that mean it is useful to do so? In other words, what benefits might accrue from an analysis of political theory as a blend of poetic, dialectic, and rhetoric? Taking political theory out of the category of dialectic and admitting that it shares the attributes of poetical and rhetorical language is not only a more accurate description of actually existing political theory, but it also allows us to ask questions about how, why, and to what effect political theory carries the appearance of truth and an accurate description of reality when it is just as poetical and rhetorical as other forms of discourse that are overtly recognized as attempts to imagine and persuade.[11] Political theory is a simulacrum of dialectic: it is a rhetorical fiction that appears faithfully to describe political reality while it is also used to create political realities. Recognizing political theory's poetical and rhetorical functions opens it up to analysis, because it takes it out of the realm of unquestionable elite and expert discourse and re-places it in the realm of the public. After all, since political theory's *telos* is to manage the public, it seems fair that the public would have some say in how it would be managed.[12] Therefore, reconceiving political theory as political fiction is a radically egalitarian attempt—radical in that it proposes a systemic paradigm shift, and egalitarian in that such a shift would allow all citizens to judge—to wrest the control of American political theory from the few and open it up to debate by the many.

A more open debate of political theory by more people should be a feature of any political community that purports to be democratic. The first step in accomplishing this goal is to recognize that political theory is not an elite discourse that corresponds to truth, but rather a form of persuasion and an act of human imagination, and that as such it can be debated as easily as any other piece of art or other influential text. Additionally, an interdisciplinary approach provides intellectual rigor and flexibility: drawing on the work of scholars in what has traditionally been thought of as structuralism, poststructuralism, mythic studies, and literature allows us to analyze political theory as poetical language that uses the structures of narrative to imagine the best form of government. Drawing on the work of scholars in what has traditionally been thought of as political science, political theory, and political philosophy allows us to analyze political theory as dialectical language that uses an analytic assessment of human nature and who should rule to describe the best form of government. Finally, drawing on the work of scholars in what has traditionally been thought of as rhetorical theory, public address, and American history allows us to analyze political theory as situated rhetorical language that rhetors adapt to specific audiences and contexts in order to persuade others that their view of the best form of government should prevail. Judged merely as dialectical language, political theory hides its potential to construct realities; judged merely as poetical language, political theory hides its potential to define politics; judged merely as rhetorical language, political theory hides its potential to create truths. Therefore, an interdisciplinary study of American citizenship allows for the analysis of the inherently poetical, dialectical, and rhetorical uses of language in political theory.

Why Did the Founders Fear Democracy?

There are significant differences between republican and democratic theories of government, both for the founding generation and for Americans today, and if we hope to thoroughly understand American citizenship we must reexamine these differences. It is easy to confuse democratic and republican theories of government, for they share one fundamental similarity: in both, "the people" are sovereign. However, political taxonomists would say that there are also fundamental differences between "democratic" and "republican" governments, which turn on how each theory answers the questions of who rules and how those who rule "administer" or act to make decisions within the government. Pure democracy is a government in which each and every citizen makes binding policy decisions for all on all questions of government ("the government of all over all" or "the government of anybody and everybody"). A republic, on the other hand, is a government based upon the will of the people, but the degree of citizen decision making can range from being almost nonexistent (assenting to the original constitution and then taking no further part in the administration of the government) to being almost ubiquitous (giving binding instructions to representatives who must faithfully mirror their constituents' will for all decisions). In short, republican constitutions can be designed to be more or less "democratic," but the two are not the same form of government. Regina Morantz points to another important difference between the two theories: democratic governments are premised upon equality, while republican governments are premised upon liberty, and the two have been thought to be incompatible.[13] In other words, republican government may be hierarchical—only some classes of people may be considered worthy of full citizenship—while democratic government has to be classless, and all people have to be considered worthy of full citizenship.[14] The United States is a republic that has embraced more inclusive practices of citizenship over the course of its history, but it has never achieved full equality or ever permitted "the government of all over all."

Most scholars interested in questions of democracy and republicanism have not recognized how the explicit difference between republican and democratic forms of government influence our conceptions of citizenship. However, Robert Ivie's recent work on the "distemper of democracy" and Jacques Rancière's work on the "hatred of democracy" are particularly helpful for thinking through the contradictions within the American political tradition. Ivie describes what he calls the "distemper of democracy" in his *Democracy and America's War on Terror;* in his view, American democracy can be understood as a construction of a wary elite who created a constitution that "displaced [political power] from the public to a ruling elite by portraying the masses in the image of a primitive Other subject to the delirium of demagoguery, not unlike the barbarian beyond the walls of the polity."[15] Ivie believes that this "image of the distempered demos" not only contributed to the rationale for a government in which the people have little power, but also justified the American "republic of fear" and "the quest to achieve a universal peace" through preemptive violence.[16] Like Ivie, Rancière believes that "hatred of democracy is certainly nothing new. Indeed it is as old as democracy itself for a simple reason: the word itself is an expression of hatred."[17] He traces the hatred of democracy from Plato to the fall of the Soviet Union and the end of totalitarianism to argue that "under the name democracy, what is being implicated and denounced is politics itself."[18] True democracy would require our accepting that "the drawing of lots" is the "the democratic procedure by which a people of equals decides the distribution of places"; therefore, our rejection of drawing offices by lot and the introduction of representation "has been the object of a formidable work of forgetting." Rancière believes that modern anti-democrats have forgotten the important truth that "good government is the government of those who do not desire to govern"; "if there is one category to exclude from the list of those who are capable for governing," he writes, "it is in any case those who set their sights on obtaining power."[19] While much of Rancière's analysis is useful here, his belief that we have openly acknowledged our hatred of democracy does not quite resonate with the American political tradition. Indeed, as the discussion of President Bush's radio address demonstrates, our political leaders often overtly and strategically embrace the term "democracy" in their discourse, even while rejecting the political system in practice. American political discourse evolved from an overt hatred of democracy in the founding generation to its strategic public embrace today.

Indeed, as scholars such as Robert Dahl have shown, there has always been anxiety about whether the people could be trusted to rule, and our founders were no different from other political theorists in this regard. Even in ancient Athens, the birthplace of democracy, political theorists had an ambivalent relationship to democratic forms of government. Plato—admittedly no friend of democracy—described it in the *Republic* as "a state in which the poor, gaining the upper hand, kill some and banish others, and then divide the offices among the remaining citizens, usually by lot."[20] And Aristotle—slightly less hostile to democracy—described it in the *Politics* as a "deviation" from a "commonwealth."[21] The word "democracy" was largely forgotten until about the mid-thirteenth century, when it was introduced into the "European political language" with the translation of Aristotle's *Politics.* David Held reports that democracy instantly "took on a pejorative connotation and became associated with the politics of the rabble; government conducted for the benefit of the poor rather than the public interest; and a form of power . . . in which the common people can be tyrannical."[22]

It is clear that prior to the rise of the Democratic Party in the latter half of the 1820s, America's political elite shared this negative connotation of both the word "democracy" and the democratic political form. "There was no controversy over the meaning of the term 'democracy' in colonial America," writes Roy N. Lokken; "colonists gave little thought to it, and the word seldom appeared in their political writings, speeches, sermons, public papers, and private correspondence." Likewise, Russell Hanson argues that "there were very few men willing to call themselves 'democrats'" in the founding generation.[23] Among the nation's elite, "democracy" invariably connoted turbulence, chaos, leveling of the social hierarchy, and mob rule. For example, an anonymous 1769 colonist argued in his "Letters in Answer to the Farmer" (written in response to John Dickinson's influential *Letters from a Farmer in Pennsylvania*) that "should the people . . . become the sovereign judges of the extent of Parliamentary authority, and a rude insulting mob exercise the powers of legislature, [we can expect] every species of confusion that is to be feared from the despotism of democracy."[24] Nor did constitutional-era Americans like James Madison think much more highly of democracy: in Federalist 10 he described democratic governments as rife with "turbulence and contention . . . incompatible with personal security or the rights of property; and . . . violent in their deaths."[25] George

Cabot's 1804 characterization of democracy demonstrated that *misodemia*—the hatred, or perhaps better, the fear, of democracy—lingered in the minds of the conservative elite into the new millennium: "I hold democracy, in its natural operation, to be the government of the worst," Cabot wrote to fellow Federalist Timothy Pickering.[26] Cabot considered democracy the worst form of government, because he did not believe mankind would ever "cease to act from impulse and habitually act from reflection."[27] In short, democracy filled many of America's elite with dread prior to its strategic rehabilitation in the second quarter of the nineteenth century.

This fear of democratic equality and mob rule—like the fear of monarchy and aristocracy—led Americans to found republican, rather than democratic, governments at both the state and national level. The founders had a concrete and specifically negative notion of "democracy" in 1787, and in their understanding it was not the same form of government as a "republic." America's founding elite deliberately chose to retain a certain level of hierarchy and therefore embraced the term "republicanism" rather than "democracy" between 1776 and 1824.

Although no substantial changes to the U.S. Constitution had occurred, in 1824 John Quincy Adams—himself no friend of pure democracy—became the first president to refer to the American government as a democracy in an inaugural address.[28] In the years that followed, Jacksonian Democrats seized the term, reclaimed and repurposed it, and made it the standard description of America's political system.[29] Yet elite Americans still believed that the people were a mob of unfit rulers. According to Regina Morantz, the words "republic" and "democracy" "ceased to connote a specific form of government, as they had for the past generation. . . . At the same time, each word projected an emotional commitment, a moral perspective, and a significant message for its hearers."[30] In other words, whereas the founding generation had debated the meaning of words like "democracy" and "republic" and had used them rhetorically for political gain, the second generation of Americans all but stopped analyzing the meaning of the terms but continued to use them rhetorically. Perhaps this helps to explain how it could be that when George Sidney Camp published a book of political theory in 1841—which he simply titled *Democracy*—his publishers felt justified in making robust claims for the book's novelty, "no work . . . having ever been published, the express design of which is to elucidate the democratic theory."[31] If the founding generation had dismissed democracy as an implausible and dangerous political system, and if the second generation had stopped debating the meanings of republicanism and democracy altogether, it would not be surprising that no books analyzing democratic theory were published prior to 1841.

Because *Founding Fictions* tells the story of how the American people were imagined to participate in their government, the fear of democracy prevalent in the founding generation is a central part of this story. However, it is important to remember that while the founding generation was generally negative toward democracy, it embraced republicanism, which was a radical and revolutionary change in 1776, and many political theorists argued for a republican constitution that was more, rather than less, directly controlled by the people. While the United States is technically a republic (and we still teach schoolchildren to pledge allegiance to the flag and "to the republic for which it stands"), modern Americans refer to their government as a democracy so frequently that they forget that it is not. Conflating democratic and republican theories of government not only profoundly inhibits our understanding of the founding generation's arguments over what it meant for the government to be based upon the will of the people (for example, does the United States prioritize liberty or equality? Are they mutually exclusive? Should our representatives mirror or filter our opinions?), but also prevents us from using the founders' analysis of the nature of republican government to assess the health of the modern American republic.

How Did the Founders Define Republicanism?

Because Americans were inexperienced with establishing, conducting, and maintaining republican governments, they could—indeed were forced to—make it up as they went along.[32] Their lack of experience with their new government meant that the term "republican" was open for construction—its meaning was ambiguous and could be interpreted differently by different people.[33] As former president John Adams crankily proclaimed in an 1807 letter to his friend the historian, playwright, and onetime Anti-Federalist Mercy Otis Warren, "there is not a single more unintelligible word in the English language than republicanism."[34] Adams was not alone in his confusion. Yet, republicanism was the "buzzword" of the Revolution, and it dominated the political discourse of the revolutionary generation. Ambiguous and ubiquitous, "republican" became an all-purpose positive descriptor: "republican mothers" sent their "republican sons" to "republican schools" for their "republican education"; "republican patriots" could deposit their "republican money" in "republican banks," and so forth.[35] The term's ubiquitous use demonstrates that it carried considerable social capital and that it had a positive connotation. Well into the second generation and beyond, Americans would continue to attach "republican" to their nouns whenever they wanted to convey a positive impression. But what did it mean for Americans to call their banks or schools "republican"? What special characteristics made something republican rather than democratic or monarchic? What did it mean for the National Lyceum, for example, to argue in 1831 that it was "more purely republican—that it has less which is anti-republican—that it addresses itself more directly and equally to all classes and ages of the community—to every man, woman, and child in our republic, than any other institution which can be named?"[36] Whatever "republicanism" was thought to mean, there was much at stake in being able to define it in America between 1764 and 1845.

As Mercy Otis Warren wrote in her 1805 *History of the Rise, Progress, and Termination of the American Revolution*, by the conclusion of the war in 1783 "some interested and ambitious men . . . endevoured [*sic*] to confound ideas, and darken opinion, by asserting that republicanism was an indefinite term." Not only did the "interested and ambitious"—clear insults in the early American lexicon that would translate to something like "greedy" and "conniving" today—purposely attempt to confuse the public's perception of republicanism by rendering its meaning ambiguous, but, Warren argued, these villains did so surreptitiously, in the private parlors of America's elite homes rather than in the town meetings and newspapers of the public sphere. It was in the whispered conversations that occurred in the privacy of "social circles" that the elite "frequently insinuated that no precise meaning could be affixed to a word." The result of this pernicious cultivation of the ambiguity of republicanism, according to Warren, was that "the people were often deceived and led to pursue a shadow instead of an object of any real stability."[37] If Warren's account can be trusted, then conniving elite politicians purposely used their connections to render republicanism "unintelligible," and the many, accepting the elite view, were forced to accept policies and constitutions that had the semblance of republicanism but not the substance. Against charges such as these, it is no wonder that Adams felt he must defend his view of the ambiguity of republicanism to Warren in 1807.

However, there *were* public debates over the meaning of republicanism (even if it was mostly elites who took part in them), so we should not accept Warren's charges against Adams and the rest of the political elite without question. Yet even if we admit that the world was not as starkly divided as Warren's assessment would suggest, her observations about the nature of the private conversations she witnessed by virtue of her membership in elite social circles point to several important implications. First, Warren seemed to believe that there was a "proper" definition of republicanism and that crafty elites intentionally obfuscated that definition because it suited their purposes—practicing a rhetorical technique that Richard Lanham would call *skotison,* to "darken it," or purposely obscure, conceal, or evade conveying meaning by hiding behind highly technical language.[38] Second, Warren's description suggests that America's elite believed there were great profits for those who could control how republicanism was defined; otherwise, they would not have bothered to worry over whether or not they could define it to their liking by cultivating its ambiguity. Third, Warren's negative characterization of the "interested and ambitious" elite men who sought to control the definition of republicanism implies that she believed that *if* the meaning of republicanism was ambiguous, then its meaning should have been publicly, rather than privately, debated and decided. And fourth, in Warren's account the many seemingly had no power to define republicanism, but could only follow the lead of their betters in recognizing its ambiguity and allowing elites to define it properly.[39] Warren's four points of analysis translate into epistemological, semiotic, and hegemonic critiques: Can we know what republicanism means? How are republicanism's shifting meanings used to gain power? Who should have the power to decide what republicanism means? In other words, Warren's analysis of how the term "republicanism" was strategically employed in her generation's public discourse demonstrates that the ability to define and control republicanism was a contest of power that was fraught with political consequences for both the many and the few.

As Warren's account of the elite discourse of 1783 attests, whoever controls the language of politics controls the people. "Republicanism" was a "keyword," or an "ultimate term," or a "god term," and as Daniel T. Rodgers argues, "Keywords . . . are words which matter enough for persons to fight over them. Not fight *for* them, though that might happen, but to fight for control *over* them—for the power to redefine, redeploy, and gain possession of them."[40] As Steven Lukes argues, behind and beneath these contests are always "disputes between contending moral and political perspectives."[41] These different "perspectives" frame or "screen" how we understand the social and political world. Yet "we can't say anything without the use of terms," writes Kenneth Burke; therefore, "whatever terms we use, they necessarily constitute a corresponding kind of screen; and any such screen necessarily directs the attention to one field rather than another."[42] Any frame is a selection of reality, and any selection of reality is also a deflection of reality. When we choose to identify with specific perspectives or traditions, we allow our world to be framed or screened by them and simultaneously divide ourselves from those perspectives that we have not chosen. Therefore, politics always starts with defining terms, because those definitions serve to create a worldview for others and each worldview endorses specific policy decisions.

Thomas Gustafson explains that the first generation of Americans was especially sensitive to the importance of this struggle over definitions; indeed, they had a "sophisticated awareness about how the struggle for interests and power was conducted through verbal means and how people could be governed, manipulated—indeed, tyrannized over—by words as well as by the rule of force and about how politics thus had to be conducted in part as literary criticism or even as a language game that could be won by those most skilled in opposing the abuse of words."[43] The meaning of the most important terms of our social and political world is destined to be fought over precisely because those are the most important terms. Politicians of the founding generation knew this and therefore struggled mightily to define the meaning of "republicanism" for their own purposes. In fact, if Gustafson's account of the struggle is accurate, any politician who did not get involved in the attempt to define republicanism was admitting that he approved of allowing others to tyrannize him and the rest of the political community. The struggle over the definition of "republicanism" therefore was a test of honor, political power, and justice for the revolutionary generation precisely because there was so much to gain for those who could control its meaning.[44]

The second generation did not contest the term "republicanism" with as much intensity as the first, and their political discourse was dominated by "descriptions of party machinations, calls to colors, [and] exhortations to victory." As we will see in chapter 5, politicians of the second generation used political terms like "federal," "republican," and "democrat" more "as propaganda for the promotion of party purposes" than to explain political theory.[45] While "republicanism" was ambiguous and ubiquitous for the founding generation, and they considered it a test of honor to struggle to retain control over its meaning, the second generation gave up the struggle over the term's meaning, called the government a "democracy," and used the rhetorical power of America's key terms to raise and retain the support of party members. The term "republicanism" was still ubiquitous, but the second generation often relied upon the founding generation's definitions, which, for better or worse, made its meaning far less ambiguous than it once was.

What Were the Features of Republican Constitutions?

When we examine how Americans made sense of the ambiguities of republican political theory, it is clear that they answered the question "What is a republican constitution?" differently in different places and as they gained more experience with independence. Bernard Bailyn has argued that colonials interpreted events between 1764 and 1776 as "danger signals, indicating hidden impulses and the likely trajectory of events impelled by them"; these "danger signals," he and others have argued, led colonials to reject monarchy and embrace republicanism.[46] Bailyn traces the colonists' theories of the dangerous decay of liberties to eighteenth-century British Opposition polemicists such as James Harrington, John Milton, Viscount Henry St. John Bolingbroke, Algernon Sidney, and Henry Neville, who helped to shape "the mind of the American Revolutionary generation."[47] Colonists eagerly learned and adopted the Opposition perspective on tyranny, yet they did not find the cure for the dangers inherent in oppressive monarchism in these writings. "What, then, are the distinctive characters of the republican form?" James Madison was still asking in his 1788 Federalist 39. "Were an answer to this question to be sought, not by recurring to principles, but in application of the term by political writers to the constitutions of different states, no satisfactory one would ever be found."[48] Americans had some understanding that a republican government would be based "upon the will of the people," would "promote liberty," and would "guarantee rights," but beyond these vague generalities Americans had no specific existing constitution to use as a model for their new governments. As Madison's argument attests, Americans had to invent and perfect republican constitutions on their own.

Like that of "democracy," the connotation of "republic" changed dramatically between 1764 and 1845. W. Paul Adams writes that prior to the publication of Thomas Paine's *Common Sense* in January 1776, republicanism fared little better than democracy in Americans' political vocabulary: it was often viewed as an inferior political system. Yet, Lance Banning believes that as Americans began to accept their new political fiction that "republicanism no longer seemed an unavoidable necessity, to be embraced with dread, but an exhilarating opportunity."[49] As I describe in chapter 2, republicanism was indeed an opportunity that Americans made the most of. An analysis of the first two generations' use of "republican" rhetoric suggests that while the term was used sparingly in official debates and proceedings prior to the 1787 Constitutional Convention, after the establishment of the national government "republican" continued to have positive associations for Americans up to the Civil War and beyond. Americans reevaluated their government between 1764 and 1787 and, deciding that republicanism was the best theory for the new nation, enthusiastically embraced the term, even if, as Madison observed, they were not sure exactly what the republican form might look like.

On May 10, 1776, the Continental Congress recommended that "where no government sufficient to the exigencies of [each colony's] affairs have been hitherto established, to adopt such government as shall, in the opinion of the representatives of the people, best conduce to the happiness and safety of their constituents in particular, and America in general."[50] Note that the Continental Congress did not explicitly state what kind of government each colony should establish—it did not use terms like "monarchy" or "republic" to constrain the "representatives of the people" from creating the best form of government for their constituents' "happiness and safety." Nor did the Continental Congress use the words "republic" or "republican" in the Declaration of Independence or in any other official congressional communication in 1776. Despite the ubiquitous use of republican rhetoric in popular discourse, the Continental Congress would not refer to America as a "republic" until December 20, 1777, when it sent a *Circular Letter to the States* that conveyed Congress's resolutions against war-profiteering and encouraged Americans to send aid to the Continental army. The "unhappy case of America," Congress didactically observed, required it to pass "laws unworthy the character of infant republics." Laws against war-profiteering were necessary "to supply the defect of public virtue, and to correct the vices of some of her sons . . . to guard against the parricide."[51] Congress referred to the American government as a "republic" on only a handful of occasions prior to 1787, and those were mostly diplomatic correspondence.[52] Yet, despite the infrequent use of the term "republican" prior to 1787, when Congress did use the term it argued that Americans were not living up to "republican" principles, which indicated that it believed republicanism was both an ideal for Americans to aspire to and the standard by which Americans' virtue and their government would be judged. In other words, in its attempt to fix meaning within shifting political terminology of the period, when Congress felt it necessary to explicitly hold Americans accountable to what it meant to be a good American citizen, it did so by comparing their behavior to ideals it labeled "republican."

Americans began experimenting with the creation of new republican constitutions as early as December 1775, when after "serious consideration" of the "unhappy circumstances" caused by British oppression, the representatives of New Hampshire, with the consent of "the free suffrages of the people," and upon the recommendation of the Continental Congress, crafted a new form of government that they "judge[d] best for the public good." Eight of the thirteen colonies ratified new constitutions in 1776 alone; although the features of these constitutions vary widely, they possess some important similarities that we can use to gauge how Americans interpreted the Continental Congress's dictate that the states form new governments for their constituents' "happiness and safety." As Thomas Jefferson recalled of the task that he and his fellow Virginians faced in 1776, the "whole code of government" had to be reviewed and "adapted to our republican form of government"; the old constitution had to "be corrected, in all its parts, with a single eye to reason, & the good of those for whose government it was framed."[53] Americans would continue to apply their reason to rewriting their constitutions in the hope of promoting the public good for many years to come.

The structures of the new constitutions were not cut from whole cloth; indeed, the new constitutions were mostly modifications of previous colonial governments with one major exception: there was no king. For example, as Montesquieu had advocated in his 1748 *Spirit of Laws,* all eight states divided the responsibilities of government among legislative, executive, and judiciary branches and among the few, the many, and the one. Yet recent experience had taught colonials the dangers of a strong executive branch; therefore, some states circumscribed the power of the executive by establishing "executive councils" and requiring the executive council to advise and give consent to all executive decisions. Also, some states gave the executive veto power and other privileges, such as embodying the militia, while others, such as South Carolina, New Hampshire, Delaware, and Virginia, explicitly prohibited the executive from using such kingly powers. Almost all states prohibited the executive from adjourning the legislature, which had been a particularly odious proclivity of royal governors leading up to 1776. Some states required that the lower house initiate all bills, while New Jersey, South Carolina, and Delaware required that only money bills originate in the lower house. All states had some kind of suffrage in which citizens—usually male freeholders—could vote for at least the lower branch of the legislature, and all states had rotation in office. Indeed, some states, including Maryland and Virginia, required that offices rotate yearly, because as Maryland argued, "rotation . . . is one of the best securities of permanent freedom." All states required their elected officials to swear some kind of loyalty oath to the constitution, and Delaware, Pennsylvania, and Maryland also required religious oaths.

Not only did the structures of the new state governments represent republican rather than monarchical theories of government, but no state allowed titles of nobility upon which an aristocracy could be formed, and South Carolina, Virginia, Maryland, and North Carolina expressly prohibited Americans from creating aristocratic titles in the future. Additionally, New Hampshire, Virginia, New Jersey, and North Carolina took advantage of the opportunity afforded by the creation of their new constitution to directly indict King George III and Parliament for their abuses of the people's trust and their usurpations of the people's power. Virginia and Pennsylvania explicitly guaranteed their constituents' rights and liberties by providing them with Bills of Rights; Delaware abolished slavery, while Pennsylvania and North Carolina expressly guaranteed their citizens the right to instruct their elected representatives. Virginia, Delaware, and Pennsylvania all referred to their new government as a "Commonwealth," while only New Jersey retained the title "Colony." Finally, the most prominent feature of the new republican constitutions was that each new government announced that the people were sovereign: New Hampshire, South Carolina, Virginia, New Jersey, Pennsylvania, and North Carolina—every state except Delaware—used the occasion provided by the creation of their new constitution to argue, as Maryland did, that all government "of right originates from the people, is founded in compact only, and instituted solely for the good of the whole." Or, as Pennsylvania made explicit, "the people of this State have the sole, exclusive, and inherent right of governing and regulating the internal police of the same . . . all power being originally inherent in the people."[54]

Therefore, while we cannot say that there was a standard form of republican government enacted by the eight state constitutions written in 1776, we can say that these constitutions shared fundamental similarities: each state argued that the new government was based upon the will of the people; all rejected titles of nobility and embraced rotation in office; all allowed male freeholders to vote in some elections; and all divided the tasks of government among three separate branches. We therefore can take these four features as representing the vanguard of American republican political theory on the eve of revolution. The process of forming and testing new republican constitutions would be repeated as the remaining states wrote their constitutions, as the Articles of Confederation were written, debated, and finally ratified between 1776 and 1781, and as the new federal Constitution was proposed, debated, and ratified between 1787 and 1789.[55] In other words, Americans spent the years between 1776 and 1789 in almost continuous contemplation and debate over how to form republican constitutions, and in the process of writing and rewriting their constitutions they solidified their political theory. Upon reflection we can say that these constitutions both reflected and created republicanism in the United States. Tautologically, America's republican constitutions constituted American republicanism, but they also reflected the republican principles that had been developing between 1764 and 1776.[56]

What Are Political Fictions?

Political fictions are narratives that political communities tell themselves about their government; like formal constitutions, they have a constitutive role in political discourse. Political fictions both create and reflect political realities, and as such they are central to any political community. We have already observed that political theory shares elements of poetical, rhetorical, and dialectical language; therefore, calling political theory "political fiction" is only another, shorthand way of making the same argument. A political fiction can be found in just about any textual artifact: paintings, poetry, newspapers, film, speeches, political theory, constitutions, photographs, debates, monuments, history, laws, and education practices, to name just a few. In short, we find examples of a nation's political fiction in any kind of text that describes or is premised upon that nation's view of its government. Each form of government will have its own political fiction; therefore, we would expect to find that particular communities at particular points in time were dominated by a theocratic fiction, a monarchical fiction, an aristocratic fiction, a republican fiction, a democratic fiction, or even an anarchic fiction. While a nation's constitution is the codification of that community's political fiction, the fiction often preexists the writing of the constitution, and therefore constitutions merely reflect emerging or preexisting political fictions for the generation that wrote them. Yet constitutions also define and delimit the political fiction of the subsequent generations and therefore are important sites for examining both the construction and the institutionalization of political fictions.

While we do not often think of it in these terms, the view of political theory as political fiction is already a part of our understanding of the American political tradition; indeed, historian Edmund Morgan partially shares this view of political theory. "Government requires make-believe," writes Morgan: "make believe that the king is divine, make believe that he can do no wrong or make believe that the voice of the people is the voice of God. Make believe that the people *have* a voice or make believe that the representatives of the people *are* the people." Yet, there are important differences between Morgan's description of political theory as fiction and mine: Morgan still appears to view political theory as primarily a form of dialectical language. "I have been troubled by the pejorative connotations attached to the word [fiction]," he writes, "but I have been unable to find a better one to describe the different phenomena to which I have applied it. . . . I do not imply deception or delusion on the part of those who employed or subscribed to the fictions examined here. . . . My purpose is not to debunk, but to explore the wonder that Hume points to, the fact that most of us submit willingly to be governed by a few of us."[57] Contrary to Morgan's apologia, a political fiction can both describe the underlying assumptions of a community's political theory *and* can be called upon to convince citizens that political policies and practices correspond to preexisting political theory. It is dangerously naive to restrict our definition and analysis of political fictions to exclude "deception or delusion" on the part of rhetors or audiences as Morgan argues. Politicians may make disingenuous appeals to political fictions that correspond neither to their own beliefs nor to the nation's constitution in order to gain and maintain power. We would be wise, therefore, to analyze how rhetors strategically employ political fictions. To be clear: political fictions *can be* deceptive, but they are not always used to deceive. Quite simply, political fictions are a blend of poetical, rhetorical, and dialectical language and should be analyzed as such.

The analysis of political theory as political fiction allows us to trace how communities use narratives, the most "pervasive forms of human thought," to organize and delimit the thinkable forms of political organization.[58] As theorists as diverse as Aristotle, Paul Ricoeur, and Walter Fisher have noted, human beings think in narrative: we constantly invent stories to explain and order our perceptions of the world.[59] Narratives are fundamental to what it means to be human and are therefore central to how we create communities—human beings cannot live and act together without narratives to organize themselves. When we analyze a nation's political fiction, we are analyzing how citizens, politicians, artists, educators, and political theorists develop and strategically employ narratives to legitimate the nation's existence, compel obedience, and maintain order. Once in place, political fictions provide a frame for understanding political practice. They are used to select certain "realities," thereby dividing their audiences/readers/citizens from other fictions or other realities. Yet, in the end, audiences (citizens) have the power to reject, modify, or ratify their fiction. Every day that citizens do not revolt is implicitly another ratification of the existing political fiction. There are more pronounced markers of support of political fictions—pledging allegiance, swearing oaths, voting, paying taxes, serving in the military, teaching others the truths of the political fiction—but, at a minimum, not revolting is a small kind of endorsement of the existing political fiction. In short, while political fictions themselves are powerful, authors and audiences are also powerful because they have the power to control how the fiction is used and whether or not it endures.

We can derive six useful points of analysis from the insightful criticisms of constitutional-era political discourse made by Mercy Otis Warren and Thomas Jefferson. First, a political fiction can be more or less *dialogic*. As Warren argued about the "interested and ambitious" elite gentlemen who attempted to obfuscate the meaning of republicanism, when founders and citizens do not mutually engage in a conversation over their political theory's meaning, that theory cannot be said to have citizen consent. Mikhail Bakhtin has argued that discourse is dialogic when it is "oriented toward the listener and his answer." According to V. N. Volosinov, the dialogic rhetor "breaks through the alien conceptual horizon of the listener, constructs his own utterance on alien territory, against his, the listener's, apperceptive background."[60] Dialogism is crucial not only for a political fiction to be fair but also for it to last. Political fictions must be the result of negotiations between authors and audiences—between founders and citizens—for as the Continental Congress argued in the Declaration of Independence, a fiction that is not dialogic is not only tyrannical but is more justly revolted against than one that has the consent of the governed.

Second, political fictions can be traced back to their *author* more or less easily. Once again, Warren's critique of the "interested and ambitious" elite gentlemen helps us to understand what is at stake when political fictions are not clearly and openly authored. If we can trace political fictions back in history and determine how we decided that a government should exist for those people in that community at that particular point in time, we can say that the fiction was clearly and openly "authored." Whether we are tracing Athenian democracy to the reforms of Solon and Cleisthenes, the British Constitution to the Glorious Revolution and the ascension of William and Mary, or the Articles of Confederation to the 1776 committee led by John Dickinson and Josiah Bartlett, in these moments in history—whether they carry the semblance of extra-human inspiration or not—we can point to specific people in specific places and determine that they wrote, spoke, and fought for those constitutions. The constitutions did not preexist the extraordinary people who helped to create them; although no one alive today can remember their origination, they were once invented.[61] When we can easily trace political fictions to their founders, we can comprehend how and why that particular constitution was invented to deal with the particular constraints faced by those particular founders. When we cannot easily trace political fictions to their founders, we may begin to think of them as unquestionable God-given truths rather than as mere human creations that can be altered.

Third, political fictions can be more or less *debated*. In September 1789, Thomas Jefferson wrote to James Madison that "the Earth belongs in usufruct to the living" and therefore that every generation should get to debate and determine its own constitution.[62] While Madison found Jefferson's logic unconvincing, Jefferson's critique offers us a way to think about the legitimacy of any political community's political fiction: citizen consent requires that one generation's constitution would not bind the next generation. Because political fictions are most legitimate when they are dialogic and because people create, sustain, and perform political fictions, they may—in fact, we hope they *would*—be debated by the population as a whole, at least initially, but preferably more, rather than less, often. Scholars of rhetoric have long attempted to determine what the norms might be for productive public debate, and while scholarly opinion has varied dramatically about whether "rational-critical" debate is possible or desirable, James Arnt Aune and I have argued that eighteenth-century "vernacular republican" public discourse was characterized by four features: an aggressive rhetoric of critique, the demand for transparency in public arguments, the rejection of elite leadership, and the belief that decisions must be made for the common good.[63] We can take these four features to be the boundary of the most egalitarian public argument known in the eighteenth-century American public sphere, and perhaps an ideal type, but a goal for a public's debate of its political fiction nonetheless.

Fourth, political fictions can be more or less knowingly *circulated*. Because political fictions are so important to a community's self-identity, and because we find evidence of them everywhere—from art and poetry to education to laws and word usage—citizen consent requires that citizens freely, knowingly, and willingly circulate the political fiction's truths. When state constitution writers in 1776 required that their citizens and officers swear an oath to uphold their constitution, they were implicitly requiring that their citizens acknowledge both that they knowingly and willing accepted that constitution's principles and that they would enact them to the best of their ability. If a political fiction does not match its nation's political theory or constitution, it is much more difficult for a citizen to freely and knowingly circulate its truths. A disjunction between what is commonly understood to be the nation's political principles and the nation's actual operating paradigm may make free and willing circulation problematic.

Fifth, political fictions can be more or less freely *ratified*. John Adams argued in 1775 that new state constitutions would be most legitimate if they were ratified by the people as a whole.[64] James Madison argued at the 1789 Constitutional Convention that it was "essential" and "indispensable" that the proposed "constitution should be ratified in the most unexceptional form, and by the supreme authority of the people themselves."[65] The founding generation was well aware that their republican fiction needed the people's assent for legitimacy; however, there was disagreement over how often the people would be requested to assent to their fiction, who would be allowed to voice their opinion, and what would happen if the people decided that they disagreed. These problems were never properly resolved and remain open questions today.

Finally, political fictions can be more or less *open* to amendment. As Federalist apologists argued in abundance during the Constitutional Convention, it did not matter whether their convention had been called expressly to amend the existing Articles of Confederation or to erect an entirely new government, for they had the right to do both. Federalists like Edmund Randolph argued that convention delegates must use their best judgment and alter their form of government as necessary. Anti-Federalists like John Lansing and Oliver Ellsworth remained unconvinced that their specific convention had been endowed with this power, but they did not argue that citizens in general should not have the power to amend or abolish their constitution as necessary. Indeed, how could they, for Thomas Jefferson and the Continental Congress had argued expressly for this right in the Preamble of the Declaration of Independence: "Whenever any Form of Government becomes destructive of these ends, it is the Right of the People to alter or to abolish it, and to institute new Government, laying its foundation on such principles and organizing its powers in such form, as to them shall seem most likely to effect their Safety and Happiness." As Jefferson and the rest of the Continental Congress avowed, if a political fiction cannot be altered or abolished as the people desire, then it is tyranny. Citizen consent requires that citizens have the opportunity either to make minor, managerial amendments to their political fiction or to make full-scale, radical changes to their political fiction.

Political fictions, therefore, can be analyzed based upon the degree to which they are dialogic, authored, debated, circulated, ratified, and open, and we can use these standards to assess the degree to which any political fiction emerges and circulates with the consent of the people. Any political fiction that claims to be of, for, and by the people would necessarily be more, rather than less, dialogic, authored, debated, circulated, ratified, and open because these are all required aspects of citizen consent.[66] No political fiction could be perfectly of, for, and by the people; hence these criteria are perhaps an ideal type that might never exist. Still, they provide a benchmark by which we can judge in what ways a political fiction emerged and continues to circulate with or without the consent of citizens.

The concept of a political fiction focuses upon the constitutive role that a nation's political theory and constitution has on that nation's political and social practices. In other words, a nation's political fiction both reflects and creates a social and political reality and provides a frame for understanding a nation's political practices. In order to clarify how *Founding Fictions* uses the concept of a political fiction in its analysis of American citizenship, it will be useful to compare it with other important ways of thinking about political ideas in context: ideology, tradition, social imaginary, and political language. An ideology, perhaps most usefully defined by Louis Althusser, "represents the imaginary relationship of individuals to their real conditions of existence," "has a material existence," "hails or interpellates concrete individuals as concrete subjects," and treats individuals as "always-already subjects."[67] Unlike a political fiction, an ideology is not clearly authored; nor is it open to debate and ratification on the part of audiences; nor do audiences have the choice to willingly suspend their disbelief in order to conform to the "reality" presented by the ideology. Both, however, are circulated and powerful and frame a political community. Like a political fiction, ideology is also a simulacrum of dialectic; those who have studied its effects have often noted its rhetorical dimensions, but its narrative structures have received less attention.[68]

A "tradition," as Alasdair MacIntyre defines it, is a "historically extended, socially embedded argument" that provides "a context" by which any practice is "made intelligible in terms of the larger and longer history . . . through which the practice in its present form was conveyed to us."[69] A tradition is a kind of narrative that appears to be a form of dialectical language by which people organize and understand their behavior and their relationship to the behavior of others. It may be possible to trace the authorship of any tradition to its originator; indeed, this aspect is often prominent in a traditional narrative. Traditions are dialogic in that individuals must agree to perform according to tradition; otherwise, as MacIntyre makes clear, the tradition will atrophy. Yet, while narratives play an important role in his conception of tradition, there is little notice of the rhetorical dimensions of traditions—the ways in which traditions persuade and frame reality is not prominent. In MacIntyre's view of tradition, "arguments" are treated as ideas rather than as persuasion; therefore, while there are important similarities between political fictions and political traditions—both recognize the importance of narrative and dialogue—the concept of tradition does not capture the rhetorical nature of political theory, and therefore the two are substantively different.

A "social imaginary," as defined by Charles Taylor, describes "the ways people imagine their social existence, how they fit together with others, how things go on between them and their fellow, the expectations that are normally met, and the deeper normative notions and images that underlie these expectations."[70] Like political fictions, social imaginaries enable people's behavior and help them understand their world and how they can act within it. Also like a political fiction, a social imaginary specifically recognizes the narrative "images, stories, and legends" that enable ideas and help to order society. However, Taylor's account of the social imaginary does not overtly recognize the role of rhetoric, dialogism, and consent in the creation, ratification, and circulation of the social imaginary, nor does it help us to comprehend how specific political systems enable specific ideas and actions. Therefore, while Taylor's social imaginary shares some important features with political fictions, they are substantially different.

Finally, the analysis of a "political language," as defined by J. G. A. Pocock, requires the identification of "the 'language' or 'vocabulary' with and within which the author operated and show[s] how it functioned paradigmatically to prescribe what s/he might say and how s/he might say it."[71] To study a political language, therefore, is to study the history of the ideas that have influenced a particular author and have delimited how he or she perceives the political community. Additionally, the study of political languages recognizes the plurality of competing and complementary influences and "idioms" with which a particular community might speak. Pocock's view of political language recognizes the authored nature of political theory—indeed, he specifically asks historians and political theorists to search out this aspect of the context of any political theory—and recognizes the rhetorical aspects of political theory—although not in quite the same way as a political fiction—yet it does not sufficiently recognize the dialogic nature of political theory, nor does it help us to understand how political languages use narratives to convey meaning. Further, Pocock's view of political language focuses primarily on the analysis of political theory; the analysis of political fictions, on the other hand, encompasses political theory but recognizes that political theory is performed in countless ways and in countless discourses every day. Therefore, the analysis of political fictions is substantively different from the analysis of political languages.

What Does It Mean to Say That Americans Were Cast as Romantic Heroes, Tragic Victims, and Ironic Partisans?

Once we recognize that political communities are invented and sustained through political fictions, we can proceed to analyze how particular fictions described citizens at particular moments, and to what effect. Northrop Frye tells us that humans use four main types of narratives in storytelling: romance, tragedy, comedy, and satire.[72] Each narrative structure is based upon how the main characters are portrayed to interact with the obstacles they face within their world; each of these narrative structures, in turn, translates into citizen story arcs within political fictions. For example, an oligarchic fiction could be populated with tragic or comedic citizens, a democratic fiction could be populated with romantic citizens, and a monarchical fiction could be populated with tragic subjects—each of the various political fictions could conceivably rely upon any of the four story arcs to describe its people. Any political fiction will have to describe who makes up its political community, and such descriptions will influence both how its people think of themselves and how its people believe that they are empowered to act within the institutional structure of their political community. As we will see, the rhetorical situations of the Revolution, the Constitution, and Jacksonian democracy required Americans to create three different citizen story arcs within the nation's political fiction: the Revolution relied upon romantic citizenship; the Constitution relied upon tragic citizenship; and Jacksonian democracy relied upon ironic partisanship. My claim here is not that everyone used these story arcs, or that these story arcs were the only ones used, or that individual people or parties only used one and not the other; rather, my claim is that these story arcs dominated the contexts in which they were formed and *that they did so for good reason*. Americans developed the romantic, tragic, and ironic story arcs because they needed them, and they were used prominently only so long as they were useful. In other words, the romantic, tragic, and ironic story arcs became repositories of *topoi;* they provided stock arguments in the form of narratives about citizens that rhetors could draw upon to persuade audiences when it was beneficial to do so.

Hayden White explains that romantic narratives are a "drama of self-identification symbolized by the hero's transcendence of the world of experience, his victory over it, and his final liberation from it. . . . [I]t is a drama of the triumph of good over evil, of virtue over vice, of light over darkness, and of the ultimate transcendence of man over the world."[73] The key features of romantic citizenship correspond neatly with White's definition: citizens were supposed to identify personally with the ideals of American republicanism; each citizen was supposed to believe that he or she was a hero who would conquer adversity—whether the "adversity" was the gun of a British regular, the corruption of luxurious British goods, or the tyranny of Parliament and the king—and once those adversities were conquered, the heroes would continue to act in the republic's best interest and ensure a safe, happy, and prosperous America. The individual citizen was portrayed as active, powerful, good-hearted, virtuous, and cheerfully willing to make sacrifices for the interests of America, and these features helped to define the individual as the patriot hero. In other words, romantic citizenship was organic: individual citizens were important insofar as they contributed to the betterment of the whole nation, which was always viewed as more than the sum of its parts.[74] Above all, romantic citizens were enabled to act for the common good.

According to White, tragic narratives reflect the "resignations of men to the conditions under which they must labor in the world. These conditions in turn, are asserted to be inalterable and eternal, and the implication is that man cannot change them but must work within them."[75] The key features of tragic citizenship correspond neatly to this definition: the corruption of the state governments and the insurrections among the people had proved that political corruption was eternal and stability was impossible under the Articles of Confederation. The citizen was not the patriot hero who would act for the common good, but rather a complicit victim of corruption. The only solution was to give more power to the central government, which would enable the system to protect order, stability, and liberty. The best Americans could hope for with tragic citizenship was for the checks and balances of the system to create equilibrium between the different branches of government and the different classes so that one group would not be able to dominate the rest. In other words, the tragic republican fiction was mechanistic: the system was more important than citizens. Tragic citizens would preserve the common good by yielding their power to the system.

Irony is not so much an explicit story arc as it is an orientation toward the language that political leaders used to describe the traditional romantic and tragic story arcs. Irony is the "figure of speech for insiders," because one has to understand a culture's enthymemes in order to understand an ironic twist.[76] Plato and Demosthenes thought that irony allowed rhetors to say two things at once by negating the literal with the figural, which meant that irony was used to evade, conceal, and pretend.[77] As the concept of irony evolved, it was no longer thought of as a mere trick of language use but as a part of the nature of life, especially by German romantics like Friedrich von Schlegel, who believed that humans inevitably sought to control the uncontrollable in life, nature, and themselves.[78] The double meanings of irony can function both to unite and to divide ideas, people, and actions, and irony is both a slippery and a crucial figure of speech. Indeed, Kenneth Burke argues that "we cannot use language maturely until we are spontaneously at home in irony."[79] To say, therefore, that America's democratic fiction cast citizens as ironic partisans is to say both that the second generation attempted to constitute citizens as romantic heroes who could not act—drawing upon the sense of irony as concealment—and that the second generation created a political fiction that it could not retain control over—drawing upon the sense of irony as unintended consequence. In the development of the citizen as ironic partisan between 1816 and 1845 we see America's political leaders struggling to maintain stability within the shifting political realities of their era by creating a democratic fiction that was ambiguously democratic.

Founding Fictions tells the story of Americans' development and strategic use of romantic and tragic citizenship and ironic partisanship: when Americans rejected the monarchical fiction in 1776, they embraced the republican fiction they had been developing (whether or not they self-consciously developed it is debatable, and somewhat beside the point) since 1764. Their new republican fiction had to appeal both to the people and to elites for the legitimacy and stability of the new governments; therefore, the colonials whom we now think of as Founding Fathers constituted Americans as hopeful and triumphant romantic citizens to motivate colonists to commit treason and support their decision to rebel from England.[80] Romantic citizenship portrayed Americans as patriotic heroes who would save the country from tyranny, protect liberty, and prevent corruption.

After the Revolutionary War had been won, however, romantic citizenship proved to provide as much instability as stability: factions within state governments, rampant disregard for the needs of the Confederacy, failure to repay Revolutionary War debts, battles between the states on boundaries and taxes, and incidents of insurrection such as Shays's Rebellion all contributed to the assessment that the romantic promise of the Revolution did not meet the needs of the thirteen states. Therefore a new view of citizenship, devoted to stability at all costs, emerged prior to and during the Constitutional Convention of 1787. Tragic citizenship constituted Americans as complicit victims of corruption who would not prevent tyranny, protect liberty, or prevent corruption. Anti-Federalists continued to appeal to the truths of romantic citizenship in their attempts to prevent ratification, and while they succeeded in convincing Federalists of the necessity of a Bill of Rights, they were otherwise unsuccessful.[81]

The second generation conflated romantic and tragic citizenship, which helped to turn romantic and tragic citizens into ironic partisans. The increase in white male suffrage after the close of the War of 1812; the increase in voter turnout, citizen meetings, petitions, and instructions; and the resulting electoral "purification" in response to the Compensation Act of 1816 forced political leaders to acknowledge that they had to pay attention to public opinion, but did not lead them to acknowledge that they also had to obey that opinion. The 1824 "corrupt bargain" charge and the long 1828 grudge match presidential campaign facilitated by the rise of the second party system turned newly active citizens into partisans who could be organized for electoral party victories. The second generation overtly portrayed Americans as romantic heroes who controlled the government, but because the Constitution's logic of tragic citizenship did not change and because party leaders hoped to constrain citizen action rather than enable it, we can see in retrospect that both Democratic and Whig Party leaders between 1824 and 1845 positioned Americans as ironic partisans—as romantic heroes who could not act except through the party system.

Romantic citizenship flattered and seduced Americans into believing that they controlled the government; tragic citizenship berated and scared them into believing that they must allow the government to control them. While the two story arcs appear contradictory, both envisioned a triumphant ending for American government even as their methods for achieving this end were opposite. It is important to note that these story arcs did not originate with the founding generation; rather, the two story arcs form the dominant features of a secularized American jeremiad.[82] Romantic citizenship corresponds to the notion that Americans are a chosen people, while tragic citizenship corresponds to the notion that Americans are not living up to their covenant or potential. Beyond where these narratives originated are the more important questions of how and why they became important expressions of American republicanism; undeniably, the two views of citizenship were crucial to the nation's understanding of itself. A revolution had been fought against tyranny in the name of "unalienable rights," and while some politicians had recognized by 1787 that there was indeed a necessity for a centralized, controlling government, the general population would not have accepted such a drastic switch in political philosophy.[83] Therefore, romantic citizenship served as an ideal, while tragic citizenship offered a safer view of republicanism for those who found romantic citizenship too democratic, chaotic, and idealistic. Elements of the romantic and tragic story arcs were often blurred in the rhetoric of the founding generation, but it was not until the second generation that the two were conflated into one view of citizenship.

America's republican and democratic political fictions therefore constituted American citizens in particular ways—as romantic heroes, tragic victims, and ironic partisans—and those ways of thinking about the role of the citizen within America's story about its government have profoundly affected how citizens think of their ability to act within the government. The goal of *Founding Fictions* is to describe and assess how Americans constructed these views of citizenship between 1764 and 1845 and how these views of citizenship might affect Americans today.

How Do We Analyze Political Fictions?

Political fictions are the defining, fundamental, and necessary foundation of any political community because, as we have discussed, human beings cannot live together in groups without narratives to organize themselves.[84] Therefore, as the founding generation was well aware, those who invent and defend political fictions—the "lawgiver" or the "founder of a commonwealth"—are destined to occupy the "ultimate peak of honor and fame" because their "dedicated effort for the community" influences the lives of others for generations to come.[85] Yet, as Thomas Jefferson wrote to James Madison on September 6, 1787, because "the earth belongs always to the living generation, no society can make a perpetual constitution, or even a perpetual law." The consequence of this logic was that, "in their natural course," the "constitution and the laws of their predecessors are extinguished . . . at the end of thirty-four years." Therefore, every subsequent generation should be "as free as if the constitution or law had been expressly limited to thirty-four years only." In retrospect, while Jefferson's theory that "the earth belongs always to the living" might have justly enabled each generation of citizens to determine its own political fiction, in practice citizens bestow so much honor and fame on lawgivers and founders—to creators of political fictions—that those fictions have the potential to become unquestionable truths, rather than fictions that expire "in their natural course."[86] For what mere citizen could ever question the honorable and famous lawgiver or founder?

Yet if honor and fame are due to those who create political fictions, then the analysis and criticism of political fictions is also honorable, because, as Jefferson observed, it is only through such an examination that political communities can ensure that their political fictions continue to meet the needs of the community. The analysis of political fictions requires that we pay particular attention to how and to what degree a political fiction is dialogic, authored, debated, circulated, ratified, and open. For, in their most benign, democratic, and optimistic uses, political fictions would pass both Jefferson's "the earth belongs always to the living" critique and Mercy Otis Warren's epistemological, semiotic, and hegemonic critiques, because all citizens would have the power to define and assent to their fiction. However, as Jefferson's and Warren's critiques imply, in their less benign, democratic, and optimistic uses, political fictions are an oppressive force, either because some citizens were prevented from defining and ratifying the fiction or because it had been manipulated against the agreed-upon initial definitions and citizens were powerless to restore their fiction to its original form. Therefore, each generation's analysis of its political fiction is honorable because it is the necessary first step toward "a free constitution," a constitution free from "force."

Founding Fictions uses a six-step process of description, evaluation, and criticism to analyze the evolution of America's political fictions between 1764 and 1845. I offer this method not as a normative model—not as the only, or even the best method of analysis—but merely as a beginning point for other scholars and citizens to consider in their own analyses of political fictions.

First, determine what kind of political system is described in the fiction: monarchy, aristocracy, theocracy, tyranny, oligarchy, meritocracy, republic, democracy, or anarchy. To answer this question we pay particular attention to the nation's political theory and judge the political fiction based upon the criterion of *who rules.* Does the fiction imagine that the ability to rule is hereditary? Is the ability to rule a gift from God? Is the ability to rule earned through strength, wealth, or merit? Should the people rule through their representatives? Should everyone rule? Should no one rule? Identifying the fiction's political system enables us to judge whom the fiction overtly empowers to rule and how the legitimacy of that power to rule is constructed. Once we determine which political system the fiction advocates, we can proceed to evaluate the fiction based upon its own logic and how well it fits the needs of the particular political community it delimits. At this stage we might ask questions such as the following: Does the political fiction accurately and transparently describe its institutional political arrangements? How do the constitutional mechanisms of power relate to the political fiction? By what criteria does the political fiction argue that it is just?

Second, determine whether the political fiction emerged from the people and whether and how it circulates with citizen consent. To what degree is it dialogic, authored, debated, circulated, ratified, or open? How so? In what ways? To answer these questions we trace the emergence of the fiction and re-create its history and evolution. Did the fiction evolve from a process of negotiation between founders and people? Did the author or authors of the fiction claim authority for it, or was the fiction portrayed as natural, ever-present, or God-given? Was the fiction discussed and debated freely among the political community? Was the fiction approved by those whom it was meant to govern? Was it open to change and amendment? Any political fiction that claims to be of, for, and by the people would necessarily be more, rather than less, dialogic, authored, debated, circulated, ratified, and open, because these are all required aspects of citizen consent.

Third, determine how the members of the political community are portrayed. Are they described as subjects, citizens, partisans, or something else? Are the people's story arcs described as romance, tragedy, satire, or comedy? Determining which kind of political system is in place is not the same as determining how the people are portrayed. For even while it may appear to be a contradiction in terms, a political fiction could describe a monarchy peopled by citizens, or a democracy peopled by subjects. Further, political fictions constitute members of a political community in specific ways—a subject's rights, obligations, and actions are very different from a citizen's, for example. Therefore, how the members of a political community are described positions them and constrains the story arcs of which they are a part. Once we determine how the people are described and delimited, we can determine what kind of story they are said to be a part of. Romances describe heroes overcoming obstacles to achieve greatness; tragedies describe insurmountable obstacles that citizens cannot overcome, but must adapt to or work around; satires describe insurmountable obstacles that citizens can neither overcome nor work around; comedies describe obstacles that citizens can only temporarily overcome, but return again or return in a different form. Once again, the kind of story arc within which the people are cast positions them in specific ways and limits how they are imagined to act. Once we determine how the people are described, we are able to assess how these fictions work to suppress or empower the people.

Fourth, determine how often, where, why, how, and to what effect the fiction is used within the discourse of the political community. Tracing the conditions of emergence, the frequency and purposes of use, the method and frequency of circulation, and the strategic employment of the fiction allows us to gauge how it influences, persuades, constrains, and enables both political communities and the people who comprise them. How does the fiction become a part of the political community? How does the community teach its fiction to its members? Does the political community self-consciously perform its fiction, does it do so surreptitiously, or is it unaware? Once we determine the circulation of the fiction, we can better assess its effects and its strategic uses.

Fifth, determine what rhetorical techniques were used within the fictions and to what effect. An analysis of the arguments, tropes, metaphors, and figures of the fiction enables us to deconstruct how the discourse persuades audiences. We might find that specific patterns of argument reappear in different places, situations, and times, which would mean that that pattern of argument is useful for rhetors who hope to persuade audiences within the frame provided by the political fiction. Any tragic story arc, for example, relies upon an argument from safety, which enables it to persuade the people that they should give up some of their power and allow the system to protect the community. Any monarchical fiction relies upon an argument from authority, which enables it to persuade audiences that one person in the community has more claim to power than any other. Different political theories and fictions would necessarily be constructed with different tropes, metaphors, and figures; an analysis of the fiction's constituent parts allows us to assess how thought is represented in patterns of imagery.

Finally, once we have determined what political system the fiction describes, whether and how citizens consented to their political fiction, how the people and their story arcs are constituted within the fiction, how often, where, why, how, and to what effect the political fiction circulates, and what rhetorical techniques and norms of discourse are explicit or implicit in the political fiction, we are prepared to assess how the fiction empowers or disempowers the people, if the fiction promotes a just political community, and if the fiction leads to emancipation or oppression. For if political fictions are the defining, fundamental, and necessary foundation of any political community, then how they function within a community and how they constitute and how they enable and delimit the people is of the utmost importance. If, like Jefferson, we desire "the will of the majority" to be "fairly" and justly expressed, scholars and citizens have an obligation to evaluate their political fictions carefully.

2
"The Revolution was in the minds of the people"
Citizens as Romantic Heroes, 1764–1776

"The Revolution," reflected John Adams in an 1815 letter to Thomas Jefferson, "was in the minds of the people, and this was effected from 1760 to 1775, in the course of fifteen years before a drop of blood was shed at Lexington."[1] Colonial Americans had once been content with their role within the empire—content with the knowledge that they were British subjects, living "under the best national civil constitution in the world."[2] But as events presented themselves to Americans, it became apparent to some that their role within the empire was not as secure as they had once imagined and that they could apparently lose their rights and liberties without notice. What to do about the encroachments on American liberty had become an intense political debate: radicals like Patrick Henry, John Adams, Sam Adams, and Thomas Jefferson would ask Americans to be patriots and defend their constitution and their liberties from British tyranny. Tories like Thomas Hutchinson and Peter Oliver argued that such "encroachments" were imagined at best, while conservatives like John Dickinson argued for reconciliation rather than revolution. In the end, the arguments of the Tories and conservatives were not compelling, and the American people were persuaded to risk their lives, their fortunes, and their sacred honor in defense of American liberty.[3]

This dramatic and significant shift in the "minds of the people" was at base a shift in the view of the role of the American citizen, and it provided the rhetorical context for the Continental Congress to create a government based upon the will of the people. In retrospect we can see that in the years prior to 1776 Americans rearticulated their political fiction and in so doing recast themselves as patriotic republican citizens. Colonial Americans had a very specific notion of patriotism: the patriot was one who defended the constitution from corruption, thereby acting above party and faction to preserve the liberty of all. Political discourse prior to 1776 had portrayed the king as the only one capable of patriotism, because only the king had the power to act. Yet "patriotism" was a contested term that both seventeenth- and eighteenth-century British Whigs and Tories attempted to define to their own advantage.[4] Perhaps the most important Tory attempt to define the patriot was Henry St. John Bolingbroke's 1738 *The Idea of a Patriot King,* a "mirror for a prince" like Machiavelli's *The Prince,* which Bolingbroke composed while in exile in France.[5] Indeed, "the idea of the Patriot King had become a commonplace in colonial rhetoric," writes William Liddle; Bolingbroke's ideal was so popular in the colonies that "writers employed it without making any reference to its author and, in some instances, these persons were probably innocent of any direct knowledge of the contents of Bolingbroke's works."[6]

Queen Elizabeth was Bolingbroke's best example of the Patriot King (making her a Patriot *Queen,* obviously): she united "the great body of the people in her and their common interest, . . . inflamed them with one national spirit: and, thus armed, she maintained tranquility at home, and carried succor to her friends and terror to her enemies abroad."[7] King George III ascended to the throne in 1761 and was the first king to have his conduct evaluated by Bolingbroke's patriotic standards. Hope in the colonies was certainly high that George III would be the Patriot King, and his "early acts also conspired to feed colonists' palpable desire to believe that the new reign had actually inaugurated the Country party program—exactly as Bolingbroke had suggested they should." It would take colonials until 1774 to finally recognize that George III was not the Patriot King but rather "the arch-conspirator against the liberties of America, the chief author of oppression and the 'Royal Brute of Great Britain.'"[8] Once colonials realized that George III was not the Patriot King who would purge England of corruption, they gave up their hope of reconciliation and moved toward revolution. Therefore, *The Idea of a Patriot King* was not only fundamentally important to the way colonials judged their political leaders, but it was central to America's shift from the monarchical fiction to the republican fiction.

The Idea of a Patriot King had been a central component of the monarchical fiction. Yet when colonials rejected that fiction between 1774 and 1776 they retained their old definition of patriotism—as a leader who would defend the liberties of the people against tyranny—and merely substituted the republican patriot for the monarchical patriot. Just as patriotism was at the center of the monarchical fiction, it was also at the center of the new republican fiction: the American citizen was now conceived of as the patriot hero who would defend liberty by eschewing parties and factions and supporting and defending the free constitution.[9] There was little room for a "patriot subject" in the old monarchical fiction, but once monarchical subjects were cast as republican citizens, patriotism could be the defining characteristic of every American.[10] The rise of the republican fiction in America between 1764 and 1776 is therefore the story of Americans learning that they could be patriotic citizens.

Reaffirming the Monarchical Fiction: Colonials as Willing Subjects

The close of the Seven Years' War in 1763 had left the British Empire with a mounting debt, one it hoped to recoup, in part, from its seemingly prosperous colonies in North America. The new policies "aimed at enhanced regulation of imperial commerce, greater control of the provinces in general, and the collection of revenue," and while these increased restrictions may have appeared to have encroached upon the rights of colonials, Parliament had optimistically expected to accomplish its goals "bloodlessly."[11] In 1763 Britain's first attempt to exert greater control over its colonies was to prohibit the settlement of western lands, which it hoped would prevent further costly hostilities between colonials and Native Americans. The Proclamation of 1763 raised the ire of western land speculators and eventually politicized landed squires like George Washington who previously had not taken an active part in political affairs, even though he had held political office for several years.[12] The Proclamation of 1763 was followed by the 1764 Sugar and Currency Acts, which increased duties on imported sugar, coffee, wine, and indigo and prevented colonials from printing their own currency; by the 1765 Mutiny or Quartering Act, which required colonials to provide for and house British troops; and by the 1765 Stamp Act, which levied the first direct internal tariff on the colonists by taxing all official papers (contracts, wills, licenses, etc.), published materials (newspapers, pamphlets), and playing cards and dice. Mercy Otis Warren remembered that the Stamp Act was an "innovation that gave a general alarm throughout the continent."[13] Remonstrances against the new restrictions poured forth from colonials, the most famous of which was written by Warren's brother; James Otis's 1764 "Of the Political and Civil Rights of the British Colonists" protested that colonials were still British subjects and retained their rights as such. In May 1765, Patrick Henry's *Virginia Resolutions to the House of Burgesses* was published and republished throughout the colonies, electrifying Americans from one end of the continent to the other. In October 1765 the Stamp Act Congress convened in New York City, declared the rights of colonials, and prepared petitions for a redress of grievances for both King George III and Parliament. In the space of two short years, colonials became politically active: pouring out their frustrations against parliamentary control in petitions and pamphlets; boycotting British stamps; and uniting in common cause. By examining each of these early responses to Parliament's attempts to increase its control over the colonies, we see how colonial leaders reaffirmed and explained their understanding of their role as British subjects. Except for the firebrand—and many thought treasonous—rhetoric of Patrick Henry, the colonial protests over the Stamp Act were largely conservative; that is, colonials hoped merely to preserve their rights as British subjects, not to expand their rights or revolt from imperial control.[14]

In the third of his 1774 "Novanglus" essays, John Adams described Boston's James Otis as "a senator, whose parts, literature, eloquence, and integrity proved him a character in the world equal to any of the time in which he flourished." Mercy Otis Warren described her brother as "a gentleman of great probity, experience, and parliamentary abilities, whose religious adherence to the rights of his country had distinguished him through the long course of years, in which he had sustained some of the first offices in government."[15] While Otis is not often remembered among the giants of the revolutionary generation, he was both well known and well respected in his day—it was his political capital that resulted in the Stamp Act Congress of 1765, for example. Bernard Bailyn describes Otis's 1764 "Of the Political and Civil Rights of the British Colonists" as "concentrated fury." Bailyn believes that its "passion" and "wildness" set it apart from other pamphlets of the day, yet as we shall see, Otis's pamphlet was a conservative plea for rights that colonials believed had been previously established, not "wild" by any means.[16]

Otis's task was to inquire "after the foundation of [colonists'] rights," which he believed others had erroneously traced back only as far as colonial charters or Magna Carta. While he believed it was his "duty" to submit to the laws of king and Parliament, anyone who preached "unlimited passive obedience and non-resistance" was "a fool and a knave [and] a rebel against common sense, as well as the laws of God, of Nature, and of Country." He granted "that the parliament of Great Britain has the undoubted power and lawful authority to make acts for the general good [and] that by naming [the laws, they] shall and ought to be equally binding, as upon the subjects of Great Britain within the realm," yet he rejected Parliament's power to make colonials "slaves" by depriving them of their liberties. For while Parliament had absolute power over British subjects, all British subjects possessed "natural, inherent and inseperable rights as men and as citizens . . . which can never be abolished . . . till the general conflagration." Otis concluded that since all British subjects retained their basic rights, Parliament's recent intrusions into colonial affairs were unjust, because Americans were entitled to "all the natural, essential, inherent and inseperable rights of our fellow subjects in Great Britain."[17] Otis differentiated between the political rights colonials had as "free born subjects" of the British government and those "natural" rights enjoyed by all "men" and all "citizens" outside of the British constitution. Yet even as he recognized the natural rights of colonials, he did not assert or demand those rights in 1764: his goal was to reaffirm colonials' political rights.

Otis's defense of colonials' political rights was therefore far from a revolutionary document. In fact, his essay was *conservative:* like other Americans in 1764, he hoped for nothing more than to preserve the political rights he believed colonials possessed as British subjects. His reaffirmation of the relationship between the mother country and its offspring included six propositions that when taken together amounted to the "first principles of law and justice and the great barriers of a free state, and of the British constitution in particular." An act of Parliament was just only when it "govern[s] by stated laws," when "those laws have no other end ultimately, but the good of the people," and when "taxes are not to be laid on the people, but by their consent in person, or by deputation." This last "principle"—no taxation without representation—was the crucial sticking point. "Now can there be any liberty," asked Otis, "where property is taken away without consent? Can it with any colour of truth, justice or equality, be affirmed, that the northern colonies are represented in parliament?" And while Otis had previously affirmed that colonials owed their entire allegiance to British law, his analysis supported the conclusion that, "as it is agreed on all hands, the Crown alone cannot impose [taxes,] we should be justifiable, in refusing to pay them." Yet, while this radical conclusion did follow from his premises, Otis was quick to back down from the radical and revolutionary answer to the problems of colonials. Rather, he argued that colonials "must and ought to yield obedience to an act of parliament, tho' erroneous, 'till repealed." With almost comical results, Otis was willing to go no further than his six propositions reaffirming British rights; he would not, and did not, challenge the political fiction of the divine right of kings.[18]

Otis had created a neat syllogism in which he first described all unconstitutional laws as tyrannical and then applied that logic to the Stamp Act, which he found "absolutely irreconcilable with the rights of the Colonists, as British subjects, and as men," and "an entire disenfranchisement of every civil right." Yet instead of calling for open rebellion against these odious laws, he concluded that it was the "duty" of colonials "to submit and patiently bear them, till [Parliament] will be pleased to relieve us." Such a conservative conclusion—so much at odds with his radical premises—belied Otis's immersion in and unwitting defense of the existing monarchical fiction. "It is a maxim that the King can do no wrong and every good subject is bound to believe his King is not inclined to do any," Otis reminded colonials. Lest his audience mistake his radical premises for actual radicalism, he reaffirmed that "it would therefore be the highest degree of impudence and disloyalty to imagine that the King, at the head of his parliament, could have any, but the most pure and perfect intentions of justice, goodness and truth, that human nature is capable of." Of course, Parliament "may have erred in [its] kind intentions towards the Colonies," it may have been "misinformed and deceived," but still "we must obey." In fact, "there would be an end of all government if one or a number of subjects or subordinate provinces should take upon them so far to judge of the justice of an Act of parliament, as to refuse obedience to it."

Otis viewed the problems facing colonials as portentous of tyranny and slavery, but he was unable to question the underlying assumptions of the monarchical political fiction. The Crown was good and could not be mistaken; colonials were subjects of the Crown; therefore, it was the duty of colonials to obey the laws established by Parliament until such time as Parliament chose to relieve them of the law's burden. Subjects were not permitted to question either the authority of the Crown or the laws made on the Crown's behalf; to do so would be "treason" and would result in "the end of all government." The monarchical fiction so completely permeated Otis's defense of colonial rights that it rendered his conclusions comically conservative. And while Otis's sentiments were on par with those of most colonials in 1764, he lost credibility with his more radical friends in Boston because of "his conservative whitewashing" of colonial grievances. When the 1765 Virginia *Resolutions* electrified the colonies with the more overtly radical doctrine that insisted upon "no taxation without representation," Otis was "at first shocked by the radicalism," and pronounced it "treason."[19]

Otis viewed colonial Americans as subjects, not as citizens, and this distinction is worth considering. If a citizen is an officer of the government, as Aristotle said, what special function or role does a subject have? Colonial subjects traced their rights to the Petition of Right of 1628, which formally protected "divers Rights and Liberties of the Subjects" such as the protection from forced taxation "without common consent by act of parliament," from forced loyalty oaths, and from imprisonment contrary to the stated laws of Britain. King Charles I believed that the Petition of Right merely "confirmed the antient Liberties of my Subjects" and that "the king's Prerogative is to defend the people's Liberties."[20] In other words, a subject did not have the power to protect his or her own liberties, but must rely upon the powerful king for protection; a subject "did not share in the king's authority," but "did have rights."[21] The monarchical fiction did not permit subjects to evaluate, question, or voice an opinion on the conduct of their government: the decisions of the king were perfect. Therefore, to evaluate or question the king was to contradict the entirety of the monarchical fiction. Otis was correct to argue that British subjects had no choice but to obey Parliament's laws, for obey was all that subjects *could* do within the monarchical fiction. His reaffirmation of colonials' rights as British subjects therefore demonstrates the dramatic transition that political theory would undergo as Americans moved from subjects to citizens over the next twelve years. Eventually, Americans would make the ability to evaluate, question, and voice an opinion on the conduct of their government the defining characteristic of the citizen.

There is no doubt that Virginia and Massachusetts led their sister colonies in reaffirming colonial rights, yet while these two colonies found common cause they at times offered incompatible arguments. "The Virginians, in their resolves, came forward, conscious of their own independence, and at once asserted *their rights as men,*" observed Mercy Otis Warren; "Massachusetts generally founded their claims on the *rights of British subjects,* and the privileges of their English ancestors."[22] On May 30, 1765, Patrick Henry had been seated as a member of the Virginia House of Burgesses for a mere nine days. His family was "neither especially wealthy nor among the province's social or political elite," yet he had a gift for oratory and "the verve of an arriviste who refused to be shackled by tradition or a stodgy elite."[23] With a bare quorum seated at the House of Burgesses, Henry introduced the *Stamp Act Resolutions,* which, John Adams declared, "did great honor to that province, and to the eminent patriot, Patrick Henry, who composed them."[24] Thomas Jefferson was then "a student of law in Williamsburg," and he remembered in his *Autobiography* how he had hovered outside "at the door of the lobby" while he listened to the "splendid display of Mr. Henry's talents as a popular orator."[25]

Henry presented seven resolutions before the House of Burgesses, all of them calculated to restore colonial liberty. The resolutions the House of Burgesses actually passed were only slightly more radical in their implications than the propositions offered by James Otis. Indeed, the first four resolutions merely echoed Otis's previous reaffirmation of colonials' rights as British subjects: British subjects could not legally be taxed without the consent of their representatives.[26] The controversial fifth resolution added little more to the argument but completed the syllogism—taking the argument further than Otis had dared or perhaps wanted to—with the radical conclusion that "the General Assembly of this Colony have the *only* and *exclusive* Right and Power to lay Taxes and Impositions upon the inhabitants of this Colony" and violations of this right had a "manifest Tendency to destroy British as well as American Freedom."[27] It seemed to follow logically that if British subjects could only be taxed with the consent of their representatives, only the House of Burgesses had the right to tax Virginians. But if this conclusion was true, then its negative was also true: Parliament did *not* have the "right and power" to tax Virginians. And while this conclusion may not seem radical prima facie, when it was read within the constraints of the monarchical fiction, for Virginians to declare that Parliament had neither the right nor the power to tax them was to threaten the fiction of the divine right of kings. Some conservative Virginians believed—with James Otis—that their refusal to consent to the power of Parliament would result in the "end of all government"; therefore the fifth resolution was recanted on May 31, 1765.

If the fifth resolution was controversial, the sixth and seventh could only be called treasonous and belligerent. They asserted that Virginians were "not bound to yield obedience" to any of Parliament's tax laws and that whoever argued that they *were* required to obey would be "deemed an enemy of His Majesty's colony."[28] The first four resolutions passed easily, the more radical and controversial fifth resolution passed by one vote after "several hours of heated debate" (but was reversed the next day), and the burgesses never voted on the last two resolutions. Although the burgesses only actually agreed to the first four resolutions, all but the fifth were printed throughout the colonies, making it appear that the burgesses had approved the most controversial, radical, treasonous, and belligerent defense of colonial liberty ever penned in America.[29] The publication of the *Stamp Act Resolutions* helped to raise public opinion against the odious laws throughout the colonies. Everywhere—but especially in Massachusetts—colonials protested the Stamp Act: pamphlets, speeches, organizations, boycotts, and riots all testified to colonials' unified dissatisfaction. Such dissatisfaction led to the first joint governing body in the colonies: the Stamp Act Congress of 1765.

"What a Blessing to us has the Stamp Act eventually prov'd," wrote Sam Adams, "when the Colonys saw the Common Danger they at the same time saw their mutual Dependence."[30] Nine colonies recognized "their mutual Dependence" and sent representatives to New York for the joint protest meeting on October 7, 1765—New Hampshire, North Carolina, Georgia, and Virginia did not send delegates. The congress believed it was its "indispensable duty . . . to procure the repeal of the act for granting and applying certain stamp duties, of all clauses of any other acts of Parliament whereby the jurisdiction of the admiralty is extended as aforesaid, and of the other late acts of the restriction of the American commerce"; therefore, "upon mature deliberation," it agreed to thirteen resolutions known as the 1765 Declaration of Rights. Along with these resolutions, it also sent petitions to the king and to both houses of Parliament. John Adams believed that the Virginia *Resolutions* and the Stamp Act Congress's Declaration of Rights "expressed the universal opinion of the continent at that time"; therefore, because the Declaration of Rights was the joint work of a majority of the colonies, it can be viewed as the representative statement of the colonial leadership during the Stamp Act crisis and as the ultimate appeal for a restoration of colonials' rights as British subjects.[31]

The first two resolutions in the Declaration of Rights described the monarchical fiction as a transactional relationship between the Crown and "His Majesty's subjects." Colonials "owe the same allegiance to the Crown . . . as his subjects born within the realm," and in return colonials were "entitled to all the inherent rights and liberties of his natural born subjects." Describing the relationship between the Crown and the colonies as quid pro quo—based upon mutual rights and obligations—allowed the Stamp Act Congress to argue Henry's "treasonous" position against the right of Parliament to tax the colonies. First, the congress argued that the "freedom of a people, and the undoubted right of Englishmen," meant "that no taxes be imposed on them, but with their own consent, given personally, or by their representatives." Second, the "colonies are not, and from their local circumstances cannot be, represented in the House of Commons in Great-Britain." Finally, "the only representatives of the people of these colonies, are persons chosen therein by themselves, and that no taxes ever have been, or can be constitutionally imposed on them, but by their respective legislatures." With one declaration the Stamp Act Congress had further radicalized the professed complaints of colonials; it now no longer seemed treasonous to assert that Parliament did not have the right to tax them. Yet the passive language of these resolutions—asserting that no taxes "be imposed on them"—signals that colonials acknowledged both that only their representatives had the right to make laws for them *and* that they had no power to make laws for themselves. In other words, the use of passive language indicated that colonials viewed themselves as subjects who did not possess the power to act.

While the Declaration of Rights drew the conclusions that Otis and the burgesses were unwilling to draw and in so doing potentially threatened the monarchical fiction, the Stamp Act Congress drew these conclusions in the name of preserving their rights as British subjects, not to challenge or destroy the old fiction.[32] For example, the preamble of the Declaration professed that members of the Stamp Act Congress were "sincerely devoted, with the warmest sentiments of affection and duty to His Majesty's Person and Government, inviolably attached to the present happy establishment of the Protestant succession." The congress desired nothing more than to reclaim colonials' rights as Englishmen and to return to their carefree days as monarchical subjects. The rhetoric of the first phase of the rise of the republican fiction can be described as *reaffirming*—colonials sought to reaffirm their rights as subjects and to revalidate their understanding of the monarchical fiction of the people within the empire.

The declarations, petitions, remonstrances, and resolutions of the colonials and their British friends proved successful; on March 18, 1766, "His Majesty was pleased to give his Royal Assent to An ACT to REPEAL an Act made in the last Session of Parliament," and with that, colonial liberty was restored. And while the citizens of Boston and other towns celebrated the "great, glorious, important NEWS" and the "Bells in all the churches were immediately set ringing," and a "day for General Rejoicing" was appointed to celebrate that the colonials' "incontestable Right of Internal Taxation remain[ed] . . . inviolate," Parliament also ominously declared that it "had, hath, and of right ought to have, full power and authority to make laws and statutes of sufficient force and vitality to bind the colonies and people of America . . . in all cases whatsoever."[33] Unfazed by Parliament's portentous declaration, colonials celebrated their reaffirmed rights as British subjects.

Challenging the Monarchical Fiction: Colonials as Patriot Subjects

On March 1, 1766, Benjamin Franklin optimistically wrote home from London that Parliament had passed the Declaratory Act "merely to save Appearances"; likewise, John Adams believed that the act "would not be executed." Franklin and Adams were wrong. In June 1767 Parliament passed the Townshend Revenue Acts, which imposed new taxes on paper, tea, glass, lead, and paint and increased the number of British customs officials in the colonies. Parliament's forceful demonstration that it meant what it had said in the Declaratory Act—that it intended to use its powers to make laws for the colonies "in all cases whatsoever"—led colonials to respond by challenging both Parliament's power and the monarchical fiction. The first and most important challenge to the prevailing political fiction was John Dickinson's 1767 *Letters from a Farmer in Pennsylvania,* which "outsold every other political tract published in America before 1776." Dickinson's *Letters* were followed in 1768 by Massachusetts's *Circular Letter* and in 1769 by Virginia's *Non-Importation Resolutions,* both of which attempted to narrow the boundaries of parliamentary rule and establish patterns of intercolonial cooperation and communication, which were absolutely essential for encouraging colonial trust and joint colonial action. In 1770 Parliament would begrudgingly repeal most of the Townshend Duties—save the one on tea—even as it continued to assert its rights to make laws for, and to levy taxes upon, colonials as it saw fit. The years from 1767 to 1770, during which colonials challenged the monarchical fiction, were therefore essentially an impasse. Colonials began to realize with Franklin that "no middle doctrine can be well maintained": either "Parliament has a power to make *all laws* for us, or that it has a power to make *no laws* for us."[34] And while Franklin was *beginning* to believe that Parliament did not have the right to make any laws for Americans, he, like most colonials, was not yet willing to reach this irrevocable and revolutionary conclusion. Yet the arguments made during the Townshend Duty controversy—like those made during the Stamp Act crisis—would help to move American public opinion in the direction of revolution and would help colonials construct their new republican fiction.

On December 5, 1767, John Dickinson, the Stamp Act Congress member who had written its Declaration of Rights two years earlier, sent his yet mostly unpublished *Letters from a Farmer in Pennsylvania* to James Otis in the hope that his senior colleague would "dispose" of the essays as he thought proper. Dickinson claimed to have written the essays "with the most ardent affection for the British colonies, the purest intentions to promote their welfare, an honest desire to assert their rights, and with a deep sense of their impending misfortunes." Yet, despite these seemingly radical beliefs, Dickinson praised Otis's "moderation" during the Stamp Act crisis and reassured him that his solutions to the "impending misfortune" of the colonies were very much in line with the reaffirming arguments of Otis's 1764 pamphlet and the 1765 Declaration. "Our cause is a cause of the highest dignity," Dickinson pronounced: "I hope it will not be disgraced in any colony by a single rash step. We have constitutional methods of seeking redress, and they are the best methods."[35] While Dickinson's *Letters* set newspapers and town meetings ablaze and "forced everyone on both sides" to ponder the precise "nature and distribution of power in the imperial system," Dickinson would cling to the monarchical fiction—eventually refusing to vote for revolution in 1776 because he still hoped for reconciliation. He conservatively "believed that mobs, sedition, and ungentlemanly violence had no part in colonial resistance to the mother country," yet he radically challenged Parliament's "right to raise a revenue in the colonies by means of external taxes," yet again, he conservatively recognized Parliament's "power to regulate colonial trade and legislate for the colonies."[36] Dickinson's arguments therefore represented the middle position between the fiction of colonials as monarchical subjects and as republican citizens. Indeed, Dickinson articulated this middle position so clearly, and his position resonated so well with colonials, that his *Letters* were published in twenty-one out of twenty-five colonial newspapers, and in three different pamphlet editions in Philadelphia, two editions in Boston, and one each in New York, Williamsburg, Paris, London, and Dublin.[37]

The *Letters* are noteworthy first and foremost because Dickinson popularized and legitimated the idea that Parliament was implicated in a conspiracy to deprive colonials of their natural rights as British subjects. "The question in these cases is not," writes the Farmer, "what evil *has actually attended* particular measures—but, what evil, in the nature of things, *is likely to attend them*."[38] Dickinson asks Americans to view recent events for what they are: colonials could dismiss the Sugar, Quartering, and Stamp Acts as "mistakes," but when these were followed by the Declaratory Act and the Townshend Duties, it was clear that trouble was afoot. According to Bernard Bailyn, conspiracy rhetoric prior to 1776 was irrefutable: "once assumed, it could not be easily dispelled: denial only confirmed it, since what conspirators profess is not what they believe; the ostensible is not the real; and the real is deliberately malign."[39] Gone were the days when James Otis could naively profess that Parliament was "mistaken" in its good intentions toward the colonies. It had become clear to Dickinson that the dire warnings of corruption penned by the British Opposition Whigs and the Country Party obtained in the colonies.

Indeed, much of the force of Dickinson's *Letters* comes from his hysterical use of *accumulatio*—the "snowball" figure that relies upon the use of a series of necessary causes and effects—to argue that each action of Parliament was portentous of a slippery slope to despotism. The Farmer believes that he clearly views the "evil" that is likely "to attend" the recent actions of Parliament. For example:

> Has not the parliament *expressly* AVOWED their INTENTION of raising money from US FOR CERTAIN PURPOSES? Is not this scheme *popular* in Great Britain? Will the taxes, imposed by the late act, *answer those purposes*? If it will, must it not take an immense sum from us? If it will not, *is it to be expected,* that the parliament will not *fully execute* their INTENTION when it is *pleasing at home,* and *not opposed here*? Must not this be done by imposing NEW *taxes*? Will not every addition, thus made to our taxes, be an addition to the power of the *British* legislature, by *increasing the number of officers* employed in the collection? Will not every additional tax therefore render it *more difficult* to abrogate any of them? When a branch of revenue is once established, does it not appear to many people *invidious* and *undutiful,* to attempt to abolish it? If taxes, sufficient to *accomplish the* INTENTION of the parliament, are imposed by parliament, *what taxes will remain* to be imposed by our assemblies? If *no material taxes remain* to be imposed by *them,* what must become of them, and the *people* they represent? . . . the late act of parliament is *only* designed to be a PRECEDENT, whereon the future vassalage of these colonies may be established.[40]

Dickinson's use of capitals and italics is meant to convey his intensity, his outrage, his speaking with wild gestures and raised voice. In short, Dickinson's Farmer is no complacent gentleman, but rather an active and determined patriot defending colonial liberty. Such intense language likely appealed to the more common sort and helps to explain both the popularity of the *Letters* and Dickinson's fame as a writer. His use of capitals and italics also helps him to convey his conspiracy argument, because the written form mimics the dire urgency of his message: There is DANGER; it is us versus THEM; we must DO something! Aside from the sense of alarm conveyed by his typesetting, the overall message of this hysterical passage was to warn colonials that if they did not protest against the Townshend Duties, they had de facto consented to Parliament's right to tax them—in perpetuity. While the duties may have seemed "trifling," Parliament hopes that colonials will consent both to the taxes and to the power of Parliament to levy the taxes, which would establish "a precedent for future use."[41]

Dickinson's repeated use of the word "intention" to describe the actions of Parliament ties together his general argument that colonials needed to find the strength actively to oppose the Townshend Duties. Because he wrote his *Letters* as a protest against the constitutionality of the Townshend Duties, the questions of whether or not Parliament has the right to tax the colonies, why Parliament's tax is unjust, and what colonials should do about the tax are central to his purpose. Dickinson argues that some colonials have made false distinctions between internal and external taxes—the Stamp Act had been odious on this view because it had created an internal tax, the traditional purview of colonial legislatures—but, Dickinson denies that Parliament has "the power . . . to lay upon these colonies any 'tax' whatever."[42] Further, if colonials admit that Parliament has the "right *to* levy a tax of one penny upon us, they have a right to levy a *million* upon us: For where does the right stop?"[43] Rather than give Parliament such carte blanche powers, colonial liberty requires that they retain the right and power to tax themselves, for if they do not, they will lose their "constitutional check upon the administration, which may thereby be brought into order without violence."[44] Therefore, because there is no difference between internal and external taxes, because Parliament does not have the power to tax colonials even one penny, and because colonials desire to prevent warfare between the people and "the administration," the people must retain the power to tax themselves. Yet, it is the "expressly avowed" intention of Parliament to tax the colonies: Parliament would "fully execute their intention"; and Parliament would "accomplish the intention" and abolish colonial liberty. Dickinson's use of the word "intention" mirrors his larger argument about the inevitable danger inherent in colonial compliance with the Townshend Duties and helps him to persuade colonials that the duties carried the semblance of conspiracy.[45]

Dickinson argues that because Parliament clearly places the rights and liberties of colonials in jeopardy, it is their duty as patriots to watch the actions of Parliament closely, to unite against the common danger, and to fight the conspiracy against their liberties. Indeed, "whoever seriously considers the matter," writes the Farmer, "must perceive that a dreadful stroke is aimed at the liberty of these colonies. I say, of these colonies; for the cause of one is the cause of all." Not only are all of the colonies threatened, but part of the plot against them is "to divide, and thus to destroy, [which] is the first political maxim in attacking those who are powerful by their union."[46] Dickinson argues that "vigilance" and "union" are the only hope for defending colonial rights. "Negligence" and "division" will lead to "distress and death," or what is worse, "shame and slavery." "For this reason," the Farmer cautions, "every man among us, who in any manner would encourage either *dissension, dissidence,* or *indifference,* between these colonies, is an enemy to *himself,* and *to his country.*"[47] Such strong talk of union was necessary because colonials had limited previous experience working together. The Stamp Act—as Sam Adams remarked—had been a "blessing" because it forced colonials to recognize their "mutual dependence," leading to the first joint American Congress. Dickinson asked colonials to unite and to cooperate, to recognize once again that the threat to each of their liberties required putting aside petty intercolonial differences. In short, colonials had to work together to preserve everyone's liberties and safety, and those who refused to contribute to common cause and obey the decisions of the many were "enemies."

Not only was it necessary for colonials to band together, not only was it their duty to protect their liberties, but Dickinson radically argues that it is their *right to judge their government.* "Ought not the people therefore to watch? To observe facts? To search into causes? To investigate designs?" asks Dickinson. "And have they not a right of JUDGING from the evidence before them, on no slighter points than their liberty and happiness?"[48] In 1764 James Otis had explicitly declared that if individual subjects or subordinate political bodies attempted to "judge of the justice of an Act of parliament," it would result "in the end of all government"; by 1767 Dickinson argued that subjects and subordinates had a duty and a right to judge their government and if they did not, then *that* would be the end of all *liberty.* Further, the standard Dickinson proposed for subjects to use when judging their government was "their liberty and happiness"—no more, no less.

Dickinson's view of the British subject's power to act was therefore dramatically different from that of James Otis or the Stamp Act Congress. The most striking feature of Dickinson's *Letters* for our account of the rise of the republican fiction is that he refuses to agree that laws are just merely because they are "imposed" upon colonials—either by Parliament or by representatives. And, perhaps even more startling, because it portended anarchism in the minds of Tories like Peter Oliver and Thomas Hutchinson, Dickinson urged colonials to evaluate, question, and voice an opinion upon the conduct of their government. In other words, Dickinson had dared to act as no subject should: he had dared to judge his government. Not only had he refused to obey, but he had encouraged other colonials to act together and judge their government for themselves. The *Letters* therefore had the potential to unleash colonials from the constraints of the monarchical fiction and turn them from subjects to citizens. But, Dickinson was not asking for revolution; on the contrary, he asked colonials to guard their rights vigilantly within the prevailing monarchical fiction, the legitimacy of which they were not to question. Like Otis, Dickinson had defended the actions of Parliament based upon the monarchical fiction. "When any laws, injurious to these colonies, are passed," wrote Dickinson, "we cannot suppose, that any injury was intended us by his Majesty, or the Lords." Therefore, while Dickinson asked colonials to take on the burdens of patriotism, he attempted to cast them as patriot subjects—a contradiction in terms. Patriot subjects could watch and critique their government, but if they found the government acting against their liberty, they could do nothing but obey.

The unintended consequence of Dickinson's call for colonial unity and for subjects to judge the government was that his cherished monarchical fiction was threatened.[49] Dickinson clearly supported the old fiction, and he could not have predicted that once colonials began to view their rights, obligations, and security in common it was but a short step to maintaining regular communication about grievances (Committees of Correspondence) and enforcing boycotts of British goods (Committees of Safety). Despite his fervent desire to retain the connection between Britain and her colonies, Dickinson unwittingly called for the exact form of cooperation that would allow colonials to build the trust necessary to revolt. That revolution would not occur for another nine years; in 1767 colonials were only beginning to learn to trust one another and were only beginning to challenge the monarchical fiction.

It is difficult to know if colonial leaders self-consciously designed their cooperation and communication strategies to move the colonies toward revolution—certainly John Dickinson and Sam Adams had different agendas, for example. Whether or not they knew that they were laying the groundwork for revolution, it is clear that cooperation and communication were the goals of the Massachusetts and Virginia legislatures in 1768 and 1769. These were no easy goals to attain. As historian T. H. Breen reminds us, "the rhetoric of common cause, however defined, had constantly to struggle against feelings of distrust and suspicion fueled by cultural and social differences."[50] Massachusetts was the first to recognize the importance of united colonial action; the avowed purpose of Sam Adams's 1768 *Circular Letter* "was to unite the colonies against British oppression." Yet, while the *Circular Letter* challenged the prevailing monarchical fiction, "it was clear in 1768 that the colonies could be united only on conservative ground," and therefore the *Letter* asked for colonial cooperation, not revolution.[51] In both 1768 and 1769 Virginia circulated its *Non-Importation Resolutions* throughout the colonies in the hope that, being "acquainted with them, [sister colonies] may go hand in hand in their opposition to measures, which [Virginians] think have an immediate tendency to enslave them."[52] The two-pronged strategy of building trust through increased communication and cooperation, begun in 1768, eventually allowed colonials to argue for more radical answers to their joint grievances and ultimately led to the destruction of the monarchical fiction.

In 1768 the Massachusetts House of Representatives had "taken into their serious consideration the great difficulties that must accrue to themselves and their constituents by the operation [of the Townshend Duties] on the American colonies." After due consideration, Massachusetts believed it "necessary" for the colonies to "harmonize with each other" and for each colony to "communicate their mind" to their sister colonies. The importance of Massachusetts's *Circular Letter* was less in its critique of the Townshend Duties or in its challenge to the monarchical fiction—indeed, the *Letter* offered no new arguments on either of those fronts—but it was important because it attempted to open a channel of communication between the colonies in the hope of building both intercolonial consensus and trust. There is no overestimating the importance of intercolonial communication to the creation of the new American republican fiction: without the ability to share grievances, to compare arguments, and to enforce boycotts, colonials would have never learned to trust each other enough to imagine a new political fiction, especially one premised upon the will of the people.[53] Breen has aptly described colonials as "inexperienced lovers" who "tentatively reached out to each other, afraid of having expressions of interest spurned and worried that the objects of their attention might turn out to be less reliable than had been assumed."[54] Indeed, Massachusetts sounded almost obsequious when addressing its sister colonies in its *Letter:* "your assembly is too generous and liberal in sentiment to believe that this letter proceeds from an ambition of taking the lead, or dictating to the other assemblies. They freely submit their opinions to the judgment of others; and shall take it kind in your house to point out to them anything further that may be thought necessary."[55] Massachusetts was gratified in its hope: every colonial legislature considered the *Letter,* and all except for Pennsylvania concurred with its sentiments. Some colonial legislatures, including Massachusetts's, were dissolved by loyal royal governors for their pains.[56] While other colonial legislatures—New York, Massachusetts, and Georgia—were harshly disciplined for agreeing to cooperate with their sister colonies, Virginia led the way in turning that disciplinary action into further proof of the necessity and benefit of colonial cooperation.

On May 17, 1769, Governor Lord Botetourt dissolved the Virginia House of Burgesses for commending the Massachusetts *Circular Letter* and approving its own *Petition to his Majesty, Memorial to the House of Lords,* and *Remonstrance to the House of Commons.* Once dissolved, the former House of Burgesses reconvened "the next day at the Apollo of the Raleigh Tavern."

And, according to newly elected burgess Thomas Jefferson, the deposed House then formed itself "into a voluntary convention, drew up articles of association against the use of any merchandise imported from Gr. Britain, signed and recommended them to the people, repaired to our several counties, & were reelected without any other exception than of the very few who had declined assent to our proceedings."[57] New York and Boston had already agreed to their own non-importation agreement, but Virginia's *Non-Importation Resolutions* "sparked enthusiastic renewal of non-importation, as colonials from Boston to Charleston intensified pressure on local merchants to close the American market to British exports."[58] Virginia thus helped to organize a colonial consensus around the consumer boycott strategy that Breen called the "distinguishing mark" and the "signature" of colonial protest prior to 1776.

Virginians declared in the *Non-Importation Resolutions* that they were "his Majesty's most dutiful subjects," avowed their "inviolable and unshaken Fidelity and Loyalty to our most gracious Sovereign, our Affection for all our Fellow Subjects of Great-Britain," and protested "against every Act or Thing, which may have the most distant Tendency to interrupt, or in any wise disturb his Majesty's Peace, and the good Order of his Government in this Colony." Despite their sincere desire to maintain the monarchical fiction, Virginians were "deeply affected with the Grievances and Distresses, with which his Majesty's American Subjects are oppressed"; they dreaded the "Evils which threaten[ed] the Ruin" of themselves and their "Posterity, by reducing us from a free and happy People to a wretched and miserable State of Slavery." Further, Virginians found that with "little Reason to expect a Redress of . . . Grievances," their only recourse for preventing the enslavement of themselves and their posterity was to "voluntarily and unanimously" resolve "to be frugal in the Use and Consumption of British Manufacturers." They therefore pledged to abide by eight non-importation resolutions in the hope that "their example as well as all other legal Ways and Means in their Power, [would] promote and encourage industry and Frugality, and discourage all Manner of Luxury and Extravagance."[59]

While Virginians hoped to use all of the "legal" means within their "power" to enforce the boycott, the *Resolutions* raised interesting legal questions. Were the *Resolutions* written by the mob or by patriots? Were they really legal or binding? Who had the power to determine if they were legal? Who had the power to enforce compliance if they were legal? After all, the House of Burgesses sat at the pleasure of his Majesty, and when Governor Botetourt dissolved them, they no longer functioned in their accorded role within the monarchical fiction. Further, the burgesses challenged the power of the monarchical fiction by defying Governor Botetourt and reconvening on their own authority, so what, then did their resulting *Resolutions* mean? Had Virginians erected their own government by their actions in 1769? According to their own declaration, they had not. Rather, Virginians had pledged to "Risque our Lives and Fortunes to maintain and defend" the monarchy, not independence. So, while the events surrounding the Virginia *Resolutions* could have led to a revolt from Great Britain, it is clear that this was not a part of the agenda in 1769.

The quasi-legal and extra-fictional *Resolutions* may not have been revolutionary in the literal sense of the term, but they led to some radical changes in colonial politics. The effects of colonial boycotts were to extend the realm of political participation to every consumer, build trust between colonials, and demonstrate that order could be maintained by an authority outside the monarchy. Importantly for our chronicle of the growth of the republican fiction, these effects of colonial boycotts allowed colonials to imagine a new form of government based upon the will of the people. The boycotts helped to turn colonials from monarchical subjects into republican citizens by politicizing the actions of average people. In short, for the first time colonials had more to do than merely obey. Dickinson had asked colonials to watch, evaluate, and judge their government, which were important features of republican citizenship, but only gave colonials limited powers to act. Boycotting British goods provided Americans with a specific realm of action in which all Americans could directly contribute to protecting their rights and liberties. Further, because participation in the boycotts was voluntary—although Committees of Safety put much pressure on colonials to comply—actively participating in the boycotts was a kind of popular ratification, or a show of support, for colonial leadership and a kind of popular rejection of the fiction of the people as subjects. The patriot subject, while a contradiction in terms, was now portrayed as a subject who possessed rights and who would take action to defend his or her liberties, rather than merely rely upon the protection of the king. Furthermore, because boycotts were organized and enforced by Committees of Correspondence and Safety, which were obviously not a part of the monarchical fiction, colonials learned that extra-fictional political associations of their own making were possible, which, in turn, demonstrated that political organizations could be created and were not God-given. In other words, in acting together to defend their own rights and liberties and in taking part in the creation and the maintenance of political decisions outside of the monarchical fiction, colonial patriot subjects began to develop a new political fiction. The patriot subject was neither a part of the monarchical fiction nor outside the monarchical fiction. Americans had proved that they would no longer willingly obey when they judged the actions of Parliament unjust.

Although we could never say that the boycotts were a complete success (there were accusations of "cheating" everywhere), they did result in a 50 percent reduction in British exports to the colonies and in the subsequent March 1770 repeal of all of the odious Townshend Duties except for the tax on tea, which was retained to bail out the failing East India Company. And while colonials merely challenged the monarchical fiction from 1767 to 1770, and the period can be described as an impasse, colonials learned that united action would achieve positive results. Colonial leaders found that quasi-legal and extra-fictional political associations could compel obedience, sustain unity, and maintain order, but only under certain conditions: first, colonials had to be persuaded that a conspiracy was afoot to take away their rights; second, they had to be persuaded that it was their duty to be vigilant, to watch, and to judge the government based upon the standards of their own liberty and happiness; and finally, they had to be persuaded that what threatened one colony's rights threatened the rights of all colonies equally. In the end, while they challenged the monarchical fiction during the Townshend Duty controversy, colonials went no further. As Dickinson's *Letters from a Farmer in Pennsylvania,* Massachusetts's *Circular Letter,* and Virginia's *Non-Importation Resolutions* all clearly pronounced, even the most radical colonials still publicly professed their allegiance to the Crown and defended the fiction of the divine right of kings. Yet despite the impasse, the patterns of cooperation and communication established as colonials challenged the monarchical fiction from 1767 to 1770 provided the context for them to begin to trust each other and to imagine a new American political fiction.

Destroying the Monarchical Fiction: Colonials as Patriot Citizens

Between 1773 and 1776, colonials began to imagine a different form of government. They began to piece together their new government based in part upon the principles they had seen work since 1765. No longer willing to play the role of obedient subjects, colonials eventually cast themselves as independent republican citizens: citizens who would control the government. Colonials persuaded themselves to embrace a future outside the monarchical fiction as they fabricated their new republican fiction. In retrospect we can see that the new republican fiction was romantic because

Americans had to believe that *they could and would prevent tyranny and protect liberty;* otherwise they would not have been able to reject the old fiction. They had to believe, or profess to believe, that republicanism would solve the problems of monarchy, that the hero would triumph in the end. Romantic by default, the new republican fiction promised the people a larger share of power: it promised that representatives would represent the will of the people; it promised that liberty would be secure; it promised that government would govern by established laws and that those laws would apply equally to both the government and the governed. In short, in the process of reaffirming and challenging the old monarchical fiction, colonials both developed the new republican fiction and found that it was tenable. Despite the fears of more conservative leaders like John Dickinson, colonials were persuaded to believe that the destruction of the monarchical fiction would not lead to anarchy, but would prevent tyranny and ensure the liberty of all. In the years between the Stamp Act and the Declaration of Independence, colonials proved that they could play the role designated for them: republican citizens.

During the Stamp Act crisis, colonials argued that Parliament did not have the right to levy internal taxes upon them; during the Townshend Duty controversy, they raised the stakes when they argued that Parliament did not have the power to levy any tax whatsoever upon them. Therefore, at the end of the challenging phase in 1770, colonials had only committed themselves as far as rejecting Parliament's power to tax them; they still retained their allegiance to the Crown and to the monarchical fiction. The years between the Boston Massacre (1770) and the Boston Tea Party (1773) witnessed a brief détente between colonials and Great Britain, then from 1773 to 1776 colonials destroyed the old monarchical fiction in successive steps. In 1774, Thomas Jefferson's *Summary View of the Rights of British Americans* pushed colonials to examine critically the conduct of King George III and demonstrated that if colonials judged their monarch based upon the patriotic criteria of their own "liberty and happiness," it was clear that colonial justice was treated with less respect than English profit. The Second Continental Congress's July 6, 1775, *Declaration of Causes and Necessity of Taking Up Arms;* July 31, 1775, *Resolution on Lord North's Conciliatory Proposal;* and December 6, 1775, *Reply of the United Colonies to the Declaration of Rebellion* raised the stakes by rejecting the power of Parliament over them and recognizing that the colonies were in active rebellion from the monarchical fiction.[60] Finally, in January 1776, Thomas Paine's *Common Sense* popularly lampooned the monarchical fiction and demonstrated the elegant simplicity of the republican fiction. Therefore, although colonials repeatedly petitioned King George III, Parliament, and the people of England for a redress of grievances between 1773 and 1776, they simultaneously embraced the fiction of themselves as citizens rather than as subjects.

Both the Boston Massacre and the repeal of the Townshend Duties occurred on March 5, 1770. With the repeal of the Townshend Duties, colonials resoundingly breathed a collective sigh of relief, tore up their non-importation agreements, and began consuming their much missed British-produced treasures. With the Boston Massacre, colonials initially demanded vengeance against the British troops, but once the soldiers were tried and acquitted of any wrongdoing and it appeared as though the whole bloody affair had been orchestrated by rebellious Boston radicals, order was restored and a relative harmony prevailed in the colonies. Mercy Otis Warren described the lull between the Boston Massacre and the Boston Tea Party as "a degree of tranquility to which we [Bostonians] had been strangers for many months." She remembered that colonials were "strongly attached to Great Britain" and that from 1770 to 1773 they "stood suspended in the pacific hope, that a change of ministry or a new parliament, might operate in their favor, and restore tranquility by the removal of the causes and the instruments of their suffering." The long-suffering colonials were "not yet conscious of our own strength, and scarcely ambitious of taking an independent rank among nations"; in short, "Americans still cherished the flattering ideas of reconciliation."[61] Warren was correct. After the repeal of the Townshend Duties and the acquittal of the British soldiers implicated in the Boston Massacre, colonials largely dropped their aggressive posture toward England: non-importation agreements were dissolved, and Committees of Correspondence were disbanded. Indeed, the methods of colonial unity were easily abrogated once common danger no longer necessitated common action. Radicals like Sam Adams knew that they "needed new tyranny and violent aggression from the mother country before we could hope to regain the ground lost." And while Adams tried to maintain colonial fear, vigilance, and unity through his contributions to the *Boston Gazette,* his orchestration of the annual Boston Massacre Oration, and his publication of the "treasonous" correspondence of Thomas Hutchinson and Andrew Oliver, he had little success fomenting rebellion until 1773, when Parliament committed another set of atrocities.[62]

Fredrick North became the new British prime minister in 1770, and while he shared Charles Townshend's goals of asserting parliamentary supremacy and defraying British taxes, he judged that a cooling-off period was necessary after the high emotions of the past five years. Parliament still maintained that it had the power to make laws for the colonies in all cases whatsoever, a premise colonials now rejected outright. Yet aside from the remaining tax on tea, which colonials sometimes avoided by smuggling and consuming Dutch tea in its stead, Lord North's policies did not initially provoke colonial outrage. That is, until May 1773, when Parliament passed the Tea Act, which gave the still struggling East India Company a near monopoly on colonial tea importation. Many members of Parliament were investors in the East India Company, and they reasoned that it need not fail when the tax collected from colonial tea drinkers could easily bail out the company. Colonial merchants, who realized that the new monopoly would cut into their tea business, were the first to cry foul. Radicals soon remembered that Lord North's ministry had committed several portentous atrocities over the past three years: colonial assemblies were dissolved; the seat of Massachusetts's government was moved to "inconvenient" Cambridge; and royal governors and judges were rendered independent of the will of the people by drawing their salaries from customs' collections rather than from legislatures' laws. By September 21, 1773, the Boston Committee of Correspondence sent out another *Circular Letter* in which it argued that "the state of public affairs still demands the greatest Wisdom, Vigilance, and Fortitude" and therefore that intercolonial cooperation and communication were more important than ever.[63]

Despite colonial protests, British tea headed to the colonies, and while New York City, Charleston, and Philadelphia were able to prevent the tea from docking, Governor Hutchinson allowed the *Dartmouth,* filled with 342 chests of tea, to enter Boston Harbor.[64] The rest of the story is well known: Bostonians refused to allow the tea to land, Hutchinson refused to allow the *Dartmouth* to sail back to England unless the proper tax was paid, and on December 16, 1773, when push came to shove, Boston Sons of Liberty steeped Boston Harbor in British tea. Lord North retaliated with the March 31, 1774, Boston Port Act and the Coercive Acts (known by colonials as the Intolerable Acts), which closed Boston Harbor until restitution was made for the destroyed tea, limited town meetings, and required those accused of inciting riot or otherwise impeding royal law to be removed to England for trial. News of the Intolerable Acts spread quickly throughout the colonies and led to renewed Committees of Correspondence, Committees of Safety, non-importation and non-exportation agreements, and, most famously, what is known to history as the First Continental Congress, which was set to meet in September 1774 in Philadelphia.

In 1765 Thomas Jefferson was a young law student who hovered outside of the House of Burgesses while Patrick Henry made his "treasonous" declamations against the Stamp Act. In 1769 Jefferson was a newly elected burgess who protested the Townshend Duties with the *Virginia Non-Importation Resolutions.* In 1774 he was elected a delegate to the Continental Congress, but he took ill en route and was unable to attend; instead, he sent along two copies of his *Summary View of the Rights of British America.* Jefferson described his argument as "the only one orthodox or tenable," which was that England and the colonies shared "the same Executive chief but no other necessary political connection."[65] Peyton Randolph was elected to the chair and circulated Jefferson's *Summary View* among the delegates, but Jefferson remembered in his *Autobiography* that although "it was read generally by the members, approved by many," it was "thought too bold for the present state of things." Perhaps his argument was just too strident for Congress. Stephen Lucas argues that the *Summary View* lost support because it argued based "on absolute and uncompromising principle," and that while Jefferson may have purported to desire reconciliation, differences could only be resolved "on his own principled terms. There were no shades of grey; America was right, England was wrong."[66] While Jefferson's *Summary View* was far too radical and therefore at odds with the *Declaration and Resolves of the First Continental Congress,* his arguments eventually became the standard justification for the destruction of the monarchical fiction. The *Summary View* helped colonials to reach consensus on revolution by giving them the rhetorical tools necessary to judge their government and by modeling patriotic republican citizenship.[67]

Jefferson's "principles" indeed articulated a stark shift in colonial support for the monarchical fiction: Jefferson was the first to declare publicly and in no uncertain terms that Parliament had no power over colonials, was the first publicly to judge and condemn the conduct of King George III, and was the first to justify the destruction of the monarchical fiction. Like Dickinson, Jefferson found the recent encroachments on colonial liberty portentous of a parliamentary plot; the actions of Parliament were "a series of oppressions, begun at a distinguished period, and pursued unalterably through every change of ministers, [which] too plainly prove a deliberate and systematical plan of reducing us to slavery." As Mercy Otis Warren observed, colonials had hoped prior to Lord North's 1773 Tea Act that a change in ministries would resolve colonial grievances, but Jefferson argued that it was evident that Lord North's ministry had pursued and would continue to pursue these same odious objectives. Indeed, Parliament's recent actions had verified that the conspiracy against colonial rights was endemic and persistent, and whether or not colonials were willing to admit it, the Intolerable Acts proved that Parliament hoped to reduce the colonies to "slavery." Jefferson built his slavery argument upon the same ground as Dickinson's conspiracy thesis: it was the clear *intention* of Parliament to reduce colonials to slavery, and the only safety from this fate was the sort of patriotic vigilant criticism of the government recommended by Dickinson and performed by Jefferson in his *Summary View.*[68]

Indeed, Jefferson's text outdid itself in its performance of patriotic vigilant criticism. Demonstrating the use of categorical thinking that Stephen Lucas calls "absolute," Jefferson concluded his summary of the odious laws of Parliament with this stinging indictment: "one of these conclusions must necessarily follow, either that justice is not the same in America as in Britain, or else that the British parliament pay less regard to it here than there." And, while his categorical reasoning defiantly led to the conclusion that Parliament had not acted with justice toward the colonies, Jefferson made clear that it was the imperial system's theoretical underpinnings that caused "the injustice of these acts." In the end, the only just colonial government would be one based upon "political principles which exempt us from the jurisdiction of the British parliament." In case Jefferson's meaning was not sufficiently clear, he added: "the true ground on which we declare these acts void is, that the British parliament has no right to exercise authority over us." While colonials had professed only that Parliament did not have the right to levy taxes upon the colonies in 1770, by 1774 Jefferson—adopting the opinion that Franklin had articulated during the Townshend Duty crisis—would have had the Continental Congress declare that Parliament had no authority over the colonies at all. The Continental Congress was nowhere near ready to make a radical proclamation that would have destroyed the monarchical fiction; instead they circumscribed just parliamentary control: "we cheerfully consent to the operation of such acts of the British Parliament, as are bona fide restrained to the regulation of our external commerce, for the purpose of securing the commercial advantages of the whole empire to the mother country." It would take until December 6, 1775, for the Continental Congress to profess Jefferson's indictment of Parliament's power to rule over the colonies.

Not only did Jefferson reject the power of Parliament over the colonies as a matter of mere "common sense," but he directly attacked the monarchical fiction by refusing to accept the ruse that the "king can do no wrong." Instead, Jefferson dared to "consider the conduct of his majesty," who after all was the mere "chief officer of the people, appointed by the laws, and circumscribed with definite powers, to assist in working the great machine of government, erected for their use, and consequently subject to their superintendance." King George III had used his prerogative (his veto power, among others) against the best interests of the colonies, rejecting colonial laws "for the most trifling reasons, and sometimes for no conceivable reason at all." This behavior was evidence that "other principles than those of justice simply have obtained an influence on [Great Britain's] determinations" and that King George preferred "the wanton exercise of this power" to justice or liberty. Further, George III had demonstrated an "equal inattention to the necessities of his people" when he allowed "laws to lie neglected in England for years, neither confirming them by his assent, nor annulling them by his negative." In 1764 James Otis declared that because "the king can do no wrong" it was "treason" merely to judge an act of Parliament and that such judgment would result in the "end of all government." Jefferson was the first to commit publicly this kind of treason—or "patriotism," depending on how one looked at the situation—by countermanding the fiction of the perfection of the king. The evidence against George III was irrefutable: he had usurped his delegated powers, condoned Parliament's injustices, and plotted against American rights and liberties. Clearly, he was not Bolingbroke's Patriot King, no matter how much colonials hoped he was.

Jefferson's final indictment demonstrated how his criticism of the monarchical fiction could logically result in the republican fiction: George III had "repeatedly" dissolved "one house of representatives" and "refused to call another, so that, the legislature provided by the laws has been out of existence." Perhaps remembering the circumstances of the composition of Virginia's 1769 *Non-Importation Resolutions,* Jefferson argued: "While those bodies are in existence to whom the people have delegated the powers of legislation, they alone possess and may exercise those powers; but when they are dissolved by the lopping off one or more of their branches, the power reverts to the people, who may exercise it to unlimited extent, either assembling together in person, sending deputies, or in any other way they may think proper."[69] In other words, according to Jefferson's argument, Virginia reverted to a state of nature when Governor Botetourt dissolved the House of Burgesses in 1769, because whenever a royal governor prorogued an assembly, all power reverted back to the people. Importantly, Jefferson did not argue that once the governor dismissed the assembly, then the assembly was no longer legal—as Tories would argue based upon their understanding of the monarchical fiction. Jefferson's bottom-up political fiction was based upon the people's unalienable right to representative government: *if the representatives were dismissed, then the government did not exist.* Therefore, Jefferson viewed prorogued and extra-fictional colonial assemblies—viewed as illegal by the British government—as the only legitimate government in

America. Such arguments as these were not only radical, they were also revolutionary. Jefferson proposed a new political fiction in 1774: a republican political fiction based upon the will of the people.

However logically compelling Jefferson's arguments may have seemed, his arguments did not persuade the Continental Congress in 1774. As Jefferson lamented in his *Autobiography,* his principles were too radical for the Continental Congress; their *Declaration and Resolves* declared that they would "cheerfully consent" to Parliament's rule over them as long as Parliament did not try to tax them. The Continental Congress was unwilling to adopt Jefferson's vigilant position against either Parliament or King George III. Despite their "alarm" at the "arbitrary proceedings of parliament and administration," and despite their perception that "such acts and measures as have been adopted since the last war . . . demonstrate a system formed to enslave America," the Continental Congress would not indict King George III for jeopardizing Americans' rights and liberties. Yet the congress did not absolve King George III of his responsibility either, nor did it profess its allegiance to the monarch or the monarchical fiction, nor did it use the obsequious language of the petition. Rather, it firmly declared colonial rights and grievances and avowed that it had agreed to a "non-importation, non-consumption, and non-exportation agreement or association," "to prepare an address to the people of Great Britain, and a memorial to the inhabitants of British America," and "to prepare a loyal address to his Majesty, agreeable to resolutions already entered into."[70] Therefore, while the First Continental Congress was unwilling to directly condemn King George III in 1774, it reestablished and coordinated colonial networks of communication and cooperation; it sanctioned such extra-fictional political associations as legal and binding; and, importantly, it announced itself as the official voice of the people of the united colonies—all on its own power and authority. Despite the Continental Congress's conservative declaration of colonial rights, Jefferson had attracted the attention of like-minded radicals with his pamphlet, and his arguments would prove useful over the next two years. In 1775 his radicalism directly confronted John Dickinson's conservatism when both contributed to the *Causes and Necessity of Taking Up Arms*—a battle that Dickinson would win. By 1776, however, Dickinson was no longer able to convince the Continental Congress that it should maintain its allegiance to the monarchical fiction.

As the Continental Congress concluded its business on October 22, 1774, it agreed to meet again "on the tenth day of May next, unless the redress of grievances, which we have desired, be obtained before that time."[71] Suspicious that Sam Adams and the rest of the Boston radicals were intentionally fomenting rebellion, Continental Congress delegates would only pledge their support *if* the British attacked. Adams returned home, where he spent the rest of 1774 and the winter of 1775 provoking General Gage and his British regulars in the hope of a violent escalation of the disagreement. By April 19, 1775, when Adams and John Hancock were on their way back to Philadelphia and Gage still had not complied with Adams's bellicose wishes, Adams dangled bait that Gage could not resist: he and Hancock, the Massachusetts Provisional Council, and the rebels' military provisions—all located in and around Concord and available for Gage's easy picking. Gage took the bait; Paul Revere made his famous ride; Adams and Hancock narrowly escaped capture; British regulars and colonial militia squared off first in Lexington and then in Concord; colonial farmers and militia poured out from neighboring towns and harassed and killed the British all the way back to Boston; and Adams and Hancock received a hero's welcome as they made their way back to Philadelphia. Once back at the Continental Congress, Adams's plan began to go awry: while delegates honored their pledges to support Boston in the event of an attack by giving military aid, he found that conservative voices prevailed and that there would be no rebellion in 1775.[72]

Despite Sam Adams's disappointment that Congress would not immediately declare independence, when delegates met in May 1775 they began to put structures into place by which they could wage war, form a permanent colonial alliance, create a treasury, form trade agreements, and distribute mail. In other words, while the Second Continental Congress was not yet willing to declare the colonies independent, it built a scaffolding of government based upon the logic of the republican fiction: the Continental Congress, as it declared in 1774, now acted as if it were the legitimate and legal representatives of the people, and it acted as if the legal representatives of the people *ruled*. Yet, while Congress was creating the means by which it could effectively manage a government, its measures were only precautionary—in case of emergency. Congress still hoped, or professed to hope, that once Parliament's treasonous plot was thwarted and colonial rights and liberties were restored, then colonials would once again resume their happy place as subjects within the monarchical fiction. In the meantime Congress would do all it could to restore the British constitution and protect colonial Americans from British tyranny. There would be several more military battles and one royal proclamation before the radicals in Congress could prevail over the conservatives.

The disagreement between the radical and conservative voices in the Second Continental Congress was readily apparent in the crafting of its

July 6, 1775, *Causes and Necessity of Taking Up Arms,* in which the more conservative John Dickinson easily prevailed over the more radical Thomas Jefferson. Jefferson and Dickinson were late additions to the June 23, 1775, "Committee to prepare a Declaration to be published by General Washington on his arrival to the camp before Boston."[73] Jefferson remembered in his *Autobiography* that he "prepared a draught of the Declaration," but that, as we might expect, "it was too strong[,] for Mr. Dickinson still retained the hope of reconciliation with the mother country, and was unwilling it should be lessened by offensive statements."[74] Dickinson's version all but scrapped Jefferson's contribution: only "the last 4 paragraphs & half of the preceding one" were included in the final version. It was probably for the best that Jefferson's version was not laid before Congress; for if the goal was reconciliation, then in style and substance Dickinson's version was the better paper of the two.

To name just one telling example of the differences between the two versions, Dickinson eliminated Jefferson's defiant description of colonials' petitions to the mother country. "We have supplicated our king at various times in terms almost disgraceful to freedom; we have reasoned, we have remonstrated with parliament in the most mild and decent language," wrote Jefferson. Dickinson's draft replaced this sentiment with the much meeker "we for ten years incessantly and ineffectually besieged the Throne as supplicants; we reasoned, we remonstrated with parliament, in the most mild and decent language." Jefferson's description of colonial petitions presumed a completely different political fiction than Dickinson's. Jefferson's republican political fiction was based upon the belief that the representatives of the people have the right to make decisions and therefore should not bow down—literally or figuratively—before the monarch, who after all was merely the "chief officer of the people." He therefore found that the "humble and dutiful" petitions of the colonial governments and Congress, which had always reaffirmed the monarchical fiction and denied that King George III (or in the case of Stamp Act petitions, Parliament) had knowingly or purposefully harmed the colonies, were written with less than republican dignity and were "almost disgraceful to freedom." On the other hand, Dickinson's devotion to the monarchical fiction would have led him to believe that Jefferson's defiant description of colonial petitions was "too strong" and "offensive" because it was not premised upon the assumption that subjects should—in fact, could *only*—supplicate their superiors in a "mild and decent" tone. The differences between these two versions were as vast as the differences between republicanism and monarchy: one was written by a citizen, the other by a subject.

Jefferson's disappointment with Dickinson's revision of the *Declaration* would turn into "disgust" when on July 8, 1775, Dickinson presented his *Petition to the King* to Congress. "Congress gave a signal proof of their indulgence to Mr. Dickinson and of their great desire not to go too fast for any respectable part of our body," complained Jefferson, "in permitting him to draw his second petition to the King according to his own ideas, and passing it with scarcely any amendment. The disgust against this humility was general." And while Jefferson and other radicals were momentarily disgusted with their colleagues who were still immersed in the monarchical fiction, they would not have to wait long before congressional opinion turned in their favor. On July 31, 1775, Jefferson's *Reply to Lord North's Conciliatory Proposal* would directly and defiantly contest Parliament's "pretended power of taxation," would argue that Parliament had "no right to intermeddle with our support of civil government or administration of justice," and would make no reference to colonials' duty as monarchical subjects.[75] On November 9, 1775, Congress learned "by authentic intelligence from London" that Dickinson's July 8 *Petition to the King* had been rejected outright on August 21, 1775, and that "NO ANSWER WOULD BE GIVEN" to colonial complaints.[76] Two days later, on August 23, King George III had accused colonials of "forgetting the allegiance which they owe to the power that has protected and supported them" and therefore proclaimed colonials to be in an "open and avowed rebellion."[77] Congress appointed Richard Henry Lee, James Wilson, and William Livingston to "prepare a declaration, in answer to sundry illegal ministerial proclamations that have lately appeared in America"; the committee reported their draft on November 29, and on December 6, 1775, Congress assented to the committee's work.

The *Reply of the United Colonies to the Declaration of Rebellion* declared the colonies free from Parliament. The *King's Proclamation of Rebellion* had accused colonials of "forgetting" their "allegiance" to the monarchical fiction; but "what allegiance is it that we forget," asked Congress. "Allegiance to Parliament? We never owed—never owned it. Allegiance to our King; Our words have ever avowed it—our conduct has ever been consistent with it." Congress had finally, clearly, and irrevocably separated itself from parliamentary control: it declared that it owed and avowed its allegiance to the king, not to Parliament. Additionally, while colonials still professed their allegiance to the monarchical fiction, they argued that their resistance did not constitute "rebellion," because it was their patriotic "duty" to resist "in those cases, in which the right to resist is stipulated . . . expressly." Not only did colonials have a duty to resist, Congress vowed belligerently that it would "risque everything, do everything and suffer everything. . . . To support our laws, and our liberties established by our laws." Next, Congress followed Jefferson's argument from the previous year's *Summary View* when it circumscribed the powers of the king based upon the logic of the monarchical fiction: "we view him as the constitution represents him: that tells us he can do no wrong. The cruel and illegal attacks, which we oppose, have no foundation in the royal authority." In other words, the monarchical fiction had represented the monarch as incapable of doing wrong; the recent acts against the colonies were wrong; therefore, King George III could not have made or sanctioned those acts; and, when colonials resisted those wrong acts, they had not resisted, but supported, the king and the constitution and had therefore remained loyal, if patriotic, subjects.

Yet, King George III had declared the colonies out of his protection. Disavowed, disowned, and disinherited, Congress argued that the principles of "reason and justice and the constitution will not prevail" and therefore that they "must report to arguments drawn from a very different source" than the monarchical fiction of the British constitution. And, to which source did Congress report on December 6, 1775? The people. "We, therefore, in the name of the people of the United Colonies, and by authority, according to the purest maxims of representation derived from them, declare, that whatever punishment shall be inflicted upon any persons in the power of our enemies for favoring, aiding, or abetting the cause of American liberty shall be retaliated in the same kind and the same degree upon those, in our power, who have favored, aided or abetted, or shall favor, aid or abet the system of ministerial oppression."[78] In the name of the people, by the authority of the people, patriots in Congress declared that it would punish the enemies of the people's liberty—be they American loyalists or British regulars. Congressional conservatives and reconciliationists must have blanched when Congress declared that it would act by authority derived from the people, rather than by authority derived from the Crown. Congress had declared Jefferson's position in his *Summary View:* when the Crown dissolved the people's assemblies, all power reverted back to the people for the people to dispense as they chose. By George III's April 23, 1775, *Proclamation,* the "traitorous" colonial assemblies were no longer legal. Once declared in "rebellion," colonials were the enemies of the Crown and their governments were subject to "the utmost endeavors" of "all our Officers, as well civil as military, and all others our obedient and loyal subjects." Britain had thus declared the colonies independent before the colonies had done so themselves, upon which Congress argued that all power reverted back to the people.

Because of George III's *Proclamation* it was clear that there was now a power vacuum—there was no longer a sovereign power in America. Congress needed either to re-create a new monarchical fiction in America by establishing its own monarchy and aristocracy, or it needed to invent a new basis for the American political fiction. Since returning to Philadelphia, the Second Continental Congress had been acting as the supreme legislative authority in the colonies: it had built an army, printed money, regulated trade, authorized colonial governments to rewrite their constitutions, established a postal system, and so forth—Congress had long assumed the powers of government, but it had not formally articulated the basis upon which its authority rested. Congress's December 6, 1775, *Reply* announced that the people were the legitimate sovereign of its new political fiction. Congress had previously assumed the role of patriot heroes defending the British constitution, but its *Reply* announced that there was a new political fiction to defend, one based primarily upon the will of the people. Therefore, the December 6, 1775, *Reply* represented a revolution in American political theory and in the American political fiction. Yet, Congress still had not declared colonial independence.[79]

Historians have often wondered why Americans declared revolution precisely when they did. Why not in 1775 after the battles of Lexington and Concord? Why not in 1773 after the Boston Tea Party? Why not in 1770 after the Boston Massacre? Why not in 1765 after the Stamp Act riots? One answer often given by historians is that Boston was at the center of these events, and many colonials believed that radicals in Boston were intentionally fomenting an unnecessary and treasonous rebellion of which they wanted no part. Boston Sons of Liberty—led by Sam Adams—were indeed at the vanguard of radicalism; only Virginia came close to matching Boston's belligerence. A frustrated John Adams believed in April 1776 that colonial public opinion was a "complicated and mighty . . . machine" that needed "management." And while Adams was impatient to move forward, he believed that other colonies were finally "advancing by slow but sure steps, to that mighty Revolution" that he had "expected for some time." Despite his impatience, Adams was shrewd enough to know that "forced attempts to accelerate their motions would have been attended with discontent and perhaps convulsions," and therefore that radicals in Boston and Virginia had to wait until laggard colonies reached a consensus on revolution.[80]

Aside from suspicions of radicals' motives, there was a second explanation for why Americans did not rebel until 1776: colonials did not know how to imagine a future outside the monarchical fiction, and without knowing how to proceed, they were mired in tradition and indecision. The fear of an unknown future caused both conservatives and radicals to argue for delay. For example, in 1767 John Dickinson had his Farmer declare, "a nation may change their king, or race of kings, and, retaining their ancient form of government, be gainers by changing. . . . But once *we* are separated from our mother country," whined Dickinson, "what new form of government shall we adopt, or where shall we find another *Britain* to supply our loss?" In other words, previous revolutions had retained the monarchical fiction but deposed specific rulers; Dickinson believed that a complete destruction of the monarchical fiction itself would cause colonials to "bleed at every vein." Unable to imagine a happy future outside the monarchical fiction, Dickinson refused to give his assent to the Declaration. John Adams was typical of other—more radical—colonials who *could* imagine a happy future outside the monarchical fiction, yet the astute Adams knew that the rest of America needed to be convinced that the future was indeed bright before any truly revolutionary action could be taken. Americans needed something to prod them toward independence, something even more pronounced than George III's renunciation of them. They needed someone to make the case for why the monarchical fiction never made sense in the first place; they needed someone to speak to them in a voice that they could understand; they needed Thomas Paine.

The penultimate step in colonials' rejection of the monarchical fiction was the publication of Paine's January 1776 *Common Sense.* Before *Common Sense,* the most widely read colonial pamphlet had been Dickinson's *Letters from a Farmer in Pennsylvania.* Paine's radicalism obliterated Dickinson's conservatism in more ways than one: "roughly one hundred times more copies of *Common Sense* were purchased in 1776" than Dickinson's *Letters* "had sold in eight years." Further, "countless others read *Common Sense* in their newspapers. . . . [C]onservatively, between January and July probably a quarter million colonists read it or heard it, roughly every other free adult living in Anglo-America."[81] Paine estimated that 150,000 copies of his pamphlet sold in America, and while some of his contemporaries—like John Adams—as well as some modern historians have claimed that he offered no new arguments, the goal of *Common Sense* was not "to persuade Congress, which was already moving apace toward Independence," but to persuade "the people whose support Congress needed."[82] The importance of Paine's pamphlet in the destruction of the monarchical fiction cannot be overestimated: Paine helped to convince Americans that the monarchical fiction was archaic and that the only just government would be one based upon the people. He therefore helped Americans outside Congress understand that republicanism was the necessary solution to colonial grievances.

The overarching goal of Paine's pamphlet was to encourage his fellow Americans to think of their duty to the future, to recognize that reconciliation was no more than "an agreeable dream," and to protect the liberty that was rightfully theirs.[83] Paine vowed to "offer nothing more than simple facts, plain arguments, and common sense" in his attack on monarchy. First of all, he asked, what was the nature of government? "Like dress," he answered, government was "the badge of lost innocence," "a necessary evil" that prevented the individual's "natural right" to govern one's self.[84] Like Locke, Hobbes, and countless other political theorists, Paine argued that the natural state of human beings—humans in a state of nature—was one of absolute freedom. A just government would provide more "freedom and security" than people would have without government in a state of nature. The most "simple" government would be best because it would be "less liable to be disordered, and the easier repaired when disordered." The simplest form of government would provide the most freedom and security, because it would be readily apparent which part of the system was out of balance, rendering it easier to correct and control.[85]

By these standards, the British constitution was a "mere absurdity!" Monarchy was "exceedingly ridiculous" because "it first excludes a man from the means of information, yet empowers him to act in cases where the highest judgment is required. The state of kings shuts him from the world, yet the business of a king requires him to know it thoroughly." In short, the British constitution was based upon "absurd and useless" principles. Monarchy was against common sense because hereditary rule and the separation of people into "KINGS and SUBJECTS" were oppressive and absurd. "For all men being originally equals," wrote Paine, "no one by birth could have a right to set up his own family in perpetual preference to all others for ever, and though himself might deserve some decent degree of honors of his cotemporaries [*sic*], yet his descendants might be far too unworthy to inherit them." Believe in the fiction of the perfection of hereditary monarchy if you like, Paine challenged, but "if there are any so weak as to believe it, let them promiscuously worship the ass and lion, and welcome."[86]

Paine argued that reconciliation with Great Britain was but "an agreeable dream" that "passed away" after the atrocities of Lexington and Concord. Four kinds of people still desired reconciliation: "interested men, who are not to be trusted; weak men, who cannot see; prejudiced men, who will not see; and a certain set of moderate men, who think better of the European world than it deserves." Paine must have been thinking of Dickinson and other conservatives in his adopted colony of Pennsylvania when he wrote that "this last class, by an ill-judged deliberation, will be the cause of more calamities to this continent, than all the other three." Paine believed that if the reconciliators used common sense, they would understand that "it is repugnant to reason, to the universal order of things to all examples from former ages, to suppose, that this continent can longer remain subject to any external power." Indeed, "small islands not capable of protecting themselves, are the proper objects for kingdoms to take under their care; but there is something very absurd, in supposing a continent to be perpetually governed by an island."[87]

"I have heard some men say," wrote Paine, "many of whom I believe spoke without thinking, that they dreaded an independence, fearing that it would produce civil wars." But "it is but seldom that our first thoughts are truly correct, and that is the case here for there are ten times more to dread from a patched up connextion than from independence." Paine believed that colonials were afraid to rebel both because "no plan is yet laid down" and because they did not recognize that American citizens possessed the "spirit of good order and obedience to continental government."[88] Believing that "a government of our own is our natural right," Paine offered his own "hints" at how the new continental government could be established. He thought that assemblies of the people should be elected annually and that they should have a president rather than a king, for "in America THE LAW IS KING." The president would be chosen by the delegates in the assembly by lot. Each state would send a minimum of thirty delegates to the assembly so that citizens would be adequately represented. State legislatures and citizens would directly elect delegates to a special convention, which, "being impowered by the people, will have a truly legal authority" to frame a "CONTINENTAL CHARTER."[89]

Paine's view of the perfect constitution was so alarmingly egalitarian that it earned him the lifelong enmity of John Adams, who wrote in an April 12, 1776, letter to wealthy Boston lawyer William Tudor that Paine's view of government was "feeble indeed—it is poor and despicable," and remembered in a June 22, 1819, letter to Thomas Jefferson that *Common Sense* was "a poor ignorant, Malicious, short-sighted, Crapulous Mass." In Paine's ideal the American citizen was decidedly active and egalitarian, which may partly explain why his view of government caused Adams—who had about as much faith in the people as he had in King George III—so much crankiness.[90] Paine demanded that his fellow Americans actively, bravely, and boldly play the part of patriotic republican citizens by giving up the dream of reconciliation and recognizing the commonsense truth that the colonies had outgrown the monarchical fiction.

The Romantic Republican Fiction: Citizens as Patriot Heroes

John Adams wrote to James Warren on May 20, 1776, that "every post and every day rolls in upon us Independence like a torrent." The sooner the better, too, for on June 7, 1776, a British fleet of 132 ships was reported to be sailing for New York, and while General George Washington readied his troops in the hope of withstanding the invasion, he knew that the relative inexperience of his men coupled with a dire lack of supplies made his situation one of "great distress."[91] Battles between colonials and British troops had been fought with encouraging success in Lexington and Concord and on Bunker Hill, and with much less success in Canada. And while some Continental Congress delegates still hoped for reconciliation and were therefore hesitant to declare independence from Great Britain, it was clear to most Americans that, independent or not, there was a war on. While one Virginian was in New York hoping to protect Americans, another Virginian, this time in Philadelphia, also hoped to defend Americans by his actions on that day. Richard Henry Lee moved that the Continental Congress consider three fateful motions. His first motion was also the most famous: "that these United Colonies are, and of right ought to be, free and independent states, that they are absolved from all allegiance to the British Crown, and that all political connection between them and the State of Great Britain is, and ought to be, totally dissolved." Yet, while Americans do not often remember his second and third motions on that day, those motions—to empower Congress to form "foreign Alliances" and to create a "plan of confederation"—were pressing concerns, especially with General Howe's fleet looming ominously.[92]

The Continental Congress knew it must make a unanimous decision for independence, so it delayed the debate on Lee's motions for three weeks while delegates gathered instructions from their respective colonies. Nonetheless, four days later, on June 11, an uneasy Congress appointed a committee of five to "prepare a declaration to the effect of the said first resolution." If they were to have any hope of successfully fighting the British and their Hessian mercenaries, Americans were desperately in need of foreign aid. With British troops hovering nearby there was no time to spare, so on June 12 Congress formed committees to address Lee's second and third motions concerning foreign alliances and confederation. In the meantime, local town meetings in Scituate, Natick, and Malden, Massachusetts, considered and voted for independence; Virginia resolved for independence and drafted its Declaration of Rights; and Delaware, Maryland, New Hampshire, and Connecticut all moved in the direction of independence. It therefore appeared that the colonies had reached a consensus on revolution when the debate on Lee's motion was reopened on July 1, 1776. Yet Lee's and Adams's hopes for independence were frustrated by the four colonies who still stubbornly refused to approve: South Carolina, Pennsylvania, Delaware, and New York.

The hero of this part of the tale is Caesar Rodney, who rode the eighty miles between Dover, Delaware, and Philadelphia that night just in time to swing his colony's vote on July 2. Now John Dickinson and Robert Morris abstained, which allowed James Wilson to cast Pennsylvania's vote for independence; South Carolina changed its mind and now approved; and New York abstained entirely until the next week, when it also voted in favor of independence. The Continental Congress thus voted for a "unanimous" independence on July 2, 1776.[93] The previous twelve years, which Americans had spent communicating and cooperating, learning to trust each other, and learning to fear the tyranny inherent in the monarchical fiction, had finally led to the American Revolution. Adams was correct when he observed that the Revolution had been achieved in the years before the battles of Lexington and Concord—those battles alone would have never resulted in revolution. The Revolution was as much a result of argumentation as it was a result of violence.[94] Upon reflection, it is clear that a specific view of citizenship emerged in the twelve years prior to 1776—especially between 1774 and 1776, when Americans shrugged off the role of sycophantic subjects and took on the role of republican citizens who would work collectively to defend liberty and prevent tyranny. Without the development of this new view of the American citizen, the Continental Congress would not have been able to construct a new government based upon the will of the people.

Republicanism had become America's new political fiction. Americans had learned through their joint action with the Stamp Act Congress, local Committees of Correspondence and Safety, and the Continental Congress that they could erect structures that could carry on the functions of government without a king or Parliament. They declared that they could *create* new governments and therefore that government was not God-given or naturally occurring, but was the product of men—of men like themselves. Monarchy had been an unjust form of government, colonials argued, because decisions were made by fiat, because laws were arbitrarily applied, because government was not based upon the consent of the governed, because neither rights nor liberty was secured. The new republican fiction resolved the problems with the old fiction by making the government accountable to the will of people in the hope that the people would rule with justice. In republican government, the representatives of the people would make decisions; debate would be open and transparent; laws would apply both to the governed and the government; justice and liberty would prevail. Whereas monarchy was the rule of the unquestionable one, republicanism would be the rule of the accountable many.

The Declaration of Independence had created thirteen independent states, but it had not created a new nation. Each former colony jealously guarded its freedom, so it is not surprising that while Congress first debated the Articles of Confederation as early as July 12, 1776, it did not approve and submit the document to the states until November 17, 1777; nor it is surprising that the states did not ratify the Articles until March 1, 1781. The Articles did not create a national government; rather, they created a confederated government, which Congress called "The United States of America," and within which each state retained its own "sovereignty, freedom, and independence, and every power, jurisdiction, and right" that was not "expressly delegated to the United States, in Congress assembled." In other words, the confederacy was "a firm league of friendship"—it was a treaty of friendship and cooperation between independent states that retained their independence—it was an alliance, not a national government. States joined the confederacy for the specific purposes of "common defense, the security of their liberties, and their mutual and general welfare." Each state pledged to "assist each other, against all force offered to, or attacks made upon them, or any of them, on account of religion, sovereignty, trade, or any other pretense whatever." Because it was based upon the republican fiction rather than the monarchical fiction, the confederacy took rotation in office very seriously. Congress would be composed of between two and seven delegates from each state, and no delegate could serve more than three years out of every six. The president would be elected to yearly terms from among the delegates and could only serve as president once every three years. To retain equality among the states, each state had one vote in Congress regardless of its size, population, or wealth. Finally, the Articles expressly prohibited any state or citizen from accepting "any present, emolument, office or title of any kind whatever from any King, Prince or foreign State"; likewise, Congress could not "grant any title of nobility."[95] American republicanism meant that each state would have its equal vote in Congress, that there would be no titles of nobility upon which an aristocracy or other hereditary government could be formed, and that offices would be rotated frequently so that no one would be able to "lay down" in office. Congress was authorized to raise an army for defense, contract debt, receive foreign ministers, and form treaties on behalf of, and only with the permission of, the states. The Articles therefore created a very weak, but republican, central government within which the individual states retained all of their own powers.

Americans developed republican governments to solve the problems of monarchy; therefore their new republican governments would be peopled by citizens rather than subjects. Citizens were often portrayed as powerful, good-hearted, virtuous, and cheerfully willing to make sacrifices for the interests of the whole, but the defining feature of republican citizens could be summarized by one word: active. Republican citizens would actively fight corruption, actively defend liberty, actively critique the government, and actively work for the common good. Unlike a monarchical subject, the new republican citizen was always described as powerful. Indeed, after twelve years of protesting arbitrary power and communicating and cooperating for the common good, there was little chance that Americans would have allowed themselves to be treated as subjects. While America's political and economic elite may not have really believed that "all men are created equal," they strategically professed the universal power of the citizen both because it provided them with justification for revolution and because it appealed to the people who would have to fight for independence. The republican citizen was only important insofar as he contributed to the betterment of the whole nation, which was always viewed as more than the mere sum of its parts. Yet, because the republican citizen both ruled and was ruled over—was a part of the whole that controlled the whole—the citizen was not believed to oppress himself. Republican freedom and liberty meant that the citizen was free to act for the common good. The republican citizen was the antithesis of the monarchical subject, whose only permissible action was to obey.

In retrospect we can see that because revolutionary rhetoric described citizens as the patriots who would succeed in their quest to win the war, conquer tyranny, and defend liberty, it constituted citizens as romantic and heroic characters. The romantic view of citizenship was decidedly hopeful—and indeed, Americans foolishly rebelled against Great Britain at the summit of that nation's power without an ally, without an army, without a navy, without money to raise, train, feed, house, clothe, or pay soldiers, without the know-how or the raw materials to make bullets, and without a plan or an exit strategy—hope was all that Americans *did* have. America's government based upon the will of the people was a wildly romantic fiction of republicanism: each American was supposed to believe that he was the hero who would conquer adversity—whether the "adversity" was the gun of a British regular, the corruption of luxurious British goods, or the tyranny of Parliament and the king. Once those adversities were conquered, the heroes would continue to act in the Republic's best interest and ensure a safe, happy, and prosperous America. In retrospect, the romantic republican hero seemingly had an impossible task, an unattainable quest. Yet, Americans did eventually prevail, which proved to many Americans that the romantic republican fiction was fact.

While the process of forming America's new republican fiction was not perfectly dialogic, debated, open, or ratified—indeed, citizens were often led by powerful elite gentlemen—there was a sense in which the new fiction was the product of an extended conversation between the many and the political and economic elite. Since Americans had begun their protest against the Stamp Act in 1764, first subjects, then citizens had been called upon to consider, support, and defend the actions of their leaders. Without the support of a significant number of Americans, there would have been no hope that the protest strategies of boycotting British goods and communicating and cooperating with sister colonies would have been effective. Furthermore, if colonial leaders had lacked the support of the majority of Americans, they would have been easily tried and convicted of treason by British loyalists. Therefore, the years between 1764 and 1776 could be read as a sustained process of forming and testing America's new political fiction. As John Adams wrote in April 1776, colonial leaders carefully monitored public opinion and only took action against Britain when they believed it would be supported by the general population. For indeed, how could they not? The colonial rebellion against the mightiest military force in the world was a foolhardy idea—with or without the support of the people. America's new republican fiction was therefore the result of a process of dialogue and debate and was open to being modified or amended as events required new institutions.

Some Americans demanded that their opinions be consulted and respected and that they be allowed to formally ratify their new republican constitutions. For example, in 1776 the "Mechanicks of New York City" argued that they had an "inalienable right" to "judge whether it be consistent with their interest to accept or reject a Constitution framed for that State of which they are members."[96] Yet, while the mechanics of New York demanded their inalienable right to pass judgment upon the work of their leaders, it was not granted. Rather, as with most states, special conventions were assembled—some delegates were popularly voted by freeholders, most were appointed—and the resulting constitutions were simply put into effect without the sanction of the citizenry. Only Massachusetts and New Hampshire allowed their citizens to ratify the new constitutions, although the practice did become widespread in subsequent years. While the new republican fiction was somewhat dialogic, debated, open, and ratified, it was not perfectly so; rather, newly powerful citizens were relied upon to support the decisions of their leaders, but they were not asked to help to make those decisions themselves—decision making in the new government was republican rather than democratic.

However, while the process of forming the new republican fiction was not perfect—and we have to remember that Americans were not only inexperienced at forming governments, but they also had no previous models, and they were in the middle of a war—the new fiction was self-consciously authored. On December 6, 1775, Congress had declared that it acted both "in the name of the people of the United Colonies" and by the people's "authority," and in so doing it had, in effect, announced and claimed title to their republican political fiction. By July 4, 1776, Congress had formally declared independence and indicted the king on charges ranging from refusing to "assent to laws" to inciting "domestic insurrections." Congress's arguments on December 6, 1775, and July 4, 1776, had claimed ownership of America's republican fiction on behalf of all Americans—the new republican fiction was of the people, for the people, and by the people. As Jefferson wrote in the Declaration of Independence, just government exists by the "consent of the governed" to secure the rights of the people, and "whenever any Form of Government becomes destructive of these ends, it is the Right of the People to alter or to abolish it, and to institute new Government, laying its foundation on such principles and organizing its powers in such form, as to them shall seem most likely to effect their Safety and Happiness."[97] The only government that could meet that criterion would be one that the people freely, willingly, and clearly took some part in creating.

3

"The American Constitution is that little *article* of HOPE, left at the bottom of *Pandora's* box of evils"

Citizens as Tragic Victims, 1783–1789

Even as the republican fiction's "self-evident truths" emerged as the justification for the newly independent states, some elites had recognized the danger inherent in its romantic promise of citizen control over the government. As the Revolutionary War raged it became clear that the confederated government was woefully unstable and therefore that America's "experiment in self-government" had not yielded the most promising results. It was no surprise to insiders like Alexander Hamilton that in the years between the 1783 Treaty of Paris and the 1787 Constitutional Convention the old threats of British tyranny were replaced by a new danger: instability.[1] Suddenly, shrewd Americans everywhere echoed the decade-old lament of John Dickinson's Farmer, who had apparently rightly feared that when Americans separated from the mother country they would be unable to "find another *Britain*" to maintain order. Not that reform-minded Americans wanted to hitch their wagon to another imperial power—far from it. What they wanted was to replace their weak confederacy with a strong, consolidated, and controlling national power that could maintain order without entangling America in old-world animosities.

Philadelphia doctor and Revolutionary War patriot Benjamin Rush wrote on February 1, 1787, that many had mistakenly confounded "the terms of the *American revolution* with those of *the late American war.* The American war is over," clarified Rush, "but this is far from being the case with the American revolution. On the contrary, nothing but the first act of the great drama is closed. It remains yet to establish and perfect our new forms of government."[2] Rush was not alone in his call for constitutional reform, for by February 1787 the steep downturn in the postwar economy had caused a tidal wave of repercussions throughout most of the states: money was scarce; loans were due; taxes were high. Creditors turned against debtors; rich turned against poor; farmers turned against merchants; and citizens turned against their government in the most spectacular and violent fashion. So it was with hopeful optimism amid dire circumstances that Rush could call upon his fellow patriots to return to the public stage for the second act of America's "great drama": creating a strong central government.

The postwar economic downturn proved to the new nation's political and economic elite that instability in government was just as dangerous to liberty as British tyranny had been. This need for stability significantly influenced the Constitutional Convention's view of the role of the citizen. The story of the road to the Constitutional Convention is well known: Alexander Hamilton and James Madison led the few delegates who had attended the Annapolis Convention in September 1786 to recommend to their states that another convention be held to revise the Articles of Confederation; Madison's "Virginia Plan" was proposed, amended, and debated by the delegates in Philadelphia; the resulting constitution was sent to the states, where it was the subject of heated factional support and opposition, but was ultimately ratified in 1789. What is less well known is why average Americans consented to the new government or how the debates over the question of representation during the 1789 debates over the Bill of Rights helped to construct a theory of republicanism that was based upon the will of the people, yet minimized the role that the people would play in controlling their government. Each of these aspects of the debates over American republicanism between 1776 and 1789 demonstrates that tragic citizenship cast citizens as complicit victims who were unable to defend themselves or their government from corruption.

In retrospect it is clear that tragic citizenship was always a part of American republican political theory and rhetoric. In later years—when Americans would choose to think of their government as a "democracy"—tragic citizenship would be banished to the backrooms of public discourse where fatcats and political power brokers did not hide their disdain for "the herd." Eventually, tragic citizenship would lurk behind and beneath the nation's professed faith in democracy and would rarely be proclaimed upon the public stage. But in 1787 the nation had not yet chosen to hide its fear of the rule of the people, and therefore tragic citizenship is conspicuous in debates over the merits of the proposed constitution and what it meant to form a government based upon the will of the people. Analyzing the rise of tragic citizenship therefore allows us to take a sustained look at the features of the dark underbelly of America's republicanism. The contentious arguments of Federalists and Anti-Federalists over the Constitution reflect a nation torn between the romantic promise of the Revolution and the tragic reality of the need for a controlling, stabilizing power. For better or worse, in the end Americans would choose stability.

Postwar Economic Woes and National Stability

The confederated states contracted about 240 million dollars in debt between 1776 and 1782; yet without any authority to tax or demand money from the states, it was unable to pay off this debt prior to Alexander Hamilton's funding plan, which was only implemented in 1790 after the new Constitution took effect.[3] Congress repeatedly attempted to resolve the financial crisis between 1776 and 1787, but it was stymied by the necessities of war, hampered by the constraints of the Articles of Confederation, and confounded by the failure of the states to cede money or power to the central government. For example, March 18, 1780, was a fairly typical day in Congress: delegates passed a resolution requesting the states "to pass laws enabling Congress to levy an impost of one per cent on all exports and imports, as a fund for sinking the emissions for carrying on the present war, to continue until a sum equal to the whole of the said emissions shall be collected."[4] Such an impost was necessary because, as the Committee on Finance reported on that day, Continental bills of credit were valued at "less than 1/40 part their nominal value, and still remain in a state of uncertainty and fluctuation." The depreciation, uncertainty, and fluctuation of the Continental currency had resulted in "great mischiefs and distress," which the Committee on Finance believed could only be reduced by each state agreeing to send (and, actually sending) "fifteen million dollars monthly" to the Continental treasury. The Board of War made the final report to the Continental Congress on that day, announcing that "70,000 lbs. of pork salted in bulk" could be got immediately if Congress would only agree to provide "10,000 dollars . . . to procure the barrels and pay the packers." Remembering that the Continental army had to eat, Congress hastily agreed to the expense. The state of wartime finances was therefore rather bleak: crumbling under the weight of massive debt with no power to procure its own relief and little hope that the states would come to its aid, Congress had to authorize purchases that it knew would sink it further into debt.

Meanwhile, most of the states were in an equally dire financial situation. "Our public affairs wear a most disagreeable aspect," wrote Massachusetts House Speaker James Warren of the perplexities of complying with congressional demands. "Every thing is resolved into money; but the great question is, how to get it?"[5] Warren was not the only one to ponder this question. Yet while many states agreed that Congress needed money, the government's financial difficulties could also be traced to those states that refused to give Congress the power "to get it." Rhode Island prevented the 1781 Impost from taking effect because it believed that "bearing hardest on the most commercial states . . . [it] would press peculiarly hard" on their state; because it would introduce "officers unknown and unaccountable" to Rhode Island's constitution; and finally, because "by granting to Congress a power to collect moneys from the commerce of these states, indefinitely as to time and quantity, and for the expenditure of which they are not to be accountable to the states, they would become independent of their constituents; and so the proposed impost is repugnant to the liberty of the United States." Rather than jeopardizing its liberty, Rhode Island preferred to "raise and collect its quota of public taxes in such a way as shall be judged most proper."[6] Defeated and still broke, Congress attempted another impost in 1783, which only nine states had granted by 1786, at which time the states were 4.5 million dollars behind in their payments to the confederacy. With states unable or unwilling to grant Congress either money or the power to raise money on their own, many frustrated congressmen threw up their hands and went back to their home states between 1784 and 1787.[7]

The Revolution had wreaked havoc on more than just the governments' finances, however. Americans voiced complaints about the economy throughout the nation: they could not access foreign ports, they had no protection for American ships from pirates and other hostile fleets, there were no willing creditors locally or abroad, debtors could not make prompt payments, internal trade was not regulated, they had no shipping rights on the Mississippi, they had no fishing rights in the Northeast, taxes were high and there was no circulating medium for exchange or the payment of taxes, and there was no protection from Native American attacks on the western frontier. In short, the postwar economic chaos affected merchants, farmers, creditors, debtors, and investors alike. The spectacular downturn in the nation's economy caused foreclosures, imprisonment for debt, and a dramatic increase in the number of lawsuits: "in 1784–1785 about 400 lawsuits were entered in the courts" of Worcester County, Massachusetts, alone, "and hence there was one lawsuit for the head of about every family in the county during these two years."[8] If the claims of the August 17, 1786, Worcester County, Massachusetts, convention can be trusted, then the only ones who profited in the postwar economy were lawyers: "an amazing flood of lawsuits has taken place [and] many industrious members of the community have been confined in gaol and many more liable to the same calamity," wrote the representatives of forty-one of the fifty towns of Worcester County; "in a word, without relief, we have nothing before us but distress and ruin." County conventions like the one in Worcester became commonplace, and petitions began to pour into the state legislatures; between 1784 and 1787, 30 percent of all Massachusetts towns sent petitions to their state representatives sitting in Boston, for example. But farmers were not the only ones to ask for relief from imminent "distress and ruin." Merchants, fisherman, creditors, and land and debt speculators all petitioned state legislatures and the Congress for help out of their economic woes.

The problems of the postwar economy were widespread, but not all of these different interests demanded the same kinds of reforms. Reforms that benefited one group (e.g., debtors or fishermen or northerners) directly harmed another group (creditors or westerners or slaveholders), and therefore the nation's economic problems were not resolved easily. As pressures on individuals increased, individuals increased pressures on their governments; as a result, the antagonisms between these different interests became explicit. For example, "many thousands of our inhabitants had been employed in the various departments of the army and navy," observed the prominent lawyer and future U.S. senator David Daggett in a July 4, 1787, oration delivered in New Haven, Connecticut, before the Society of Cincinnati; "some indeed returned to plentiful fortunes—some to peaceful industry. Yet, many, destitute of property, and the means of acquiring it, could only think of supporting themselves by the sweat of the brow. The idea was intolerable." With no sympathy for the plight of the yeoman farmers in his and neighboring states, Daggett, like many of his class, found the financially distressed simply lazy and unpatriotic:

> It led them to despise their country, disposed them of the patriotic sentiments, and fitted them to sow the seeds of civil discord. . . . These soon found the scene changed, and that an industrious pursuit of some constant employment would alone support them. This they could not submit to, and ascribed the declension of their fortunes to the badness of the times, scarcity of case, and a thousand other causes. The alarming state of our finances, compelled the legislature to lay heavy taxes. They caused the most bitter complaints. They parted with their property with the utmost reluctance. Is this liberty—is this independence they say—How preferable the years of 1772 or 1773!—We were told during the struggle for freedom, of happy days—of quiet enjoyment

> of our possessions—of "sitting under our own vines and fig trees"—
> But how different the situation![9]

Daggett's own economic position only allowed him to mock the distress of others; without sympathy or empathy, Daggett hurled abuse and sarcasm instead of offering aid and support. Likewise, an equally unsympathetic contributor to the *Pennsylvania Gazette* found the supposed economic woes of those who complained of a "decay of *trade*" to be "without foundation": "it should rather be said there is a decay of *traders.* A few merchants are sufficient to import and see all the goods America requires." The writer recommended that "those of them who complain of hard times betake themselves to the cultivation of the earth, or to the establishment of some useful manufacture. Until ninety-nine out of an hundred of the citizens of America are farmers, artificers or manufacturers, we can never be rich and happy."[10] This often-reprinted lament told lawyers like Daggett a thing or two about who or what was to blame for America's economic troubles. As both of these perspectives demonstrate, Americans on opposite sides of the credit divide saw little merit in the arguments of their antagonists. Without a common enemy to unite them, Americans turned against one another; seemingly, private interest had trumped concern for the common good.

Rather than resolving the growing crisis, county conventions and petitions to state legislatures only intensified the growing animosities among the different financial sectors of American society. Mostly these petitions came from yeoman farmers who "proposed remedies to neutralize the demands of creditors" in the hope of preventing being "confined in gaol"—as Worcester County had lamented—from the want of a circulating currency when "hard money" was scarce. Indeed, the emission of paper money was the most frequent demand, and "over half of all town petitions and every county convention specifically asked for a paper currency."[11] Although the petitioners dutifully claimed to "humbly seek protection and redress from the wisdom of your Honours," their request for "a portable representation of property" and aid in "induc[ing] the man of wealth to deposit that wealth in the lands and products of his country, rather than in speculations of publick securities, or in a commercial line," raised the ire of their intended audience more than it elicited the hoped-for relief. Many elites believed that the repeated calls for paper money were "repugnant to all honesty" because the paper currency began depreciating as soon as it was printed, "yet is tender in all payments equal to gold and silver," and therefore would allow debtors to pay off their loans and taxes at a significantly reduced rate.[12]

The elite response to the petitions in Massachusetts in particular dismissed the claims of the beleaguered and attributed nefarious motivations to their pleas. The many citizens who assembled "in conventions" only did so "to do acts treasonable to the state, and to concert measures to defraud their own and the publick creditors." Subsistence farmers were cash-poor, even though they had plenty of land and crops for exchange; yet these farmers were roundly denounced in newspapers, and the petitioning citizens were exhorted to "cheerfully pay, as far as they are able, their own private debts, retrench their idle, unnecessary expences, and contribute their portion to support a government of their own making." The Americans who attended these conventions were "desperate in their circumstances, and devoid of principle . . . destitute of property, without reputation, hardy and factious in their tempers, and eminent only for their vices and depravity." That these conventions and petitions would destroy the government seems to have been a pretty common perception among the state's elite. For example, Massachusetts chief justice William Cushing believed that petitioners were "endeavouring to stir up insurrection and tumult," the result of which could only be despotism. "If we cannot abide by the Constitution the few years so solemnly agreed upon," said Cushing, "there is no chance of our ever having another government by general consent and agreement—but we must remain in a state of nature, until a government of force shall arise to bend and control our stubborn, divided wills." The extra-constitutional conventions had returned Massachusetts to a state of nature in its most violent form: the state of war of all against all. "For let every man depend upon it," lamented Cushing, "as the present government and constitution fall, which are so vigorously struck at by conventions—all private right and private property will fall with them, and left wholly at the mercy of the most idle, vicious and disorderly set of men in the community."[13] Likewise, "Worcester" warned in *Worcester Magazine* that petitioners disturbed the public's peace and safety and, as such, that they ought to be treated as criminals and traitors: "Government, except in a few instances, has been too lenient, but it is hoped that such exertions will be made, when necessary as will cause all those, who in the future shall dare to disturb the publick tranquility, to lament their folly and wickedness."[14] Indeed, as "A Citizen" charged, the goal of these villains was nothing short of destroying the "present happy government."[15] For as a "Freeman" believed, "when we had other *rulers,* committees and conventions of the people were lawful—they were then necessary; but since I *myself* became a ruler, they cease to be lawful—the people have no right to examine my conduct."[16]

Although the petitions came from town and county meetings, and therefore were extra-constitutional in most states, they were still mere petitions. Although many creditors perceived the petitions as menacing anarchy, there were very few riots prior to 1785, which demonstrates that Americans initially attempted to work within the established system for a redress of their grievances. In response to the petitions, some states, such as Rhode Island, emitted paper money to relieve the farmers' distress. Others, such as Massachusetts, passed laws that harmed, rather than helped, the interests of the farmers—laws "hedged in with so many exceptions and conditions that they brought no relief and failed to soothe popular irritation."[17] Elites in these states, fearing that the petitions portended anarchy rather than orderly republican government, generally ignored, chastised, and punished petitioners for peaceably seeking a redress of grievances.[18] In return, some of the beleaguered farmers believed their new republican government was no less despotic than the monarchy had been in 1776, and they took direct action to prevent tyranny.

Between 1785 and 1787 seven of the thirteen states—Maryland, New Hampshire, Connecticut, Pennsylvania, South Carolina, Virginia, and Massachusetts—saw economic riots and court closures. New Hampshire farmers, for example, "surrounded the legislature at Exeter" and made demands that would frighten any member of the ruling elite: "paper money, the abolition of debts and taxes, and the equal distribution of property."[19] The state militia quickly drove them away. Yet, according to David P. Szatmary, Americans all over the country made similar demands. In May 1785 farmers attacked South Carolina's Camden courthouse "in a demonstration against debt collections, successfully blocked the consideration of debt suits, and sent the judges scurrying home." In Virginia, "husbandman formed associations and boycotted property sold at auction. Others flooded the legislature with petitions for paper money and tender laws," and "the King William County courthouse 'with all the records of the county, was burnt down.'" In June 1786 "a tumultuary assemblage of the people" closed the Charles County, Maryland, courthouse; "yeoman in Hartford and Calvert counties organized public boycotts against government sales of debtor property"; and "farmers in Cecil County circulated unsigned handbills that threatened state officers with violence in the event of government seizure of property for unpaid taxes." New Jersey farmers "refused to pay taxes and blocked attempts by sheriffs to auction debtor property. . . . In July, 1786 Jersey farmers assaulted the Elizabethtown debtor court, planted a stake in the ground, and impaled an effigy of Governor William Livingston on the pole." In November 1786, two hundred Pennsylvania yeomen, "about twenty armed with guns, and the rest with clubs, marched into York, and by force attempted to rescue some goods and chattels that had been executed for taxes." In January 1787, Pennsylvanians assembled "at the house of Justice Sherman, where a public sale of some cattle seized for taxes was to have been held, and effecting a rescue of them."[20] And between August 1786 and June 1787 a reported nine thousand people in Massachusetts—calling themselves Regulators, wearing their old Revolutionary War uniforms, and carrying a sprig of hemlock in their hats—took part in the most famous agrarian insurrection: Shays's Rebellion. While the economic riots, court closures, and attacks against military provisions in Massachusetts were a striking example of the people's discontent, the disaffection represented by Shays's Rebellion was by no means limited to that state. On the contrary, in the two years leading up to the Constitutional Convention in Philadelphia, Americans in more than half of the states had taken some kind of direct action against their local and state governments.

The response to the rebellions was swift. Rebels won brief victories—debtors' courts were temporarily closed in Massachusetts, South Carolina, Virginia, and Maryland, but were soon reopened. Again, the most dramatic actions took place in Massachusetts: Governor James Bowdoin declared the state in an "open, unnatural, unprovoked, and wicked rebellion," which meant that the rebels were "open enemies" of the state. The enemies of the state were hastily suppressed by government troops; disqualified from serving as jurors or as elected officials; disenfranchised; prohibited from teaching, innkeeping, and retailing liquor; and chased into New York and Vermont.[21] Between 1787 and 1789 at least "two hundred" rebels "were convicted of treason, insurrection, riot, seditious acts, treasonable practice or kindred offences"; the state jailed, fined, and threatened to execute the convicted, but they were eventually pardoned so long as they swore an oath of loyalty to the state.

While the states managed to suppress the insurrections, the lasting legacy of the rebellions was to demonstrate to elites that the people could not be trusted to prevent corruption, anarchy, or tyranny. Indeed, some elites began to believe that the people were the *source* of corruption, anarchy, and tyranny. By the time Daniel Shays and company were rebelling in Massachusetts, a movement had already been under way to reform the confederacy. However, with only five states sending delegates to the September 11, 1786, Annapolis Convention, we could hardly say that the reform movement had had broad support prior to Shays's Rebellion.[22] With rebellions occurring in seven states, many of the nation's leaders soon recognized that something drastic must be done to bring order to the chaos.

The economic and political elite resoundingly hoped that by strengthening the loosely constructed confederacy they might be able to control unruly states and citizens. For example, Secretary of War Henry Knox, who was rumored to be a secret monarchist, wrote to George Washington on October 23, 1786, that "a formidable rebellion against reason, the principles of all government, and the very name of liberty" had occurred in Massachusetts, the goal of which was to "annihilate all debts public and private, and have agrarian laws, which are easily effected by the means of unfunded paper money, which shall be tender in all cases whatsoever." His solution to the crisis was to strengthen the central government, which he hoped would "secure our lives and property."[23] In turn, Washington wrote to Henry Lee on October 31, 1786, that the accounts of the insurrections throughout the country "exhibit a melancholy proof of what our trans-Atlantic foe has predicted; and of another thing perhaps, which is still more to be regretted, and is yet more unaccountable, that mankind when left to themselves are unfit for their own Government. There are combustibles in every state, which a spark might set fire to."[24] The "combustibles" both frustrated and terrified elites like James Madison, who wrote to Edmund Pendleton on February 24, 1787, that "the late turbulent scenes in Massts. & infamous ones in Rhode Island, have done inexpressible injury to the republican character in that part of the U. States." He feared that the result of the tumult would be the establishment of monarchy or the "partition of the Union into three more practicable and energetic Governments." Madison believed that the latter plan was "a lesser evil," but he hoped that "the danger of it will rouse all the real friends to the Revolution to exert themselves in favor of such an organization of the Confederacy, as will perpetuate the Union, and redeem the honor of the Republican name."[25] The sentiments of Knox, Washington, and Madison could be multiplied many times over among the economic and political elite: the rebellions, riots, and insurrections proved that "mankind when left to themselves are unfit for their own Government," and the only hope of perpetuating the union, redeeming the "honor of the Republican name," and securing "lives and property" would be to reorganize the confederacy. Therefore, in the summer of 1787, reform-minded Americans headed to Philadelphia to see what could be done to preserve union, order, and republicanism.

The Need for Stability and the Constitutional Convention

The Constitutional Convention delegates were at once bold and shrewd. A secret convention during the sweltering summer months in Philadelphia set the scene for fifty-five men from twelve states—Rhode Island refused to send delegates—to abolish the Articles of Confederation and devise a new constitution. Like Americans prior to the Revolution, these delegates were well aware of how the dangers of corruption, tyranny, and instability endangered liberty; and, also like the Americans of 1776, they hoped to change the system of government to prevent these harms. Yet they hoped for a managerial, rather than a radical, change in the nation's political fiction—they did not hope to swap their republic for an aristocracy or an monarchy, for example. Therefore, delegates differed dramatically from revolutionaries in how they viewed the causes of "this dreadful class of evils" and in their proposed solutions to end it.[26] Convention delegates blamed average citizens for corruption rather than King George III and Parliament, and in so doing they reconceived how the average citizen would function in the republican fiction. Indeed, the romantic republican hero—so prevalent in discussions of political theory between 1764 and 1776—seldom surfaces in these debates. Revisiting the arguments made over those four long, hot, and tense months in 1787 allows us to reconstruct how the founding generation developed and justified this new view of citizenship.

During the debates, convention delegates put forward three claims that, when read together, demonstrate how the logic of the new constitution was different from the logic of the Revolution. While there were many differences of opinion about how to reform the American government, those who made the trip to Philadelphia that summer tended to be united on one point: something drastic must be done to create stability. Quite simply, the first claim of the convention was that instability existed in every part of the American government. For example, on May 29, 1787, Virginian Edmund Randolph began the convention by reminding his fellow delegates that the "laxity of government every where" portended the "prospect of anarchy" in America.[27] Likewise, in a long speech on June 19, James Madison delineated the "confusion and ruin" of the confederacy and argued that it was damaged beyond repair.[28] As Madison recounted much later in his life, the "distracted and disheartening condition of the union" meant that "the Federal authority had ceased to be respected abroad" and "at home it had lost all confidence and credit." Furthermore, "the unstable and unjust career of the States had also forfeited the respect and confidence and credit between man and man."[29] The country was disrespected at home and abroad, and its lack of authority meant that, as delegate after delegate complained, Americans could not carry on the basic functions of government, let alone preserve liberty and prevent corruption.

Delegates offered theories of the purpose and scope of a just government in their attempts to solve the rampant instability. Government existed, Madison—who spoke more than anyone else at the convention—argued on June 6, to provide "more effectually for the security of private rights, and the steady dispensation of Justice." These, therefore, were the criteria by which he believed a constitution should be judged, and "interferences with these were evils which had more perhaps than any thing else, produced this convention."[30] Explanations for the confederacy's weaknesses abounded. "Bad governments are of two sorts," Pennsylvanian James Wilson argued: "first, that which does too little. Second, that which does too much: that which fails thro' weakness; and that which destroys thro' oppression. Under which of these evils do the U. States at present groan?" asked Wilson. "Under the weakness and inefficiency of its Government," he answered.[31] Prompted by the occasion of the Constitutional Convention, Americans who were not in Philadelphia also pondered the nature and scope of the problems of the confederacy. For example, during the convention's first week the *Baltimore Gazette* urged the delegates to remember that the Articles of Confederation "were made for the temporary purposes of war" and that while they "were as wisely drawn as the then situation of the country would permit," they had since "become a loose, incomplete agreement, totally inconsistent with its own principles." Specifically, "the United States in Congress, have *exclusive right and power* for the following purposes without being able to *execute* one of them": "They may 'make and conclude treaties'; but can only *recommend* the observance of them. They may appoint Ambassadors; but cannot defray even the expences of their tables. They may borrow money in their own name, on the faith of the union; but cannot pay a dollar. They may coin money; but cannot purchase an ounce of bullion. They may make war, and determine what number of troops are necessary; but cannot raise a single soldier. In short, they may DECLARE every thing, but can DO nothing."[32] As Randolph, Madison, Wilson, and the *Baltimore Gazette* all argued, the weaknesses in the Articles of Confederation facilitated corruption and prevented stability. Solving the crisis required a new way of thinking about the role of the citizen, for by the logic of romantic republicanism, when corruption occurred, republican heroes could be called upon to cheerfully sacrifice, think of the common good, defend liberty, and prevent tyranny. However, as delegates lamented, romantic republican heroes were in short supply.[33]

The second claim in the convention's view of republicanism therefore was that individual citizens had proved that they were not the patriot heroes who would prevent corruption. There are two parts to this claim: the first part argued that average citizens are not patriot heroes and therefore that they could not be trusted to prevent corruption; the second part argued that whether or not average citizens are patriot heroes, recent experience had proved that they either cannot or will not prevent corruption. The first was prima facie a negative view of citizens, while the second was more surreptitious but equally negative. In either case, average citizens could not be trusted. "We must take man as we find him," Alexander Hamilton believed, "and if we expect him to serve[,] the public must interest his passions in doing so. A reliance on pure patriotism had been the source of many of our errors."[34] As Charles Cotesworth Pinckney made clear, "he differed from gentlemen who thought that a choice [of representatives] by the people would be a better guard against bad measures, than by the Legislatures," for he believed that "the latter had some sense of character and were restrained by that consideration."[35] Likewise, Edmund Randolph argued that the "general object" of the convention "was to provide a cure for the evils under which the U. S. labored; that in tracing these evils to their origin every man had found it in the turbulence and follies of democracy" and that "some check therefore was to be sought for against this tendency of our Governments."[36] Madison believed that the widespread failure of the people to act in the interest of the common good proved instructive: "the lesson we are to draw from the whole," he observed, "is that where a majority are united by a common sentiment, and have an opportunity, the rights of the minor party become insecure."[37] Indeed, as delegate Elbridge Gerry of Massachusetts argued, "the commercial and monied interest would be more secure in the hands of the State Legislatures, than of the people at large. The former have more sense of character, and will be restrained by that from injustice."[38] With elites' lives and property endangered by the "follies of democracy"—by a government composed of people who have no "character" and no "pure patriotism"—delegates argued that Americans must resign themselves to ameliorating the threat posed by corruption by any means necessary, including giving more of their own power over to the government.

The individual citizen was portrayed as childlike—as a complicit victim of corruption at best, and as the source of corruption at worse. According to Gouverneur Morris, "children do not vote . . . because they want prudence, because they have no will of their own." And while some delegates, like John Dickinson, might argue that since a "great mass of our Citizens is composed at this time of freeholders" they would "be pleased" with a freehold restriction on suffrage, Morris argued that eventually a majority of the citizens would not rise to the level of freeholders, and therefore that since "the ignorant and the dependent can be as little trusted with the public interest" as children, the constitution should explicitly declare who was worthy of the right of suffrage and who was not.[39] On the question of suffrage, South Carolinian John Rutledge believed there was no difference between "a mediate and immediate election by the people," for it was quite the "same thing to act by oneself, and to act by another." Since there was no real difference between direct democracy and representation, why not just grant the states suffrage? After all, "an election by the Legislature would be more refined than an election immediately by the people."[40] As Morris's and Rutledge's comments implied, most convention delegates seemed to believe that they were above average citizens.

In fact, many delegates believed that childish citizens, rather than elected officials, were to blame for the problems in the state governments. According to Gerry, childish citizens had allowed themselves to be duped by "pretended patriots," had voted the "the worse men" into office, and had been "daily misled into the most baneful measures and opinions by the false reports circulated by designing men."[41] "The people can not know and judge of the characters of Candidates," argued Maryland delegate John Mercer; therefore, "the worse possible choice will be made."[42] Or, as Connecticut delegate Roger Sherman protested, the people "immediately should have as little to do as may be about the Government." After all, "they want information and are constantly liable to be misled."[43] Morris was adamant that if delegates gave "the votes to people who have no property," the people would only "sell them to the rich who will be able to buy them." Morris believed that average citizens' views would never control the government whether or not they were given the right of suffrage, because "the man who does not give his vote freely is not represented"; instead, "the man who dictates the vote" is.[44]

Therefore, the third claim in the convention's view of republicanism was that the best that Americans could hope for in a government based upon the people was for the checks and balances of the system to create equilibrium so that one group would not be able to dominate the rest. "It was more than probable," Madison warned the convention, that they were "digesting a plan which in its operation would decide for ever the fate of Republican Government." Delegates "ought not only to provide every guard to liberty that its preservation could require, but be equally careful to supply the defects which our own experience had particularly pointed out." One serious defect of the Articles of Confederation, according to Madison, was that it did not protect the rights of the minority. America was not "one homogeneous mass, in which every thing that affects a part will affect in the same manner the whole"; rather, the majority of the people "labour under all the hardships of life, and secretly sigh for a more equal distribution of its blessings" and continually threaten the property of "those who are placed above the feelings of indigence." The people "may in time outnumber" those with property, and when this occurs, "according to the equal laws of suffrage, the power will slide into the hands of the former." The confederacy was already plagued with this class of evils: "debtors have defrauded their creditors. The landed interest has borne hard on the mercantile interest. The Holders of one species of property have thrown a disproportion of taxes on the holders of another species."[45] Protecting the property rights of the minority would not be easy, because the "danger [had] to be guarded against on republican principles."[46] Therefore, since the minority interests had to be weighed against the majority interests, building checks and balances into the system was the only hope for protecting the liberty of both consistent with republican principles.

Delegate after delegate argued that Americans must turn to the system to prevent tyranny. Even when delegates argued that the miserable state of American government was not entirely the fault of the citizenry, they still argued that the people were like children who could not be trusted to prevent the harm, and therefore that the system must be buttressed to prevent the danger. For example, James Wilson believed that the government ought to mirror the people: it ought "to possess not only first the *force,* but second the *mind or sense* of the people at large." Further, unlike Rutledge, Wilson believed that there was a difference between direct democracy and representative government: "representation is made necessary only because it is impossible for the people to act collectively." Yet, even while arguing that the best possible government would be one in which the people were fairly represented, Wilson still argued that the people's "mind or sense" had to be diffused into large districts, because "bad elections proceed from the smallness of the districts which give an opportunity to bad men to intrigue themselves into office."[47] Wilson believed that while the government should mirror the people, the structure of government must be arranged such that the people will not be required to defend liberty and prevent corruption because the people had proved that they could not be trusted with this important responsibility. A balance had to be struck between giving too much power to the people and too little, because as Madison argued, while the Constitution had to refine "the popular appointments by successive filtrations," he did not want that idea to be "pushed too far," because completely disenfranchising the people would also cause instability. Madison's metaphors were as mixed as his desire to rest the government on the people but not allow them to control it: "the great fabric to be raised would be more stable and durable," he said, "if it should rest on the solid foundation of the people themselves, than if it should stand merely on the pillars of the Legislatures."[48] In other words, in Wilson's more simple metaphor, the new constitution was a "pyramid" and the real power was at the top, which was "a considerable altitude" away from the base. The people were as distant from real power as any part of the pyramid *could* be and still be considered a part of the whole. Yet the "confidence of the people" was necessary; therefore the people ought to be included in a minor but important way—they would be the foundation of the pyramid. The government would still be based upon the will of the people, but their will would be diffused so that they could not cause too much mischief.

The delegates had developed a new republican fiction in three short moves: first, instability existed in every part of the American government; second, individual citizens had proved that they were not the patriot heroes who would prevent corruption; and third, the best that Americans could hope for in a government based upon the will of the people was for the checks and balances of the system to create stability. Whereas revolutionary republicanism had argued that average citizens were precisely the people who could and would prevent corruption, the Constitutional Convention delegates argued that recent experience had proved that this was simply false. Therefore, the new constitution created a consolidated national government with internal checks on power to abate the growing regional, sectional, and state differences among the thirteen states. In effect, the new constitution offered Americans who found romantic citizenship too "democratic," "leveling," and "dangerous" another legitimate interpretation of how to define average Americans' role within a republican government.

In retrospect we can see that this view of the role of the citizen in government is tragic because it asked Americans to resign themselves to the harsh reality that corruption was either so ubiquitous or so powerful that it could not be overcome. Corruption existed, and while its effects might be temporarily mitigated, there could be no hope that romantic republican heroes would ever successfully eradicate it. In short, tragic citizenship asked Americans to recognize that they could not be patriot heroes. Stability was the best that could be hoped for. Hence the best a republican constitution could do was to balance interests against each other in such a way that no one part would be able to oppress either the other parts or the whole. Average Americans must look to the system to fulfill the role previously imagined to be occupied by themselves—the system would cheerfully sacrifice, think of the common good, defend liberty, and prevent tyranny—so that average citizens did not have to.

The delegates, however, were not "men of little faith." They believed that stability could be achieved—it even could be "easily done," as Charles Cotesworth Pinckney argued, if only power was distributed "in such a manner, and for such limited periods, as while it gives a proper degree of permanency to the Magistrate, will reserve to the people, the right of election they will not or ought not frequently to part with."[49] Pinckney, like a majority of his fellow delegates, romanticized the power of the system to resolve the problems of corruption and instability. The delegates who made the trip to Philadelphia hoped to take direct action against instability and corruption. In so doing, they acted the part of romantic republican heroes—as Benjamin Rush had asked them to do earlier in the year—in their attempt to save the Republic from harm. That they did so by arguing that average citizens were *not* romantic republican heroes can be taken either as one of the great ironies of American history or as evidence that the assembled delegates viewed themselves as substantially different from the average citizens whom they denigrated.

Why Did Americans Accept Tragic Citizenship?

South Carolinian Pierce Butler wisely cautioned the convention that they "must follow the example of Solon who gave the Athenians not the best Government he could devise; but the best they would receive."[50] Expediency required that delegates consider whether the people would accept the drastic changes that they had made to the confederacy. Massachusetts delegate Nathaniel Ghorum, for example, believed that the convention "must consult" the people's "rooted prejudices" when devising the new constitution if they hoped for "their concurrence in our propositions."[51] One could argue therefore that the people acted as a fifty-sixth delegate (of sorts) throughout the debates. Yet delegates also argued that either the public will was not known, could not be known, or was immaterial, because the public did not know what was best for America. "If the opinions of the people were to be our guide," Madison argued, then "it would be difficult to say what course we ought to take," for "no member of the Convention could say what the opinions of his Constituents were at this time"; nor could any member "say what [the people] would think if possessed of the information and lights possessed by the members here; and still less what would be their way of thinking 6 or 12 months hence." Delegates argued further that because they knew what was best, the convention should act as it saw fit—as long as they could later persuade Americans to accept their decisions. "We ought to consider what was right and necessary in itself for the attainment of a proper Government," said Madison; "a plan adjusted to this idea will recommend itself." And if the plan did not recommend itself, then "the respectability of this convention will give weight to their recommendation of it. Experience will be constantly urging the adoption of it, and all the most enlightened and respectable citizens will be its advocates."[52] In other words, Madison believed that if there happened to be opposition to the proposed constitution, delegates would be able to use the convention's respectability and their own experience and prestige to persuade Americans of its merits.

Some process of ratification, therefore, was always on the minds of convention delegates. However, there was much debate over whether the constitution would be ratified by the people or by the state legislatures. Madison insisted that popular ratification of the proposed constitution was "essential," because "the articles of Confederation themselves were defective in this respect, resting in many of the States on the Legislature sanction only." This, in turn, allowed states to claim that their laws should take precedence over federal laws and led to the problems of *imperium in imperio.*[53] Elbridge Gerry, on the other hand, "seemed afraid of referring the new system" to the people, because "at this time [they have] the wildest ideas of Government in the world." He believed that "great confusion" would be the result of "a recurrence to the people," for they "would never agree on any thing" and he did not "see any ground to suppose that the people will do what their rulers will not."[54] Edmund Randolph believed that state "demagogues" would "spare no efforts to impede that progress in the popular mind which will be necessary to the adoption of the plan"; since these demagogues had complete control over the state legislatures, Randolph thought that the constitution stood the best chance of success with ratification conventions called specifically for the purpose.[55] After all, as Benjamin Franklin reminded the delegates, "it is of great consequence that we should not depress the virtue and public spirit of our common people" by failing to have them voice their opinion about their new government.[56] On June 12, 1787, the vote on whether to send the constitution to the states for popular ratification was nearly even, but those states in favor of it won by a margin of six to five.[57]

The convention submitted the proposed constitution to the states immediately; once it was read, it instantly drew admirers and detractors. There seemed to be a general consensus among America's economic and political elite that the new constitution had fundamentally changed the role of the average citizen within the government—some thought for the better, some thought for the worse. Virginian Edmund Pendleton, for example, wrote to Madison on October 8, 1787, to express his satisfaction with the new constitution. Pendleton believed that "a Republic was inevitably the American form," and despite his fear that republics often suffered from the "Natural danger [of] Popular Tumults & Convulsions," he approved of this constitution because, while it recognized that "the People" were "the Origin of Power," it prevented them from acting "personally; [they] can only exercise their Power by representation."[58] Likewise, Pennsylvania's November 14, 1787, *Carlisle Gazette* lauded the fact that America would soon adopt the proposed constitution. The *Gazette* believed that Americans would soon recognize that "such a government is more safe, and more respectable, than that which admits of popular licentiousness. They will then acknowledge that safety cannot exist in a government where there is no check but the voice of the people at large."[59] On October 29, 1787, the *Boston Gazette* published a satirical dialogue in which the staunchly Federalist Mr. Cutbrush rebuffed his Anti-Federalist interlocutor, Mr. Schism (believed to be former governor James Warren), for deserting the interests of his class in favor of the interests of the mass: "it appears to me," said Mr. Cutbrush, "and to almost all of my neighbours, that the American Constitution is that little *article* of HOPE, left at the bottom of *Pandora's* box of evils, which are so thick upon us at this day." Mr. Cutbrush "tremble[d] for the consequences" if "this last resort of the wretched" was not ratified, "for despair makes men mad indeed."[60] These Americans, then, seemed satisfied that the new constitution would improve the relationship between the citizen and the government, because it removed the threat of the "evil" of citizen participation.

On the other hand, New York ratification delegate Melancton Smith believed that the change in the relationship between the people and the government portended tyranny rather than stability or "safety." "Our duty is to frame a government friendly to liberty and the rights of mankind, which will cherish and cultivate a love of liberty among our citizens," Smith argued on June 23, 1788. "If this government becomes oppressive it will be by degrees: it will aim at its end by disseminating sentiments of government opposite to republicanism; and proceed from step to step in depriving the people of a share in the government." Further, Smith believed that the proposed constitution was evidence that "a change" had "taken place in the minds of many in this country in the course of a few years" and that "many who are ardent advocates for the new system, reprobate republican principles as chimerical" or as "fictions or fancy." Smith believed that these pretended republicans "ought to be expelled from society" and that their constitution ought to be rejected.[61] Americans like Smith, therefore, seemed quite dissatisfied with the way the new constitution changed the relationship between the citizen and the government.

It is fairly easy to grasp why America's elite would argue the merits of the proposed constitution: the stability promised by strengthening the government would improve the economy by guaranteeing contracts, preventing the states from printing money, creating interstate commerce laws, and reducing the national debt. However, it is more difficult to understand why average Americans would vote to approve a form of government that had the semblance of republicanism but not the substance. In other words, why did Americans accept the new tragic citizenship? Why did they agree with the nation's economic and political elite that they could not be trusted to defend liberty and prevent tyranny?

To answer this difficult question we must first turn our attention to the nuts and bolts of the ratification process. A total of 1,648 votes were cast by state delegates at the thirteen ratifying conventions between 1787 and 1790. Of those, 1,071 votes were cast in favor of the constitution and 577 were cast against it.[62] It is true that some states—Delaware, New Jersey, and Georgia—voted unanimously for the constitution, but these states had the fewest number of delegates—popular opinion was diffused into very large voting districts. The votes were much more contentious in the states with the largest number of delegates—Massachusetts, North Carolina, and South Carolina—in which popular opinion was much less diffused. The approval margin in the two most powerful states—Virginia and New York—was only ten and three votes, respectively.[63] Some town or county voters required their candidates to swear to a particular position on ratification before election day began, some gave instructions to their representatives after they had elected them, and some refused to give instructions at all. Most delegates acted consistent with their community's instructions; however, when delegates diverged from the instructions of their community it was almost always when they had been instructed to vote against the constitution and they preferred to vote for it. Anti-Federalists in Massachusetts, Pennsylvania, and Delaware complained of voter intimidation, suppression, tampering, and violence—there were no such complaints made by Federalists. Finally, each state had a freehold qualification for voters, which required a certain length of residency, a specific amount of property in land, a certain profit off of that land, and that citizens had been assessed and had paid their taxes in the previous year (as difficult as it had been for many Americans to find the hard money to pay their taxes between 1786 and 1788).[64] Therefore, the legitimacy of the American government rests on the 1,071 votes cast by state delegates at ratifying conventions; voting for those delegates was restricted to freeholders, may have been irregular, and the elected delegates may not have voted consistent with their community's wishes.

One could argue, therefore, that this was not the most stable foundation for the base of the federal pyramid. Yet, let us assume that everyone who was qualified and had the desire to vote was able to do so and that delegates cast their votes as their community had instructed them at all times. What else besides these structural issues could account for Americans approving a constitution that purposely restricted their ability to control the government? Perhaps Madison's confident belief that the constitution would be approved because of the respectability of the convention and the experience and prestige of the convention delegates merits consideration, for when convention delegates left Philadelphia they embarked upon a public relations campaign the likes of which America had never seen before.

Americans roundly congratulated themselves for electing to the Constitutional Convention men who were esteemed for their patriotism, intelligence, wealth, and power. For example, as early as April 14, 1787, the *Massachusetts Centinel* anticipated that "much good" would result from the "Convention at Philadelphia" because "the deliberations of the sages and patriots" who had been elected to reform the Articles of Confederation could not "but produce the most salutary measures."[65] Likewise, in Pennsylvania on June 25, 1787, "Civis" pronounced the "hope and desire of all good men" that the "distinguished characters . . . who compose the Convention" would "strain every nerve to establish a permanent and well adapted system of republican government." Further, "with such a great and good patriot as Washington at their head," the writer gushed, "may we not expect the most salutary measures will be recommended?" Although the convention had released no information about its progress in June 1787—indeed, they had just begun deliberations—he believed that the states should "join unanimously in adopting the plans" even if "it should affect" their "petty interests."[66] In other words, the prestige of the convention was so great that Americans should agree to any plan of government that it might put forward. Indeed, the *New Haven Gazette* reported, Americans had resoundingly demonstrated their determined "sincerity" to reform the Articles of Confederation by electing "men of the most distinguished characters for wisdom, knowledge, integrity, and patriotism to meet in a General Convention."[67] The convention was always referred to as the "Honorable

Convention" or the "the late Honorable Convention" because, as "A Jerseyman" argued in the *Trenton Mercury* on November 6, 1787, "our celebrated statesmen" had "gone through a four-months' labor of investigation," and such efforts deserved Americans' respect. Further, if America did not approve the plan of these "men of acknowledged abilities and disinterested patriotism," who would be better able to "undertake again the arduous task?"[68] As Madison had predicted, and as these many references to the respectability of the convention attest, calling upon the respectability of the convention—its ethos—had the potential to persuade Americans to ratify the constitution. The logic beneath this strategy was a very simple argument by authority: convention delegates were celebrated patriots; convention delegates said that the constitution was good; therefore, the constitution was good. Trust them, trust it.[69]

The only rupture in this logic of the unified respectability of the convention came from the thirteen convention delegates who left Philadelphia before the proceedings had ended, some of whom reported back to their home states that things were not going well at the convention. Federalist propagandists easily dismissed these reports as premature hearsay. More difficult to dispatch were the objections of the three delegates who remained until the end of the convention but refused to sign: Edmund Randolph, George Mason, and Elbridge Gerry. Randolph later changed his mind and voted with Federalists at the Virginia ratifying convention, but Mason and Gerry continued actively to oppose ratification, thereby drawing much criticism from the constitution's proponents. Federalists helped Americans resolve the contradiction caused by the disagreement over the respectability of the convention by roundly attacking the character of Gerry and Mason. They argued that Anti-Federalists did not deserve the same esteem that their Federalist colleagues did and therefore that their negative opinions of the convention were suspect. For example, "A Landholder" (Connecticut delegate Oliver Ellsworth) accused Gerry of delaying his objections until it was too late for delegates to change the constitution, of conspiring with other Anti-Federalists, and of having personal economic reasons for objecting. In a befuddling turn, "Brutus" (Tobias Lear) argued that Mason, "a man of acknowledged abilities and great influence," had taken an "undue advantage of his influence" and that he had opposed the constitution "in a clandestine manner" by handing out as many copies of his *Objections to the Federal Constitution* as he could to anyone who would take them.[70] Federalists thus attempted to defend the respectability of the convention by impugning the reputations, motivations, and tactics of the convention's Anti-Federalist dissenters.

Not only did Federalists draw upon the respectability of the convention in their appeals to citizens and state delegates, but convention delegates returned to their home states and argued that the expertise they had acquired as members of the convention meant that they had superior knowledge of how the Republic should be structured. Every state allowed former Constitutional Convention delegates to serve as state ratifying convention delegates—apparently finding no conflict of interest in having the men who wrote the document sitting in judgment upon their own work. Many Federalists took advantage of this oversight and sought election to state conventions: of the fifty-five delegates in Philadelphia, an astonishing twenty-nine attended their own state conventions—twenty-four of those twenty-nine voted to ratify.[71] Rhode Island—the only unrepresented state in Philadelphia—was the only state in which *no* Constitutional Convention delegate sat. Indeed, Madison's second prediction—that "experience" would "constantly urg[e] the adoption" of the proposed constitution—appeared to have come true. Although Madison argued at the Constitutional Convention and in Federalist 10 that "no man is allowed to be a judge in his own cause, because his interest would certainly bias his judgment, and, not improbably, corrupt his integrity," *he* was so eager to be elected to the Virginia convention that he left his duties at the Congress meeting in New York and hurried home to campaign for his own election—something that elite gentlemen considered beneath them in eighteenth-century American politics. When prospects did not look good for his election in his home county (Orange), he considered standing for election in Westmoreland and agreed to give the first public speech of his career to citizens in Orange in the hope of attaining their votes. He was successful. George Washington was one of the few Constitutional Convention delegates who had scruples about the conflict of interest: he refused to stand for election in Fairfax County, Virginia, because he thought it would negatively affect his reputation for Cincinnatus-like disinterestedness.[72]

Although only 29 out of the 1,648 votes cast during the ratification process came from former Constitutional Convention delegates, the influence of those delegates in the state conventions cannot be overestimated. Former Philadelphia delegates were elected to the most prestigious offices at the state conventions—at least two served as presiding officers—and delegates were able to claim that they had a special knowledge of the reasoning of the convention, which often gave them the edge over their Anti-Federalist antagonists. For example, Pennsylvania delegate and former Constitutional Convention attendee James Wilson constantly reminded his Anti-Federalist interlocutors that he knew more about the constitution than they did and that their opposition to the new government was simply due to the fact that they were misinformed. Further, because they had been through the process that led to the structure of government under consideration, former Philadelphia delegates were often better prepared to argue the merits of the plan and to neutralize the harms of the Anti-Federalist opposition. Therefore, as Madison had predicted, Federalists used their experience to great effect as members of their state conventions.

Madison's third reason for believing the constitution would be ratified was the high level of Federalists' personal prestige. And indeed, because the Constitutional Convention enjoyed such respectability and because so many convention delegates were elected to their state conventions, the prestige of the Federalists in the state conventions largely outmatched that of their Anti-Federalist opponents. While Madison had believed that Federalists' prestige would help to ensure ratification, according to Anti-Federalists like Massachusetts delegate Amos Singletary, Federalists used their prestige for pernicious ends: "these lawyers, and men of learning, and moneyed men . . . talk so finely and gloss over matters so smoothly, to make us poor illiterate people swallow down the pill." Indeed, Federalists "expect to get into Congress themselves," charged Singletary, "they expect to be the managers of the Constitution and get all the power and all the money into their own hands, and then they will swallow up all us little folks, like the great Leviathan."[73] Whether or not we agree with Singletary that state conventions pitted the "poor illiterate people" against "the great Leviathan" in a contest for power and money, it is clear that Federalists used their prestige both inside and outside the state conventions in their attempt to win the contest over ratification. The most striking example of Federalist attempts to use their prestige to make Americans "swallow down the pill" was their effort to control access to free and open public debate about the merits of the constitution. Anti-Federalists in New York, Boston, Philadelphia, Providence, and Hartford charged Federalists with preventing newspapers from publishing their essays against the constitution and with tampering, delaying, or "disappearing" their private letters and Anti-Federalist newspapers. These charges are nearly impossible to prove, because Federalists did not have complete control over the nation's newspapers and mail. Yet, the Federalists did enjoy the assistance of editors like Benjamin Russell of the *Massachusetts Centinel,* who flatly refused to publish Anti-Federalist essays, or, if he published one, would also publish three Federalist arguments against it. There was at least one instance of stolen private Anti-Federalist correspondence being made public: Pennsylvania Supreme Court justice George Bryan's March 7 and March 12, 1788, letters to former Pennsylvania assemblyman John Ralston were intercepted and published in the March 26, 1788, Federalist *Pennsylvania Gazette.* Therefore, it is also impossible to dismiss completely these charges of Federalist trickery.[74]

Many Anti-Federalists who suffered under the Federalists' highly effective public relations campaign may have believed with "Brutus Junior" that "artful and ambitious" Federalists were "determined to cram this government down the throats of the people before they have time deliberately to examine it."[75] But such determined cramming did not prevent the most resolute Anti-Federalists from gaining seats at their state conventions. The convention debates between high-powered Federalists and Anti-Federalists—the showdown between James Madison and Patrick Henry in Virginia, for example—provide yet another perspective on why American voters ratified the constitution. For when elites were evenly matched for prestige, knowledge, and skill, arguments turned to questions of safety and stability, and rhetorical strategies played off the ambiguities of republican political theory in the most dramatic and spectacular fashion.

For example, the speech of Revolutionary War hero and popular Virginia governor Patrick Henry on June 5, 1788, at the Virginia state convention has long been regarded as one of the most memorable of his eloquent career.[76] His main antagonist was James Madison, who, though no great public speaker, had worked tirelessly to get his "Virginia Plan" through the four months of debates in Philadelphia, had written a large number of the *Federalist Papers,* and had kept up constant communication with the nationwide network of Federalists. In short, Madison knew the constitution better, his motivation was greater, and his strategies were honed sharper than any other Federalist in the country. This, then, was no simple contest between the "little folks" and the "Leviathan," but a stunning showdown between two of America's political all-stars.

Henry's arguments at the Virginia convention, like those of other members of the Anti-Federalist elite, championed states' rights while appealing to delegates' fears of a tyrannical, consolidated federal government. His first, and from his perspective the most damning, critique of the proposed government concerned the simple distinction between "we the States" and "we the people" found in the new constitution's preamble. In his attempt to determine exactly how to judge the drastic changes that these few words revealed, Henry ran through the catalog of available political systems. Was the proposed government a monarchy? A confederacy? It certainly was not a democracy, in which the "people retain all their rights securely." Henry believed that these few words were evidence of a "radical" plot to create a "consolidated Government" that "endangered" Americans' "rights and privileges" and "relinquished" the "sovereignty of the States."[77] As Henry performed a close reading of the proposed constitution, he drew out the consequences of this "alarming" shift: "the rights of conscience, trial by jury, liberty of the press, all your immunities and franchises, all pretensions to human rights and privileges, are rendered insecure, if not lost, by this change." Not only should Virginia delegates be alarmed by this threat to their rights and liberties, but their "tame relinquishment of rights" was not "worthy of freemen." In the apotheosis of eighteenth-century insults, Henry questioned whether delegates lacked "that manly fortitude that ought to characterize republicans." Saying that delegates lacked republican fortitude was another way of arguing that they had fallen victim to the outrageously false fear appeals of Federalist propagandists: "we are told there are dangers; but those dangers are ideal; they cannot be demonstrated."[78] For while Henry "acknowledge[d] that licentiousness is dangerous" and therefore "that it ought to be provided against" and admitted "that the new form of Government may effectually prevent it," he also believed that in so doing it would "oppress and ruin the people."[79] Therefore, Henry's Anti-Federalist argument was fourfold: first, the new constitution fundamentally changed the government; second, this fundamental shift portended a loss of American liberty; third, Federalist fear appeals could not withstand scrutiny; and fourth, romantic republican heroes—seemingly in short supply among the Federalist delegates—were required to defend liberty and prevent the ratification of the proposed constitution. Henry attempted to turn the Federalists' fearful arguments back against them: Federalists thought of themselves as romantic republican heroes saving the Republic, but Henry asked delegates to see them for the would-be tyrants they really were. "Whither is the spirit of America gone?" lamented Henry. "Whither is the genius of America fled?"

When Madison arose to answer Henry's charges the following day, he implored delegates to render judgment "by a calm and rational investigation." He belittled Henry's bombastic style and his fearful description of the constitution and asked instead for a calm deliberation that was more suited to his own debating skills. We can almost hear the reticent Madison sneer when he asked that "Gentlemen, in displaying their abilities" would "condescend to prove and demonstrate, by a fair and regular discussion" rather than by "giving opinions, and making assertions."[80] While disdainfully acknowledging Henry's "abilities," Madison criticized Henry for his attempt to persuade delegates based upon the fear of tyranny and for his name-calling based upon the logic of romantic citizenship. Madison, therefore, purported to raise the conversation above mere fear appeals. "He told us," Madison said, summoning all of the power in his small frame to bellow, "that this Constitution ought to be rejected, because it endangered the public liberty, in his opinion, in many instances." Yet Henry's claims rested upon "general assertions of dangers, without examination." For example, Henry had "suggested that licentiousness has seldom produced the loss of liberty; but that the tyranny of rulers has almost always effected it." Madison believed that if Virginia delegates would only conduct a "candid examination of history," they would recognize that "turbulence, violence, and abuse of power, by the majority trampling on the rights of the minority" have been the "cause of factions and commotions, which, in republics, have more frequently than any other cause, produced despotism."[81] Madison had arranged for each delegate to receive a copy of the *Federalist Papers* (its authorship was not known at the time) before the convention began. This allowed him to refer to his not-yet-famous argument in Federalist 10 against factions, majorities, and pure democracy, in the hope that his audience was already familiar with his extended arguments against these evils.[82] Madison then turned the argument from attacking the constitution as the perpetrator of tyranny to defending the constitution as "the only possible remedy"; all the while "evil" and dangers were lurking, leaving "the principles of republicanism" in need of protection.[83] In retrospect we can see that even though he had promised to forgo fear appeals in favor of rational argument, Madison still attempted to persuade through the fear of tyranny, although his version of tyranny was the view of factions and democracy described in Federalist 10.

What does the showdown between Henry and Madison tell us about how elites argued among themselves when they were equally matched for power and prestige? Henry's and Madison's arguments share two important similarities: first, the ambiguous meaning of republicanism allowed them both to claim that threats to republicanism existed and that their plan for the government was the only republican solution to the problems of the republic; second, both claimed that only their solutions to the supposed problems of the Republic would provide liberty, safety, and stability. Both of these political titans' arguments therefore hinged upon fear appeals, for each was wise enough in the ways of political argument to know that the only argument that could beat a safety argument was another, even more frightening, safety argument. But who had presented the better case for the dangerous threats to republican liberty? Where did the *most* danger reside? Did danger rest with a consolidated government that might protect elites from "licentiousness" but would surely also deprive them of their much-cherished rights and liberties, as Henry argued? Or did more danger reside in the majority "trampling" the rights of the elite minority, as Madison argued? The two views were incompatible and required different courses of action, for in one the new constitution was the evil, and in the other it was the cure. Madison's speech and the nearly monthlong efforts of other Virginia Federalists triumphed; on June 25, 1788, Virginia became the tenth state to ratify the constitution when it voted eighty-nine to seventy-nine in its favor. It would seem, then, that Virginia's political elite had been convinced of the veracity of the constitution's new view of citizenship.

To return to our original question, what can this analysis of the ratification process tell us about why Americans accepted the tragic republican fiction? We first observed that the structural elements of ratification—who was allowed to vote, whether or not state delegates voted consistent with their constituent's wishes, whether or not there was voter fraud and intimidation—raised serious questions about the legitimacy of the 1,648 votes cast in the thirteen states during the ratification process. We next turned our attention to the Federalist public relations campaign articulated and supervised by Madison: Federalists relied upon arguments by authority in their claims that the respectability of the Philadelphia convention meant that Americans should accept whatever constitution the convention saw fit to create; Federalists used the experience gained in Philadelphia to take over their state conventions, and as a result a large number of Federalists passed judgment on their own work; and Federalists may have used their prestige to suppress Anti-Federalist sentiment from circulating in the public sphere. Finally, we examined how Federalist and Anti-Federalist elites used fear appeals and played off of the ambiguity of republicanism to argue the merits of the new constitution when they were evenly matched for power and prestige. Any one of these factors in isolation might not have been effective enough to prevent Americans from rejecting the constitution if they had recognized—along with Anti-Federalists like George Mason, Melancton Smith, and Patrick Henry, among others—that it represented a fundamental threat to their ability to control the government and a drastic shift in the republican fiction. Yet, when the structural elements of the ratification process were combined with the Federalists' impressive public relations campaign and the use of savvy safety arguments and the rhetorical possibilities inherent in the ambiguity of republicanism, it is clear that Anti-Federalists were simply no match for Federalists.

However, one aspect of ratification has yet to be addressed: while we could accuse Federalists of heresthetic rhetrickery, we also must recognize that Federalists offered a specific plan, were hopeful about the possibility of achieving stability, and asked the nation to move forward toward a happy future.[84] Anti-Federalists did not offer a specific plan to solve the harms that every American had felt since the close of the Revolution; rather, they merely criticized the new constitution without offering a viable alternative. In the end, their failure to produce a specific plan to resolve instability meant that Americans did not have much of a choice: when forced to choose between known instability and economic ruin or an unknown future under the new constitution, Americans found the unknown more appealing.[85] Indeed, average citizens knew the problems of the economy and instability all too well. They had tried to work within the system, but that had failed; they had tried riots and insurrections, but that had failed; might the Federalists' new system be the solution? In the end, Americans had little choice but to accept the new constitution's tragic citizenship: it promised to provide stability, which they had been convinced was the best anyone could hope for in a government based upon the will of the people.

Tragic Citizenship and Amending the Constitution

Once ratified, the new Constitution was set to go into effect in the spring of 1789. Bowing to pressure from the state ratifying conventions, the First Congress proposed the amendments to the Constitution now collectively known as the Bill of Rights. Two debates over the proposed amendments directly affected the role of the citizen in the national government: the ratio of representatives to constituents and the right of citizens to instruct their representatives (the latter being a part of the almost nonexistent debate over freedoms of religion, speech, press, assembly, and petition). The debates in the House over these amendments reveal much about the conflicted views of how average citizens should act in the national government and demonstrate the confusion over the precise form of government Americans had ratified. For our purposes, revisiting these debates demonstrates that Federalists were quite self-conscious about the logic of tragic citizenship and that they continued to support that logic even after ratification.

Constitutional Convention delegates intended the lower branch of Congress to represent the people, so delegates granted the House of Representatives the powers to originate laws, levy taxes, conduct war, and control the budget in the name of the people. The only time George Washington gave his opinion on any question in Philadelphia was when he asked delegates to change the ratio of representatives to citizens because he believed that as representation had been constructed it was an "insufficient security for the rights and interests of the people."[86] Yet even when the delegates altered representation from one for every forty thousand inhabitants to one for every thirty thousand, Anti-Federalists like Brutus still decried the scheme of representation as unfit to "declare the sentiments of the people."[87] At the heart of the controversy over representation was the question of whether the representative would "mirror" or "filter" his constituents' opinions.[88] Anti-Federalists tended to believe that the representative should faithfully mirror the opinions of the citizens, so they advocated for more accountability in the form of increased communication between the representative and the represented, increased numbers of representatives, binding instructions, and direct and frequent elections.[89] As we have seen, Federalists tended to distrust the opinions of the people and therefore hoped that representatives would filter and diffuse public opinion and that they would make independent decisions based upon their own analyses. Representation was therefore a crucial and contentious issue, because it reflected the founders' hope and fear that the people would rule.

We have already discussed the Constitutional Convention delegates' arguments against giving the people too much power or responsibility in the new constitution. However, not all Americans were convinced that the people's opinions should be dismissed so hastily. For example, during ratification the Anti-Federalist Brutus argued that "a free government" could only be defined as one in which the "people . . . give their assent to the laws."[90] If a scheme of representation was going to be used rather than direct democracy, then "the manner of the choice and the number chosen" would have to be such that the representatives of the people would "possess, be disposed, and consequently qualified to declare the sentiments of the people." For, if representatives either "do not know, or are not disposed to speak the sentiments of the people," then "the people do not govern, but the sovereignty is in a few."[91] In Brutus's judgment, Federalists advocated a government that could not rightfully be considered free. This view of representation places a high premium on the role of deliberation—that is, deliberation between representatives and their constituents—in the decision-making process. While Brutus's essays were circulated and commented upon throughout the nation, his criticism of the proposed constitution did not persuade delegates in New York or elsewhere to reject the new government.

Yet as state after state held ratifying conventions, it was clear that many delegates were as unsatisfied with the new constitution's idea of representation as Brutus was; Massachusetts and Virginia demanded a Bill of Rights to resolve these problems and protect the people from their government. On July 21, 1789, the House of Representatives elected a committee of eleven to "take the subject of amendments to the Constitution of the United States generally into their consideration, and to report thereupon to the House."[92] The Committee on Amendments submitted its report to the Committee of the Whole on August 13, 1789, igniting debates that raged until August 24, 1789.[93] One of the more contentious debates on the amendments centered around the ratio of representatives to the represented: Federalists like Fisher Ames believed that having fewer representatives would ensure that gentlemen would retain control over the government. "By enlarging the representation," Ames argued, "we lessen the chance of selecting men of the greatest wisdom and abilities; because small district elections may be conducted by intrigue, but in large districts nothing but real dignity of character can secure an election."[94] While Ames sought to justify his elitism with arguments about the purity of large districts, Massachusetts representative and former Anti-Federalist Elbridge Gerry, who acted over and over as the gadfly in the Bill of Rights debates, accused Ames of promoting his own aggrandizement at the cost of his constituents: "now I wish to know, whether he means that we should establish our own importance at the risk of the liberties of America," asked Gerry; "if so, it has been of little avail that we successfully opposed the lordly importance of a British Parliament." "I hope," implored Gerry, "that gentlemen will be inclined to give up some part of their consequence to secure the rights of their constituents."[95] According to Gerry, arguments like those made by Ames smacked of an attempt to make the House of Representatives aristocratic and "at the risk of the liberties of America." At stake in this debate was much more than the rate of representation: Ames hoped to purify the most democratic branch of government by instilling it with "dignity," while Gerry hoped that by guaranteeing "liberty" the House would be as democratic as possible.

The debate over representation was clearly a continuation of the debate in Philadelphia and at the state conventions about the proper role of the people within a republican government. While Ames retained his disdain for the average citizen, Gerry, who had been as fearful of the people as anyone else in Philadelphia, now acted as the champion of the people's right to adequate representation. Eventually, Ames, Gerry, and the rest of the Committee of the Whole would compromise, the Senate would approve the amendment, and the states would reject it.[96] The debate over representation was followed by an even more contentious debate over whether average citizens should have the constitutionally guaranteed right to instruct their duly elected representatives.

The debate over the right of instruction was initiated by South Carolina representative Thomas Tudor Tucker on August 15, 1789, during the debate over the freedoms of religion, speech, press, assembly, and petition. Massachusetts representative Theodore Sedgwick had argued that "the right of the people peaceably to assemble and consult for the common good" should be struck from the amendment because "he feared it would tend to make them appear trifling in the eyes of their constituents; what, said he, shall we secure the freedom of speech, and think it necessary, at the same time, to allow the right of assembling?" After all, said Sedgwick, "if people freely converse together, they must assemble for that purpose."[97] While Sedgwick found the freedom of assembly redundant, Tucker argued to retain the words because "they were recommended by the States of Virginia and North Carolina." Additionally, Tucker argued that North Carolina and Virginia had requested that the House amend the Constitution with a "declaration that the people should have a right to instruct their representatives," this being the "most material part" of the freedoms of speech, assembly, and petition.[98] In retrospect, we can see that this question was so contentious precisely because it exposed the disjunction between romantic citizenship, in which the people were supposed to control the government and defend liberty, and tragic citizenship, in which the people had no power to act.

The first to rise to speak on Tucker's amendment was Massachusetts representative Thomas Hartley, who argued that the right of instruction was not necessary because citizens had the right of suffrage. Further, Hartley believed that the amendment, if adopted, would introduce the "real evils" of public opinion into House deliberations. "I have known within my own time so many inconveniences and real evils arise from adopting the popular opinions on the moment," argued Hartley, "that although I respect them as much as any man, I hope this Government will particularly guard against them." And while the government was supposed to have been an act of "we the people," Hartley believed that if representatives were bound to listen to public opinion, "the great object which this Government has been established to attain"—namely, stability—"will inevitably elude our grasp on the uncertain and veering winds of popular commotion."[99] "Instruction and representation in a republic appear to be inseparably connected," observed Virginia's John Page. "To doubt the authority of the people to instruct their representatives will give them just cause to be alarmed for their fate." Further, Page believed that if Hartley's "dangerous doctrine" prevailed, it would be "subversive of the great end for which the United States have confederated."[100] The alarm rung by both Hartley and Page over the fate of the new government would be a consistent theme throughout the debate on instructions: representatives argued as if the fate of the entire republican experiment would depend upon this one phrase's defeat or success, and in retrospect, perhaps it did.

James Madison clarified that the people's freedoms of speech, petition, and assembly were all secured, but if other representatives believed that "the people have a right to instruct their representatives in such a sense as that the delegates are obliged to conform to those instructions, the declaration is not true." As Madison elaborated his point, he offered his view of the proper role of the people in republican government: "my idea of the sovereignty of the people is, that the people can change the constitution if they please; but while the constitution exists, they must conform themselves to its dictates."[101] In what may be his most concise description of his view of republican government, Madison argued that the people's role was to assent to the government initially, and thereafter merely to obey. He therefore accorded a very minimal role to the people: they were not meant to participate in the government or defend liberty actively; rather, they were to approve the efforts of the Constitutional Convention delegates and then do nothing more. Elbridge Gerry challenged Madison's opinion of the role of the people: "he says the people have a right to alter the constitution, but they have no right to oppose the Government"; "If, while the Government exists, they have no right to control it," observed Gerry, then "it appears they have divested themselves of the sovereignty over the constitution." In other words, if Madison's opinion of the role of the people was correct, Gerry argued, it was hypocritical for the House to continue the charade that the government was based upon the people; rather, "our language, with our principles, must change, and we ought to say that the sovereignty existed in the people previous to the establishment of this Government." "But," Gerry said, diffusing the harsh tone of his argument, "I trust, sir, too much to the good sense of my fellow citizens ever to believe that the doctrine will generally obtain in this country of freedom."[102] That Gerry backed down from his barb against Madison suggests that he did not quite believe that Madison's definition of republican government was consistent with the general consensus. Perhaps to Gerry's surprise, other House members concurred with Madison.

Turning to the question of the nature of the new government, Maryland representative Michael Jenifer Stone argued that allowing constituents the power of instruction "would change the Government entirely; instead of being a Government founded upon representation, it would be a democracy of singular properties . . . wherein all laws are made immediately by the voice of the people."[103] Once again Gerry rose to challenge the definition of republicanism: "the gentleman from Maryland (Mr. Stone) had said that the amendment would change the nature of the Government, and make it a democracy. Now he had always heard that it was a democracy; but perhaps he was misled, and the honorable gentleman was right in distinguishing it by some other appellation; perhaps an aristocracy was a term better adapted to it."[104] Gerry once again used hyperbole to argue that the position against the amendment was inconsistent with the consensus opinion of republican government; yet this time he did not back down from his argument, which suggests that he was beginning to understand the precise nature of the opposition to instruction: foes of the amendment did not trust the people to control the government; they wanted public opinion to be as diffused as possible; they wanted representatives to filter their constituents' will.

Gerry was not alone in his fight for representative-as-mirror rather than representative-as-filter. Virginian John Page would rise again to support the citizens' ability to instruct their representative. Page believed the amendment was "strictly compatible with the spirit and the nature of the Government; all power vests in the people of the United States; it is, therefore a Government of the people, a democracy." As Page continued he offered a view of the role of the people in the government that could only have made Ames, Hartley, Madison, and Stone roll their eyes at its naïveté: "If it were consistent with the peace and tranquillity of the inhabitants, every freeman would have a right to come and give his vote upon the law; but, inasmuch as this cannot be done, by reason of the extent of territory, and some other causes, the people have agreed that their representatives shall exercise a part of their authority. To pretend to refuse them the power of instructing their agents, appears to me to deny them a right."[105] No one arose to address or to refute Page's argument that the people had a right to give their "vote upon the law"; no one arose to discuss whether or not the people had the "power of instructing their agents"; no one arose to disprove that the House was denying the people "a right"; no one arose to debate whether the government was, in fact, a democracy. When the vote was called, the amendment that would have guaranteed citizens the right to instruct their representatives, control the government, and protect liberty lost ten to forty-one.

Tragic Citizenship: Citizens as Complicit Victims

In January 1787, just prior to the Constitutional Convention, Philadelphian Benjamin Rush called on American patriots to create a stable republican government, "PATRIOTS of 1774, 1775, 1776—HEROES of 1778, 1779, 1780! Come forward!" Urged Rush: "Your country demands your services!—Philosophers and friends to mankind, come forward! Your country demands your studies and speculations! . . . Hear her proclaiming, in sighs and groans, in her governments, in her finances, in her trade, in her manufactures, in her morals, and in her manners, 'THE REVOLUTION IS NOT OVER!'"[106] In other words, Rush believed by 1787 that Americans had already become apathetic—that the heroes and patriots of the Revolution had abandoned their efforts on behalf of the common good. Rush was not alone; as we have seen, many of America's elite agreed with him that Americans were not acting as the patriot heroes promised by the Revolution. The new constitution's tragic citizenship was meant to form a government that was based upon the will of the people, but one that would safely remove the caprices of public opinion from actual governing. While many Americans believed that the new constitution was essentially an extension of the American Revolution, savvy observers knew better. "The phantom of Democracy that has seduced the people is about to disappear," France's minister to America, Comte de Moustier, wrote to his colleague on August 2, 1788. His was a less sanguine view of the transition from romantic to tragic citizenship than Rush's: "The credulous majority, intoxicated by the noblest hopes that is allowed itself to be fed, has itself forged the bonds by which sooner or later the Leaders of the people will be able to subjugate and control them after having appeared to want to obey them."[107] The new constitution was still republican, yet as Comte de Moustier observed, the people had allowed themselves to be subjugated and controlled by the Federalists' fear appeals.

In retrospect we can see that the many Americans who petitioned their governments for debtor relief prior to 1787 were merely acting the part provided for them as romantic citizens. Petitioners believed themselves to be actively working to defend their constitutional rights and liberties—they believed they were acting on behalf of the common good. However, America's economic and political elite either did not perceive these petitions in quite this way or, if they did believe that average Americans were playing the part of romantic republican heroes, then such a belief caused them to recognize precisely how dangerous romantic citizenship could be for established power structures. Therefore, America's economic and political elite argued repeatedly between 1787 and 1789 that corruption unfortunately existed in America; that individual citizens had proved that they were not the patriot heroes who could prevent it; that Americans must resign themselves to ameliorating the threat posed by corruption by any means necessary, including giving more power to the government; and that doing so would enable the system to prevent the corruption that individuals could not or would not stop. The individual citizen was portrayed as childlike, as a complicit victim of corruption at best, and as the source of corruption at worse. The best that Americans could hope for was for the checks and balances of the system to create equilibrium between the different branches of government and the different classes so that one group would not be able to dominate the rest.

Yet in hindsight, perhaps New York Anti-Federalist Brutus's criticism should have received more consideration. If the definition of a free government is one in which citizens are able to share a voice in the creation of the laws they must obey, how can citizens ever "voice" their opinions about the laws within the structure of representative government? If there is no dialogue between the representative and the citizen, how can the government ever be "free"? House members ensured that the citizen would not be able to instruct their representatives in 1789; how, then, could the people's will be exercised over the government? Federalists did not answer these questions adequately; they elided the questions by banishing the concept of democracy to the margins of realistic political practices and by defining republicanism ambiguously. The founding of the United States thus highlights the crux of the problem of democratic deliberation in a republic: when the people rule through their representatives, what influence should the opinions of the people have in their representatives' decision making?

The tragic view of citizenship argued that citizens could not be depended upon to fight corruption actively; nor would they actively defend liberty, critique the government, or work for the common good. Tragic citizenship thus gave citizens very little to actually *do* within the new national government. As Madison argued in 1789, "my idea of the sovereignty of the people is, that the people can change the constitution if they please; but while the constitution exists, they must conform themselves to its dictates."[108] The constitution required the approval of the people for legitimacy, but beyond that, republicanism was a "*gratis dictum,*" as Thomas Jefferson argued in a December 1787 letter to Madison about James Wilson's argument against a Bill of Rights.[109] The republicanism of the constitution had the appearance of empowering the people, but not the reality. In comparison to romantic citizenship, tragic citizenship significantly reduced the possibility of citizen action within the government. Yet, despite the new, less optimistic view of citizenship that emerged between 1786 and 1789, the new republican fiction was authored, dialogic, circulated, ratified, and open, and thus, while it granted the people less power, it was still somewhat enabling of the people. As we have seen, the constitution's new republican fiction was not perfectly dialogic, ratified, or open, but despite the structural problems involved in the ratification process, it still went through some kind of approval process and was not forced upon the people by fiat. Further, while the tragic citizen was constituted as a complicit victim of corruption rather than as a patriot hero, Americans were still portrayed as citizens rather than as subjects. Therefore, while the new republican fiction privileged the nation's economic and power elite more than it did the average citizen, it only modified America's republican government; it did not radically change the system to an entirely different form of government. In short, even after the adoption of tragic citizenship, the nation was still a republic.

4
"Who would not have been willing to have died such a death?"
Citizens as Reified Patriot Heroes, July 4, 1826

That John Adams and Thomas Jefferson died on the same day is fascinating; that they died on the Fourth of July is surprising; that the Fourth of July on which they died was America's Jubilee—its fiftieth anniversary—is a very strange coincidence. If in retrospect we can acknowledge that the deaths of Adams and Jefferson on America's Jubilee were fascinating, surprising, and strange, then we must recognize that for a nation already participating in patriotic panoply, the twin deaths were nothing short of "miraculous." Americans faced a hermeneutical choice in 1826: they believed the deaths of Adams and Jefferson were no mere coincidence, but were rather a meaningful event orchestrated by Providence as a sign to tell the nation something important about itself. But the sign was ambiguous: Were the twin deaths an omen that the Republic would end with its founders? Or, did the deaths demonstrate that the Republic would outlast its founders? Because the twin deaths were so surprising, every American was "immediately affected"; because the providential sign was so ambiguous, Americans commemorated the lives of Adams and Jefferson by telling themselves a story about the nation's past, present, and future that gave clarity to the ambiguity.

The yearlong celebration of America's Jubilee, beginning with the long-awaited return of Revolutionary War hero Marquis de Lafayette and ending with the deaths of Adams and Jefferson, provided a fitting backdrop for a rededication to the fiction of a predestined, providential, and heroic American republic. Americans could not help but rationalize, mystify, and embellish the strange events of the Fourth of July, and in so doing they conflated the nation's two views of citizenship. The founding generation freely and openly admitted that there were two different ways to think about the citizen's ability to act within the republican fiction, and Adams and Jefferson in particular—admittedly, long after their opinions had much political weight—at least attempted to explain their differences and persuade one another of the merits of their perspectives. However, by the 1826 Jubilee, differing views of citizenship would become hidden and America's political leaders would no longer willingly debate their different views of human nature, liberty, and republicanism. The story of the discourse of 1826 marks two important shifts in America's political fiction: first, Americans covered their republican fiction in the divine-right narrative of the old monarchic fiction; second, Americans reduced the romantic and tragic views of citizenship into one.

Adams and Jefferson: "Rival Friends"

While many members of America's political and economic elite met in Philadelphia in the summer of 1787 in the hope of crafting a stable republican government, two "stars" of the Revolution watched the proceedings anxiously from across the Atlantic. Serving as America's ministers to Britain and France meant that as much as they might have liked to have joined their colleagues in Philadelphia, John Adams and Thomas Jefferson could only influence the new constitution from a distance. They eagerly sought information about the new constitution and the ratification process and freely passed on information and opinions to anyone who would listen. Neither thought the proposed constitution was perfect, but both seemed to hope that with a few modifications—both insisted that it needed a bill of rights, for example—it could answer the needs of the thirteen states by balancing stability and individual freedom. Adams would have liked a stronger executive branch; Jefferson would have liked executive term limits. These differences in assessing the new constitution did not affect their collegiality or friendship, however. While residing in Europe, the two men regularly exchanged letters that were both professional and personal, each pledging his respect, affection, and friendship to the other. In short, Adams and Jefferson were mostly like-minded friends and colleagues prior to their return to the United States to serve as vice president and secretary of state in the new government.

Nor did their friendship abate once they returned home. Even when Jefferson became increasingly suspicious of Adams's "obnoxious" behavior as president of the Senate, his reported penchant for ostentatious carriages, and his rambling *Discourses on Davila,* the pair remained socially cordial, even if Jefferson sought out Adams's opinion less frequently than he had when the pair had been in Europe. Likewise, while Adams did not approve of the tumult of the French Revolution as Jefferson did, he seems to have believed that while Jefferson romanticized the violence in France, he had at least retained his sensibilities about American government. Indeed, while the pair's relationship was not what it had been—Jefferson turned increasingly to his Virginia colleagues James Madison and James Monroe for advice—there was no open hostility, and with Jefferson heading up the State Department and Adams serving as vice president, there was no reason for their different views of government to directly confront each other. Adams and Jefferson's warm friendship ended abruptly with the May 1791 publication of Thomas Paine's *Rights of Man.*

Alexander Hamilton's plan to rescue the nation's finances—assumption of state debts, a national bank, and paying premium prices to current note holders—caused Jefferson, Madison, Monroe, and a network of like-minded others to grow wary of a Federalist "cabal" as early as 1789.[1] By June 16, 1792, Jefferson wrote to the Marquis de Lafayette that "a sect has shewn itself among us who declare they espoused our new constitution, not as a good and sufficient thing itself, but only as a step to an English constitution, the only thing good and sufficient in itself in their eye." He wrote to Thomas Paine three days later that "high and important characters . . . need your lessons in republicanism. . . . It is but too true that we have a sect preaching up and panting after an English constitution of King, lords, and commons and whose heads are itching for crowns, coronets and mitres." Yet despite Jefferson's belief that "too many of our legislature" had "become stock jobbers and king-jobbers," he believed that Federalists were "preachers without followers, and that our people are firm and constant in their republican purity," as he wrote to Lafayette, and that the people were "firm and unanimous in their principles of republicanism," as he informed Paine.[2] Jefferson therefore believed that his view of republicanism was that of a majority of Americans and that those who disagreed with his views were at odds with the public. To Adams's dismay, Jefferson grouped Adams with the rest of the Federalist "jobbers" even though Adams steadfastly claimed to avoid any party affiliations.

Adams disapproved of financial speculators like Hamilton and his friends and was therefore decidedly not a "stock-jobber"; yet the accusation that Adams was a "king-jobber" could not be so easily dismissed. After reading his 1787 *Defence of the Constitutions of Government of the United States of America* and his 1790 *Discourses on Davila,* suspicious Americans found good reason to infer that Adams held monarchical sympathies.[3] His dense and lengthy ruminations on human nature, political theory, and constitutional construction led many Americans to believe he had professed a preference for monarchy and aristocracy above republican government. For while Adams admitted that appointing "officers by lot"—pure democracy—would have been a "more rational choice" for American constitutions, he believed this could not have been done. Rather, stability required that "gentlemen, that is to say, friends and connections of the rich, well-born and well-educated members of the house," would occupy positions of power. If the government was not run by the elite, Adams feared, "the community will be filled with slander, suspicion, and ridicule against them, as ill-bred, ignorant, and in all respects unqualified for their trusts; and the plebeians themselves will be as ready as any to join in the cry, and run down their characters." In other words, "division, faction, sedition, and rebellion" could be prevented only if the elite controlled the government, because the people would never respect a government controlled by themselves. Adams's *Defence* therefore fit with the Federalist discourse of 1787–89: the people could not be trusted to control the government. However, Adams's spin on prevailing Federalist sentiment was to argue that the people could not be trusted because human beings *would always want to look up to others.* Adams believed that hierarchy was natural and pervasive and that governments should reflect and protect preexisting hierarchies.[4] For, as Adams argued in his *Discourses,* "emulation next to self preservation will forever be the great spring of human actions, and the balance of a well ordered government, will alone be able to prevent that emulation from degenerating into dangerous ambition, irregular rivalries, destructive factions, wasting seditions, and bloody civil wars."[5] Therefore, the best form of government would promote and protect stability by dividing power among the three classes and would separate executive, legislative, and judicial powers, thereby enabling a strong executive in combination with the rich, wellborn, and well educated to take their natural and rightful leadership positions. To be fair, Adams did not believe the United States should be a monarchy; nor, however, did he believe republican government was right for every nation. Rather—and this was what got him into trouble with Jefferson and his friends—he believed France and England should retain their monarchies either because they had no cause for complaint against their current governments or because they were unprepared for the responsibilities of self-rule. In any case, Adams argued that both American and European constitutions should promote and protect natural hierarchy.

Edmund Burke's *Reflections on the Revolution in France,* which espoused opinions similar to those in Adams's *Discourses,* had been well received by Federalists when it appeared in America in 1790. Madison, Jefferson, and Monroe each believed that political principles like Burke's and Adams's were less than republican, and they sought to encourage the circulation of Thomas Paine's 1791 *Rights of Man*—an attack on Burke's *Reflections*—to controvert the "jobbers" and serve as a reminder of how a "true republican" viewed republicanism, liberty, and the American and French revolutions. Madison sent Jefferson his copy of Paine's pamphlet and asked Jefferson to send it on to House clerk Jonathan Smith, who, in turn, passed it on to Benjamin Franklin's grandson "Benny" Bache. Bache had just begun a career as the editor and printer of the anti-administration *Philadelphia Aurora* and was happy to publish Paine's pamphlet, believing it vindicated the political theories of his hero and grandfather.[6] Amid the swirl of networking, gossiping, and accusing, Jefferson found reason to include a note to Smith along with Paine's pamphlet stating that "he is extremely pleased to find it will be reprinted here, and that something is at length to be publicly said against the political heresies which have sprung up among us. He has no doubt our citizens will rally a second time round the standard of *Common Sense.*"[7]

It was odd that Jefferson used the third person to refer to himself, his opinion of Paine's work, the propriety of Adams's political theories, and his hope that Americans would endorse his view of republicanism. Perhaps the nonconfrontational Jefferson had hoped that such a distancing technique would provide a kind of plausible deniability should Adams ever hear of the part he had played in the publication of *Rights of Man.* Perhaps he had counted on his comments being made public and had simply put his note in a form conducive to publication. Whether or not Jefferson had intended to minimize his perceived participation or facilitate his comment's publication, Bache published it at the top of his edition of Paine's *Rights of Man.* Not only did Bache include Jefferson's note, but he also put it into the first person, which meant that Americans throughout the nation read that Jefferson openly declared that he was "extremely pleased" and had "no doubt" about Paine's work. Jefferson's note, attributed to him specifically, was also published as an encomium to the book in advertisements and newspaper notices throughout the country. Adams, enraged by the comments, knew just who Jefferson believed was spreading "political heresies." John Quincy Adams burst onto the national political stage by taking up his pen to defend his father's honor and their mutual views of republicanism, Paine, and the correct ordering of government in a series of essays published in Boston's *Columbian Centinel* and reprinted nationwide under the pseudonym "Publicola."

"I confess," wrote Publicola in the first essay of the series, "I am somewhat at a loss to determine, what this very respectable gentleman means by *political heresies.* Does he consider this pamphlet of Mr. Paine's as the canonical book of political scripture? As containing the true doctrine of popular infallibility, from which it would be heretical to depart in one single point?" If so, then Jefferson's words were meant "like the Arabian prophet, to call upon all true believers in the *Islam* of democracy, to draw their swords, and, in the fervor of their devotion, to compel all their countrymen to cry out, 'There is but one Goddess of Liberty, and *Common Sense* is her prophet.'"[8] There was more than one legitimate view of republicanism, Publicola argued, and as much as Jefferson might believe his was the only correct and proper view, he was mistaken. For the remainder of 1791 and into 1792, Brutus, Agricola, A Republican, The Ploughman, and The Watchman filled newspapers with angry responses to Publicola's treatment of Jefferson and Paine, to which Publicola willingly replied. With that a line in the sand, so to speak, between Federalists and the opposition had been drawn.

At first Jefferson attempted to explain away the Paine mishap. He wrote letters to Adams and Washington claiming that the insult was not intentional, that he had meant to give no offense, and that his comment was taken out of context, without his permission, and blown out of proportion by Publicola and other Federalist troublemakers.[9] Neither Washington nor Adams seems to have been convinced by Jefferson's transparent apologetic strategies. It did not take long for Jefferson to learn that his encomium to Paine—whether intentional or not—had positioned him as the champion of the opposition, at which time he ceased apologizing. Taking their cue from Bolingbroke, among other British Whig writers, eighteenth-century gentlemen profaned political parties, and none more vehemently than Jefferson. Yet he seems to have been able to convince himself that *they* acted like a party, that *they* were a faction, while *he* was just upholding traditional republican values. Such a belief made it much easier for Jefferson to organize his network of like-minded friends. In the spring of 1791 he and Madison went on a monthlong "botanizing excursion" in the Northeast to meet and enlist members for the opposition. They also established and helped to finance an opposition newspaper—Phillip Freneau's *National Gazette*—in November 1791. Their organizing efforts were successful. "Upon political subjects we perfectly agree and particularly in the reprobation of all measures that may be calculated to elevate the government above the people," Monroe pledged to Jefferson in a June 17, 1791, letter.[10] It was one of many letters that Jefferson would receive from well-wishers who wanted to declare that he was their standard-bearer.

Jefferson resigned from Washington's administration on December 31, 1793, "retiring" to tend to his garden and organize his first presidential election campaign. Jefferson placed second to Adams in 1796, by which time the new president and vice president represented warring political parties.[11] A tumultuous four years followed in which Adams pursued a "half-war" with France and passed the Alien and Sedition Acts (one of his first targets was Benny Bache), and in which Jefferson and Madison openly called themselves and their friends "Republicans" and secretly authored the Virginia and Kentucky Resolutions.[12] Jefferson's triumph in the "Republican Revolution of 1800" ended Adams's political career; he slunk away from Washington, D.C., at four in the morning without witnessing Jefferson's inauguration, and the pair barely spoke until 1812. Mutual friend Benjamin Rush engineered the reconciliation between Adams and Jefferson in 1812, at which point the pair rebuilt their friendship and famously corresponded for the next fourteen years.[13]

On October 16, 1809, Rush wrote Adams in a transparent attempt to cajole him into reconciling with Jefferson. Rush had had a dream, he said, in which his son was reading a book of American history that told the story of Adams writing a letter of congratulations to Jefferson on his retirement, to which Jefferson "instantly replied . . . and reciprocated expressions of regard & esteem."[14] In Rush's dream the pair then continued their correspondence until they "sunk into the grave nearly at the same time full of years and rich in the gratitude and praises of their country . . . and to their numerous merits and honors, posterity has added, that they were RIVAL FRIENDS."[15] Adams wrote back that Rush's dreams had the tendency to put him "in spirits for a Month" but that he had "no other objection to [Rush's] dream but that it is not history," although, he added mysteriously, "it may be prophecy."[16] Rush's words were prophetic indeed. Adams wrote a short note to Jefferson on January 1, 1812, and sent him John Quincy Adams's then recently published *Lectures on Rhetoric and Oratory,* to which Jefferson responded, beginning the conversation that Lester J. Cappon calls "a rich and voluminous correspondence that has no counterpart in any other period of American intellectual history."[17]

A string of letters in the summer and fall of 1813 offered the former friends an opportunity, as Jefferson wrote, "not to die before we have explained ourselves to each other."[18] These letters of explanation allowed the pair to directly confront one another's views of aristocracy and republican government. On August 14, 1813, Adams wrote to Jefferson with a translation and discussion of the ideas of the Greek aristocrat Theognis, challenging Jefferson to controvert Adams's (and Theognis's) view of hierarchy and aristocracy. "Has Science or Morals, or Philosophy or Criticism or Christianity," asked Adams, "advanced or improved, or enlightened Mankind upon this Subject, and shewn them, that the Idea of the 'Well Born' is a prejudice, a Phantasm, a Point no point, a Grape Fly away, a dream?"

Adams clearly believed that human nature had *not* advanced past hierarchy and that it never would; distinctions among human beings were an "Ordinance of God Almighty, in the Constitution of human nature, and wrought into the Fabric of the Universe." And while idealistic "Philosophers and Politicians"—like Jefferson—"may nibble and quibble . . . they never will get rid of it. Their only resource is, to control it."[19] Adams's classification of the wellborn in the cosmic trilogy of God, nature, and universe demonstrated that well into his retirement he had retained his view from the *Defence* and the *Discourses* that hierarchy was natural, powerful, and ubiquitous. "Who are the aristocrats," Adams asked; "Philosophy may Answer 'The Wise and Good.' But the World, Mankind, have by their practice always answered, 'the rich, the beautiful, and well born.'"[20] Adams sided with the world and mankind when he further argued to Jefferson that "beauty, wealth, birth" could, and always would, overshadow more rational characteristics such as "genius and virtues." Adams relegated the opposing view of aristocracy to mere "philosophy," idealistic theory.[21]

"I agree with you that there is a natural aristocracy among men," Jefferson wrote Adams, clarifying that "the grounds of this are virtue and talents." "There is also an artificial aristocracy," he continued, "founded on wealth and birth, without either virtue or talents." Like Adams, Jefferson believed that there were important political consequences implicit in his and Adams's perspectives. "May we not even say that that form of government is the best which provides the most effectually for a pure selection of these natural aristoi into the offices of government," asked Jefferson. "*You* think it best," he accused Adams, "to put the Pseudo-aristoi into a separate branch [or] chamber of legislation where they may be a protection to wealth against the Agrarian and plundering enterprises of the Majority of the people. I think to give them power in order to prevent them from doing mischief, is arming them for it, and increasing instead of remedying the evil."[22] "You suppose a difference of Opinion between You and me, on the Subject of Aristocracy," Adams sighed in response to Jefferson's rebuke, but "I can find none."[23] Adams's view that there were no differences between his and Jefferson's positions on aristocracy cannot withstand scrutiny, for while Jefferson proclaimed that liberty required that talent and virtue would always triumph over beauty, wealth, and birth, Adams believed that liberty could be preserved by making "Offices of great Power and Profit . . . hereditary," which Jefferson would never condone.

Although Adams and Jefferson had both long since retired from active politics, each had retained his old view of republicanism, liberty, and the causes and cures of corruption. Both continued to openly describe citizens as tragic victims and romantic heroes. These differences were more substantial than mere political party differences; indeed, Adams's and Jefferson's views were fundamental expressions of how government could best be formed based upon the known conditions of human nature. In other words, the first generation of Americans had legitimate differences of opinion about the best form of government, and when they were honest with one another about it, when they attempted to "explain ourselves to each other," they found themselves offering incompatible perspectives. Yet, while Adams's tragic citizenship and Jefferson's romantic citizenship were indeed at odds, there was something endearingly earnest about their willingness to articulate and defend their respective positions to one another. In the spirit of mutual respect and philosophical dialogue, they freely and openly admitted their biases. However, by 1826 the second generation's differing views of citizenship would be hidden and America's political leaders would no longer allow their different views of human nature, liberty, and republicanism to be debated publicly.

While the second generation's hesitation to earnestly debate political theory may have prevailed for quite some time, the most dramatic example of this tendency can be found in the discourse surrounding the deaths of Adams and Jefferson.[24] For despite their well-known and manifestly divergent views of republicanism, upon their deaths Adams and Jefferson would be hailed as the "twin stars" of liberty as if they had always been in perfect agreement about how best to protect liberty. Revisiting how Americans interpreted the deaths of Adams and Jefferson allows us to view the second generation of Americans struggling to determine what America means, how to remember the Revolution, and how to imagine the future of the republican experiment. In the process of commemorating the fiftieth anniversary of July 4, 1776, and the lives and deaths of Adams and Jefferson, Americans would read the deaths as a sign of the nation's divine origin, as proof of American exceptionalism.

Jefferson and Republican Heroes

Jefferson's "Last Letter" is one place to begin when considering how the political discourse of 1826 conflated and confounded history and reduced the previous generation's romantic and tragic citizenships into one. Jefferson—too weak to walk, nearly deaf, and hardly able to hold his pen—spent the year of the Jubilee—the last year of his life—writing letters attempting to clarify party differences and his own political principles for the second generation.[25] Because of his poor health—the "sufferings of sickness," he wrote in the letter—Jefferson believed that this might well be his last opportunity to communicate directly to the public and influence how Americans understood what he believed America stood for. Indeed, Jefferson lay prostrate in a coma—and determined to survive until the Fourth, according to family lore—for most of the days between when he wrote the letter and July 4.[26] The circumstance of the composition of his letter was directly related to the celebration of American independence, so it is no surprise that his letter would echo the sentiments of the Declaration of which he, and the rest of the nation, was so proud.[27] Jefferson's "Last Letter" functioned as a farewell address; he used it to remind Americans of the revolutionary generation's struggle for liberty and to ask the current generation to continue that struggle. Jefferson's public dénouement allowed him to frame July 4, 1776, as a part of the current generation's republican past and future. Jefferson was as concerned as his fellow founders with how history would remember him, and he considered his authorship of the Declaration one of the three most important acts of his lifetime (the other two were authoring Virginia's statute for religious freedom and founding the University of Virginia); therefore his letter to the public took on added significance as his last chance to communicate the importance of this work.

"I should, indeed, with peculiar delight have met and exchanged there personally," Jefferson lamented as he expressed his regrets to the nation, "with the small band, the remnant of that host of worthies who joined with us, on that day, in the bold and doubtful election we were to make for our country, between submission or the sword." While poor health had rendered him unable to attend the celebration in the nation's capital, he praised such celebrations as evidence that "our fellow citizens, after half a century of experience and prosperity, continue to approve the choice we made."[28] The Declaration that Americans all over the nation would gather together to celebrate on July 4, 1826, was "the signal of arousing men to burst the chains under which monkish ignorance and superstition had persuaded them to bind themselves, and to assume the blessings of self-government." Jefferson most certainly exaggerated the Declaration's purpose and impact on Americans in 1776, for he knew that while Americans had learned to treasure the document and its sentiment by 1826, at the time of its writing it was considered no more than "a formal justification of an act already accomplished."[29] As Jefferson's version of history makes clear, the sentiment expressed in the Preamble was irrefutable proof that all Americans agreed in 1776 that citizens were supposed to rule over their government, which was a highly debatable claim in 1776, 1826, or beyond. Jefferson's exaggeration of the Declaration's immediate impact therefore helped him to tell a hyperbolic story of the revolutionary generation's devotion to equality, liberty, and citizen rule in the hope that despite historical realities, Americans would remember the founders as unimpeachable romantic republicans.

Jefferson hoped that Americans would view the Jubilee as a celebration of the "free right to the unbounded exercise of reason, and freedom of opinion" promised by the Declaration and that the celebration would refocus the nation's attention on "the rights of man." For he believed that "the general spread of the lights of science has already laid open to every view the palpable truth that the mass of mankind has not been born with saddles on their backs, nor a favored few booted and spurred, ready to ride them legitimately, by the grace of God." As Douglas Adair has demonstrated, Jefferson borrowed the "booted and spurred" imagery from the June 26, 1685, gallows speech of Colonel Richard Rumbold.[30] While he did not invent the imagery himself, Jefferson was able to use his light and equestrian metaphors with great effect in his "Last Letter." In combination with his belief that reason and freedom had spread through science to illuminate the dark reaches of both mankind's minds and political institutions, his use of Rumbold's riding metaphor asked Americans to rededicate their reason to defending their liberty from tyranny. His larger narrative was supported by his use of metaphors—what George Campbell called "an allegory in miniature" and Giambattista Vico called a "fable in brief"—to tell Americans a story about the triumph of reason and the many over ignorance and the elite.[31] Reason was natural, like light; the mass was born free, like a horse. Therefore in Jefferson's story the founders believed that equality was light and natural and that elite rule was dark and unnatural.

Not only did Jefferson invoke the founders' romantic citizenship and their commitment to equality, liberty, and freedom, but he hoped that Americans' commemoration of July 4 would "forever refresh our recollections of these rights, and an undiminished devotion to them," thereby rededicating all Americans to Jefferson's version of history. As each year brought another July 4 and another opportunity for Americans to devote themselves to liberty, more Americans would be folded into the great responsibility of defending their liberty from the elite riders who believed they were the legitimate rulers of the many. In short, Jefferson offered the celebration of July 4 as a parallel to romantic citizenship. The purpose of July 4 commemoration was to remind Americans of the dangers of tyranny and, just as important, to recruit new Americans into the "host of worthies," the "small band" who defied "submission" and chose the "sword." For, as Jefferson remarked, the number of heroes remaining from 1776 was indeed small. Jefferson's "Last Letter" attempted to constitute his generation as liberty-loving republican heroes, the commemoration of July 4 as active recruitment for patriot heroes, and all Americans who participated in the celebrations as the heroes who would fight future tyranny. While most Americans in 1826 did not enjoy the right of suffrage, and many Americans did not enjoy *any* freedom, Jefferson hoped that merely joining in July 4 celebrations would equal romantic citizenship and liberty.[32] Whether or not we judge his light and equestrian metaphors as allegory or fable, it is clear that Jefferson chose them specifically to express his hope for an American future that he would no longer be a part of.

Jefferson's romantic story of the Revolution and his romantic view of American citizens were nearly identical and endlessly bound up with one another. The "small band," the "host of worthies" were romantic heroes; America's Jubilee was evidence that the current generation "continue[s] to approve the choice" they had made for liberty. There were no "chains" on romantic heroes; they had the "free right to the unbounded exercise of reason and freedom of opinion." Americans still had an "undiminished devotion" to their liberties and would defend those liberties against "monkish ignorance and superstition," against those who believed there were a "favored few" who may "legitimately" dominate the whole. That Jefferson's attempt to frame the public's memory of the founders, the Declaration, the present, and the future was a hyperbolically romantic narrative that barely resembled reality need not matter if Americans recognized something of themselves or who they hoped to be in his discourse. Jefferson's words in this letter would be recalled time and again as prescient and comforting when the nation learned of the deaths of the "twin stars of liberty" on July 4, 1826.

Not only was this romantic story central to Jefferson's "Last Letter," but it also permeated the discourse surrounding the commemoration of the lives and deaths of Adams and Jefferson. This message could not have come at a more opportune time. The 1820s, wrote historian Arthur M. Schlesinger Jr., "were a decade of discontent, born in depression, streaked with suffering and panic, shaken by bursts of violence and threats of rebellion."[33] As Schlesinger notes, no matter where one looked for signs of stability in the 1820s—the economy, religion, class relations, political parties, migration patterns—one was likely to be disappointed. Specifically, as Charles Sellers notes, "as never before, young adults and nuclear households were forsaking kin and neighborhood to wander from place to place."[34] The movement of Americans from the country to the city and from established eastern states to newly developing western states and territories reflected the emerging "market revolution" that had wrecked havoc on every familiar aspect of Americans' day-to-day lives. Massive westward expansion, industrialization, and the concomitant extension of the franchise had badly frayed traditional political alignments based upon deference, class, and old-world notions of patronage, leading to a crisis of leadership the likes of which Americans had not experienced since the turbulent years between 1764 and 1776. Could this crisis be mitigated by the romantic citizenship of Jefferson's "Last Letter"? Jefferson's letter argued that the founders were heroes and so were the rest of Americans; therefore there was no crisis in leadership, because each citizen was a leader who would act to ensure a triumphant future for the nation. While Jefferson's view of citizenship and republicanism had not changed since the Revolution, his rearticulation of romantic citizenship in 1826 helped to remind the second generation that they could be romantic heroes.

Making Sense of the Twin Deaths

Thomas Jefferson, in his eighties and nearly bankrupt, took ill sometime in late June 1826.[35] University of Virginia professor of medicine Robley Dunglison attended him alongside grandsons Thomas Jefferson Randolph and Nicholas P. Trist and several servants. While accounts of his last days differ, all describe Jefferson as intent to survive until the Fourth of July. On Monday, July 3, he refused the opiate laudanum that Dr. Dunglison had been administering steadily for several weeks, and according to Trist he asked fervently around midnight, "Is this the Fourth?" Sensing that Jefferson really needed to hear that it was, Trist lied, to which Jefferson replied, "Ah, Just as I wished."[36] Dr. Dunglison remembered that Jefferson asked him if it was the Fourth around 7 p.m. on July 3, to which he replied, "It soon will be." Thomas Jefferson Randolph recalled that his grandfather's last words occurred when he awoke around 4 a.m. on July 4 and barked orders at his servants. He apparently awoke again at 10 and 11 on the morning of the Fourth and "fixed his eyes intently" on Randolph, but he had little pulse and was unable to speak. He died at 12:50 p.m. with the bells of Charlottesville ringing out the Jubilee celebration in the distance.

According to his wishes, Jefferson was buried quietly at Monticello on July 5, 1826, with an obelisk tombstone of his own design, which read:

> Here Was Buried
> THOMAS JEFFERSON
> Author of the Declaration of American Independence,

Of the Statute of Virginia for Religious Freedom,
And Father of the University of Virginia[37]

Mindful of the story that Americans would tell about him, Jefferson instructed posterity to remember him not for the offices of power he held but for defending liberty and founding the University of Virginia.[38]

John Adams, at ninety-one, seems to have been in much better health than Jefferson in the weeks leading up to his death. While Adams was too weak to write letters and was almost blind, he had left his home as late as July 1 and was reported to have had conversations with people on July 4. He awoke on July 4 and reportedly exclaimed, "it is the glorious Fourth of July—God Bless it—God bless you all." Later in the day, Reverend John Whitney visited Adams to ask him for a toast for the local Quincy Jubilee Celebration. Adams reportedly provided him with "Independence forever. And not a syllable more." Of those who attended Adams on the Fourth there is disagreement about what his last words were. Chief Justice William Cranch of the District Court of Washington, D.C., wrote: "In the course of the day he said, 'It is a great and good day.' And that his thoughts were dwelling on the scenes of 1776, is evident from the last words he uttered, which were 'Jefferson survives.' But alas! At that very moment, the spirit of Jefferson had already flown." President John Quincy Adams, who was in the capital for the Jubilee, wrote in his journal that his father's last words were inaudible but that Jefferson's name was distinguishable; Adams's niece Louisa Smith corroborates this last account. Over four thousand Americans reportedly attended his funeral, but Adams, who had not written a public letter about the Jubilee, had not written an epitaph for his grave.[39] Unlike Jefferson, Adams did not attempt to instruct Americans about how best to remember him. He likely thought the attempt futile. "Your Character in History may be easily foreseen," Adams complained to Jefferson in 1813. "Your Administration, will be quoted by Philosophers, as a model, of profound Wisdom; by Politicians, as weak, superficial and short sighted. Mine, like Pope's Woman will have no Character at all."[40] A grumpy Adams was even more explicit about how he believed history would treat him in an 1809 letter to Benjamin Rush: "Mausoleums, statues monuments will never be erected to me. Panegyrical romances will never be written, nor flattering orations spoken, to transmit me to posterity in brilliant colors. No, nor in true colors. All but the last I loathe."[41] He was wrong, of course; history has not remembered Adams quite as he would choose, but there were many "flattering orations spoken" to transmit him "to posterity in brilliant colors."

Newspapers printed black announcements; cities held mock funerals; eulogies were written and delivered to the thousands of citizens who gathered in memorial; in short, in 1826 the nation gathered in collective mourning for the fallen founders. "Jefferson and Adams were twin stars that shone with resplendent glory, during the whole eventful struggle of the revolution," wrote Georgetown's *Metropolitan.* "They have descended together to the tomb, and the prayers and blessings of their countrymen follow them. Their services, in conjunction with the happy coincidence of their deaths, have secured them an imperishable niche in the temple of fame. The late anniversary will be hailed as a glorious era in the annals of liberty, and we most sincerely trust will be solemnized with pomps, shows, games, sports, guns, bells, bon-fires and illuminations, until the end of time." The *Metropolitan* also hyperbolically proclaimed that "from the moment the melancholy tidings were received, every political feeling was banished; our citizens only remembered that these illustrious men were the promoters of their country's independence, and had hallowed it by their death." Whether or not "every political feeling" *actually* "was banished," Americans all over the country asked each other to view the twin deaths as both a "happy coincidence" and as a stunning display of America's chosen status. "Indeed, if the world had asked a sign to prove the *divina origine* of our compact," argued the *Metropolitan,* "it would have it in the *miracle* of their simultaneous demise, on the Jubilee of American Freedom."[42] When confronted with the shocking news of the twin deaths of Adams and Jefferson many Americans made sense of the strange coincidence, like the *Metropolitan,* by resoundingly declaring the deaths a providential sign of American liberty.

"Felicitations upon the illustrious death of your father," Secretary of State Henry Clay wrote in congratulations to President John Quincy Adams on July 25, 1826. "Who would not have been willing to have died such a death? Without indulging in a spirit of superstition, it is impossible to contemplate the dissolution of your father and Mr. Jefferson without believing that it has been so ordered to produce a great moral effect upon the American people, their liberty and their institutions." Clay's sentiment, while seemingly grotesque in its celebration of Adams's death, summarizes the prevailing wonder and corresponding acceptance of the "illustrious" simultaneous deaths. People everywhere were shocked by the events of July 4, 1826, but, like Clay, understood upon reflection that this "happy coincidence" had been "so ordered" by Providence to demonstrate American exceptionalism.[43]

News of Jefferson's death spread quickly through Charlottesville, Virginia, on July 4, 1826; likewise, news of Adams's death spread throughout

Quincy, Massachusetts, on the day of his death. However, the news slowly made its way to the rest of the country. Typically, the preparations that were already under way to honor whichever founder the city had heard about first were delayed when the news of the other's demise was received. For example, Georgetown mayor John Cox sent a memo to the Boards of Aldermen and Common Council to report that while the city had begun "to adopt measures in relation to the death of the venerable *Thomas Jefferson,*" it was forced to abandon the plan when it learned that "his compatriot, the venerable JOHN ADAMS, had also died on the same day." As Cox reported, the "additional event was well calculated to excite the feelings" of the citizenry. Georgetown eventually decided "that as in their lives they had been united in the great cause of liberty, so in their deaths the honors due their memory should not be divided." These "honors" included that a day be set aside for an observance, that there be an oration by Francis Scott Key, and that citizens would "wear crape on the left arm for thirty days." These same kinds of "pomps, shows, games, sports, guns, bells, bon-fires and illuminations," as the *Metropolitan* had called them—quoting from Adams's July 2, 1776, letter to Abigail after the Continental Congress had voted for revolution—occurred all over the country.[44]

To say with Mayor Cox that the deaths of Adams and Jefferson were "well calculated to excite the feelings" of Americans in 1826 seems a gross understatement. For two of the most important founders—and two of the three remaining signers of the Declaration of Independence—to have died on the same day and for that day to be the fiftieth anniversary of the Fourth of July was simply too much coincidence for most Americans to ignore. A coincidence such as this *had to mean something,* many Americans reasoned. But what did it mean? For the Americans of 1826 who were searching for meaning there were at least two possible interpretations of the deaths. Clearly, the deaths of Adams and Jefferson were a sign from Providence, but were they a sign of the "*divina origine*" of American republicanism, or were they an "omen," a curse, on the Republic? While the deaths could have been interpreted as a portentous omen, as trivial, or as something else entirely, Americans resoundingly asked each other to view them as "illustrious" evidence of Providence's approval of their people, liberty, and institutions. American jeremiadic rhetoric had prepared citizens to watch for such divinely inspired events; indeed, the rhetoric of republicanism had been built upon such narratives of predestination, corruption, and redemption.[45] The constitutive discourse surrounding the "apotheosis of 1826" raised Adams and Jefferson above mere heroic men; it reified the deaths as monuments to the perpetuity of the nation.

For example, on July 25 the *Vermont Gazette* reported the remarks made in Washington by Treasury Secretary Richard Rush, the son of that old reconciliator Benjamin Rush, in honor of the fallen heroes. The younger Rush observed that Adams and Jefferson had "lived through such a long generation of men—had begun to live so long anterior to the oldest of us now on the stage—anterior even to the foundations of the Republic itself—foundations which they laid—that it seems difficult, at least in the first moments of their decease, to regard the Republic in disjunction from their presence." But, Rush argued, it only *seemed* difficult to conceive of the Republic existing without the protection of twin stars of liberty, for the nation would continue. Yet, Rush was aware that it took great effort to understand the deaths as a blessing rather than as a curse. He described what most Americans must have felt when he said that the deaths "presented aspects affecting and awful." "Let us repeat," said Rush: "Nothing like this has occurred before, and it will not be matched again. It is impossible! It seems a vision, under which the people stand at gaze; something out of the course of nature; a drama of solemn, heavenly grandeur, which the uplifted curtains of the Jubilee has suddenly revealed to the wondering, entranced rivetted eyes of an assembled nation. We should pronounce it romantic if we did not believe it providential." While Americans gazed in solemn wonder, trying to determine what the vision provided by the simultaneous deaths meant, Rush attempted to constitute the deaths as a sign of "heavenly grandeur."[46]

Rush's eulogy made two important points: first, it expressed the surprise and wonder that many Americans felt upon learning about the deaths; second, it sought to channel such bewilderment, to frame the deaths as a positive sign of the health of the Republic. Certainly, Rush admitted, it was difficult to think of the nation without its heroic founders, but they were not gone. No, they had left a legacy of liberty, an example of virtue, and it was now up to those "on the stage" to receive that legacy and live by their example. That Rush felt compelled to channel the "gaze" of the public, to constitute the events as "grandeur" rather than "awful," demonstrates that there was a need for such a framing—that there was fear that at least some Americans might misconstrue the deaths as a curse and fail to see their "sublimity." The twin deaths of Adams and Jefferson on the nation's Jubilee were not only "affecting and awful" but also incomprehensible, "impossible," "out of the course of nature." Rush's speech was typical of those given by leaders on the nation's political stage: the negative interpretation of the deaths was often acknowledged, only to be quickly dismissed and replaced by a view of the events as "glorious." Eulogists often attributed the deaths to the invisible hand of Providence, thereby acknowledging their own insignificance when confronted with the splendor of the founders and their "illustrious" deaths. For indeed only the founders or Providence could have acted so heroically. In his speech, Rush portrayed Adams and Jefferson as a model of virtuous republican heroes who had triumphed over adversity in the service of their country. It was now up to those on the nation's political stage to wipe away "the vision" of the deaths, to learn the important lesson that the nation *could* continue on without Adams and Jefferson, and to follow the path begun by the founders.

Turning the nation's gaze away from the immobilizing vision of the deaths would not be easy. For example, Philadelphia's *National Gazette* believed that the twin deaths made "a coincidence so striking that it has immediately affected every person, and in a former age would have been deemed ominous, or at least a special dispensation of Divine Providence." As Rush had in his eulogy, the *National Gazette* acknowledged that the shocking events could be construed as "ominous"; and, also like Rush, the editors quickly dismissed such thinking as belonging to "a former age." The editors in Philadelphia were correct that the coincidence "immediately affected every person," but they were incorrect that the coincidence would not be viewed as a "special dispensation of Divine Providence," for this is exactly how most Americans described July 4, 1826.[47]

The editors of the *Charleston Courier* were representative of the other Americans who described the coincidence as a providential blessing of America, its institutions, and its people. "While the public contemplation was drawn eagerly to the remarkable fact, that MR. JEFFERSON had died on the very anniversary of the natal day of our Liberties," the *Courier* observed, "a day identified with his own undying fame, the surprise and wonder of all are increased, by the still more extraordinary circumstance, that MR. ADAMS departed this life on the same day." "It would seem as if they enjoyed the peculiar favor of Heaven," wrote the *Courier* as it attempted to mitigate the "surprise and wonder" people felt by giving the strange events a positive, romantic story: "such was the duration of their lives, and such the marvelous coincidence of their deaths. The day, remarkable as it was before, will never return without strong recollections of the PATRIOTS it has taken away, as of the Liberties it gave. Fortunate day! The threshold of freedom upon earth—the threshold now of happiness above."[48] The July 8 *New York American* went even further than the *Courier* in pronouncing the deaths with hyperbolic wonder and willing acceptance when it reported that it remembered "nothing in the annals of man so striking, so beautiful, as the death of these two time honored patriots on the jubilee of that freedom, which they devoted themselves and all that was dear to them, to proclaim and establish."[49]

The use of hyperbole—"nothing in the annals of man"—by newspapers such as the *Metropolitan,* the *Courier,* and the *New York American* would normally signal that Americans should not take the newspapers' claims of the deaths' wonderful magnificence literally. However, these exaggerated claims were used with such ubiquity that it seems plausible that Americans were meant to take them at face value, to believe that there was really *nothing more beautiful in the history of the world* than having Adams and Jefferson die on the fiftieth anniversary of July 4, 1776. Like Rush's eulogy, newspaper accounts also attempted to constitute the deaths as providential proof of American exceptionalism: the deaths were the most beautiful event in the history of the world; such an event was clearly important and must be understood properly; Americans should read the deaths as a "fortunate day" that proved the "peculiar favor of Heaven." Providence had reached down from the heavens to take Adams and Jefferson on the fiftieth anniversary of the Declaration of Independence to show Americans how much God approved of the nation and its institutions. Americans were not supposed to question the logic of this story—Does God really favor destitute slaveholders? How about the cantankerous and vain? Is God a republican?—rather, Americans were merely supposed to recognize the sublime beauty of the deaths. The press's use of hyperbole was useful in their efforts to influence how Americans read the deaths, because while the hyperbole heightened the sense of "wonder," it also helped Americans to understand the deaths as "wonderful." Contrary to Jefferson's belief that the "lights of science" had triumphed in America, Americans preferred to make sense of the deaths by telling themselves a story riddled with what he would have called "superstition."

Americans seemingly concurred with the *Charleston Courier* and the *New York American* by resoundingly proclaiming the deaths "fortunate" and pouring out their affection in public ceremonies. For example, Richmond, Virginia, held ceremonies of "the most impressive description" to honor Jefferson and Adams on July 12, 1826. On an "unusually fine" day, the procession, four deep, began at Capital Square and marched past the Union Hotel and the U.S. Bank. When the procession ended back at the Square, "the immense assembly of people" took their seats under the canvas tent that had been constructed "over the large four-sided Gothic Arch, which had been erected on the eastern end of the Capital in honor of Lafayette" to hear the eulogy delivered by Attorney General William Wirt.[50] The procession was part of Virginia's larger effort to honor the heroes. Upon learning of Jefferson's death, the "Governor and Council of the state of Virginia" resolved that all state buildings "be hung in mourning," that the state Guard House bell "be tolled throughout the day," that guns be fired every hour on the hour from sunup to sundown, that state officials "wear badges of mourning for one month," and that citizens of Virginia "cheerfully unite in any other measures manifesting respect and veneration for the memory of the deceased."[51] Indeed, if the account of Elizabeth Wirt is considered, American life essentially froze momentarily in unified adoration. "The bells have been tolling all day for Mr. Jefferson—and the papers which announced his death this morning were all in mourning. I understand we are to have a mock funeral," Elizabeth wrote to her husband. A mere two days after Jefferson's death, she retold one of the popular stories about the deaths that had made them seem more romantic, heroic, and providential, "What a glorious and well-timed exit he made! On the 4th of July and *at the very hour* in which the declaration of independence was first read."[52] In fact, Jefferson had not died at the hour the Declaration was first read. The Continental Congress voted to declare independence on the morning of July 2, 1776, debated the Drafting Committee's Declaration until July 4, and it was not read aloud to the public until July 8.[53] Nonetheless, people all over the country, like Wirt, had begun to believe that Jefferson died "at the very hour" that the Declaration was first read. It is somewhat surprising that she missed the connection between the Eighth of July and the Declaration because as the *Masonic Mirror* and others reported, "[John Adams] was 8 years older than Mr. Jefferson; Jefferson 8 years older than James Madison; Madison 8 years older than James Monroe; Monroe 8 years older than John Quincy Adams. This is truly a singular coincidence."[54] Singular indeed.

Such embellishment likely helped people to understand the strange twin deaths on such an important day, but it also helped to build a bridge between the past, the present, and the future. By further exaggerating the amazing coincidence of the simultaneous deaths, Americans made certain that the events would be seen as "glorious" rather than "ominous." Americans added to the republican fiction by reaffirming that Adams and Jefferson were romantic heroes and by placing the average citizens who attended funerals and perpetuated the hyperbolic stories as characters in the drama of the republican fiction itself. As Jefferson argued about the July 4 celebrations, if all Americans could participate in mourning the heroes, then all Americans were citizens responsible for protecting liberty. Mock funerals could be found in just about every city and town around the country. Such observances, memorials, and eulogies not only allowed Americans to grieve and pay their respects but also tied the nation together—however briefly—in celebration of the romantic story of American exceptionalism. Not only did all Americans once again become active characters in the story of American republicanism, but the end of Adams's and Jefferson's lives reinforced the end of the revolutionary generation and the assumption of power by those who inherited the Revolution. The deaths therefore marked the segue between generations by allowing the second generation of Americans to grieve for, to make peace with, and to supplant the founders.

Eulogists like Daniel Webster made the theme of transition central to their speeches. While mock funerals, memorials, and eulogies were held and delivered all over the nation, Webster delivered the most famous eulogy in Faneuil Hall on August 2, 1826. On that day Bostonians crowded into the "Cradle of Liberty" to hear Webster's second speech in less than a month.[55] President John Quincy Adams was among the crowd dressed in black for Webster's two-hour speech; it would be one of many eulogies he would hear over the next several weeks. Webster believed that the deaths were "poetry" that could only have been written by the hand of "Divine Providence." Adams and Jefferson were "patriots" who had "fallen; but so fallen, at such age, with such coincidence, on such a day, that we cannot rationally lament that the end has come." Yet, while it was important for Americans to recognize that the lives of Adams and Jefferson were "gifts of Providence" and that their "happy termination" was proof of providential care, this framing had largely been accomplished by the day of Webster's eulogy. The main purpose of Webster's eulogy was to ask Americans to go one step further; his goal seemed to have been nothing less than the perpetuation of the nation itself. The generation that inherited the Revolution was once again asked to believe that with the deaths of Adams and Jefferson they had finally *truly* inherited the Revolution.

Webster rearticulated the importance of the transition between the generations that had become a recurring theme by August 2, 1826. "Let us not retire from this occasion," he admonished, "without a deep and solemn conviction of the duties which have developed upon us. This lovely land, this glorious liberty, these benign institutions, the dear purchase of our fathers, are ours: ours to enjoy, ours to preserve, ours to transmit." The nation was not only theirs to keep but also theirs to protect. "Our fathers, from behind, admonish us, with their anxious paternal voices; posterity calls out to us, from the bosom of the future; the world turns hither its solicitous eyes," warned Webster, "all, conjure us to act wisely, and faithfully, in the relation which we sustain." There it was: the republican past, present, and future all unveiled for the generation that inherited the Revolution. The founders, posterity—in fact, the *whole world*—had its eyes upon Americans in this moment to see if they would act wisely, to see if they would faithfully maintain the republican experiment, willing them to be romantic heroes. Webster's story was therefore that the deaths functioned as a proof positive "sign" that the nation was protected by Providence: the sublime coincidence of the simultaneous deaths of Adams and Jefferson could only be read as a glorious event in the nation's history because it was so improbable that it had to have been arranged by God to teach Americans that they must be the world's guardian of liberty.[56] Adams and Jefferson died in the most unbelievably heroic fashion, which Americans told themselves meant that romantic heroism was still possible. The astounding coincidence of the simultaneous deaths of two of America's founders on the fiftieth anniversary of the Fourth of July allowed Americans to hope that they were indeed a chosen people, a chosen nation, a chosen continent.

Transition and Conflation: Citizens as Reified Patriot Heroes

In his 1825 inaugural address, John Quincy Adams had confidently proclaimed that Americans held "no difference of principle, connected with the theory of government," and therefore that "our political creed is, without a dissenting voice that can be heard, that the will of the people is the source and the happiness of the people the end of all legitimate government upon earth." Such perceived unanimity in American political theory brought President Adams great comfort. "Standing at this point of time," he observed, "looking back to that generation which has gone by, and forward to that which is advancing, we may, at once, indulge in grateful exultation and in cheering hope. From the experience of the past, we derive instructive lessons for the future."[57] The Jubilee celebration itself, as Adams foretold, was a deliberate moment of recognition for the close of the revolutionary generation as much as it was a moment of reaffirmation of America's republican fiction. What Adams could not have known in 1825 is that while the nation paused to commemorate American republicanism with its Jubilee celebration, two of its most important founders would have "sunk into the grave," leaving the nation to wonder about its destiny. Initially, the coincidence led some Americans to wonder if the deaths of Adams and Jefferson might be a "curse on the republic" or a portentous "omen." Contrary to the confident and hyperbolic panegyric offered by newspapers like the *Metropolitan,* some citizens wondered if the deaths of their heroic founders signaled the end of the republican experiment, rather than its "*divina origine.*" If the deaths were not ominous, others wondered, who would defend the liberty of Americans now that the "twin stars" were gone?

In other words, the discourse surrounding the deaths of Adams and Jefferson reveals Americans in an overt and dramatic hermeneutical struggle with their recent past and their potential future. The discourse of 1826 was marked therefore by the tensions inherent in the transition between the first and second generations and by the questions of how to interpret the deaths of the founders. These tensions and ambiguities provided an invitation for the nation's leaders to retell the story of America and American citizenship. That there was something unique about the Americans of 1826 has already been recognized: Joyce Appleby believes that they were defined by being "born between Independence and 1800" and therefore that this generation's task was to "fashion the revolutionary affirmations that gave the United States a national culture replete with purposes, heroes, taboos, prescriptions, symbols, and celebrations."[58] Yet, George B. Forgie argues that the Revolution had cast a long shadow over the lives of the second generation that was difficult to escape; he believes that the shadow of the founders' heroism prevented the possibility of truly heroic action until the Civil War.[59] In other words, an entire generation of Americans had been rendered bystanders to greatness because they had had the misfortune of following in the footsteps of the all-too-heroic founders. Perhaps, then, the deaths of Adams and Jefferson marked the moment when the generation that inherited the Revolution finally came into their own. Merrill D. Peterson has argued that "the passing of Jefferson and Adams was a dramatic moment in the growth of American self-consciousness." He believes that the deaths produced "a fable" that "explained the miraculous, brought men into a community of loyalty and belief, and turned the nation's loss into a triumph."[60] Likewise, Andrew Burstein argues that 1826 was a "moment when two critical generations reaffirmed their connection," and therefore was the moment when "the rising generation" embraced "its political inheritance."[61] If these accounts are correct, July 4, 1826, was a pivotal moment when Americans expressed what they believed to be their nation's political principles and claimed their place on the nation's political stage.

Hannah Arendt argues that storytelling and commemoration are two of the most important kinds of actions human beings can undertake because they help to define political communities. Communal stories have the power to define not only what occurred but how we think about what has occurred. As Arendt reminds us, "*who* somebody is or was we can know only by knowing the story of which he is himself the hero—his biography, in other words; everything else we know of him, including the work he may have produced and left behind, tells us only *what* he is or was."[62] Americans told stories about who and what America was in abundance as they celebrated first the Jubilee and then the lives and deaths of Adams and Jefferson. The yearlong celebration of America's Jubilee had allowed citizens across the nation to reflect on America's story; in so doing, the remaining members of the revolutionary generation attempted to define their version of their life's events—who, rather than what, they and America were. The deaths of Adams and Jefferson gave the generation that inherited the Revolution the opportunity to attempt to craft a meaningful story of the nation's past in which they could find a place for themselves in the nation's future. Hence there was much at stake in the hermeneutical moment prompted by the fiftieth anniversary of July 4.[63] In retrospect, when we read the frenzy of newspaper reports, memorials, eulogies, and mock funerals together we can see that while Americans often acknowledged that there were different ways to interpret this stunning coincidence, they generally told each other a hopeful and romantic story about the triumph of the nation and its citizens. This romantic story helped to constitute the generation that inherited the Revolution, not as mere bystanders to heroism, but as romantic heroes themselves.

The "apotheosis of 1826" raised Adams and Jefferson above mere heroic men; it *reified them as monuments to romantic citizenship and liberty.* As Adams and Jefferson might have desired, the discourse of 1826 equated them with Bolingbroke's Patriot King. Yet the discourse of 1826 could only accomplish this reification by hyperbolic exaggeration and by conflating and confounding historical personalities and events. Jefferson and Adams were "twin stars" of liberty: they believed the same things, championed the same causes, and sought to effect the same vision of government, by the same principles, by the same means. Contrary to history, the commemoration of the lives and deaths of Adams and Jefferson unified all difference. The effect of such conflation, confusion, reductionism, and mysticism was to celebrate an *unproblematized* account of the first generation's contestation over republicanism and to reinforce the notion that all American citizens were the romantic patriot heroes who would save the Republic from corruption. Note that tragic citizenship is conspicuously absent from the accounts of the deaths, the embellishments of events, and from the eulogies. Tragic citizenship simply did not belong to such nostalgic accounts of America's destiny. Adams's and other Federalists' views of republican citizens had all but disappeared in the American political discourse of 1826. Tragic citizenship warned Americans to be wary of the dangers of citizen control, which made it decidedly un-useful for an optimistic reading of the deaths as a sign of America's chosen status. For if the deaths proved that Americans were objects of providential care, how could any American be portrayed as a tragic victim?

Americans commemorating the lives and deaths of Adams and Jefferson faced a hermeneutical choice in 1826: Were the deaths a hopeful sign from Providence, or were they an omen? Americans resoundingly declared the meaning of the deaths, republicanism, and themselves hopeful and romantic. When the second generation constituted the founding generation as unified romantic heroes, the nation as unified in liberty and freedom, and the second generation as romantic heroes, they delimited the rhetorical choices available to describe who and what could count as "American." For while public discourse proclaimed that Providence had proved America's status as the land of romantic republicans in 1826, many Americans still believed that the people could not be trusted to prevent corruption and defend liberty. Yet, Americans did not rationally interrogate the profound choice they had made when they banished tragic citizenship from their political fiction. There was no space in America's political discourse for these views to be discussed and debated; tragic citizenship had disappeared, yet no actual changes to America's constitutions had been made. In other words, as we have seen, America's constitutions were based upon the logic of tragic citizenship; therefore, if romantic citizenship really was going to prevail, all constitutions would have had to have been re-written, re-debated, and re-ratified. None of this was done in 1826. What the discourse of 1826 had changed, however, was the willingness of America's political elite to freely and openly admit that they still believed—along with John Adams and the Federalists of 1787–89—that the people were not romantic heroes.

"Adams and Jefferson are no more," Daniel Webster said as he summarized the sentiment of the nation in 1826. "They are no more. They are dead. But how little is there of the great and good which can die!" Eulogies like those delivered by Webster and Rush asked Americans to recognize that the deaths of Adams and Jefferson were a providential sign of the "*divina origine*" of America. Such a manifest sign of God's approval meant that Americans should recognize themselves as a chosen people, on a chosen land, with a chosen government. The discourse surrounding the deaths of Adams and Jefferson told Americans that those deaths were proof of American exceptionalism.[64] Americans had believed themselves to be a chosen people for as long as they occupied space in the New World, but the deaths of Adams and Jefferson *proved* that they were, in fact, chosen.[65]

As Americans made sense of the deaths in 1826 they thus clothed republicanism in the divine-right narrative of the monarchical fiction. The twin deaths of Adams and Jefferson proved that American republicanism was divinely sanctioned, which not only added further legitimacy to the fiction but also made it unquestionable.[66] In other words, if Providence approved of America's republicanism, then republicanism was the only legitimate form of government for the nation. Therefore, Americans not only conflated the romantic and tragic views of citizenship but also reinforced this reification by giving it divine sanction. The "cheerful unity" of 1826 turned the secular into the sacred by articulating the predestined, providential, and hence unquestionable logic of romantic citizenship.

The history of Adams and Jefferson's political differences would have been well known to the second generation of Americans, so the willful elision of those differences could be interpreted as further evidence of Americans' belief in the notion of citizen control—if citizens could control American history, they could certainly control America. Or, what is more likely, perhaps all of this talk of "cheerful unity" and the banishment of "every political feeling," as the *Metropolitan* had hoped, could be viewed as a ploy to appropriate romantic citizenship for partisan purposes. This was certainly the case if we view the scene through the eyes of one disgruntled "Democrat," who argued that Daniel Webster had no business giving his famous eulogy of Jefferson. "A Democrat" smelled a rat in Webster's speech: he believed that Webster and other "federalists" were abusing this notion of "cheerful unity" to use Jefferson's name, image, and political philosophy for disingenuous party ends: "The appointment of such men as Daniel Webster to eulogize the character and life of Thomas Jefferson; a circumstance, so inconsistent in itself, that no republican who has attentively observed the state of parties for the last twenty-five, or even from ten to fifteen years past, can view without disgust. The men who have done little else than abuse and contemn Mr. Jefferson during the whole of his political *life,* appear to have seized on the occasion of his *death,* not merely as a means of displaying their great talents and erudition, but as a political ladder to rise to popularity and public honor."[67] In other words, while Americans were demonstrating their ability to control the Republic by their immediate, unified historical revisionism of Adams and Jefferson as romantic heroes who triumphed over the dangerous threat of corruption and bequeathed to the second generation a land of ubiquitous freedom and liberty, politicians found that extolling the virtues of Adams and Jefferson would play well with the masses. Indeed, as "A Democrat" charged of Webster and his fellow "federalists," savvy politicians were attempting to channel "the gaze" of the unsuspecting public, to use their erudition to climb the "political ladder" and thus to gain honor and high office for themselves by riding the coattails of the founders.

As is indicated by the derisive account of Jubilee politicking by "A Democrat," by 1826 party politics had reached a new prominence in America. Politicians in the age of Jackson emphasized party "discipline," broke away from "the old ideal of national unanimity, or of a consensus transcending party," and embraced "the useful, the constructive contributions of political competition and conflict."[68] While decidedly not a friend of Daniel Webster, Andrew Jackson was the most successful of those hoping to ride Jefferson's coattails up the political ladder. Indeed, the 1826 Jubilee fell in the middle of the long campaign leading up to the 1828 grudge match between John Quincy Adams and Jackson, which Sean Wilentz has characterized as the "Era of Bad Feelings."[69] Although Jefferson had refused to anoint Jackson as the inheritor of his tradition, Jackson persuasively rearticulated Jefferson's romantic citizenship for his own purposes. The 1826 Jubilee celebrations fell in the middle of the buildup to the 1828 election; therefore, it is not surprising that we would find politics in these epideictic ceremonies, for it appeared as though the Jubilee represented a transition as much as a celebration. The deaths of Adams and Jefferson marked the transition between the generations, but they also marked the transition between America's republican political fiction and its democratic political fiction. We can make more sense of what was at stake in the commemoration of Adams and Jefferson in 1826 if we take a sustained look at the development of America's democratic fiction.

5

"I will not look up to the weather-cock of popularity, to see which way the gale is blowing"

Citizens as Ironic Partisans, 1816–1845

"The men who have preached these doctrines," Noah Webster groused of Jacksonian democracy in 1837, "have never defined what they mean by the people, or what they mean by democracy, nor how the people are to govern themselves, and how democracy is to carry on the functions of government."[1] As Webster's complaint attests, the rise of Jacksonian democracy in America was precipitated by three distinct ruptures in American political discourse: first, the word "democracy" began to have positive connotations for many Americans; second, Americans began to describe their government as a democracy rather than as a republic; and third, the word "democracy" itself was all but drained of its precise, technical meaning in popular usage.[2] These shifts in American political discourse were not unrelated; indeed, one could argue that if not for this last shift—if the word "democracy" had continued to denote and connote "the government of all over all"—then the first and second shifts might not have occurred at all and Webster would not have had cause to be so grumpy. By draining "democracy" of its traditional meaning without clearly defining who the people were, what democracy was, how the people would govern themselves, or how the Constitution would be changed to create a democracy, Jacksonians helped to create an ambiguously democratic political fiction in America.

The long and convoluted history of the rise of the democratic fiction began with the political turmoil of the 1790s, extended through the War of 1812, and reached its apotheosis with the rise of the second party system during the long 1828 presidential campaign. As we have seen, the first generation's political battles occurred, in part, because of different views of human nature and the best form of government for the new nation. The founding generation frequently questioned whether America should be a monarchy, an aristocracy, or a republic; they questioned what it meant to form a republic; and they questioned what kinds of policies supported republican government. As we saw in the previous chapter, by 1826 the second generation had accepted republicanism as the divinely sanctioned best form of government for the United States, which meant that the second generation no longer had the same need to debate republican political theory. With the Republic firmly established, the major debates of the second generation focused more upon questions of legitimacy, expediency, and practicality than upon the best political theory. The second generation questioned whether or not the existing republican Constitution permitted policies such as internal improvements, financial monopolies, nullification of federal laws, and the extension of slavery. These battles were still fought with intense vigor, but they were much less about interrogating political theory than the founding generation's battles had been. This shift had a marked effect on America's political discourse: it provided the rhetorical context for the rise of the democratic fiction and the shift from Americans as romantic and tragic citizens to Americans as ironic partisans.

To be sure, the first generation was filled with partisanship. Yet, while Federalists and Republicans supported party newspapers and rallied around party candidates and party measures, they also self-consciously argued that they were no party—they spoke for the people, for republicanism, and for the common good, they said. They always portrayed their opposition, however, in the most negative terms possible—as partisans who hoped to subvert liberty. For example, James Madison was in the process of forming his own party in 1792 when he wrote that all political parties were "evil" in the party newspaper that he and Thomas Jefferson had just financed.[3] Likewise, George Washington famously cautioned in his 1796 farewell address that parties were "potent engines, by which cunning, ambitious, and unprincipled men will be enabled to subvert the power of the people and to usurp for themselves the reins of government, destroying afterwards the very engines which have lifted them to unjust dominion."[4] Despite Jefferson's 1801 attempt to render his Federalist opponents silent "monuments" when he proclaimed in his first inaugural address that "every difference of opinion is not a difference of principle. . . . We are all Republicans, all Federalists," the Federalist Party continued to offer Americans different opinions and different principles until its collapse after the 1815 Hartford Convention.[5] The 1816 election of James Monroe ushered in the "Era of Good Feelings," in which all Americans supposedly became like-minded members of the Republican Party.[6] With only one national political party between 1816 and 1824, Americans who had previously identified themselves as Federalists either temporarily dropped out of national politics or joined forces with the more conservative wing of the Republican Party. Indeed, with no legitimate opposition, Monroe would have won a unanimous reelection in 1820 if the quick-thinking William Plumer had not cast his vote for John Quincy Adams, thereby narrowly preserving George Washington's distinction as the only American with this honor.

Yet, despite the unanimity that the designation "Era of Good Feelings" would seem to indicate, the 1820s hardly lacked important political battles. Like the period between the end of the Revolution in 1783 and the Constitutional Convention of 1787, the 1820s were filled with massive state-level political unrest caused in part by a dramatic downturn in the economy, westward expansion, industrialization, and popular demands for political reform. And, like Federalist efforts to regain stability by abolishing the Articles of Confederation and creating a new centralized government in 1787, politicians of the second generation sought to preserve stability by channeling demands for democratic reform into a centralized network for political action: the newly created second party system. The new-style politicians of the second generation would find the democratic fiction useful for harnessing the people's demands for increased political participation and organizing the newly enfranchised white male population to help them to win elections. In so doing, politicians of the second generation positioned Americans not so much as romantic heroes or as tragic victims, but rather as partisans who political leaders hoped would act within the confines of the party system.

The Compensation Act of 1816: From Republican to Democratic Representation

Perhaps the most interesting debate over the average citizen's ability to control the government occurred not during the era we call "Jacksonian democracy" but in the middle of the 1816 presidential election. The public outcry over the Compensation Act of 1816, which would have raised congressional salaries for the first time since 1789, resulted in the largest turnover of incumbents in the House of Representatives in the nation's history—70 percent of the Fourteenth Congress did not win reelection to serve in the Fifteenth—and led not only to the repeal of the act but also to an extended debate over the nature of representation.[7] In other words, the debates over the Compensation Act revived the questions from the 1787–89 ratification debates over whether and how the government was based upon the will of the people. In the end Congress would vow that *vox populi, vox dei,* and it would rescind the Compensation Act against its representatives' better judgment. However, while Congress had little choice but to obey the will of the people on this matter, it did so only begrudgingly.

Convinced that designing demagogues had caused the public outcry as part of a plot against Congress, the people's outrage over the act only seemed to reaffirm that average citizens were complicit victims of corruption. In the end the controversy over the 1816 Compensation Act marked the change from republican to democratic representation by requiring politicians to seek and maintain popularity.

The matter began simply enough on March 4, 1816, when Kentucky representative Richard M. Johnson—Martin Van Buren's future vice president—urged his colleagues to change the rate and method of their compensation, a power explicitly granted to the House by the Constitution. Johnson argued that changing the rate of compensation from six dollars per day, the rate established in 1789, to fifteen hundred dollars per year would facilitate the "dispatch of public business, a more punctual attendance of the members of Congress to their duty, and . . . shorten the sessions of Congress."[8] Virginia representative John Randolph warmly supported Johnson's bill as an act of "manliness," "frankness," and "independence, which deserves not only the thanks of this body, but the approbation of the nation."[9] Randolph was not alone in his support of the bill; of the many representatives who got up to speak on the merits of the proposed act, only four spoke against it. South Carolina representative Benjamin Huger was the act's most vocal critic. In a speech that took up the better part of March 7, he explained that he disapproved of the act because "it wore too much the appearance of disguise and concealment." Shifting the method of payment from a per diem to a salaried amount prevented his constituents from having "an opportunity of making a fair comparison between the present allowance, and what it was now proposed to raise it to."[10] Not only did the proposed method of compensation prevent transparency, but Huger believed that the "retrospective operation" of the act was unjust, because when representatives had been elected "they well knew they would be entitled to six dollars a day, and no more."[11] Furthermore, while other representatives believed that the "liberality of their constituents would confirm" their voting themselves a pay raise "without a second thought," Huger "thought very differently." Although "he had as much confidence in the liberality of those whom he immediately represented" as any of his colleagues, when he considered that taxes and tariffs were unusually high in 1816 he "could not find it in his conscience to draw upon their liberality for a gratuity and an addition to his pay at such a moment, and under such circumstances."[12] Huger did not know how he (or, by implication, his colleagues) could return "home and acknowledge that under such circumstances, and at the close of so bloody and expensive a war, he had voted for, or even neglected to oppose an increase of pay to himself."[13]

Huger's speech received lengthy responses from Representatives John Randolph, Henry Clay, Thomas Grosvenor, and John C. Calhoun, each of whom defended the Compensation Act as necessary, fair, and proper. Despite Huger's efforts, the House rushed through the act after just four days—passing it on March 8 by a vote of eighty-one to sixty-seven. The Senate spent even less time debating the act; it quickly passed the act by a vote of twenty-one to eleven with a minimum of discussion on March 14.[14] President James Madison signed the Compensation Act into law on March 19, and congressmen began drawing their new salary immediately. While Representative Huger had believed that his colleagues had "sneered and laughed" at him for his opposition to the act, he was right about how his constituents would react.

At first, newspapers like the *Federal Republican* and *Niles Weekly Register* merely reported the progress of the proposed act as part of their regular coverage of congressional business and did not comment on it either positively or negatively. Yet as early as March 25, the *Examiner* explained that the Compensation Act was "a measure, whereby the representatives and senators in congress, under the pretext of 'altering the mode,' double the amount of their compensation." Not only had Congress doubled its pay, the *Examiner* argued, but it had done so "even though the constitution prohibits any senator or representative from holding any civil office, the emoluments of which have been increased during his period of service." All of this might not be so bad, the *Examiner* argued, if the nation had not been "much embarrassed in its pecuniary concerns."[15] The *Examiner* drew from Huger's analysis to argue that the act was duplicitous, unconstitutional, and financially reckless. However, because Congress itself would benefit from the act, when newspapers like the *Examiner* applied such unfavorable labels to the act they were also applying those labels to the men who had passed the legislation. Therefore, in the *Examiner*'s analysis *Congress* was intentionally duplicitous; *Congress* acted against the Constitution; and, *Congress* was financially reckless. In short, the *Examiner* believed that romantic republican heroes were in short supply in the Fourteenth Congress. The *Examiner* was far from the only newspaper to indict Congress for passing the act.

The June 17 *Federal Republican* likewise abhorred the act and indicted Congress for poor judgment at best and treachery at worst. "The indignation of the people is raised to such a pitch by this unexampled measure," wrote the *Federal Republican,* "that the names of those members from

Maryland, who voted for it, are stuck up at all the taverns, stories, blacksmith's shops and cross roads in the country." The people were justly outraged, the *Federal Republican* believed, because it was "intolerable that the same set of men who plunged the country into a bloody and expensive war, who have imposed upon the nation, impoverished as it is, the heaviest taxes, whose mismanagement caused an alarming derangement of the finances and the circulating medium, the people think it dishonest and cruel in these men, to vote such an immense sum in their own pockets before any relief is given to them." The writer decried the "rank aristocratic language" of the representatives who had argued that the pay raise was necessary because it would enable them to "live like gentlemen" in Washington, D.C.; "such is the difference between the professions and the actions of self styled republican gentlemen or your *gentlemen republicans.*"[16] The *Federal Republican*'s aggressive and inflammatory denunciation of the Compensation Act and Congress modeled how the standards of romantic citizenship could be used to judge whether or not Congress had acted against the common good; Americans seemingly took notice.

As the August 3 *Western American* reported, perhaps there is no "more effectual way of ascertaining the public sentiment on any subject of a public nature than by watching the movements of the people on a public occasion." Citizens throughout the nation had gathered on July 4 to express "the real displeasure the sovereign people harbor towards those unprofitable servants, whose highest ambition has been self aggrandizement." Indeed, "scarcely a celebration" could be found that did *not* denounce the act and the Fourteenth Congress. For example, the citizens of Paris, Kentucky, raised their glasses when they heard: "may the 14th Congress, at the ensuing session, rise from its present sordid abasement, pure, uncontaminated, and unpensioned; through the chastising spirit of an enlightened people"; citizens in Lebanon, Pennsylvania, toasted to "the 14th Congress—May the $1500 characters be supplanted by honest and disinterested republicans"; the citizens of York, Pennsylvania, perhaps put the matter the most succinctly: "the next Congress: more business and less pay."[17] While these public toasts ranged from elaborate arguments to pithy slogans, they were united in their disapproval of Congress and the act. Like the newspaper accounts, citizens and community leaders indicted Congress for its corruption; now, however, the people were lauded as republican heroes watching, judging, and critiquing their representatives. While Fourth of July toasts reflected the pervasive negative public sentiment, they were neither official nor legal mechanisms for expressing the public's outrage. The people officially expressed their displeasure with their representatives, Congress, and the Compensation Act through the many local public meetings and state legislatures that voted to give instructions to Congress to repeal the act.

For example, the July 4 *Pittsfield (Mass.) Sun* reported that the legislatures of New Hampshire and Rhode Island had "voted their disapprobation of the double pay which Congress voted to themselves" and "voted instructions for the repeal of the new Compensation Law."[18] Massachusetts went even further by voting to instruct "their Senators and Representatives in Congress to use their influence to effect the repeal of the present compensation act" and by urging their representatives to amend the Constitution so that "no law varying the compensation for services of Senators and Representatives in Congress shall take effect until an election of Representatives shall have intervened."[19] The grand jury of Chittenden, Vermont, expressed its "disapprobation of a late act of congress, raising, by salary, the pay of its members about three-fold its former establishment; and at a time when the public burdens hung heavy on the farming interest."[20] A county meeting in Chester, Pennsylvania, protested that "high salaries (especially when made so by the incumbents) is evidence of a declension of the spirit of liberty, fraught with progressive evil, and ought to meet with a decided and determined check from those citizens who wish to return their liberty and rights, and transmit them unimpaired to posterity."[21] On August 26 the citizens of Fluvanna, Virginia, "convened by public notice at the court house" and unanimously adopted instructions for their representative, Hugh Nelson. Fluvannians exercised their "constitutional right, as a portion of the American people, to review the conduct of their Representatives" and avowed "their utter disapprobation of this law, which in every point of view appears to them indefensible." Not only did the citizens of Fluvanna enact romantic citizenship when they wrote that they believed that they had a constitutional right to investigate, judge, and censure their representatives, but they also ordered that their proceedings and resolutions be delivered directly to Representative Nelson and that the whole correspondence be published in the *Richmond Enquirer.* Nelson wasted no time in responding to his constituents; the *Enquirer* was able to publish his dutiful response alongside the censure. "I acknowledge myself flattered by the polite and approbatory style of this communication," wrote Nelson, who had perhaps wisely abstained from voting on the act in March. "And without hesitation," he assured his constituents that he was "influenced by a conviction of the impropriety of the measure, as well as by a just sense of respect for their instructions," and therefore that his "best exertions shall be used to procure the repeal of the Compensation Law."[22] Nelson's mollifying assurances to his constituents allowed him to retain his seat in Congress; many of his colleagues were not as fortunate.

On August 17 the *Washington City Weekly Gazette* observed that "many persons are struck with surprise at the violent discussions in the public prints, apparently occasioned by the compensation law." The *Gazette* believed that there was more at issue than merely the Compensation Act. "In reality there is a deep and radical dissatisfaction in the minds of many," wrote the *Gazette,* and such dissatisfaction could only lead to a political "purification." The *Gazette* was not "of those who impiously proclaim *vox populi vox dei*—that the voice of the people is the voice of God! because we have seen in other countries the most horrible deeds perpetrated in the name, and by the consent, of the people." However, wrote the *Gazette,* "it is the people who must purify representative government from political vices; and if, in effecting that purification, they go a little beyond the strict line of propriety, it is better to bear with their honest mistakes than to submit to the knavish practices of others." In other words, the *Gazette* applauded the people's outrage as the appropriate action of romantic heroes: American citizens watched, critiqued, and fought against the corruption of those who "laid down in office" and used their power against the common good. The *Gazette* finished with a warning that must have made congressmen blanch at its implications: "One benefit will inevitably result from the current political agitations: the representatives of the people will be taught to know that they are not the people themselves, a circumstance which individuals who have long continued in power are very apt to overlook."[23] The *Gazette* was correct both in its assessment that the people would act to "purify" Congress and in the lesson that Congress would learn from the purification. Throughout the nation local communities and state legislatures held meetings, condemned the act and Congress for passing it, and demanded that their representatives vote to repeal the act immediately. And while Federalists and Republicans blamed one another for the act, the people "purified" incumbent members of both parties during the 1816 election.

Indeed, within weeks of the Compensation Act's becoming law, the April 29 *Columbian* had directly connected any representatives' likelihood of reelection in the 1816 polls to whether or not he had voted for the act. "No man ought to be elected from this state," warned the *Columbian,* "who would be unwilling to vote for the repeal of that law."[24] On June 15, John C. Calhoun wrote to Alexander J. Dallas that he expected "great changes in this part of the Union at the coming election. The compensation bill is much objected to. I find in my own district very considerable dissatisfaction at it."[25] As one of the act's most vocal supporters, Calhoun was right to worry about his reelection. In response to the public outcry over the act, representatives made speeches and sent letters in the hope of appeasing their constituents. For example, Kentucky representative Stephen Ormsby, who had voted in favor of the act, vowed that he was "in heart and principle a democratic republican" and that as such it was his "duty to consult" his constituents' will and to "faithfully represent it; or having mistaken it, to be always ready to correct any error into which misapprehension has led me."[26] Despite his pledge "to effect a repeal of the present (compensation) law," Ormsby was not reelected to the Fifteenth Congress. In Ormsby's Kentucky, newspapers and citizens were particularly aggressive in their demands that their representatives act with appropriate contrition. Representative Joseph Desha was forced to "publish a contradiction to the report, (which has been circulated to his injury,) that though he voted against the Compensation Law, he really wished it to pass, and encouraged others to support it." Desha decried the rumor as "palpably false, and a base calumny" and offered "incontestible evidence" to support his claims. He was reelected to serve in the Fifteenth Congress. Fellow Kentucky representatives Speaker of the House Henry Clay and Richard M. Johnson had both warmly supported the act and therefore, as the July 11 *Country Courier* reported, "the opposition to Messrs. Clay and Johnson has every appearance of being very powerful and leads us to expect that they will hereafter be allowed to repent in leisure, of their greediness, in pushing through the compensation bill."[27] While Clay and Johnson succeeded in their elections, 70 percent of their colleagues from the Fourteenth Congress did not. Even Benjamin Huger, "the most strenuous opposer of the compensation law," could not "secure his re-election," losing by 319 votes to newcomer James Ervin.[28] One incumbent, New York representative Enos T. Throop, finding that his "services as a representative" did not meet "with the approbation" of his constituents, resigned his office so that others "better qualified to execute the important duties" could be elected.[29] In Throop's New York alone, citizens removed twenty out of twenty-seven incumbent representatives from office, thus exercising the principle of rotation in office to a greater degree than they ever had before.[30] With citizens actively watching, critiquing, and judging their representatives, it appears as though the Compensation Act prompted citizens to act as romantic heroes preventing corruption and defending their liberty.

Newspapers generally encouraged the people to act as romantic heroes, both by modeling active citizenship (practicing the "watchdog" function of the press) and by prompting the people to judge and take action against

Congress. For example, the July 6 *National Register* wrote that "this state of occasional fermentation is to be expected under a government, organized like ours; and is, perhaps, a state to be desired, as it indicates a vigilance and activity in the people, from whom all power emanates, conducive to the preservation of our liberties and essential to the salvation of the republic."[31] The July 12 *Western Monitor* published an essay by "One of the People," who argued that "the people have taken the matter into their hands, and I hope they will not lay it down until all the members who supported the law are deprived of the power of offending again by a similar act."[32] Likewise, "Honestes" wrote in the October 29 *People's Advocate* that he did not place "a blind confidence in the leaders of the republican party" and that he would not uncritically trust "their opinion of men and measures." The *Niles Weekly Register* applauded the "vigor of the people which so manfully opposes what displeases them"—that is, for acting the part of romantic heroes.[33] Yet, while many newspapers encouraged romantic citizenship, many others remarked on the dangerous consequences of the people's sudden political awakening.

The July 20 *Essex Register* agreed that "in our government the popular will must be obeyed," and it believed that "if the disapprobation of this law be general among the people," it must "be repealed or modified at an early day," even "though the public interest should certainly suffer by it."[34] The July 23 *New York Evening Post* was astounded by the nation's active citizens. It could find nothing "parallel, in the annals of any civilized country where the very body who enacted a statute, were obliged, during the very session in which they passed it," to repeal it.[35] The December 19 *Albany Advertiser* thought the whole mess "a miserable affair to distract the nation" away from the real issue: "the expenditure of a hundred millions of dollars in a war, by which the nation has gained not a single object for which the war was made."[36] The August 9 *Daily National Intelligencer* argued that "artful demagogues" riled the people against Congress and the Compensation Act in order to "build their popularity"; likewise, the November 16 *Albany Advertiser* believed that the act itself was "got up rascally" in order "to set people talking about it, so that they might not have their attention drawn to the *main point,* which is the election of Monroe."[37] Whether or not designing demagogues had led the people to critique Congress was an impossible question to answer definitively: certainly newspapers had published negative accounts of the Compensation Act and Congress; certainly the people had taken part in July Fourth toasts and public meetings; certainly 70 percent of Congress was "purified"—these were all indisputable facts—but, did the people rise up against Congress on their own, or were they manipulated into acting against their best interests by demagogues? No one could say for sure, but representatives made the question a major part of the discussion over the act when they returned to Washington for the "lame duck" second session of 1816–17.

When Congress resumed on December 2, 1816, it was a foregone conclusion that it would repeal the Compensation Act, yet debate over its repeal took up a majority of the House's time until January 23, 1817. While part of the debate focused upon the pragmatic questions of congressional compensation—should Congress repeal the act, should representatives repay the extra monies received during the last session, should the Fourteenth Congress set a new amount for compensation or leave that to the Fifteen Congress, and so forth—the pragmatic debate over the act was largely superseded by a debate over whether and how *vox populi, vox dei*. Most representatives granted that the government should be responsible to the will of the people, but they wondered how the public will should be expressed; they wondered whether the people had a natural right to instruct their representatives; they wondered whether representatives should mirror or filter their constituents' will; and they wondered how they could faithfully mirror their constituents' will without looking as if they had stooped to demagoguery. In other words, the public's negative response to the Compensation Act of 1816 set in motion an extended debate over whether and how America's republican government would be based upon the will of the people the likes of which the nation had not seen since 1789.

"The Fourteenth Congress," Henry Adams wrote, "for ability, energy, and usefulness, never had a superior, and perhaps, since the First Congress, never an equal." Yet, after the long summer of public scrutiny, these illustrious leaders "returned to Washington mortified, angry, and defiant, disgusted alike with the public and with public service."[38] Adams was mistaken when he surmised that there was "little of permanent interest or value" in the debates over the act's repeal, for representatives dramatically reinterrogated American republican political theory during these extended debates, and when they affirmed that *vox populi, vox dei* they not only changed how America's political fiction described representation but also implicitly recognized that America's political fiction was undergoing a major shift itself. New York representative Thomas Grosvenor declared unequivocally on January 18 that "the people were the sovereign, of this country. From them emanated all the powers of Government. This is now the settled doctrine of the civilized world, and he must be a madman or an idiot in this Republic who would dispute it."[39] Every representative who got up to speak either for or against repealing the act demonstrated that he was neither madman nor idiot by agreeing with Grosvenor that the government was based upon the will of the people. Yet, while the public fury over the Compensation Act did not make representatives question republican government itself, it did lead them to debate how the will of the people would be properly exercised in a government based upon the people's will.

Some representatives believed that Congress had a clear idea of public opinion and that representatives' decisions should simply "obey" that opinion. For example, Virginia representative Phillip Barbour believed that "no measure, since the institution of this Government, had excited so much dissatisfaction, as the one now proposed to be repealed . . . from one extremity of the Union to the other, there had been an almost concurring sentiment of disapprobation."[40] Likewise, Massachusetts representative Albion Parris called the public's opinion a "burst of disapprobation from Maine to Georgia, and from the Atlantic to the most remote settlements on the frontier" that spoke "loudly . . . in a voice that cannot be misunderstood, in a manner that must and ought to be respected, because it promulgates the will, and the deliberate will, of the sovereign and paramount authority of this country."[41] For representatives like Barbour and Parris the matter was simple: the public had clearly spoken its will, and representatives should obey public opinion and repeal the Compensation Act.

Whether or not Congress had heard the "deliberate will" of the people was a contentious issue for representatives like Richard M. Johnson, who acknowledged that while "the poor compensation bill excited more discontent than the alien or sedition laws, the quasi war with France, the internal taxes of 1798, the embargo, the late war with Great Britain, the Treaty of Ghent, or any one measure of the Government, from its existence," such excitement was "artificial and unnatural"—the product of "hobby riders," "popularity traps," and "designing men."[42] Virginia's John Randolph agreed with Johnson that the controversy over the act had "assumed a character, had put on an appearance and quality, which did not belong to it." While he was "not prepared either to affirm or deny that the sentiment which the gentleman had said pervaded the whole continent, was the ruling sentiment," he did believe that "if a sentiment exists in the public mind, it is entitled to weight."[43]

The problem was, how could representatives ever know what public opinion really was? Pennsylvania representative John Ross flatly declared that "he was too well acquainted with the instability of public opinion, to make it a rule of action."[44] Likewise, Representative John Hulbert of Massachusetts believed that Barbour and Parris had "mistaken the clamor of newspapers, and the noise of party spirit, and factious demagogues, for the voice of the nation." Hulbert argued that he had a high "respect for the cool and deliberate opinions of the people," but he believed that Congress had "heard no such opinion on this subject."[45] Indeed, Thomas Grosvenor categorically refused to "accept the toasts and harangues with which the 4th of July meetings may have frighted honorable gentlemen." Nor would he "accept those indecent resolutions which interested demagogues may have persuaded their knots of partisans to adopt at their electioneering conventions." Nor would he "recognize the officious intermeddlings of State Legislatures upon a subject with which they have no Constitutional concern."[46] Massachusetts representative Elijah Mills promised to "pay the utmost deference and respect" to public opinion, but only when it met impossibly high standards. Mills would submit his vote only to the "calm, deliberate, and dispassionate opinion of the people, coolly expressed, upon a subject fairly before them, with a full knowledge of all the facts necessary to enable them to come to a decision."[47] While Mills dared to dream of an ideal of public opinion based upon complete information and calm rationality, such a standard clearly obviated actually existing public opinion, especially, in his judgment, the public's opinion regarding the Compensation Act. The representatives who refused to obey public opinion treated citizens as tragic victims—as irrational, passionate, unknowledgeable fools who could be led easily by demagogues and who certainly could not be trusted with public decisions.[48]

"In what way," asked Representative Albion Parris in exasperation, could "public sentiment be collected, except from public expression?"[49] In response to such categorical rejections of what he viewed as the clear evidence of the public's disapprobation of the act, Parris recognized that the question over whether or not representatives correctly understood public opinion was fundamentally a question over the right of instruction. Recall that the First Congress had considered making the right "to instruct their representatives" a part of what we now call the First Amendment freedoms of religion, speech, press, assembly, and petition, but that representatives like James Madison dismissed the right of instruction as against republican principles.[50] "The right of freedom of speech is secured," Madison clarified for his colleagues in 1789, "the liberty of the press is expressly declared to be beyond the reach of this Government": "The people may therefore publicly address their representatives, may privately advise them, or declare their sentiments by petition to the whole body; in all these ways they may communicate their will. If gentlemen mean to go further, and say that the people have a right to instruct their representatives in such a sense as that the delegates are obliged to conform to those instructions, the declaration is not true."[51] When Madison explained in 1789 that citizens could publicly or privately address and advise their representatives and they could petition Congress, but they had no right to give binding instructions to their representatives, few of his colleagues were willing to argue that citizens did or should have the right of instruction. By 1816 Madison would be completing the eighth and final year of his presidency, and many representatives would come out strongly in favor of the right of the people to instruct their representatives. Indeed, many of America's second generation of politicians would argue that American republican government meant nothing if the people could not give binding instructions to their representatives.

For example, Kentucky representative Joseph Desha applauded his colleague Richard M. Johnson "for willingly attending to the wishes of the people, and subscribing to the principle of instruction," which Desha argued was "the very essence of representative government." After all, argued Desha, "to deny that the people have a right to instruct their agents, is striking at the very nature of our Government."[52] Although Desha appeared confident in his view of republicanism, whether or not the right of instruction was consistent with the Constitution was quite controversial. Some representatives, such as Albion Parris, believed that "on all usual subjects of legislation, the people have a right to be heard; say what we may, they will be heard, and not only heard, but they will be obeyed. With them resides the sovereign power, with them the physical strength," but Desha and Parris were in the minority.[53] A flabbergasted Representative John Tyler of Virginia—the future president known as "His Accidency"—made the first speech of his congressional career when he stood up to inquire "if, indeed, all his political ideas had been drawn from a wrong source?" Tyler "had always understood that what powers were not expressly given by the Constitution, were retained. He would ask, then, where had the right to instruct been yielded up by the people?"[54] In other words, the people had *a natural right of instruction,* and as Kentucky representative Micah Taul explained, "such powers as they have not . . . given, they have expressly retained." Further, if representatives wished "the people to not exercise this right," argued Taul, then they must "call upon them to give it up."[55] The representatives who believed, contra Madison's 1789 explanation of the First Amendment, that the people had a constitutional or a natural right to instruct their representatives argued for a far more democratic view of government and a much more romantic view of citizenship than constitutional-era Federalists would have thought prudent. Other representatives demonstrated the republican prudence that Parris, Tyler, and Taul lacked.

For example, Delaware representative Thomas Clayton argued that "if this right to instruct exists, it must be a perfect, absolute, and unconditional right; and if it exists in any case, it exists in all cases." Yet, argued Clayton, "were a majority of this nation here assembled, they could enact no one law. They have parted with that portion of their authority to Congress, and having no right to act of themselves . . . they cannot instruct us to act for them; if they attempt it, their instructions are not obligatory."[56] In other words, citizens could only act outside the legislature; representation did not mean delegated power, it meant fiat power. Thomas Grosvenor dramatically attempted to hold representatives to the letter of the law when he held up a copy of the Constitution and demanded that representatives point to precisely where in the Constitution the right of instruction could be found: "there is none to be found. It would have stained its fair pages, for it would have attempted an absurdity, to grant and retain by the same instrument the same power and authority to secure a right in the nature of things incapable of execution."[57] Clayton and Grosvenor were joined by New York representative Peter Wendover, who quipped that if citizens really did have the right of instruction, he would "have demanded of my constituents to remain in perpetual session, either in bulk or by proxy, and send me my instructions from day to day, as I might be called to act; and, also, instruct me how to vote."[58] South Carolina representative John C. Calhoun was perhaps the most exasperated by the drawn-out debate over the right of instruction. "The car of this House on this subject is sealed against truth and reason," proclaimed Calhoun. And, "what has produced this magic spell? Instructions!" Calhoun believed that if the right of instruction existed, the people must have "resolved the Government into its original elements, and resumed to themselves their primitive power of legislation" without his knowledge. He demanded to know if his colleagues would make themselves "trimmers" or follow the "political weather-cock." "I too am an advocate for instructions," Calhoun bellowed. "I am instructed. The Constitution is my letter of instruction. Written by the hand of the people, stamped with their authority, it admits of no doubt as to its obligation. Your very acts in opposition to its authority, are null. This is the solemn voice of the people, to which I bow in perfect submission. It is here the *vox populi, vox dei*."[59] The voice of the people was the voice of God; the people had expressed their voice when they ratified the Constitution; Calhoun believed that the people could do no more.

The problems with whether representatives correctly knew the will of the people, whether citizens had the right of instruction, and whether representatives had to obey public opinion and instructions could be reduced to the question of whether representatives should mirror or filter their constituents' will. For, as Massachusetts representative John Hulbert explained, there was not "a single objection against the measure worthy of notice" except for the "senseless clamor" of public opinion; Hulbert wondered if representatives would so easily "give up our opinion and oppose the dictates of our own consciences? Shall we now repeal this law which we so lately passed, and which we still deem essential to our country's good?" Hubert believed that they should not; indeed, he believed that doing so would be a "gross violation of our public duty, and a cruel act of self degradation."[60] Hulbert swore that "until he could change his opinion, he would never change his vote," but much to his frustration, many of his colleagues did not possess this same independent spirit.[61] "I feel no humiliation," protested New York representative John Taylor, "while avowing that I stand here to express for my constituents, and as their representative, what they themselves would express if personally present, and possessed of the same information upon which I act."[62] North Carolina representative Lewis Williams believed that American republicanism was based upon the fundamental truth that "the people are the sovereign power in this country. Hence, I lay down the broad principle, that they must be right; in other words, that they can do nothing wrong, and ought to be obeyed."[63] Virginia representative Phillip Barbour believed not only that representatives should reflect the "image of the feelings and sentiments of their constituents" but that there would be "an end of representative Government" if they failed to mirror their constituents' will.[64]

While many representatives agreed with Barbour that republican government required that their constituents' will be mirrored in Congress, many others agreed with Grosvenor that mirroring their constituents' opinions was "most repugnant to our system of government, most degrading to our rulers, and most destructive to our prosperity."[65] Grosvenor believed that "the true theory and spirit of our representative Government" could be reduced to one principle: "responsibility for conduct, not control over it."[66] In other words, as Tyler explained, Grosvenor argued that the people's "sovereignty consists alone in the miserable power of turning out their Representatives at the termination of their period of service"; while representatives remained in office, the people had no right to instruct them.[67] Grosvenor believed that Tyler and others who believed that representatives should mirror the opinions of their constituents had a "total misconception of the theory and nature of our system"; they confused "the checks upon the abuse of power by their rulers, retained by the people" with the "right at all times to interfere with all their acts, and to participate in the exercise of all their powers and duties."[68] Representatives who hoped to work for the common good could not mirror their constituents' will because, as John Randolph quipped, "there are some subjects on which we are better qualified to give than to receive instruction."[69]

The Compensation Act was completely repealed on January 21, 1817, which returned congressional salaries to the old per diem of six dollars.[70] As we have seen, congressional debates over repealing the act dramatically revisited the questions of republican government but did not result in any kind of unanimity about whether and how the average citizen could act to control the government. Some representatives, like Albion Parris, believed that the public's critical response to the act "augurs well for the purity and stability of our republican institutions" because it demonstrated "that the people are jealous of what they deem to be their rights; that they are watchful over the conduct of their public agents."[71] The public's critical response proved that they could and would act as romantic heroes—and that was a good thing. Likewise, Kentucky representative Thomas Fletcher applauded the "happy form of our Government" in which the citizens were enabled to "investigate, and think for themselves, and withdraw confidence from such of their public servants as may attempt to lay the foundation for oppression and self-agrandizement [*sic*]." Fletcher believed that this kind of active citizenship was "one of the great securities against slavery and despotism; a principle not acted upon in any other part of the world," but other representatives saw the matter differently.[72] Hulbert believed that the repeal of the act would "surely hang us on one of the horns of this dilemma. We must either confess ourselves guilty of extreme rashness in the vote we gave last session or of cowardice in the one we now give."[73] In other words, no matter what course representatives chose, they had already lost, for as Georgia representative Richard Henry Wilde observed, the House had already "receded from the front of empire." The House had once been the "favorite of the American nation, the first and most important branch of the Government—the immediate image of the people." But, it had "been losing and continued to lose . . . that rank and power in the Republic originally belonging to them." The public fury over the Compensation Act only proved to representatives like Wilde that the government had become seriously disfigured, that it "was no longer what those who made it intended it should be."[74] Representative Joseph Hopkinson of Pennsylvania believed the repeal of the act would be "absolutely destructive of the very principles and uses of republican representative Government" and would create "a mere democracy."[75] Evidence of Americans' ability to enact romantic citizenship—the meetings, Fourth of July toasts, and purification of incumbent representatives—thus caused more than a little nervous excitement in many representatives, for even if the people only had the right to enforce rotation in office and "purify" the government, in 1816 they had proved that they would act on that right.

In retrospect we can see that part of the controversy over the Compensation Act can be attributed to the shift in the nation's political fiction that was beginning to occur in 1816. Younger politicians like Virginia's John Tyler, Kentucky's Micah Taul, and Massachusetts's Albion Parris were not only new to national politics—each was in his first term in 1816—but each was born after the 1783 Treaty of Paris, and two were not yet born when convention delegates met in Philadelphia in 1787. These new political leaders had new ideas about America's political fiction and about America's citizens, but they met with opposition from the established leadership of the first generation who still controlled the Senate, the executive branch, and the judiciary. Because the public's outrage over the Compensation Act turned so many long-established representatives out of office, the new-style politicians of the second generation gained office on the promise of obeying their constituents' instructions and repealing the act. Such a clear example of the people watching, critiquing, and judging their representatives could not be ignored; politicians now understood that they must bow to what John Randolph called the "great Leviathan of popularity."[76] While representatives acknowledged that they must now pay attention to popular opinion and worried if their decisions in Congress would be well received by their constituents, they still denigrated the public's opinion as irrational, ill-informed, and capricious. When public opinion was compared to a "political weather-cock," an instrument that pointed in whatever direction the wind carried it, then it is clear that representatives continued to view citizens as tragic victims of corruption. Now, however, representatives realized that they had to manage the "political weather-cock," or else succumb to an electoral purification driven by others who would dictate which way the wind blew.

If republican representation was based upon the ideal of disinterested gentlemen who would use their best judgment to act for the common good, then the controversy over the Compensation Act demonstrated that republican representation was no longer tenable. There were now simply too many voters, too many newspapers, and too much partisanship for representatives to be able to claim the same elite superiority over their constituents that they once could. The new democratic representation evidenced with the public outcry over the act meant that more than ever before, representatives had to at least pay attention to the will of their constituents—even if they did not receive instructions or mirror their constituents' will—because they faced an increased risk of suffering an electoral "purification" if they did not. America's political leaders were thus placed in the position of "popularity hunters" and were forced to pay attention to the direction of the "political weather-cock." Even if they hoped to remain disinterested gentlemen, political leaders increasingly found the old republican representation impossible. Yet, as the many representatives who spoke against repealing the act explained, while the pragmatic politician was increasingly attendant to managing his popularity, citizens technically still had no constitutional right to give binding instructions to their representatives. While the Fourteenth Congress in 1816 was far more willing to argue that the people might have a natural right to instruct their representatives than the First Congress had been in 1789, no one introduced an amendment to the Constitution that would guarantee the people a right of instruction. Citizens could privately "advise" their representative or publicly petition Congress for a redress of grievances, but except for their biannual vote, they had no recourse for actively influencing the decisions made by their representative. In short, the new democratic representation dictated that representatives must be popular, but they still need not listen to public opinion.

The nature of representation had fundamentally changed with the debates over the Compensation Act: the nation was shifting from republican representation supported by the rhetorics of hierarchy, stability, and concern for the common good to democratic representation supported by the rhetorics of (white male) equality, citizen control, and concern for popularity. While the public outcry over the 1816 Compensation Act marked the beginning of the change from the republican to the democratic political fiction, this shift reached its apotheosis between the presidential elections of 1824 and 1828, which marked the movement from republican to democratic campaigning.

The Elections of 1824 and 1828: From Republican to Democratic Campaigning

The 1814 Treaty of Ghent not only concluded the War of 1812 but also led to two unintended consequences in American politics. First, the end of the war allowed Americans to continue their massive westward movement into the frontier, which resulted in the establishment of six new states between 1814 and 1828 and the extension of suffrage to all white males in the new states and territories, which, in turn, threatened the existing restrictive suffrage laws in established states. By 1828 only five of the twenty-four states in the Union retained their old freehold property requirements, although six additional states still had taxpayer qualifications.[77] Not only had the number of voters increased, but the new voters were far less deferential than their predecessors had been, which meant that as representatives lamented during the debates over the Compensation Act's repeal, they increasingly had to make decisions based upon their popularity—they had to follow the "political weather-cock"—rather than upon their independent judgment.

The second unintended consequence of the end of the War of 1812 was the destruction of the Federalist Party, largely due to the public's negative perception of the Hartford Convention. Twenty-six Federalists met with their colleagues in closed session in Hartford, Connecticut, between December 14, 1814, and January 4, 1815, in the hope of addressing what they viewed as the ills caused by the war and by the presidencies of Thomas Jefferson and James Madison. The Republican press's treatment of Hartford Federalists was unambiguously negative: newspapers throughout the nation declared Federalists unequivocal "traitors." One newspaper in May 1815, for example, demanded that Federalists "throw off the mask" and reveal that they "really are flaming monarchists, high-churchmen, lovers of thrones, princely idleness, and ornamental ribbons."[78] By the 1816 presidential election the Federalist candidate Rufus King could only win three states' electoral votes, and James Monroe would win the presidency in a landslide: 183 Electoral College votes to King's 34. Federalists would never run another candidate for president, and Monroe would run unopposed in 1820. The Republican Party controlled American politics between 1816 and 1824, when the veneer of the "Era of Good Feelings" finally gave way to expose the intensely bitter political campaigning of the 1824 and 1828 presidential elections.

After 1816, white males increasingly had the right of suffrage in America; new democratic-style campaigning allowed political leaders to organize these new voters to win elections. The election of 1824 highlighted the important changes that had occurred between the first and second generations: the massive movement of Americans to the West, the dramatic rise of self-made men, the increasing antagonism between slaveholders and non-slaveholders, and the beginning of the second party system. Of these changes, perhaps the one most directly relevant to the shift from the republican fiction to the democratic fiction was the willingness of two of the candidates to seek and campaign for office overtly. The founders' old "republican" code rejected party and campaigning and mandated that statesmen disinterestedly serve to promote the interest of the public good; the second generation's new "democratic" code embraced party and campaigning and mandated that politicians serve to promote the interests of their party. To be sure, Federalists and Republicans did all of these things to a degree, but they would never admit to it (recall Jefferson's 1791 transparent apologia to Washington and Adams over the publication of Paine's *Rights of Man,* for example). Therefore, that members of the second generation would willingly admit that they belonged to a party, would campaign to win the support of their party, and would promise to serve the needs of their party once in office was not only a dramatic shift in American political practice and political discourse but also an abrogation of traditional views of party, faction, virtue, and liberty. The party tactics developing in 1824 would dominate by the 1828 election.

This shift from republican to democratic campaigning was triggered by one event in particular: the 1825 "corrupt bargain" between John Quincy Adams and Henry Clay. For whether or not Adams and Clay exchanged the presidency for the position of secretary of state, the mere possibility that they might have forever gave the lie to the old republican claims of disinterest. Therefore, the election of 1824 demonstrates how the second generation moved from politics based upon faction—the personal ties of "friendship" between a gentleman and his supporters—to politics based upon party—the impersonal ties of loyalty between a politician and his party.[79] Each of the four candidates—John Quincy Adams, Henry Clay, William Crawford, and Andrew Jackson—had his own network of "friends" who actively worked toward his election, even as Adams protested that he would do "absolutely nothing" to promote his own election.[80] Likewise, Jackson's letters prior to election day show him deeply committed to supporting the will of the people, determined not to campaign, and apprehensive that "designing demagogues" would steal the election. His having served as Monroe's secretary of state made Adams the heir apparent, but Monroe refused to endorse any candidate, and Adams was not popular outside the Northeast. Crawford had the support of the Republican caucus and was therefore the presumed front-runner until Jackson's friends discredited the caucus system and demanded that nominations move to the state level.[81] As fate would have it, Crawford had a massive and incapacitating stroke, thereby disappointing his supporters and wreaking even more havoc upon the already confused election.

As the state vote tallies became known in December 1824, it was clear that Jackson would win the popular vote but that he would not have enough electoral votes to win the presidency. The election was thrown into the House of Representatives, where each state would cast a single ballot for one of the three candidates who had the largest number of electoral votes: Jackson (99), Adams (84), or Crawford (41). When Congress reassembled on December 7, the state votes and the resulting electoral impasse were already well known. Congressmen descended upon the city prepared for political battle, and Washington was awash in negotiations, rumors, and plots until the House made its selection on February 9, 1825. According to reports by Clay, Jackson, and Adams, each candidate's friends attempted to form an alliance that would win his man the presidency. With Crawford incapacitated, most speculated that the presidency must come down to Adams or Jackson. Intriguers also realized that there was one person who could swing the election any way that he wanted: Henry Clay. "My position in relation to the friends of the three returned candidates is singular enough and often to me very amusing," Clay wrote to then Kentucky newspaperman and future member of Jackson's Kitchen Cabinet, Francis Preston Blair, on January 8, 1825. What had Clay so amused? "In the first place they all beleive [*sic*] that my friends have the power of deciding the question"; and second, the intriguers believed that Clay had "the power of controlling my friends." Clay professed that he despised his awkward position, yet he found himself continuously accosted with "disinterested homage and kindness," and while he reported to Blair that he "almost wish[ed] that it was in my power to accomodate [*sic*] each of them," he knew he would have to make a "choice of evils."[82] In other words, Clay recognized that there were games afoot and that he had a powerful, but complicated, role to play. For while each candidate's friends flattered Clay in the hope of gaining his vote, they also implied that there would be trouble for him if he did not vote their way.

In fact, Clay had already made too many promises and accepted too much flattering praise by the time he wrote his January letter to Blair. By mid-December 1824, Pennsylvania representative James Buchanan whispered to Tennessee senator John Eaton—Jackson's most devoted friend—that Clay and Adams had been in secret negotiations and that a bargain would soon be reached. With the publication of the accusation of the Adams-Clay bargain, Clay now understood that he was in the game too deep. For no matter what course of action he took—vote for Adams, vote for Jackson, accept the secretary of state from Adams or Jackson or not at all—he would still appear guilty. Indeed, his position was so precarious that Clay believed that Jackson's friends had intentionally accused him of malfeasance when they knew that it was not true in order to ruin his career. In response he published a "card" in the January 31 *Daily National Intelligencer* calling the anonymous author of the "corrupt bargain" accusation "a base and infamous calumniator, a dastard and a liar."[83] On that same day, in a dramatic move calculated to defend his honor, Clay temporarily stepped down as Speaker to address the House directly on the accusation of bargaining for the presidency and to request that a special committee be formed to establish his innocence.

While his claims of innocence might be true, it was also the case that Clay had opened himself up to suspicion by soliciting Adams's private company on two occasions prior to Adams's election and on two more occasions between Adams's election and Clay's nomination. On January 9, Clay met with Adams and informed him that he would vote for him; on January 29 they met and discussed the election; on February 11, two days after the House gave Adams the presidency, Adams offered Clay the secretary of state position; on February 17 Clay accepted. Yet, aside from these general topics, we know very little about what transpired during these private conversations—Adams's *Diary,* usually a great source of information, provides little detail. There is no hard proof on either side of the "corrupt bargain" question, although it certainly appeared to many at the time that Clay was guilty, despite his protestations to the contrary. Not only did the circumstantial evidence (the meetings, the known bargaining, Adams's election, Clay's new position) implicate Clay, but Kentucky was the only state in the Union to give its congressional delegation voting instructions, which Clay ignored. On December 24, 1824, the Kentucky Legislature explicitly instructed Clay to vote for Jackson, and Clay knew of his state's instructions at least by January 10, 1825, if not before. Therefore, when Clay preferred Adams to Jackson it appeared to Jackson and his friends as though Clay had betrayed his state, the will of the American people, the West, and his own honor.

John Quincy Adams was sworn into office on March 4, 1825, "with a pomp and ceremony of guns and drums," Jackson reported to New York politician and future embezzler Samuel Swartwout, "not very consistent in my Humble opinion with the character of the occasion."[84] Despite this rebuke, Jackson had participated in the day's events and was "the first (after Mr. Monroe) to tender his hand and congratulations to Mr. Adams."[85] It appeared that Jackson had coolly accepted his defeat until the next day when, while seated as one of Tennessee's two senators, he was asked to confirm Henry Clay as secretary of state. Enraged at what they believed was evidence of the "corrupt bargain," Jackson and thirteen of his friends refused to approve "the *Judas* of the West" who had "closed the contract" and now only needed the Senate's approval before he received his "thirty pieces of silver."[86] Clay was confirmed anyway. As Jackson left Washington in disgust in the early spring of 1825, he told anyone who would listen to him along the route home about the corrupt bargain between Adams and Clay. "I had esteemed [Adams] as a virtuous, able and honest man," Jackson lamented in an October 7 letter to Henry Lee. When the rumors of the corrupt bargain began to circulate, Jackson would not believe them, but instead he had "manifested pubicaly [*sic*] a continuation of the same high opinion of his virtue." Then, the "rumours became facts," and since that moment Jackson knew that he would have to defend "the principles of the constitution."[87] By October 1825 the Tennessee Legislature had already renominated Jackson for the 1828 election.[88]

Convinced that "designing demagogues" had subverted the will of the people and now controlled the government, Jackson vowed revenge and immediately began an open campaign for the 1828 presidency. While Jackson seems to have never trusted Clay, he had believed that Adams was of the old republican code; therefore, the "corrupt bargain" proved to Jackson that his trust had been misplaced and that the republican code was a sham.[89] Such evidence of corruption freed Jackson to pursue the presidency as he would have pursued any other affair in which his honor was at risk. Much of this party rancor would come as a surprise to Adams, who had happily proclaimed in his inaugural address that because there existed no "difference of principle, connected either with the theory of government or with our intercourse with foreign nations," the "baneful weed of party strife was uprooted." Yet, despite Adams's distinction as the first president to refer to the United States as a "democracy" in an inaugural address—a "confederated representative democracy," to be exact—his December 6, 1825, first annual message made him appear much less than democratic.[90] To Jackson's disgust, Adams had urged Congress not to be "palsied by the will of our constituents" when considering the necessity of internal improvements like schools, canals, and roads.[91] Adams therefore seems to have retained the old view of republican government: parties were bad, the government was based upon the will of the people, but if the people did not know what was best, enlightened statesmen should act against the people's wishes and make decisions for the common good. Jackson was unimpressed with Adams's professions of republicanism; he believed that the kind of elitist thinking evident in Adams's annual message had contributed to the subversion of the people's will during the 1824 election. Therefore, the election of 1824 provided the context for the rise of the Democratic Party between 1824 and 1828, the acceptance of the new overt campaign tactics and the political parties that ran such campaigns, and the shift from republican-style to democratic-style politicking.

A large part of the rise of the new democratic-style campaigning can be attributed to Andrew Jackson's personality and disposition. Jackson was "a man of a noble and commanding presence, tall, straight, with a military air and mien that made a strong and favorable impression upon every one at first sight." He was the kind of man who naturally would be "placed in command," and he was known to have "very urbane and graceful manners," especially when ladies were present. Yet Jackson was also "haughty and overbearing, impatient of restraint and irascible in temper; opposition in any shape aroused his anger, which was fierce and unrelenting." Indeed, anyone who "crossed his path, thwarted his purposes, or held opinions in opposition to his own . . . was looked upon as an enemy." Jackson "never forgave" his enemies, but "there was no service in his power he would not render" to his friends.[92] In short, Jackson was a proud leader who acted as he saw fit, refused to be questioned, and rewarded his friends and punished his enemies.

Such was the reputed disposition of the man whom Henry Clay had dared to antagonize. Indeed, it was Jackson's well-known violent temperament that gave Clay reason to reject Jackson's candidacy in the first place. Clay told a friend that he preferred Adams because the election of Jackson, a mere "Military Chieftain," would have been "fraught with much danger to the character and security of our institutions."[93] Clay was right. Jackson was violent, and his single-minded campaign for the presidency was violent retribution against Clay, whom he despised. For example, Jackson viewed Clay's March 26, 1825, "Address to the People of the Congressional District," a lengthy defense of his part in the election, as "the dying struggle of a political gambler." The speech was evidence that Clay had "abandoned his political principles, and the expressed wishes of his constituents are sacrificed at the altar of self-agrandisement [*sic*]." Clay had "whiningly" asked his constituents for "forgiveness for his corruption," Jackson mocked, "because all this was done with the sole view of bringing himself into the office of Secretary of State."[94]

Jackson's first campaign goal was to expose the plot between Adams and Clay and demonstrate to Americans that the "corrupt bargain" had robbed them of their choice of president. Clay's friends began a gossip-fueled counterattack that caused Jackson to spend the next four years in a blind rage attempting to defend himself and destroy his enemies. It appears that the campaign strategies of both Clay's Republicans and Jackson's Democrats centered upon an attempt to control Jackson's famous temper. The Republicans hoped to provoke Jackson into losing his temper to such a degree that he would do something that would expose him as rash, violent, and unpresidential.[95] Likewise, Jackson's own party hoped to protect him from losing his temper so that he would *not* do something that would expose him as rash, violent, or unpresidential. Therefore, the campaign of 1828 centered not on grand issues or even on differences in policy, but upon whether Jackson's enemies could drive him to violence. This was definitely a new style of campaigning.

Republicans attacked Jackson on every aspect of his life that he held dear: his reputation, his honor, his military record, his patriotism, his wife, and his mother. Jackson's correspondence between 1825 and 1829 reveals him in a state of war against rumor, accusation, and innuendo. The entirety of these years seems to have been devoted to writing angry letters demanding evidence to support his and his family's innocence and coordinating the public defense of his reputation.[96] Clay and his friends' attacks were indeed vicious: they said that Jackson was violent, that he lacked good judgment, that he had conspired with Aaron Burr's treasonous plot in 1806, that he had cowardly retreated from New Orleans and had to be ordered back by President Monroe in 1814, that he had wantonly killed six American soldiers in Tennessee, that he had executed British citizens in Florida by fiat, that he was a "negro trader," that he had seduced his wife (Rachel) away from her husband (Lewis Robards), that Rachel was still married to Robards when Jackson married her, and that his fifty-years-dead mother, whom Jackson claimed "had not a speck upon her character," was actually a "prostitute who intermarried with a Negro," which resulted in his "eldest brother" being "sold as a slave in Carolina."[97] Miraculously, Jackson fought these personal attacks without engaging in physical violence. "My philosophy is almost worn out," an exasperated Jackson wrote to Brigadier General Richard K. Call on August 16, 1828, "but all my enemies expect is to urge me to some rash action, this they cannot do until the election is over." It is unclear which vindication Jackson dreamed of more: winning the presidency or avenging his honor. One way or another, he promised, "there will be a final settlement," and his enemies' "day of retribution must come."[98]

These character attacks were based upon the old republican campaigning logic of political party as faction—they were designed to separate Jackson from his political friends who were thought to follow his lead because of his status and reputation. If Jackson could be proved to be violent or dishonorable, the logic seems to have been, then his friends would surely desert him. Indeed, Jackson's letters often acknowledged that he understood the rules of Clay's game. Jackson wrote to Tennessee representative Sam Houston on December 15, 1826, that he was "determined to unmask" the "perfidy, meaness [*sic*], and wickedness, of Clay, naked before the american people." Jackson was not entirely innocent of playing these games, for as he also told Houston, "I have lately got an intimation of some of his secrete [*sic*] movements, which, if I can reach with positive and responsible proof, I will wield to his political, and perhaps, his actual destruction."[99] Jackson did not cause Clay's actual destruction, but he was able to skillfully maneuver through each trap set for him. What Clay and his supporters did not well understand when they attacked Jackson based upon the logic of faction was that the rules of the game had changed. Jackson's campaign operated according to the new democratic campaigning logic of political party as loyal organization rather than as faction. In other words, Clay's character attacks were destined to fail because he presumed that Jackson would not organize and mobilize a party that would support him despite the rumors. Jackson succeeded by building a loyal nationwide coalition and using that coalition to refute the charges against him and launch attacks upon Adams and Clay.

While Jackson managed the personal attacks against him, he was in no way the mastermind of his coalition or its new democratic campaign tactics. The real mastermind behind the Jackson campaign was New York senator Martin Van Buren. For the past decade, Van Buren and his Albany Regency had been crafting a new style of party politics based upon loyalty to party above all else. What we now call the second party system was orchestrated by men who had a "passion for organization"—a "passion that would have seemed strange, possibly even sinister to their predecessors."[100] Van Buren had originally been a Crawford man, but with Crawford out of national politics Van Buren transferred his efforts to Jackson's election. When Van Buren and his loyal political friends joined forces with Jackson's and John C. Calhoun's supporters, they formed a coalition between the "the planters of the South and the plain Republicans of the North."[101] The new-style professional politicians founded pro-Jackson newspapers, promised government jobs to the party faithful, and pressed state officials into the service of the national organization. The leaders of the new "political machine" had learned that even without the "aristocrat's wealth, prestige, and connections," they could still rise to power by enlarging their constituency and by compelling obedience with strict "party unity" achieved by any means necessary. In other words, Jacksonians ran their political campaign much like their hero might have run a military campaign: troops were rallied, organized, and trained and then used to attack the enemy.[102]

The Democrats' new political machine "reached into every neighborhood [and] inducted ordinary citizens of all sorts into active service."[103] For example, Major Allen Campbell wrote to Jackson from Louisville on February 4, 1827, with a detailed description of his statewide organizing efforts. "With the cooperation of about half a dozen, intelligent and zealous friends," Campbell wrote, he had created a "System of Committees, from a Principle or Central Committee at Louisville, down to Sub-Committees into every ward of the Town, and Captains Company in the Country." Not only was "the organization of the Committee Plan . . . expected to be in full and successful operation, before the next August elections," but the goal of the new organization was to give both Jackson the victory and to ensure the "resuscitation and success of our local . . . cause," thereby binding the local and the national politicians together. Statewide committees like Campbell's were formed throughout the Union and kept in close communication with one another through letters, party newspapers, and party leaders—although not Jackson—touring the nation to shore up votes. South Carolina representative James Hamilton Jr. reported to Jackson that he and Van Buren would make just such a campaign tour together in 1827–28. "After the adjournment" the two partisans would travel "to spend Van Buren's Spring in Carolina and Georgia," and the next summer Hamilton would "join [Van Buren] at the North, and pass it with *our friends*."[104] Unlike Jefferson and Madison's surreptitious 1791 "botanizing excursion," which they had commenced for similar purposes, Hamilton and Van Buren would openly campaign for Jackson.

Because the Democratic coalition included "politicians of all creeds, sections, and interests," Jackson "exercised extreme caution in defining his position on current issues."[105] Supported by a shaky and testy coalition and backed by a party machine that demanded loyalty to party but not necessarily to principles, Jackson found no need to reveal his own political principles during the 1828 campaign. He managed his political image by leaving his positions on the most controversial topics of the day purposefully vague. For, as Jackson noted, "my real friends want no information from me on the subject of internal improvements and manufactories, but what my public acts has afforded. . . . Was I now to come forth, and reiterate my political opinions on these subjects, I would be charged with electioneering views for selfish purposes . . . and I was determined not to furnish food for my enemies to annoy me with."[106] Referring Americans to his past "public acts" was a useful rhetorical strategy not only for evading Republicans' attacks but also for maintaining Democratic Party unity. Democrats understood that the election would be won by keeping their coalition together—that loyalty and unity were paramount—and therefore that it was best to remain silent about controversial topics rather than alienate party members. Yet, Jackson's refusal to reveal his positions—whether motivated by Clay's trickery or not—meant that there was little debate of substantive issues during the 1828 campaign.

Rather than focus on questions of policy, Jackson and Van Buren's campaign attempted to destroy Clay's reputation and convince Americans that Adams was a closet Federalist, disguised as a Republican. Although Jackson could never fully prove the "corrupt bargain" charge, with Clay leading the smear campaign against Jackson it was not difficult to find reason to impeach him as "the basest, meanest, scoundrel, that ever disgraced the image of his god." For, as attack after attack on Jackson's character appeared in print it became clear that there was "nothing too mean or low for [Clay] to condescend to, secretely [*sic*] to carry his cowardly and base purpose of slander into effect; even the aged and virtuous female, is not free from his secrete combination of base slander."[107] Jacksonians indeed well pilloried Clay as an intriguer. For example, "Obediah Penn" wrote in the July 7, 1828, *United States Telegraph* that "among men of desperate station in life . . . the spirit of slander is not to be wondered at: it is ever the subterfuge of paupers in character and intellect, and the bosom companions of desperate demagogues." "Friend Clay," wrote Penn, was just of this sort. Penn believed that Clay had "no excuse for the ruffian-like attack upon the character of an unoffending, virtuous woman," and he was warned that he would be held "altogether responsible for [Republicans'] calumny, and the infamy and its consequences must rest on [Clay] alone."[108] Yet, while Jackson's friends could take a small measure of gleeful pleasure in Clay's rumormongering tactical errors, Adams could not be connected directly to the odious slander. Jackson and his supporters knew that Adams would have to be attacked by a different strategy, and they knew just where he was most vulnerable: he was Publicola.

While Jacksonians' attacks on Clay focused upon his personal perfidy, the attacks on Adams focused upon his political perfidy—Adams was repeatedly tarred as "hostile to popular government." To make these charges stick, Jacksonians resurrected Adams's 1791 Publicola essays, argued that Adams and his father held the same monarchist views of government, and offered "proof" that Adams had either always been a Federalist or had switched parties so often as to be a man of no political principles at all—or, a "great political weather-cock," as one antagonist called him.[109] Early in 1827,

Pennsylvania representative Samuel D. Ingham—who would later become secretary of the treasury and a member of Jackson's Kitchen Cabinet—published a closely typed, two-column, twenty-one-page excoriation of Adams that served as the Democratic Party's anti-Adams rhetorical playbook. Ingham's "An Exposition of the Political Character and Principles of John Quincy Adams" was a magnificently orchestrated attack that argued "by historical documents and incontestable facts" that Adams was "educated a Monarchist"; that he was "always hostile to Popular Government" and "its great bulwark, the Right of Suffrage"; that he had "affected to become a Republican only to attain the power to pervert and degrade the Democratic Party"; and that his goal was nothing short of "establish[ing] the United States an Aristocratical and Hereditary Government."[110] Pro-Jackson newspapers throughout the nation used sections of Ingham's "Exposition" so frequently that its contents became the stock phrases of the American political lexicon during the election, Jackson's administration, and beyond.[111]

Ingham was hard pressed to find overt evidence of Adams's supposed monarchist tendencies, but there was much in his father's published writing that could be construed as favoring hereditary government. Ingham therefore went to great lengths to recount the many passages from John Adams's *Defence* and *Discourses* that might lead to the conclusion that John Quincy Adams's "lessons of political instruction" had been designed to thoroughly inculcate a "hatred of republican government."[112] The elder Adams had denigrated Jefferson's Republican Party as "'disorganizers,' 'enemies to law, order, and religion'; in a word as 'Jacobins' and 'DEMOCRATS'; which appellations were intended to designate the abettors of every vice which the author of the '*defence*' had characterized as the concomitants of popular government."[113] John Quincy Adams's Publicola essays, according to Ingham, were a "defence of royalty" that "breathe in almost every line, a disguised hostility to republican principles, and the same devotion to monarchy which is found in the writings of his father."[114] Throughout the "Exposition" Ingham thus compared and contrasted the political thoughts of the two Adamses and argued that they held identical views—both preferred monarchy or hereditary government of some kind. The sum total of the *Defence,* the *Discourses,* and Publicola's essays proved without question that "Mr. John Q. Adams' . . . democracy has been merely affected."[115] Yet, while Ingham had offered much proof to substantiate the claim that the father could be read as a monarchist, the son was guilty only by association. Despite Ingham's repeated claim that the two were identical, his rhetorical strategy—using the opinions of the elder Adams to condemn the younger—was simply a legerdemain—a sleight of hand. There was no proof that the younger Adams preferred hereditary government; in fact, his views of government were surprisingly similar to Jackson's. Furthermore, while Ingham and the rest of the Democratic Party argued that the Adamses were "affected" (pretended) democrats, the Adamses flatly rejected that either of them had ever attempted to masquerade as such. Both father and son were firmly republican, they had always argued; in retrospect we can see that they both supported the Constitution's tragic republicanism.

Because Jacksonians wanted to demonstrate that they were on the side of Thomas Jefferson, and that John Quincy Adams was not, Ingham's pamphlet focused on Adams's flippant 1791 retort—in which he called Jefferson the "Islam of Democracy" in return for Jefferson calling John Adams's *Defence* and *Discourses* "political heresies"—and turned it into the Jacksonians' battle cry. Jefferson *was* their "Mahomet," Jacksonians argued, and he *had* called them to "rally around the standard of *Common Sense,*" and they *did* rally around that standard, and anyone who did *not* was a Federalist, a "monarchist," an "anti-democrat," and "betrayed the will of the people." Thus it was that Jacksonian democracy took its rhetorical form and shape. By seizing the ground of their opposition and turning it to their own benefit, Jacksonians developed not only a winning rhetorical strategy but also a party ethos.[116] This tactic also mirrored how Jacksonians responded to Clay's character attacks—his attacks upon Jackson's character, they argued, showed precisely how debased *Clay's character* was. The whole logic of the Jacksonian campaign was to turn discourse back upon itself by conflating, redefining, or ambiguously defining terms and then using those definitions to claim superiority over their enemies. The discourse surrounding the election of 1828 can be described as little more than a "he said"/"we said" campaign of invective, evasion, attacks, and counterattacks.

The tone of the 1828 campaign and its rhetorical strategies were defined almost immediately after the Senate confirmed Clay as secretary of state, for Jackson had used his troping (language-turning) technique as early as February 22, 1825.[117] On January 28, 1825, Clay wrote to the president of the Virginia Court of Appeals, Francis T. Brooke, explaining why he would vote for Adams rather than Jackson; in his letter he derided Jackson as a mere "Military Chieftain," and therefore unfit for the presidency. Clay's letter was reprinted in pro-administration newspapers as early as February 12—a mere three days after the election. Enraged, Jackson fired off a retort in a February 2 letter to Samuel Swartwout that was widely republished and commented upon in pro-Jackson newspapers. A brief examination of Jackson's use of troping demonstrates that his rhetorical strategies left his adversaries with little to do but retreat and admit defeat. First, Jackson feigned confusion about what Clay could have meant by the insult, which implied that Clay's worldview was very different from his own—"It is for an ingenuity stronger than mine to conceive what idea was intended to be conveyed," Jackson wrote quite innocently. Second, Jackson interrogated the idea behind the insult and defined it to his advantage—"It is very true that early in life, even the days of boyhood, I contributed my mite to shake off the yoke of tyranny, and to build up the fabric of free government," he said flatly. "If this can constitute me a 'Military Chieftain,' I am one." Third, Jackson took on the insult as his badge of honor, thus turning Clay's intended harm into not only his defining characteristic but also a benefit to the nation—"Our lives were risked, privations endured, sacrifices made, if Mr. Clay pleases, Martial Law declared, not with any view of personal agrandisement [*sic*], but for the preservation of all and everything that was valuable, the honor and safety and glory of our country. Does this constitute a 'Military Chieftain'?" Fourth, Jackson further turned Clay's attack to his own advantage when he observed that if Clay's worldview had not been so disordered, he would have acted precisely as Jackson had—"Mr. Clay never yet has risked himself for his country, sacrificed his repose, or made an effort to repel an invading foe." And finally, Jackson further exaggerated the potential harm caused by Clay's disordered worldview, which overwhelmingly turned Clay's attack back against him: "Demagogues I am persuaded have in times past, done more injury to the cause of freedom and the rights of man, than ever did a 'Military Chieftain.'"[118] Once the turn was complete, Jackson would wear the "Military Chieftain" slur with pride and Clay would have to explain why he thought it was bad to serve the country, why he had not served the country himself, and what he had meant by accusing Jackson of serving his country, and he would have to defend himself from the charge of demagoguery. In short, Jackson argued as aggressively as he dueled.[119] Tactics such as these allowed Jacksonians to control the discourse leading up to the 1828 election and contributed to Jackson's landslide victory over Adams.

The Jacksonians' rhetorical strategies did more than contribute to a Democratic Party victory, however; they forever changed America's political fiction. During the election of 1828, Jacksonians seem to have discovered that republicanism was not the same as democracy. Furthermore, they discovered that republican tragic citizenship was a close relation to aristocratic, oligarchic, or monarchic tragic citizenship. They therefore derided the Adamses' republicanism as evidence of anti-democratic sentiment. Yet, while tragic republicans were portrayed as closet monarchists, Jacksonians said nothing about romantic republicans, who were also not democrats. Nor did Jacksonians acknowledge that the Constitution was premised upon republican political theory and, therefore, that the Adamses' political theory was technically correct. In other words, Jacksonians called romantic republicans "democrats" and called tragic republicans "monarchists," the effect of which was to further conflate the real differences between the different forms of government, confuse the different views of how the people should rule, and institutionalize the democratic fiction. The Adamses were forthcoming both about their belief that the people were sovereign and about their fear that too much power might be given to the people. By using the Adamses' tragic republicanism against them for the purposes of name calling without interrogating its ideas, Jacksonians turned it into caricature.

The most careful observer of American political discourse would have been confused by the Jacksonians' campaign tactics; indeed, the term "democracy" had been used with promiscuous abandon since the House had made Adams president in 1825. For example, prior to the 1828 campaign the word "democracy" was mostly used in its traditional—and pejorative—sense, as when on March 4, 1817, the *Connecticut Journal* proudly proclaimed that "it has been our *exclusive* glory to have successfully resisted the arts of the demagogues of democracy from the commencement of our union." Likewise, the March 27, 1817, *Boston Gazette* asked its readers if they were "so enamoured with the experiment of democracy in this State as to wish it to be repeated? Few and evil have been the years of its reign in Massachusetts!" In other words, we see the word "democracy" used—by Federalists, no doubt—to refer to a despised system of government in which demagogues control the people. About this time, however, we also begin to see the term used less to refer to the system of government and more to refer to the *demos*—to the people as a whole. For example, the *Connecticut Journal* feared the "Idol of Democracy," the "heterogeneous mass of Democracy," and the "bellowings of Democracy" in its news reports of 1817; likewise the *Newburyport Herald* and the *Rhode Island American* both derided the "leaders of Democracy." By 1822 the *Boston Commercial Gazette* would use it in a slightly different sense, to refer to the lowest of the three classes in society—"Aristocrat, Middling Interest, or Democracy"—while the *Newbury Herald* would equate it with "revolution" and "jeopardy." Democratic discourse began to have first a neutral, and then a positive, connotation just prior to the 1824 election. For example, in 1823 the *New Hampshire*

Patriot, the *Watch Tower,* and the *Eastern Argus* referred to "the democracy of the nation" without a positive or negative valence. The *Portsmouth Journal of Literature and Politics* endorsed a candidate in 1823 by arguing that "his political principles, imbibed at the fountain head of democracy, and formed during the purest period of the republic have remained untainted." By 1826 democracy was not only positive but something that must be protected and defended—at least according to the *New-Hampshire Patriot and State Gazette,* which charged that there was a plot to create a "great New-England Adams party" whose goal "was to demolish any vestige of democracy." By May 13, 1828, we see political terms applied without rhyme or reason, such as in the *New-Hampshire Gazette:* "should there be a mixture of federalism with democracy in the Convention, then the Convention would not probably receive the full and entire confidence of the republican yeoman." And by November 21 of that year, the *Eastern Argus* argued that the election could be reduced to a "single question between Jackson and Adams," for the differences between the two men were nothing short of the choice between "democracy and federalism" and Jackson's election would certainly "restore democracy."[120]

This confusing use of political terminology can be more easily understood if we recognize that Americans had stopped using these terms as political theory and had begun to use them as party names, or as interchangeable with a party's name. Words like "federalism," "republicanism," and "democracy" had become empty signifiers through a process that the Greeks would have called *antonomasia*—"name swapping." They had lost their traditional meanings and had ambiguously taken on new meanings; discourse had become so distorted that the election of 1828 can be described as a "Thucydidean crisis," a moment when "words lose their meaning."[121] Words were used strategically to represent ideas that were entirely different from their traditional meaning, the effect of which was to allow the Democratic Party to lay claim to the democratic fiction and to accuse Republicans like John Quincy Adams of monarchism. This rhetorical strategy meant that for some observers it appeared that democracy had indeed triumphed once Jackson was elected. "The spirit of '76 is reviving," wrote the *Pittsfield Sun;* "the republicans are putting away the doctrines of amalgamation, and enlisting under the banners of Democracy." Not only had democracy triumphed, but the Revolution—the "spirit of '76"—had been recast as democratic, which might have been surprising to those who had created the republican fiction to fight King George III and Parliament in the years leading up to 1776. Yet, while newspapers like the *Sun* gushed over the new revival of old democracy, other newspapers, like the *Salem*

Gazette, feared that the government was "controlled by the dictates of unprincipled demagogues" and they tried to fight the name-swapping practices of the Democrats. "Such government," wrote the *Gazette,* "is an aristocracy in fact, although a democracy in form."[122] Whether or not the *Gazette* was right to fear the fact or the form of the government, it was clear that with the "cause of democracy," the "ranks of democracy," and the "leaders of democracy" all behind the Democratic Party, the party of Adams, Clay, and Webster would find it difficult to win elections for the next twelve years.

On December 11, 1828, after he learned of his triumph over Adams, Jackson wrote a letter to Brigadier General John Coffee in which he thanked "the great ruler of the universe for his kind and protecting care, particularly for his preserving Mrs. J. and myself, unhurt." For while the "combined and corrupt minions of a profligate administration" had "wield[ed] all its patronage to destroy" his family with "wicked slanders," he and his loyal coalition were able to effectively turn "those slanders to recoil upon their own heads and fall harmless before us."[123] Jackson had achieved his victory, but at what cost to himself and the nation? For what Jackson did not know when he wrote his thankful victory letter was that his beloved wife, Rachel, would die from a heart attack eleven days later—Jackson always believed that the stress of the campaign had killed her—and that he would have to travel to Washington alone and depressed. Still in mourning as he slowly made his way across the country, he was forced to accept the hearty congratulations of Americans along the way; yet without Rachel, Jackson's triumph had seemed to him as much less than a complete victory. When Jackson arrived in the nation's capital he pointedly did not pay President Adams a courtesy visit; likewise, Adams became the second president and the second member of the Adams family to refuse to attend the inauguration of his successor.[124] While Jacksonians celebrated their victory, Adams's supporters were less sanguine about the Democratic Party triumph. "His friends have no common principle—they are held together by no common tie," Daniel Webster wrote of Jackson in a February 23, 1829, letter to his brother Ezekiel. "My opinion is that when he comes he will bring a breeze with him. Which way it will blow, I cannot tell," he wrote in another letter that month. "My *fear* is stronger than my *hope.*"[125] Once Webster saw the deluge of "hungry friends" flood the capital to claim their promised political appointments, he knew that his worst fears had materialized and that the "breeze" of Jacksonian democracy had brought the mob with it.[126] While it was true that Jackson's campaign and victory had induced thousands upon thousands of loyal Democrats to travel to Washington to take their place at the general's side, Webster's fear that the government would actually be run by the people was not realized. For while the election of 1828 had forever changed campaign tactics and political language, it had not actually changed the Constitution from a republic to a democracy.

If republican campaigning was based upon building a network of political "friends" who supported a candidate because they trusted that his concern for his reputation and status would lead him to make disinterested decisions that would protect the nation's stability, then the elections of 1824 and 1828 demonstrated that republican campaigning was no longer tenable. The increase in the electorate, the "corrupt bargain" charge of 1825, and the long, bitter campaign of 1828 had fundamentally changed the way America's political leaders sought office. Political leaders need no longer "retire" to their mansions in order to mastermind their political campaigns; they need no longer pretend to be a Cincinnatus who only reluctantly took power and gave it away at the first opportunity. Rather, the new democratic campaigning meant that political leaders openly campaigned for office by giving speeches, hiring newspaper editors, canvassing for votes, attacking their opposition, and organizing their national network of loyal partisans. While republican elections were essentially negotiations for power among the political elite and only ratified by those white males qualified to vote prior to the extension of suffrage in the 1820s, the new democratic elections were far more popular. In fact, the percentage of qualified white males who cast their vote for president jumped from 26.9 percent in 1824 to 57.6 percent in 1828 and would rise to 80.2 percent by 1840; the deluge of new voters made republican-style campaigning impossible.[127] Organizing voters therefore became the "passion" of politicians, campaigns were run as political battles, and political appointments were a part of the "spoils of the enemy." The new democratic campaign tactics forever changed America's political fiction, for once the people were brought into the political process and made to believe that their party's victory was also their victory, there was no going back to republican campaigning. In short, the election of Andrew Jackson in 1828 signaled the triumph of America's new democratic political fiction, but what can be said of how the new democratic fiction treated the ability of average citizens to rule?

Active Citizenship and Jacksonians' Democratic Fiction

Jacksonians did not single-handedly change America's political fiction from republican to democratic. As we have seen, that change had begun as early as 1816, while Jackson was still a "Military Chieftain" and the first generation still controlled national politics. Jacksonians did, however, retain control over the nation's politics from 1828 to 1840 during the most dramatic shifts in the nation's political discourse and political practices, which is why we often associate Andrew Jackson with the rise of American democracy. As I have shown, the rise of what we think of as Jacksonian democracy can be understood more profitably as the rise of America's democratic fiction. In retrospect, we can see three important facets to the rise of America's democratic fiction: first, the shift from republican to democratic representation, which forced political leaders to consider the opinions of the people, even if they were not constitutionally bound to obey them; second, the shift from republican to democratic campaigning, which allowed political leaders to actively seek office and required that they organize average citizens to support party candidates and policies; and third, the change in the use of the word "democracy" in American political discourse, which allowed political leaders to conflate and confuse aristocratic, republican, and democratic political theories for political ends. Yet, none of these changes to representation, campaigning, or word usage made any changes to the nation's Constitution. This point cannot be stressed enough, because any nation's constitution is the codification of its political theory, and the nation's political fiction may or may not correspond to its political theory. In this case the nation retained its republican political theory and its republican Constitution, but adopted a new way of imagining, or rhetorically constructing, its government. When we reexamine the rise of Jacksonian democracy, therefore, we find that Jacksonians helped to change the nation's political fiction but not its Constitution or its political theory.

It is one thing to say that the new democratic fiction confused republican and democratic political theory; it is quite another to examine how the nation's political leaders treated the average citizen's ability to control the government within the new democratic fiction. If, as political leaders avowed in both 1789 and 1817, the protected freedoms of speech, press, assembly, and petition constituted the primary ways that citizens could actively control the government within constitutional constraints, we would hope to find that the nation's new democratic fiction made every effort to protect these rights. Examining how Jacksonians responded to the citizens who protested against Indian removal and slavery allows us to gauge how the nation's new democratic politicians treated the rights of active citizenship.

According to Martin Van Buren's 1854 *Autobiography,* President Jackson "sedulously employed the power with which the People had clothed him" to pursue the four "most prominent" objects of his domestic agenda: first,

Jackson removed "the Indians from the vicinity of the white population [to] their settlement beyond the Mississippi"; second, he stopped "the abuses of power of the Federal Government in regard to internal improvement"; third, he opposed "the re-incorporation of the existing National Bank"; and, fourth, he arrested "as far as possible the abuses that had crept into the legislation of Congress upon the subject of protecting duties."[128] Van Buren argued that while Jackson's record largely elicited a "full share of public applause," he believed that "the credit which has been awarded to him for the effective aid he rendered to his Country by his policy in respect to Indian Affairs and by the success with which it was executed has fallen far short of his desserts."[129] Believing that Jackson's Indian removal policy, which ended in the "Trail of Tears" during Van Buren's own administration, had not been appreciated properly, Van Buren provides a detailed defense of the forced removal of the Creek, Choctaw, Cherokee, Chickasaw, and Seminole tribes from Georgia, Alabama, and Florida to the west of the Mississippi. Van Buren believed that the "factious opposition" to Jackson's removal policy attempted to "promote the interests of party at the expense of the highest interests of the Country, upon grounds which were not tenable and for avowed purposes which were not practicable."[130] Jackson's enemies "hoped to drive him to acts of violence which would destroy his popularity," but Jackson "pursued his policy with his accustomed energy and perseverance, and his labors were ultimately crowned with complete success." In the end, Van Buren believed that the "great work" of Indian removal "was emphatically the fruit of [Jackson's] own exertions. It was his judgment, his experience, his indomitable vigour and unresting activity that secured success. There was no measure, in the whole course of his administration of which he was more exclusively the author than this."[131] In short, Jackson heroically defended the common good when he overcame the "partisan agitators" and the "factious opposition" to implement his successful removal policy. However, despite Van Buren's apologetic retelling of the removal saga, Jackson's policy still has not received what Van Buren believed was its "full share of public applause."

One need not focus on the tragedy of the eight thousand Native American lives lost from starvation, disease, and forced march to understand why Jackson has not received the praise that Van Buren thought proper. Indeed, if we examine the story from the perspective of whether or not Jacksonians encouraged or discouraged active citizenship, then the Indian removal policy might still appear less praiseworthy than Van Buren's version of the story would indicate.[132] Indian removal was always controversial, even before President Jackson's December 8, 1829, first annual message announced it as a primary object of his administration. As his message explained, the American policy toward the Native American populations had always been "to introduce among them the arts of civilization, in the hope of gradually reclaiming them from a wandering life." Yet, while on the one hand the United States professed a desire to "civilize," it also often practiced another policy "wholly incompatible with its success": Americans had "at the same time lost no opportunity to purchase their lands and thrust them farther into the wilderness." To resolve the apparent conflict in policy, Jackson "informed the Indians inhabiting parts of Georgia and Alabama that their attempt to establish an independent government would not be countenanced . . . and advised them to emigrate beyond the Mississippi or submit to the laws of those States."[133] Jackson's first annual message asked Congress to pass legislation to allow him to facilitate and oversee the Indian removal.

Like the public outcry over the 1816 Compensation Act, the public response to the Indian removal policy was swift, vocal, and uniformly against the forced removal of the Native American tribes. The January 6, 1830, *Baltimore Patriot* reported that citizens gathered at a meeting in New York with the express "purpose of memorializing Congress upon the subject of the removal of the Indians"; not only did New Yorkers write their own petition, but they resolved to recommend to their "fellow citizens in different parts of the country, to petition Congress on behalf of the Cherokee and other southern tribes of Indians, that they may be sustained in the undisturbed enjoyment of their national and social rights, and that the honor and good faith of this nation may be preserved."[134] The January 20 *New York Daily Advertiser* reported that public meetings had already been held in Hartford, New Haven, Philadelphia, Boston, and New York at which concerned citizens expressed a "strong and general sentiment . . . against the necessity, the justice, and the humanity of the removal of the Indians."[135] Indeed, religious and women's groups organized petition campaigns in "unprecedented" numbers "overwhelming traditional forms of political participation" and generating "the most intense public opposition that the United States had witnessed."[136]

To the exasperation of Jacksonians, Americans petitioned Congress in record numbers against removal. Jacksonians used newspapers like the *Pittsfield Sun* to mock the "infatuation" of "a few who have taken no pains to inform themselves upon the subject," but the petitions continued to roll into Congress.[137] As early as January 11, 1830, representatives debated whether or not to receive the petition "from a meeting of the citizens of New York, praying the interposition of the General Government to protect the Southern Indians from injustice and oppression." Representative Wiley Thompson of Georgia questioned "the propriety of entertaining every petition or memorial which may be addressed to Congress, whether it be the result of an accidental meeting at a grog shop or not."[138] For the remainder of the day, representatives debated whether or not to follow their traditional procedure and refer the petition to the Committee on Indian Affairs or order the petition to be laid upon the table, never to be debated or considered by Congress at all.[139] The House eventually decided to receive the petition, but largely because its representatives did not want the subject of Indian removal debated by the Committee of the Whole. Jackson packed both the House and the Senate's Committees on Indian Affairs with men favorably disposed to his policy, and by May 26 both chambers had passed removal bills by narrow margins.[140] The Cherokee tribe appealed to the U.S. Supreme Court, which ruled in its favor in two decisions: the March 18, 1831, *Cherokee Nation v. Georgia* and the March 3, 1832, *Worcester v. Georgia.* President Jackson patently refused to support the Court's decision—"John Marshall has made his decision, now let him enforce it," Jackson reportedly said—and forced Indian removal became the nation's official policy.[141] Native Americans began their Trail of Tears as early as 1831, but removal was not completed until 1847. In total approximately sixty thousand people were forced off of their lands and made to march across the South to the new lands west of the Mississippi; about eight thousand of those people did not survive the journey.

"Thus far we have succeeded against the most corrupt and secrete combination that ever did exist," President Jackson wrote of removal opposition in an August 25, 1830, letter to Major William B. Lewis. "I'm sure the stand the Executive has taken was not anticipated by their wicked advisors," he gloated.[142] Jackson viewed the public meetings and petition drives of religious organizations and women's groups as a corruption of the right to petition, and he saw the Supreme Court rulings in support of the Native Americans as part of the plot of the "secrete combination" who worked together against his policy. Jackson was able to conquer the wicked by organizing counter-petition drives, packing important committees with friendly members, and using his network of newspapers to mock the efforts of citizens. His initial record of promoting active citizenship is therefore dubious: rather than respecting the petition drive of average citizens as the effort of romantic heroes controlling the government and acting for the common good within constitutional limitations, Jackson used the power of his office and party to overwhelm dissent. He thought of the citizens who disagreed with his policy as enemy combatants who would have to be defeated, rather than as friends to be persuaded. Yet, even though representatives considered rejecting Americans' anti-removal petitions outright or ignoring them by laying them upon the table, the House at least continued to receive the petitions, thereby respecting this fundamental right of active citizenship.

The mass petition campaign against Indian removal was unsuccessful in changing Jackson's policy or its implementation, but it had a tremendous long-term impact upon American politics, for it represented the first massive, nationwide petition campaign and it inducted women into active citizenship in a manner not seen since they had participated in nonconsumption protests prior to the Revolution. The participants of the anti-removal campaign would become the leaders of American abolitionism, and they would use their petition campaign strategy to create an even greater nuisance for Jacksonians. Defeated in their hope to prevent forced Indian removal, social reformers like Arthur Tappan, Angela and Sara Grimke, and William Lloyd Garrison turned their attention to the abolition of slavery in the District of Columbia—the only place where Congress could constitutionally abolish the "peculiar institution." The movement from the abolitionist policies of "gradual emancipation" and "colonization" to "immediatism" was directly related to reformers' experiences with the Indian removal question, because once reformers realized that forced removal was akin to forced colonization, the vanguard of abolitionism began to accept that they needed to agitate for the immediate abolition of slavery.[143]

While still at the margins of power and public opinion, abolitionism was becoming more vocal and more strident in its demands, which led to the innovation of new, more confrontational tactics such as the "mail bombing" of the South—mailing abolitionist newspapers into slave states—in the summer of 1835.[144] President Jackson demanded that Congress consider bills to silence the northern abolitionist "traitors to the Union" in his December 7, 1835, annual message. The mail bombing of the South was not only "destructive of the harmony and peace of the country" but also "repugnant to the principles of our national compact, and to the dictates of humanity and religion." He therefore asked Congress to pass a federal law that would "prohibit, under severe penalties, the circulation in the southern States, through the mail, of incendiary publications intended to instigate the slaves to insurrection."[145]

Both the House and the Senate considered bills consistent with Jackson's request to prohibit the abolitionists' freedoms of speech and the press, but Congress refused to pass Jackson's policy. The House buried the bill, never to debate it in the Committee of the Whole. The Senate created a special committee made up mostly of southerners who, like Jackson, viewed abolitionists as miserable fanatics, but John C. Calhoun made sure that Jackson's bill did not pass. Calhoun, always fearful of federal power, refused to grant the federal government the power to determine which publications should be excluded from the mail, because he wanted each state to have the power of censoring the mail as it saw fit. While the question of censoring the abolitionists' mail excited a small amount of debate, on December 16, 1835, both branches of Congress erupted over whether to accept abolition petitions when Maine representative John Fairfield introduced his petition from "172 females, praying the abolition of slavery and the slave trade in the District of Columbia."[146] According to William Lee Miller, 176 abolition petitions, with a total of 34,000 signatures (15,000 from women) had been submitted to Congress in the 1835–36 session alone.[147] "According to House rules," explains Miller, "the first thirty days of a congressional session were all petition days" in which the people's voice was admitted into public debate. "Thereafter, as the House got down to business, only every Monday was a petition day."[148] The House clerk called out the state names one by one in geographical order from North to South, and if a representative had a petition to put before the House, he would rise, summarize the plea of the petition, and recommend that the petition be referred to the appropriate committee for action. In the case of abolition petitions the House would routinely refer the petitions to the Committee on the District of Columbia and allow the petitions to sit there without ever debating them in the Committee of the Whole.

However, the recent mail bombings of the South had followed a long line of events that many southern slaveholders read as portending bloody slave revolts: the debate over the Missouri Question in 1819–20; Denmark Vesey's potentially deadly insurrection in South Carolina in 1822; New York's final elimination of slavery in 1827; David Walker's publishing of the *Appeal* in 1829; William Lloyd Garrison's publishing of the *Liberator* in 1831; Nat Turner's leading sixty fellow sufferers on a forty-eight-hour rampage in Southampton County, Virginia, and the Virginia legislature publicly debating abolition in 1832; the American Anti-Slavery Society's vowing to fight for immediate abolition, agitating for the abolition of the slave trade in Washington D.C., and publishing its four newspapers devoted to immediatism in 1833; and, in the summer of 1835, Mississippi's Madison and Hinds counties erupting in a panic over rumors of a white-led slave revolt. Recent history, therefore, had taught southern representatives that miserable fanatics—both white and black, free and enslaved—were determined to cause a "servile war," which could only lead to the deaths of slaves, the loss of property, and the destruction of the Union. In order to prevent this grim fate, New York representative John Cramer immediately moved that Fairfield's December 16, 1835, petition "be laid on the table; which was agreed to" 180 to 31.[149] Two days later, Massachusetts representative William Jackson attempted to present another abolition petition from "sundry citizens of Massachusetts, praying Congress to provide for the immediate abolition of slavery within the District of Columbia; which he moved to refer to a select committee."[150] South Carolina representative James H. Hammond immediately "moved that the petition be not received" so that citizens would understand the House's "decided seal of reprobation on them, by peremptorily rejecting them," which the House agreed to after intense debate.[151]

As many representatives observed, Hammond's tactic meant that American citizens essentially lost their right to petition the government for a redress of grievances, for while citizens could continue to submit petitions to Congress, they were not received or acted upon, and therefore did not contribute to the nation's deliberations. In other words, if in 1816 representatives debated whether or not citizens' critical petitions must be *obeyed,* by 1835 representatives debated whether or not their critical petitions would even be *received.* Between 1835 and 1838 both houses of Congress practiced the procedure of "peremptorily" rejecting abolition petitions by calling for the question of a petition's reception and then quickly moving that the question of whether or not to consider to receive the petition itself be tabled. On January 28, 1840, the House passed a standing resolution (House Rule 21) against the reception of abolition petitions so that representatives did not have to go through the trouble of peremptory rejection.[152] This procedure allowed Congress to make petitions disappear from debate without referring them to any committee and without any debate over the question of abolition, but it also prevented public opinion—both for and against slavery—from entering Congress.

From 1835 to 1844 thousands upon thousands of abolition petitions flooded into Congress, but Congress did not receive them. John Quincy Adams, who had been elected as a representative from Massachusetts in 1831, fought mightily to restore average citizens' right to petition their government for a redress of grievances, but he was largely unsuccessful. Both the retiring president, Andrew Jackson, and the incoming president, Martin Van Buren, agreed on the prudence of "peremptorily" rejecting abolition petitions, and the Democratic Party held majorities in the House and Senate for most of the years between 1835 and 1844 while the petitions were rejected. Yet, the rejection of the people's petitions was more than a mere party issue—the cooperation of both parties was necessary to sustain the peremptory rejection policy—and the Democratic Party controlled the House in 1844 when House Rule 21 was rescinded. Members of both parties agreed that Congress should reject abolition petitions because they believed the petitions to be too dangerous: the petitions threatened southern slaveholders' lives and livelihoods; threatened the new second party system's national coalitions; threatened all politicians' popularity; and threatened the Union itself. Abolition petitions were simply too dangerous, and most politicians would rather sacrifice the reception of the petition than their personal or political safety. Once again the people had overstepped their boundaries and had attempted to enter their dangerous opinions into the legislature; once again the people's opinions were rejected in the interest of preserving stability. Rejecting the abolition petitions was certainly the most prudent action Congress could take, but it was also a rejection of the average citizen's ability to watch, critique, and judge the government. If, as James Madison argued in 1789, the First Amendment guaranteed the citizen's freedoms of assembly, petition, and speech, and if these were the primary mechanisms for average citizens actively to control the government, then it is clear that the potential for active citizenship was easily abrogated for safety and stability. In other words, as our brief discussion of Indian anti-removal and abolitionist petitions demonstrates, politicians of the second generation—whether they were willing to admit it or not—did not encourage American citizens to control the government any more than the founding generation had. In both theory and practice, the nation's new democratic fiction was really no more democratic than the nation's old republican fiction had been, except that more white males could, and did, vote.

Yet if average citizens were no more enabled to control the government than they had been before, why did Jacksonian democracy appear to represent the "rise of the common man"? The common man did indeed rise: the massive increase in white male suffrage, voter turnout, public meetings, and petition drives certainly created the impression that the people controlled the government more than ever before, and politicians like Andrew Jackson helped to cultivate that perception. For example, Jackson's July 10, 1832, "Veto Message Regarding the Bank of the United States" was a masterful defense of the rights of the common man. "It is to be regretted," argued Jackson, "that the rich and powerful too often bend the acts of government to their selfish purposes. Distinctions in society will always exist . . . but when the laws undertake to add to these natural and just advantages," the "humble members of society—the farmers, mechanics, and laborers—who have neither the time nor the means of securing like favors to themselves, have a right to complain of the injustice of their Government."[153] As his angry veto explained, Jackson believed the president should protect the people from those who would use the government for their own advantage. Likewise, perhaps still stinging from the 1824 "corrupt bargain" that gave John Quincy Adams the presidency, Jackson asked Congress to abolish the Electoral College because "to the people belongs the right of electing their Chief Magistrate; it was never designed that their choice should in any case be defeated, either by the intervention of electoral colleges or by the agency confided, under certain contingencies, to the House of Representatives."[154] Jackson also asked Congress to promote rotation in office by amending the Constitution to include executive and congressional term limits. Seven out of eight of Jackson's annual messages included such pleas to abolish the Electoral College and implement term limits, but Congress did not approve Jackson's requests. Therefore, the Jacksonians' record on empowering the people to control the government is frustratingly ambiguous: sometimes Jackson treated the people as enemies, while at other times he treated them as sovereign. A brief examination of Jackson's March 4, 1837, farewell address may help us to resolve the contradiction.

Andrew Jackson won the 1828 election over John Quincy Adams in a landslide; he defeated Henry Clay in 1832 by an even bigger margin. During his eight years in office he would destroy the bank, suppress the Nullifiers, censor the Abolitionists, and remove the Indians; he would fire his cabinet, veto more bills than any previous president, and introduce the "spoils system" to "reward his friends and punish his enemies."[155] When he wanted to retire, Jackson even named his successor—his most loyal political friend, the "Little Magician," Martin Van Buren.[156] In short, Jackson consolidated power in the executive branch and, as his Whig critics charged, acted more like "King Andrew" than any president properly should. Yet, Jackson justified each of his actions by appealing to the authority of the people. If he acted like a king, Jackson demurred, it was only to protect the people, the Union, and the Constitution. As Van Buren was sworn in on March 4, 1837, Jackson took the opportunity to give a farewell address—he was only the second president to do so—in which he informed the nation of "the leading principles upon which" he had "endeavored to administer the Government."[157]

Jackson followed George Washington in using his farewell address to caution the nation that the Union must be preserved, the federal government's powers must be limited, and the liberties of the people must be protected. Jackson characterized his presidency as one of "prompt decision" and "energetic action"; indeed, he had "fearlessly encountered" adversity because he knew that "the continued and unbroken confidence" of the people would "sustain" him through "every trial." Thus supported by the will of the people, Jackson took on all adversaries in the people's name: "Indian tribes" and "foreign powers" were no match for him. "Artful and designing men" who "persuade themselves . . . that they are laboring in the cause of humanity and asserting the rights of the human race" and supporters of the American system "who wished to enlarge the powers of the General Government" were routed. Nullifying "State politicians" were vanquished. And, perhaps most hated of all, the "corporations and wealthy individuals" who supported "paper money," speculated in "public lands and various kinds of stock," and conspired with the "Bank of the United States"—capitalists of all kinds who had "waged war upon the people"—were crushed. In short, as Jackson had found the people "continually beset by enemies" he had continually devoted his presidency to defending the people from the people's enemies. Because President Jackson was a fearless warrior, the people were safe.

But, Jackson warned, the enemies of the people "will continue to besiege the halls of legislation . . . and will seek by every artifice to mislead and deceive the public servants" and therefore, without his protection, the people must "look [to themselves] for safety and the means of guarding and perpetuating" their "free institutions." Indeed, "eternal vigilance by the people is the price of liberty": "In your hands is rightfully placed the sovereignty of the country, and to you everyone placed in authority is ultimately responsible. It is always in your power to see that the wishes of the people are carried into faithful execution, and their will, when once made known, must sooner or later be obeyed; and while the people remain, as I trust they ever will, uncorrupted and incorruptible, and continue watchful and jealous of their rights, the Government is safe, and the cause of freedom will continue to triumph over all its enemies."[158] That the uncorrupted people would keep the government safe seems simple enough, but we could ask, along with Noah Webster, whom did Jackson mean by "the people"?[159] Jackson's people were a very specific segment of the American population: "the farmer, the mechanic, and the laboring classes of society." The people were, without exception, white and male. Slaves did not count as people, nor did women or Native Americans. In fact, in Jackson's view the proper rulers of the government were precisely those middle- and lower-class white males who were most likely to defend the South from the "weak men" who "cast odium upon their institutions." Jackson's people would never "disturb [southern] rights of property," because they knew that such action would be "in direct opposition to the spirit in which the Union was formed, and must endanger its safety."[160]

Indeed, the movement to extend the right of suffrage and allow the people to vote directly for electors—"egalitarian republicanism for whites," as William W. Freehling has called it—was necessary to ensure the continuation of the "peculiar institution," because for the first time the North had a larger population than the South, which threatened the southern stronghold in the House of Representatives.[161] With the House no longer solidly for slavery, with determined abolitionists gaining support in the North, with petitions flooding into Congress to end the slave trade in the District of Columbia, with the economy becoming more and more modern and therefore less and less reliant upon slave labor, and with Virginia actually debating abolition in 1832, slavery was in its most precarious position in American history.[162] This fact, perhaps more than any other, accounts for whom Jackson despised as a "villain" and whom he lauded as "the people." Native Americans occupied land that American slaveholders could have exploited; the Whigs' American system taxed southern slaveholders for the benefit of northern capitalists and further threatened the profitability of the slave economy; abolitionists attacked slavery as debased and impugned the honor of the South, thereby threatening southern lives and livelihood; and capitalists and bankers were doubly damned because they prohibited the easy expansion of slavery with all of their "speculating" and "credit schemes" and at the same time their paper money and stock supported the northern capitalists. In other words, "Jackson's party organization institutionalized racially-selective egalitarianism. The party rallied white male commoners to shape decisions. . . . John Quincy Adams and fellow Whigs were tagged with the unpardonable American label: undemocratic about whites."[163] Therefore, to answer Noah Webster's question, Jacksonian democracy was not really very democratic, nor was it meant to be.

We could say many interesting things about Jackson's use of the rhetoric of republicanism in his farewell address—how he relied upon the republican analysis of liberty, which does not include equality; how he feared that liberty was constantly threatened by a lack of virtue; how he defended his consolidation of power in the executive branch as consistent with how a Patriot King would act to protect his subjects; and how he exhorted Americans to be patriotic republican heroes themselves and jealously guard their own liberties—but such an analysis would not help us to understand how Jackson helped to construct the democratic fiction. Rather, we have to consider what he did not say and how what he did not say relates to what we would have expected him to say. After twelve years of promising power to the people and successfully destroying the enemies of the people, surely his farewell address would wax poetic about the strength of the American democracy and the triumph of Jacksonian democracy itself. We would certainly expect his address to mimic the proliferation of democratic rhetoric that had saturated the nation since the House had made Adams president in 1825. But, no, as it turned out, Jackson did not use the word "democracy" at all in his address. When he referred to the American political system, which he found occasion to do five times during his speech, he always called it a "republic." Americans were "citizens of this great Republic"; the "history of republics" like America's was full of "fatal divisions"; disunion would ruin "this great and glorious Republic"; Americans must adhere to the "principles of economy, which ought to characterize every republican government"; and finally, "the progress of the United States under our free and happy institutions has surpassed the most sanguine hopes of the founders of the Republic." In other words, while Jackson had spent twelve years promising Americans democracy and had in the process helped to change the nature of American political discourse, in the end, when he finally told Americans what he thought about their nation's political theory, he told them that he had left the government just as he had found it; he had left the government a republic.

Between 1824 and 1836 the Democratic Party successfully used the democratic fiction to appeal to average citizens' desire for political power and equality. Yet there were Americans who did not join the Jacksonians in proclaiming the wondrous joy of the triumph of the democratic fiction. John Quincy Adams joined a long (and losing) chorus of linguistic purists when he wryly observed that party names such as "Republicans" and "Democrats" were "appellations which had the advantages of recommending them to the Special favor of the people and at the same time stigmatizing their adversaries by the implication that they were anti-republican, monarchists, and aristocrats."[164] By the 1840 election the Whigs would successfully employ the Democrats' democratic fiction, using it to get their man of "Hard Cider and Log Cabins" elected, although William Henry Harrison was a member of a family that had ruled in America since well before the Revolution, which meant that he was not at all a man of the people.[165] That the people fell for the Whigs' disingenuous performance of the Democrats' democratic fiction would cause much consternation among those who had promised to trust the will of the people above all. For, if the democratic fiction could help the Whigs to win elections, Democrats like Orestes A. Brownson lamented, then of what use was it for the Democratic Party to laud the power of the people? Yet, by 1845 the Whigs had lost the presidency once again; exasperated, they published a journal devoted to clarifying the positions of the parties for, as they explained, "every thing has a character of some kind, but it is not always easy to discover what it is. The trouble in this case is, that a mere name, and falsely assumed, as we have seen, has been made a convenient external, universal habit for the party, covering all sorts of form and feature."[166] As the Whigs and the Democrats both well understood, America's democratic fiction could function as a powerfully enticing legerdemain with which a party could ambiguously promise power to the people to gain political power for themselves and for their preferred constituency.

Yet, when the Democrats seized the "Islam of democracy" quip from John Quincy Adams and turned it into their defining characteristic and their badge of honor, they could not have known that the unintended consequences of their troping would be that they would lose control over the democratic discourse they had set loose. Once Democrats promised power to the people and the people believed that they were all-powerful, there could be no retreating back to the open acknowledgment that the government was based upon the will of the people but that the people did not actually control the government. Democratic discourse was set free, which allowed it to become the rallying cry of beleaguered and disempowered citizens everywhere. Eventually, Americans would use the Democrats' democratic fiction to end slavery and gain universal suffrage, but it would take several generations to accomplish those worthy goals. The democratic fiction was therefore maddeningly ambiguous: political leaders at times used it ironically as a legerdemain, while citizens at times used it earnestly as a tool to fight injustice and oppression.

The democratic fiction could and would be used by politicians of all political stripes and by both the political elite and average citizens, but what can we say about whether it had citizen consent? As the democratic fiction emerged and circulated, was it knowingly and freely chosen by the people? Recall Mercy Otis Warren's 1805 epistemological, semiotic, and hegemonic critiques of how the founding generation cultivated the ambiguity of republicanism. When citizens are prevented from defining and assenting to their political fiction or it is manipulated against agreed-upon definitions, then the political fiction does not have citizen consent. Judging the democratic fiction by the criteria of whether or not and how it was dialogic, authored, debated, open, and ratified allows us to gauge citizen consent. First, dialogism is crucial both for a political fiction to be just and for it to last: as Jefferson argued in the Declaration of Independence, any government that does not have the consent of the governed is not only tyrannical but is more likely to be revolted against than one that does have the consent of the governed. What would it mean to argue that Jacksonians had the consent of the governed in 1828 when they claimed that the United States was a democracy rather than a republic? For the rise of the democratic fiction to have been dialogic, there would have to have been an extended conversation between Democratic Party leaders and citizens that clearly and unambiguously identified the terms of the debate and the changes that would be made to the Constitution to enable the government to become a democracy, at a bare minimum. As we have seen, Democratic Party leaders offered no such conceptual clarification, nor did they allow for the kind of freedom of speech, thought, and dissent necessary for true dialogue to occur. Without dialogism, Jacksonians replaced America's republican political fiction with the democratic fiction by fiat.

Second, a political fiction is authored when it is portrayed as a human creation that can be altered, rather than as a God-given or natural, and hence unquestionable, truth. Although in retrospect we can trace the institutionalization of the democratic fiction to the actions of political leaders between 1816 and 1845, Jacksonians, in particular, did not acknowledge their authorship of the democratic fiction to Americans in 1828 or after. When Jacksonians triumphed they resoundingly proclaimed that they had returned the nation to its democratic roots, thus claiming that they had not authored the fiction but that they had only called upon America's true democratic Constitution, which preexisted their campaign efforts. By refusing authority, the Democratic Party used the ethos of the founding generation as "eulogistic covering" for their attacks upon the founding generation's republican fiction.[167] In order to make their democratic fiction credible they argued that they followed in the Jeffersonian democratic tradition, even though Jefferson specifically rejected this claim in 1825. The importance of Jacksonians' attempt to lay claim to Jefferson's "image" gives added significance to the commemoration of Adams's and Jefferson's lives and deaths in 1826 and the related conflation of romantic and tragic citizenship: such manipulation allowed Jacksonians to claim that Jefferson was a democrat. Once the democratic fiction was clearly dominant but ambiguously authored, it appeared natural, uncontroversial, and unquestionable. The democratic fiction became the standard by which Americans described their government, and they believed that—aside from the pernicious influence of Federalists or Whigs—the nation had always been a democracy.

Third, a political fiction is most just when citizens freely debate its merits and when it is open to being amended. Democrats attacked tragic republicanism by turning it into caricature without interrogating its assumptions or offering a different set of political principles. The Democratic Party's use of the democratic fiction thus stifled debate over America's political fiction and its political theory, which meant that America's political fiction and political theory were no longer open to change or amendment—they were no longer debatable. George Sidney Camp argued as much in his *Democracy* when he observed that "if a man were seriously to propose for our adoption monarchical or aristocratical institutions, he would be overwhelmed with public obloquy."[168] A politician need not even go so far as to pronounce in favor of monarchy or aristocracy. For, if any American politician of the second generation had admitted publicly that he believed that the government should be based upon the will of the people, but that he feared giving the people too much power in the government—as John Quincy Adams had done—then he would have been immediately tarred a monarchist. In other words, the limits of what was sayable had changed profoundly with the rise of the democratic fiction, but the fear of the people remained a prominent feature of American political theory and practice. Therefore, because Democrats had turned democracy into the only legitimate political theory, the rise of the democratic fiction allowed politicians to hide behind the appearance of democracy without fear that citizens would seriously interrogate what they meant by that term.

Finally, a political fiction is just when it is ratified by the people as a whole, and if it cannot be altered or abolished as the people desire, then it is a kind of tyranny. We could argue that because Americans voted for the Democrats in 1828 and because they adopted the Democrats' democratic fiction, the democratic fiction was ratified. However, because Americans did not intentionally deliberate and vote for its ratification and because the Democrats' democratic fiction was a legerdemain that promised what it did not intend to deliver and because Jacksonians professed to have not changed the political fiction at all, but to have only restored that which had been altered by others, we cannot say that the democratic fiction was properly ratified in 1828 or beyond. In other words, because the Democrats surreptitiously changed the republican fiction into the democratic fiction without dialogue or debate, it could not have been legitimately ratified.

The democratic fiction was circulated, however, and it continues to circulate with promiscuous abandon. The Jacksonians' democratic fiction was used in so many different places and it had so many different meanings—"democracy" was a word "covering all sorts of form and feature," as the Whigs said—that it could appeal to all. Yet, dissevered from its technical political theory, it became an empty signifier.[169] The sheer ubiquity of its use coupled with its flattering praise of the people made the democratic fiction a powerful political fiction that endured because it served the interests of both the powerful and the powerless.

The Democratic Fiction: Citizens as Ironic Partisans

"Statesmen are gamesters," David Crockett wrote in an 1845 diatribe against Martin Van Buren, "and the people are the cards they play with."[170] Statesmen like Jacksonian and Albany Regency member William L. Marcy willingly admitted that political parties played the game to win and that "to the victor belong the spoils of the enemy."[171] However, while Democrats like Marcy flaunted their ability to "reward their friends and punish their enemies," they were less forthcoming about the language games they used to win or the effects of those games on the nation's view of citizenship.[172] By organizing citizens into party members; by running campaigns as party battles; by demanding submission to party law; by contesting elections for the purpose of party advantage; by using the spoils system to maintain party power; and by changing the nation's political discourse without changing the Constitution or its fundamental principles, political gamesters created the democratic fiction in America. As we have seen, the rise of Jacksonian democracy did not change the country from a republic to a democracy, but it did change Americans from citizens to partisans. Citizens had demonstrated that they would act to judge the government, that they would conduct electoral "purifications," and that they would voice their opinions in the legislature. The organization of citizens into partisans helped to mitigate the dangerous threat of public opinion and active citizenship by providing another layer of separation between citizens and the government.

"We hold it a principle," the *Albany Argus* declared in 1824, "that every man should sacrifice his own private opinions and feelings to the good of his party and the man who will not do it is unworthy to be supported by a party, for any post of honor or profit."[173] Indeed, Van Buren's "political maxim" was that organization should be a "logical pattern of political behavior that was based upon consistency, complete loyalty once a decision was made and discipline not just in thought but in deed."[174] The Democratic Party knew that its main political weapon was its loyal, unified party members, so it made every effort to organize citizens into partisans who they hoped would act in lockstep with the national organization. Jackson and Van Buren's organization spoke to its constituent members through the pages of the *United States Telegraph* and the *Albany Argus,* whose "words were recognized as stating the party's law" and whose editorials were reprinted and commented upon nationwide.[175] In other words, the Democratic Party's view of active citizenship was strict conformity to party law; members who did not act with the party found themselves at war with the entire organization. Dissent was foolish against the overwhelming force of a nationwide network of politicians who pledged to act in unison. Van Buren's view of party and its application in the Democratic Party's organizational structure and operations was thus premised on unity, vigilance, and submission: partisans would act together because in unity there was strength; partisans would vigilantly defend the decisions, actions, and interests of the party; partisans would submit their own opinions to the party line.[176]

While the people demonstrated that they could and would act the part of romantic heroes when they petitioned Congress against the Compensation Act, Indian removal, and slavery, some political leaders viewed such evidence of active citizenship as a threat that needed to be controlled. When active citizens were portrayed as a "most corrupt and secrete combination" and their opinions were mocked, silenced, and outmaneuvered, there was little incentive for citizens to attempt to control the government outside of the party structure. While on one hand the democratic fiction promised power to the people, on the other hand it denied those who would be active—whether "miserable fanatics" or not—the ability to freely watch, judge, and critique the government. Yet, while Democrats and Whigs denied average citizens their right to petition the government for a redress of grievances, American citizens were not treated as tragic victims. As we saw in our analysis of the 1826 deaths of Adams and Jefferson, it was not possible to publicly proclaim the *divina origine* of American republicanism and still also proclaim that citizens were unworthy, tragic victims. With so many more citizens voting, meeting, and petitioning, political leaders had to fear the "great Leviathan of popularity," which meant that citizens could no longer be ignored. Political leaders learned that the new, active citizenry could be organized from the smallest ward to the national organization and that party newspapers would keep citizens well informed of party perspectives. Political leaders learned that active citizens' meetings, petitions, and purifications posed the dangerous problem of instability, but that organizing citizens into loyal partisans could be a benign solution that allowed political leaders to retain control and stability.

Therefore, the rise of the democratic fiction in conjunction with the rise of democratic representation and democratic campaigning allowed political leaders to fundamentally recast citizens from romantic heroes or tragic victims into ironic partisans. Representatives would absolutely mirror and obey the will of the people, except when they did not want to; representatives would seek the people's approval and maintain their popularity by speech making, job promising, and party organizing. Citizens would act by supporting their party and their party's policies, or else their opinions and criticisms would not be allowed to enter into public debate. The differences, therefore, between a republican romantic hero and a democratic ironic partisan were as pronounced as the differences between republicanism and oligarchy: whereas romantic heroes would actively fight tyranny and protect liberty by critiquing the government and defending the Constitution, ironic partisans would protect their party by obeying the party leaders' commands. As the Democrats and Whigs used the democratic fiction they professed to defend the rights of the people, but in all practicality the organizational structure of the new party system allowed for little input from those below the Kitchen Cabinet or the leadership of the state organizations. Democrats and Whigs may have professed that the people were sovereign and that representatives merely obeyed their will, but when the people's will diverged from party policy, public opinion was ignored. America's republican Constitution was characterized by representation, hierarchy, and stability. As we have seen, the Constitution was designed to filter the will of the people through representation, to preserve hierarchy and prevent equality, and to provide stability at all costs. The democratic fiction promised the people participation and equality, which, if put into practice, would have made the government profoundly unstable. Therefore, as the democratic fiction emerged and was practiced between 1816 and 1845 it was no more democratic than the republican fiction had been between 1776 and 1815. More white male citizens had the right of suffrage, but the people's increased desire to control the government through voting, meeting, and petitioning was still viewed with deep skepticism by the nation's political elite.

If a citizen is one who actively controls the government for the common good, as Aristotle says, then the democratic fiction portrayed citizens ironically. Irony is the trope of negation and obfuscation: it allows rhetors to say two things at once. Irony is the language of insiders: it signals to insiders that the apparent is not the actual. When political leaders used the democratic fiction they did so ironically, to promise to give away the power that they knew would make the nation fundamentally unstable. When citizens used the democratic fiction they did so earnestly, to demand the power that they knew was rightfully theirs. There was an ironic gap between the democratic fiction's use of the term "democracy" and the nation's republican political theory and Constitution. There was another ironic gap between the democratic fiction's portrayal of average citizens as all-powerful and average citizens' declining political power. When citizens were portrayed as ironic partisans they were sporadically involved, which meant they could only actively control the government through their vote for representatives; they were a part of a system or network apart from the whole, which meant that republican concern for the common good no longer applied to them; and they were directed by powerful others, which meant they were not empowered to act to control the government as individuals, but were empowered through their association with their party. Citizens were now neither romantic heroes nor tragic victims, but rather semi-powerful partisans who could be more easily organized and controlled.

Conclusion

There is a "practical absurdity," writes Michael Calvin McGee, in the "contradiction between our claims to popular sovereignty and our commonplace judgments of the popular will." For comparison, "who would say that the 'King' is sovereign, but in the next breath deny the 'King's' ability to resist sophists, accuse him of such ignorance that he cannot tell his own interest, and then top the argument with the claim that public ethics force officers of state, who owe their power to the 'King,' to pay no attention to him."[1] As McGee observes, a citizen, unlike a monarch, is often portrayed as the victim of sophists, demagogues, and his or her own ignorance. Ethics requires that the people rule, but only through the filtering mechanisms of representation and party politics. Yet, while McGee's argument resonates with my analysis in this volume, the story of American citizenship is more complicated than McGee suggests. The story of American political discourse between 1764 and 1845 demonstrates that America's political fiction cast citizens in three very different roles: romantic heroes, tragic victims, and ironic partisans. McGee's observation about the "practical absurdity" in America's political fiction certainly applies to the view of citizens as tragic victims, but it does not capture the tenor of the view of citizens as romantic heroes or as ironic partisans. While McGee's analysis does not reflect all of the first two generations' views of citizenship, it does help us focus our attention on the contradictory ways we have learned to think about the power of the average citizen. On the one hand, we tell ourselves that American citizens are sovereign and all-powerful; citizens control the government that is based upon their will. On the other hand, we tell ourselves that American citizens are sovereign but not all-powerful; citizens cannot be trusted to control the government that is based upon their will. For better or worse, we think of citizens as heroes, victims, and partisans, and we often view them in all three ways simultaneously. America's political fiction is sufficiently ambiguous and malleable to accommodate each of these characterizations without causing the inherent contradictions to become so absurd that the fiction collapses upon its own inconsistencies—no small feat, to be sure. America's political fiction is a complexly woven story of the nation's political theory, its political practices, and its people. Despite its ambiguities and contradictions, America's political fiction has allowed the nation to endure for over two hundred years, exceeding the most sanguine expectations of its founders.

America's Political Fictions and Citizenship

Americans between 1764 and 1776 rejected the monarchical fiction and the characterization of the people as subjects and embraced the republican fiction and characterized themselves as citizens. The monarchical fiction had been premised upon the supposed perfection of the monarch, which made all laws perfect and unquestionable. When "odious laws" were passed against the people's best interest, the people could do nothing but obey and hope that the monarch would choose to relieve them and protect their rights and liberties. Indeed, the only permissible action for subjects within the monarchical fiction was to obey. Americans believed that there would be "an end of all government" if a subject were to watch, investigate, judge, and question the monarch or Parliament in any way. Yet, while the monarch was the unquestionable sovereign upon whom all political power rested, the monarchical fiction circumscribed the power of the king by requiring that he care for and protect subjects' liberties. As Americans became more and more disillusioned with King George III and Parliament between 1764 and 1776, they also became more disillusioned with the monarchical fiction and their role as subjects. Once it became clear that "justice is not the same in America as in Britain," once Americans began communicating and cooperating with one another, once Americans began actively watching and critiquing their government, once Americans began to act together on their own authority, and once Americans could imagine a happy future outside the monarchical fiction, they cast themselves as citizens rather than as subjects. When Americans declared independence, they also declared that the people were the new sovereign of their government: the government was now based upon the will of the people rather than the will of the monarch.

Because the people were now sovereign, Americans drew from republican political theory to construct both their new state constitutions and the Articles of Confederation. The application of republican political theory to America's constitutions in 1776 meant that the new governments rejected titles of nobility, embraced rotation in office, allowed male freeholders to vote in some elections, and divided the tasks of government among three separate branches. Americans had learned to think of the good citizen as someone who watched and critiqued the government; who worked together through committees of safety and correspondence and Sons of Liberty organizations; who boycotted English imports and exports; and who risked life and fortune to fight British oppression. Patriotism meant critiquing the government, rejecting party and faction, defending the constitution, and working for the common good. Because the Revolution required the participation of citizens to succeed, Americans portrayed themselves as active patriots who cheerfully sacrificed for the common good. Yet the governments that Americans erected, while dramatically more accountable to the will of the people than the old colonial governments had been, did not give the average citizen much power to control the government. While every state allowed citizens to vote in at least some elections, all states except Vermont had either a freeholder or a taxpayer qualification, which restricted the right of suffrage to landed property holders and taxpayers. The new republican fiction portrayed the good citizen as a hero who would triumph over the forces of oppression, thereby preserving and defending liberty from corruption, yet the new constitutions were not democratic. Some citizens had the right of suffrage, and some states guaranteed their citizens the right to instruct their representatives and other freedoms (speech, assembly, press, and petition, for example), but citizens did not make direct, binding decisions on matters of public policy. The new republican fiction portrayed its citizens as more powerful and active than they had ever been portrayed before, but their realm of activity was restricted. Within the legislature, the new romantic citizen would rule through his representatives; outside the legislature, the new romantic citizen would act for the common good.

However, once romantic citizens became convinced that they were sovereign, and once they had seen the power of their own actions, the political elite found it difficult to contain American citizens' actions to their designated sphere. The dramatic downturn in the economy after the close of the Revolution in 1783 led to increased public meetings, petitions, and resolutions from the people requesting that the government pass debtors' relief laws. When the government did not respond as the petitioners had hoped, citizens took direct action against the government by marching and drilling, intimidating local officials, and closing down county courts. The people's rebellions and insurrections led political leaders to question whether the people could be trusted to stop corruption, protect liberty, or sacrifice for the common good. Many of the delegates at the Constitutional Convention believed that the people were more like children or complicit victims of corruption than romantic heroes. Therefore, delegates created a new consolidated government designed to guarantee the stability and liberty that the state governments, the Articles of Confederation, and the people could not provide. Federalists hoped that the new constitution's checks and balances would enable the "government to control the governed and . . . itself," thereby limiting citizens to their proper realm of action. The Bill of Rights explicitly granted individual citizens the freedoms of speech, press, assembly, and petition, but citizens were only directly represented in the House of Representatives, the ratio of representation was considered quite high, and citizens had no right to instruct their representatives. Suffrage laws were left up to the individual states, which retained their freeholder and taxpayer qualifications. The new constitution was still premised upon republican political theory—the people were still sovereign—but the people were no longer imagined as romantic heroes.

During the Constitutional Convention and the ratification debates, Federalists described citizens as complicit victims of corruption who could not be trusted to act as romantic heroes and who had proved that they would not confine their actions to their appropriate realm. The goal of constitutional reform was to create a stable system of government that would give the general government control over the states and the people. The Constitution's new republican fiction was therefore tragic: it asked Americans to accept the fact that the forces of corruption were simply too great to overcome, which meant that stability was the best that Americans could hope for. The stability of the system was now of the utmost importance, Federalists argued, because only a stable system would protect liberty and justice. The Constitution's good citizen would agree to confine his actions within constitutional limitations and would agree to allow the system to control the whole, defend the common good, and protect liberty. The new national government was still republican, and while it did not place additional constitutional limitations upon the citizen's ability to act to control the government—indeed, very little actually changed for the majority of American citizens—the story Americans told themselves about who they were in relation to their government, corruption, and liberty had fundamentally changed. The romantic citizen was now viewed as a dangerous threat to stability and liberty; the active citizenship praised in the years leading up to the Revolution was no longer portrayed as prudent or desirable. When Americans accepted the new tragic citizenship, they allowed themselves to be constituted as victims rather than as heroes. Once citizens were viewed as victims, it was far easier for political leaders to justify exclusionary voting practices, ignore public opinion, and enact policies without citizen consent. While many Anti-Federalists believed that the new "consolidated government" infringed upon states' rights, very little resistance was made to the new government on behalf of the right of citizens to actively control the government. The need for stability had triumphed over romantic citizenship.

Federalists successfully instituted the constitutional reforms necessary to create a stable government. By the nation's 1826 Jubilee only three signers of the Declaration of Independence remained alive to remind the second generation about the revolutionary generation's romantic struggle for liberty and independence. Americans believed that the July 4, 1826, deaths of John Adams and Thomas Jefferson were a sign from Providence, but the sign was ambiguous. Americans wondered whether the deaths were an omen of the impending end of the Republic or a glorious sign of the nation's *divina origine.* The second generation chose to believe the latter, and in so doing they clothed America's republican fiction in the unquestionable divine-right narrative of the old monarchical fiction. Such an astounding coincidence as the twin deaths of two of America's most important founders on the fiftieth anniversary of the Declaration of Independence was so improbable that it could only be read as a sign from God that American republicanism was itself divine. In telling themselves this story, Americans conflated the very real differences between Adams's and Jefferson's views of republicanism: despite historical realities, Americans chose to believe that Adams and Jefferson were the "twin stars of liberty" who held the same views of government, the same views of how to protect liberty, and the same views of how to imagine American citizenship. In short, after the deaths of Adams and Jefferson "every political feeling was banished."

Not only did revolutionary republicanism and constitutional republicanism become identical, but in reifying Adams and Jefferson as monuments to liberty, Americans also conflated romantic and tragic citizenship. They once again described themselves as romantic heroes who chose the sword over submission and who refused to accept the ruse that some were "born with saddles on their backs" while others were born "booted and spurred, ready to ride them legitimately, by the grace of God." Jefferson's "Last Letter" had helped to frame the Jubilee as the triumph of the romantic hero; the eulogies, memorials, and commemorations of Adams and Jefferson allowed Americans to read the twin deaths consistent with Jefferson's framing. Americans throughout the nation exaggerated the deaths as the most beautiful event in the "annals of history" and demonstrated that they had a part to play in the romantic fiction when they took an active part in commemorating the founders. In so doing, Americans resolved the hermeneutical crisis prompted by the twin deaths, pronounced the deaths "fortunate," and constituted themselves romantic republican heroes. Because tragic citizenship had been justified by appealing to the natural hierarchy between leaders and citizens, it no longer applied in a fiction in which no one had the God-given right to rule over another. Because tragic citizenship had been crafted in opposition to the romantic citizenship that the Jubilee and the deaths of Adams and Jefferson celebrated, it could not be invoked to make sense of the deaths or reassure Americans that the deaths were fortunate. Yet the logic of the nation's constitutions continued to be based upon the need for stability. Americans celebrated the chaos-making romantic citizen while simultaneously reaffirming the continuity of constitutional republicanism. The good citizen of the Jubilee was asked to recognize the sublimity of the twin deaths, participate in celebrating revolutionary republicanism and romantic citizenship, and continue the work of the founding generation by supporting a Constitution based upon the disempowering logic of tragic citizenship. Americans made sense of the twin deaths by claiming that romantic republicanism had divine sanction, which made republicanism unquestionable and pushed tragic citizenship to the unmentionable backstage of America's political fiction.

The new divine-right narrative of American republicanism in 1826 was possible, in part, because of the long and bitter political campaign leading up to the 1828 grudge match between Andrew Jackson and John Quincy Adams. Since the 1815 signing of the Treaty of Ghent, average citizens had sought a more active part in American politics. The citizens who moved into the frontier after the War of 1812 demanded—and were granted—universal white male suffrage, which threatened the exclusionary suffrage practices of the established eastern states. Not only did citizens demand their right to vote for their representatives, but they also began assembling, petitioning, and instructing their representatives in a manner reminiscent of the turbulent years between the close of the Revolution and the Constitutional Convention. Political leaders were made forcefully aware of how citizens could use their powers in the controversy over the 1816 Compensation Act, which resulted in 70 percent of representatives losing their seats in that year's election. Representatives suddenly realized that they needed to watch which way the "political weather-cock" blew and that the "great Leviathan of popularity" ruled. Yet, while citizens had demonstrated that they would actively investigate, watch, and judge their government to prevent corruption, representatives refused to accept that the public outcry was genuine, that the public's opinion was well informed, or that the people had the right to instruct their representatives. While more representatives argued that republicanism meant that the government must obey the people—that the voice of the people was not only the voice of God, but also belonged in the legislature—many continued to find the ideal of representative-as-mirror dangerous and a betrayal of the fundamental principles of American republicanism. The controversy over the Compensation Act therefore marked the transition from republican to democratic representation, which was ambiguously democratic at best.

The democratic representation that emerged in 1816 was followed closely by the shift from republican to democratic campaigning with the "corrupt bargain" of 1824. Andrew Jackson won the popular vote but did not have an Electoral College majority; this threw the election into the House of Representatives, where Henry Clay used his political capital to swing the vote to John Quincy Adams, despite the fact that his home state had instructed him to vote for Jackson. Jackson believed that Clay—the "Judas of the West"—had betrayed the will of the people in exchange for the office of secretary of state, and he swore to avenge himself and the people. Between 1824 and 1828, Jackson and his new Democratic Party organized voters into a national coalition, hired party newspaper editors, and promised jobs to the party faithful. Clay and his Republican Party allies conducted a dramatic smear campaign impugning Jackson's honor and judgment, but Jackson was able to turn the "wicked slander" against Clay until it "recoiled against his head." Jacksonians attacked John Quincy Adams for being a closet Federalist at best and a monarchist at worst and claimed that Adams despised the rule of the people, resurrecting Adams's 1791 "Islam of democracy" quip and turning it into the Democratic Party's battle cry and their party's ethos. In so doing, Jacksonians called romantic republicans "democrats" and called tragic republicans "monarchists," which allowed Jacksonians to turn language against itself by ambiguously defining terms like "democracy," using words that had traditionally represented specific political theories without rhyme or reason, and turning Adams's tragic republicanism into caricature. Jacksonians took advantage of the increase in white male suffrage to organize citizens as partisans who would follow the dictates of the party leadership and who would view the triumph of the party as a triumph for the common good. The election of 1828 therefore signaled the shift from republican campaigning to democratic campaigning and from the republican fiction to the democratic fiction.

Democrats had helped to change the nation's political fiction, but as Jackson's 1837 farewell address made clear, they had not changed the nation from a republic to a democracy. In fact, the Jacksonians' history with the people's freedoms of speech, assembly, press, instruction, and petition—the traditional freedoms of active citizenship—had not been good. The controversy over Jackson's Indian removal policy resulted in public protest meetings, citizens instructing their representatives to vote against removal, and the nation's first large-scale petition drive. Religious groups and women petitioned Congress in record numbers, but Jacksonians mocked the reformers in party newspapers, held counterprotest meetings, packed important committees with friendly representatives, and generally treated the reformers as enemy combatants who could only be destroyed, not persuaded. The Indian removal petition campaign led to an even larger campaign to abolish slavery in Washington, D.C., which resulted in the "mail bombing of the South" and so many petitions flooding into Congress that members of both parties and both houses agreed that national stability and their personal and political livelihoods required them to "peremptorily" reject the petitions without receiving them. Once again the people had dangerously overstepped their constitutional limitations by attempting to enter their opinions into the legislature; once again they were prevented from acting in the name of promoting and protecting stability. The democratic fiction was therefore ambiguously democratic: while Jackson had justified his actions as necessary to protect the people's liberty, he had also consolidated power in the executive branch; while seven out of eight of Jackson's annual messages had requested that Congress amend the Constitution to abolish the Electoral College and create executive and legislative term limits, Congress refused; and while both the Democrats and the Whigs used the democratic fiction to help them win elections, the people's freedoms of speech, press, and petition were easily abrogated to protect safety and stability.

The democratic fiction was ambiguously democratic, and citizens were portrayed as ironic partisans who were all-powerful, but only within the limitations of the constitutional and party systems. The party system now functioned to add another layer of separation between the people's dangerous opinions and the government: it helped to contain and constrain citizen action so that it would not escape its designated sphere and threaten the nation's stability. Citizens could watch, investigate, judge, and critique the government, but only when authorized to do so by their party. Citizens could use their newfound right of suffrage to "purify" government, but such electoral purifications were now highly organized party campaigns and not left to the caprices of public opinion. When citizens attempted to critique their government on their own—when they organized successful petition drives against favored party measures, for example—they were intimidated, mocked, ignored, and silenced. The democratic fiction portrayed citizens both as powerful romantic heroes and as incapable of action outside the party structure. Therefore, citizens were now partisans, and partisans were ironically powerful—they could only use their power when directed by powerful others. Irony is the figure of distance; it negates the literal with the figural. In this case, the democratic fiction distanced Americans from their republican political theory and simultaneously affirmed that American citizens are all-powerful, while constraining their power. Although more white males could and did vote, the majority of Americans gained little political power with the shift from the republican fiction to the democratic fiction between 1816 and 1845.

Each fiction and each view of citizenship was a product of, and appropriate to, its immediate context. For example, what if the Revolution had been justified with tragic citizenship instead of romantic citizenship? Would Americans have been motivated to win a war against the mightiest military power in the world if they had been portrayed as complicit victims of corruption? It is not likely. What if the new constitution had been based upon the logic of romantic citizenship rather than tragic citizenship? Would romantic citizens have provided the stability necessary to rescue the economy and allow Americans to build a new nation? Perhaps, but because elites were so convinced that the licentiousness of the people would lead to economic ruin, it is unlikely that they would have supported such a government. What if the deaths of Adams and Jefferson had been interpreted through the lens of tragic citizenship instead of creating romantic heroes out of the second generation? Would the nation have overcome the destabilizing transitions between the first and second generations if they had been portrayed then as complicit victims of corruption rather than as romantic heroes? It is doubtful, because the historic crisis of leadership of 1826 could have been resolved only by each American believing that he was the romantic hero who had inherited the Revolution. What if Jacksonians had continued to employ the republican fiction instead of the democratic fiction? What if they had continued to think of Americans as citizens instead of as partisans? What if they had portrayed partisans as tragic victims rather than as romantic heroes? Would they have successfully won the presidency, maintained stability, and preserved the Union? It is not likely, because the extension of suffrage and the increased attempts to influence the legislature meant that the republican fiction's logics of protecting stability through hierarchy and representation were no longer tenable—those who tried to invoke the old republican fiction's logics often found themselves on the wrong side of an electoral "purification." Furthermore, Jacksonians' new democratic fiction could not have been peopled by citizens, because its logics of equality and participation had already proven to be profoundly unstable—the nation could not have long endured if the opinions of the "miserable fanatics" had been allowed to enter into the legislature. Stability required that newly empowered Americans be portrayed as partisans who would work for the good of the party; Americans had to believe that a party victory would ensure the common good. Finally, partisans had to be portrayed as romantic heroes because the party leadership needed their members to believe that they could actively control the government, that a vote for the party was a step toward ending corruption, and that the forces of good would triumph over the forces of evil if they acted in lockstep with their fellow party members and obeyed the dictates of the party leadership. The democratic fiction had to portray newly empowered citizens as romantic heroes, but it had to confine those heroes to their appropriate realm of action; therefore, ironic partisanship successfully captured the tenor of the new American democratic citizen.

Americans developed the romantic republican fiction, the tragic republican fiction, and the ironic democratic fiction in response to their existing political contexts, which is precisely why America's political leaders found each fiction so useful. America's political fictions helped the nation commit treason and win an impossible victory over the mightiest military in the world; they helped the nation rebound from an economic collapse and create an improbable stability in a new nation that had witnessed numerous insurrections and rebellions; they helped the nation resolve the hermeneutical crisis prompted by the deaths of Adams and Jefferson and transfer power to the second generation; and they helped the nation maintain stability despite the new dangerous threat of increased suffrage and participation prompted by the failure of the rhetorics of deference and hierarchy. America's political fictions created and maintained a stable, powerful nation, but did they enable the people to act to control the government? No, they did not. Therefore, as Michael Calvin McGee notes, there is a "practical absurdity" to America's republicanism, at the heart of which is a fundamental contradiction. But the contradiction is not "between our claims to popular sovereignty and our commonplace judgments of the popular will," as McGee argues, for the incompatibility of these two beliefs is only a symptom of the contradiction. The fundamental contradiction at the heart of American republicanism is between the *government's need for stability* and the *citizen's desire for active participation*. Popular governments are profoundly unstable, because when the people rule then there can be no settled question, no unquestioned rule, no ruling power, and no powerless citizen. Therefore, America's political leaders have simply dismissed public opinion as irrational, ill-informed, and the product of demagogues, because in so doing they are provided with a justification for ignoring public opinion and preserving stability. America's political leaders knew all too well that when the people did not confine their actions to the realms of military defense, epideictic celebration, and political party—when they tried to enter their opinions into the legislature's deliberations—there was chaos and instability.

Founding Fictions has used an interdisciplinary approach to tell the story of how Americans invented, debated, and enacted American republican political theory between 1764 and 1845, and in so doing it has approached political theory as a combination of poetical, rhetorical, and dialectical language. Thinking of political theory as political fiction has allowed us to analyze how and why the nation's political theory was constructed against other alternatives and how it responded to the prevailing ideas in circulation within its immediate context. This approach has allowed us to think about the relationship between America's political theory and the stories Americans tell themselves about their government; it has also highlighted the inherently constructed nature of political theory. We found that sometimes the nation's political fiction accurately reflected the nation's political theory and constitution, and at other times we found an ironic gap between what was portrayed as the nation's political theory and the logic of its existing constitution. We found that the nation developed, and its political leaders and citizens strategically deployed, specific political fictions because they found them useful for coping with specific contextual constraints. We found that America's political fiction was the result of the people's imagination, which meant that it was not an unquestionable elite discourse but rather the joint creation of Americans.

From the critiques of savvy political observers like Mercy Otis Warren, of idealistic romantic republicans like Thomas Jefferson, and of apprehensive Anti-Federalists like Brutus we learned that any political fiction could be judged based upon whether and how it was dialogic, authored, circulated, debated, ratified, and open, and also that political fictions could be said to have more citizen consent when they met more, rather than fewer, of these six characteristics. Our analysis of the Revolution's republican fiction found that despite the nation's inexperience with republican constitution creation, there was a strong sense of dialogism between political leaders and citizens, because without the support of the mass of the people political leaders would have certainly been hung as traitors. The years between 1764 and 1776 witnessed Americans debating, ratifying, and knowingly circulating the truths of the republican fiction they jointly authored. While we could not say that the construction of the Revolution's republican fiction was perfectly dialogic, authored, circulated, debated, ratified, or open, it did appear to have enough citizen consent for Committees of Correspondence and Safety to effectively manage the government after the collapse of the monarchical fiction and motivate citizens to participate in the war effort.

The new Constitution was overtly constructed in a secret enclave in 1787, but it did go through a rigorous process of debate and ratification—even if only a few Americans were actually allowed to vote on it. The Constitution was decidedly authored; indeed, the prestige of the Constitutional Convention had been used as one of the more persuasive arguments in its favor. The new Constitution was also specifically open to amendment and was overtly and knowingly circulated. This much is true of the nation's new Constitution, but what can we say about the nation's new tragic republican fiction? Was it also predominantly dialogic, authored, circulated, debated, ratified, and open? It is difficult to say with certainty whether or not citizens accepted that they were tragic victims rather than romantic heroes, especially because of the accusations of heresthetic rhetrickery during the ratification process and because "vernacular republicanism" endured well into the 1790s. Yet, while romantic citizenship may not have been eradicated, citizens accepted the new Constitution and allowed it to provide the stability that the nation's political elite desired.

The way Americans responded to the deaths of John Adams and Thomas Jefferson on the nation's Jubilee conflated romantic and tragic citizenship and gave America's republican fiction divine sanction, but it did not change the nation's Constitution. There is a sense in which Americans ratified the interpretation of the deaths as providential when they participated in celebrating the lives and deaths of the founders, but there was little interrogation of what it meant to banish tragic citizenship to the unmentionable backstage of the nation's political fiction. Furthermore, while the nation celebrated the specific authors of the nation's political fiction and circulated their fiction in great abundance, they also seemingly clothed that fiction in an unquestionable and unauthored divine-right narrative. If America's republican fiction was providential, then it was no longer created by the people or open to their amendment. Therefore, the way Americans responded to the deaths of Adams and Jefferson allowed them to make sense of the startling coincidence, but it also fundamentally dissevered America's political fiction from its authors and rendered it less debatable, less open to amendment, and therefore, ultimately, less dialogic.

The rise of the democratic fiction during the era of the common man was partially a response to the changing political dynamics that preceded it—the increase in white male suffrage, the increase in citizen participation, the rise of organized political parties—and partially the result of the need to recraft the nation's political fiction to accommodate the new political circumstances without sacrificing stability. The nation's second generation of political leaders developed the democratic fiction by using ambiguously defined political theories for the purposes of party name calling and by pointing back to the founding generation as the inventor of their democratic fiction. Therefore, the democratic fiction was less dialogic, debated, or clearly authored than we would hope it would have been. Because of the dramatic rise of mass politics and voter turnout, there is a sense in which the democratic fiction was ratified, but because Jackson refused to reveal his political positions leading up to the 1828 election, it is unlikely that voters knew precisely what they were voting for. The democratic fiction circulated with great abandon, but it was less open to change and amendment than citizen consent would require. Citizens were told to judge their government by the standards of "democracy," but the democratic fiction allowed that word to be drained of its precise technical meaning, thereby hindering citizens' ability to judge whether or not their government was performing as they would wish. The rise of the democratic fiction made conflict over America's political theory nearly impossible. As we have seen in the Jacksonians' treatment of the Adamses' tragic republicanism, and as Regina Morantz, Russell L. Hanson, Arthur M. Schlesinger Jr., Sean Wilentz, and just about every other historian of American politics argues, after the triumph of Jacksonianism it was difficult for politicians of the second generation to admit publicly that they feared the rule of the people—even if they did.[2] Americans had all become democrats with the rise of the democratic fiction, which moved the locus of political debate from political theory to political action—political action organized by party and professional politicians. Therefore, the rise of the democratic fiction was enabling—not of the people, certainly, but of party conflict. The "Era of Good Feelings" had minimalized party conflict; the democratic fiction thrived upon it.

How Does *Founding Fictions* Contribute to Our Understanding of American Citizenship?

"The principle of the sovereignty of the people has acquired, in the United States, all the practical development which the imagination can conceive," Alexis de Tocqueville wrote in his 1835 *Democracy in America.* "It is unencumbered by those fictions which are thrown over it in other countries, and it appears in every possible form, according to the exigency of the occasion. Sometimes the laws are made by the people in a body, as at Athens; and sometimes its representatives, chosen by universal suffrage, transact business in its name, and under its immediate supervision."[3] Making no distinction between the laws the people enacted directly and those they enacted through their representatives, and unable to imagine a *more* democratic political community, de Tocqueville optimistically reported the triumph of democracy in America. Yet, as we have seen, his analysis did not accurately reflect the state of American politics in 1835, which was ambiguously democratic at best. Any narrative of American citizenship that begins with *Democracy in America,* therefore, must be reexamined to take into consideration the conflicted, paradoxical nature of how Americans imagined citizenship between 1764 and 1845.[4] *Founding Fictions* makes a necessary correction to Tocquevillian optimism by offering a different story of American citizenship. Above all, *Founding Fictions*' narrative of American citizenship reveals an important contradiction in American political theory and practice: national stability and active citizen participation are fundamentally at odds.

Two scholars have also recently directly revisited de Tocqueville's analysis of American citizenship. *Founding Fictions*' story of American citizenship supports both Michael Schudson's and Rogers Smith's arguments that de Tocqueville's original analysis was too optimistic and therefore that we have not really witnessed a decline in active citizenship.[5] Yet, while Schudson and Smith are certainly correct that basing our understanding of modern citizen apathy and civic decline upon *Democracy in America* leads to an overestimation of the health of active citizenship during the Age of Jackson, this is only part of the story.[6] For as *Founding Fictions* describes, America's republican and democratic political fictions constituted American citizens as romantic heroes, tragic victims, and ironic partisans, and they did so for good reason. Therefore, the ways in which de Tocqueville overestimated active citizen control over the government and the enduring prevalence of his optimistic read of American citizenship helped to perpetuate the view of American citizens as romantic heroes, even though citizens were often treated as tragic victims and ironic partisans. We might even say that de Tocqueville's *Democracy in America* has helped to cultivate the ambiguity of American democratic citizenship by conflating republican and democratic forms of government and by conflating romantic and tragic citizenship. While Schudson's and Smith's reevaluations have helped us to recognize some of de Tocqueville's errors, neither has fully accounted for the effects of those errors on America's political fiction or how tragic citizenship contributed to citizen apathy today.

Founding Fictions' analysis of how America's republican and democratic political fictions constituted Americans as romantic heroes, tragic victims, and ironic partisans likewise supports and expands Jacques Rancière's analysis of the "hatred of democracy" and Robert Ivie's analysis of the "distemper of democracy." Both Rancière and Ivie recognize that the political elite have traditionally hated, feared, berated, and trivialized the active participation of the people. In Ivie's analysis, America's political elite used the "metaphor of disease" to "demote" American citizens "from the role of decision maker to that of bystander" in 1787.[7] In Rancière's analysis, "the term democracy . . . does not simply mean a bad form of government and political life. It strictly means a style of life that is opposed to any well-ordered government of the community."[8] Yet, while *Founding Fictions*' story of American citizenship can be read as a more detailed discussion of how and why the "irony of democracy" emerged between 1764 and 1845 by chronicling how and why romantic and tragic citizenship and ironic partisanship emerged within their specific contexts and how these narratives of citizenship were strategically employed by political elite and average citizens, *Founding Fictions* does more than merely support Ivie's and Rancière's analysis: it expands upon it. For in Rancière's analysis the political elite have always overtly acknowledged their *misodemia*—their hatred of the people—even though it is clear that in the American political tradition, at least, the political elite have at times strategically embraced citizens as romantic heroes and at other times have openly positioned citizens as tragic victims and at still other times have positioned citizens as ironic partisans while proclaiming them romantic heroes. In Ivie's analysis, James Madison's and other Federalists' hatred of democracy was replaced when the "Jacksonian party, in effect, became the symbolic vehicle for steering a democratic course against Federalist currents of conservatism," which, in turn, set in motion "a long slide toward diminished confidence in political rhetoric and popular rule."[9] *Founding Fictions*' narrative of American citizenship likewise describes Madison's *misodemia,* but it argues that Jacksonians' use of the democratic fiction was less of a clear repudiation of Federalists' tragic republicanism than the 1828 campaign might have made it appear. Indeed, as we have seen, the tragic distrust of the people and their dangerous opinions has been a feature of America's political fiction and America's Constitution since 1787, because such distrust is inherent in the structural design of the Constitution and in the political theory upon which the Constitution was constructed.

The Constitution was overtly designed to protect stability by constraining citizen action to what political leaders believed was its proper realm: outside the legislature. Citizens were sovereign—the government was based upon the will of the people rather than upon the will of the monarch—but their dangerous opinions would be filtered through the stabilizing mechanism of representation. Therefore, the tragic logic of America's Constitution is fundamentally at odds with a romantic conception of citizenship like Michael Hardt and Antonio Negri's, which seeks to shift from a government based upon the will of "the people" to a government based upon the will of "the multitude." Hardt and Negri recognize that their conception of the multitude, which they define as a political community that "is not unified but remains plural and multiple" and is composed of "an active social subject, which acts on the basis of what the singularities share in common," contradicts established forms of sovereignty by re-conceiving the people as "living flesh that rules itself" by "acting in common."[10] Hardt and Negri ask political communities and citizens to celebrate the sporadic, carnivalesque participations of the multitude, which they believe will facilitate "the government of all over all." *Founding Fictions*' analysis indicates that however appealing Hardt and Negri's abolition of sovereignty and embrace of the rule of the multitude might be, the political elite will always view the participation of the many with deep skepticism and will always seek new ways to prevent active citizen participation—whether sporadic and dispersed or not. In other words, while the concept of the multitude solves the problems of an oppressive view of "the people" that arbitrarily conflates all difference, it does not solve the inherent tension between stability and active citizen participation. Hardt and Negri's romantic and heroic view of active political participation across borders, boundaries, nationalities, and socioeconomic status would indeed compound the threat of dangerous citizen action for those who believe that citizen action is a threat. The romantic citizenship of the multitude is far more democratic than the tragic citizenship of the traditional and constitutional notions of the sovereignty of the people. Such a conception would equal a revolutionary change in American political theory and America's political fiction, which makes it unlikely, even though it is potentially desirable.

Finally, *Founding Fictions*' narrative of American citizenship demonstrates how Benjamin Barber's "infantilized citizens" are the logical consequence of limiting citizen actions to war, party, and consumption.[11] In other words, if the realm of citizen action continues to be restricted to outside the legislature; if democratic deliberation continues to be thought of as destabilizing chaos; if the people continue to have no right to instruct their representatives; if the traditional freedoms of active citizenship—petition, assembly, press, and instruction—continue to be ignored, trivialized, and trigger partisan attacks, then there can be no hope for active citizenship, and citizens will continue to act more and more as consumers rather than as romantic heroes. Therefore, views of citizenship as "discursive action," or citizenship enacted outside the legislature, reflect a resignation that tragic citizenship is either desirable or the best that can be attained and further contribute to prevent citizen action. If there is one lesson found in *Founding Fictions*' story of American citizenship, it is that if we hope to promote active citizenship we must recognize that America's republican public sphere has never been the sphere for citizens; America's public sphere has always been the sphere for political leaders. We must therefore at a minimum restore the view of citizens as romantic heroes and restore the traditional freedoms of active citizenship and reconceive America's public sphere as democratic rather than republican.

The fundamental contradiction between the nation's need for stability and our desire for active citizenship cannot be resolved easily, for so doing would require that political leaders embrace and celebrate instability. Embracing instability would require political leaders to imagine active citizens the way Thomas Jefferson imagined rebellion in 1787: it would require political leaders to acknowledge that "a little rebellion now and then is a good thing, and as necessary in the political world as storms in the physical."[12] In other words, if we are to resolve the fundamental contradiction of American republican government, we must recognize that Jefferson was right and Madison was wrong; we must trust that instability is natural and productive and necessary to protect liberty; we must recognize that stability is *not* the best we can hope for. Political leaders must recognize that the people will make mistakes, but also that because *vox populi, vox dei* the people must be obeyed.

Notes

Introduction

1. Aristotle, *Politics,* ed. Ernest Barker (Oxford: Oxford University Press, 1946), 3:1276b–79a.

2. Scholars across disciplines study the questions of citizenship. I have found the following particularly useful: Michael Shudson, *The Good Citizen: A History of American Civic Life* (New York: The Free Press, 1998); Michael Hardt and Antonio Negri, *Multitude: War and Democracy in an Age of Empire* (New York: Penguin Press, 2004); Ronald Beiner, *Theorizing Citizenship* (Albany; State University of New York Press, 1995); Robert D. Putnam, *Bowling Alone: The Collapse and Revival of American Community* (New York: Simon and Schuster, 2001); Jürgen Habermas, *The Structural Transformation of the Public Sphere: An Inquiry into a Category of Bourgeois Society* (Boston: MIT Press, 1991); Craig Calhoun, *Habermas and the Public Sphere* (Boston: MIT Press, 1993); Benedict Anderson, *Imagined Communities: Reflections on the Origins and Spread of Nationalism* (New York: Verso, 1991; Robert W. McChesney, *Rich Media, Poor Democracy: Communication Politics for Dubious Times* (Urbana: University of Illinois Press, 1999); Aristotle, *Politics,* trans. H. Rackham (New York: Loeb, 1932); Walter Lippmann, *The Phantom Public* (New York: Transaction Press, 1993); John Dewey, *The Public and Its Problems* (New York: Swallow Press, 1954); Benjamin R. Barber, *Consumed: How Markets Corrupt Children, Infantilize Adults, and Swallow Citizens Whole* (New York: Norton, 2007); Vanessa Beasley, *You, the People: American National Identity in Presidential Rhetoric* (College Station: Texas A&M University Press, 2004); Kevin Michael Deluca and Jennifer Peeples, "From Public Sphere to Public Screen: Democracy, Activism, and the 'Violence' of Seattle," *Critical Studies in Media Communication* 19 (2002): 125–51.

3. International Institute for Democracy and Electoral Assistance (International IDEA) Strömsborg, SE-103 34 Stockholm, Sweden, 2008, http://www.idea.int/vt/survey/voter_turnout_pop2-2.cfm.

4. Michael C. McGee, "'Not Men, but Measures': The Origins and Import of an Ideological Principle," *Quarterly Journal of Speech* 64 (1978): 141–54, 142;

Michael C. McGee, "In Search of 'The People': A Rhetorical Alternative," *Quarterly Journal of Speech* 61 (1975): 235–50.

5. The goal of *Founding Fictions* is not to try to examine all of the dominant ideas or aspects of culture and society between 1764 and 1845, but to examine specifically how Americans described and debated their republican government. It tells the story of how Americans invented a narrative to support their constitutional order; it is the story of how America explained its republicanism to itself. Liberalism and Protestantism certainly influenced the founders, but they are not a part of the story of the republican fiction, and therefore are not the focus of this book. Americans knew themselves to have radically and revolutionarily changed their political system from a monarchy to a republic. Therefore, we must accept their own judgment of what they had done between 1776 and 1789. Taking this perspective is not meant to diminish the claims of those who would argue that liberalism and Protestantism greatly influenced Americans; it is meant to meet our forebears on their own terms and to assess the governments they thought they had created. For more on the founders' relationship to religion see Isaac Kramnick and R. Laurence Moore, *The Godless Constitution: The Case against Religious Correctness* (New York: Norton, 1997).

6. Kenneth Burke, *Rhetoric of Motives* (Berkley: University of California Press, 1969), 41.

7. Maurice Charland, "Constitutive Rhetoric: The Case of the Peuple Québécois," *Quarterly Journal of Speech* 73 (1987): 133–50; James Boyd White, *When Words Lose Their Meaning: Constitutions and Reconstitutions of Language, Character, and Community* (Chicago: University of Chicago Press, 1984), 286–91; Ernesto Laclau and Chantel Mouffe, *Hegemony and Socialist Strategy: Toward a Radical Democratic Politics* (London: Verso, 1985); James Jasinski, "A Constitutive Framework for Rhetorical Historiography: Toward an Understanding of the Discursive (Re)constitution of 'Constitution' in *The Federalist Papers*," in *Doing Rhetorical History: Concepts and Cases*, ed. K. J. Turner (Tuscaloosa: University of Alabama Press, 1998), 72–92; James Jasinski "Constituting Antebellum African American Identity: Resistance, Violence, and Masculinity in Henry Highland Garnet's (1843) 'Address to the Slaves,'" *Quarterly Journal of Speech* 93 (2007): 27–57; Nathaniel I. Cordova, "The Constitutive Force of the Catecismo del Pueblo in Puerto Rico's Popular Democratic Party Campaign of 1938–1940," *Quarterly Journal of Speech* 90 (2004): 212–33; Michael Leff and Ebony Utley, "Instrumental and Constitutive Rhetoric in Martin Luther King Jr.'s 'Letter from Birmingham Jail,'" *Rhetoric and Public Affairs* 7 (2004): 37–51.

8. For more on the debate among rhetoricians between texts and contexts see Michael C. Leff and Fred J. Kauffeld, eds., *Texts in Context: Critical Dialogues on Significant Episodes in American Political Rhetoric* (Davis, Calif.: Hermagoras Press, 1989); Barbara Warnick, "Leff in Context: What Is the Critic's Role?" *Quarterly Journal of Speech* 78 (1992): 232–38; Michael Leff, "Things Made by Words: Reflections on Textual Criticism," *Quarterly Journal of Speech* 78 (1992): 223–31; Steven Mailloux, "Rhetorical Hermeneutics Revisited," *Text and Performance Quarterly* 11

(1991): 233–49; Robert J. Branham and W. Barnett Pearce, "Between Text and Context: Toward a Rhetoric of Contextual Reconstruction," *Quarterly Journal of Speech* 71 (1985): 19–37; Martha Solomon, "The Things We Study: Texts and Their Interaction," *Communication Monographs* 60 (1993): 62–69; Michael Calvin McGee, "Text, Context, and the Fragmentation of Contemporary Culture," *Western Journal of Speech Communication* 54 (1990): 274–89; Raymie E. McKerrow, "Critical Rhetoric: Theory and Praxis," *Communication Monographs* 56 (1989): 91–111; Kent A. Ono and John M. Sloop, "The Critique of Vernacular Discourse," *Communication Monographs* 62 (1995): 19–47; Michael Leff, "Textual Criticism: The Legacy of G. P. Mohrmann," *Quarterly Journal of Speech* 72 (1986): 377–90; G. P. Mohrmann and Michael C. Leff, "Lincoln at Cooper Union: A Rationale for Neo-Classical Criticism," *Quarterly Journal of Speech* 60 (1974): 459–68; Michael C. Leff and Gerald P. Mohrmann, "Lincoln at Cooper Union: A Rhetorical Analysis of the Text," *Quarterly Journal of Speech* 60 (1974): 346–59.

9. Kathleen Turner, ed., *Doing Rhetorical History: Concepts and Cases* (Tuscaloosa: University of Alabama Press, 1998), 2.

10. Hayden White's *The Historical Imagination in Nineteenth-Century Europe* (Baltimore: Johns Hopkins University Press, 1973) and *Tropics of Discourse: Essays in Cultural Criticism* (Baltimore: Johns Hopkins University Press, 1978) have greatly influenced my understanding of the writing of history.

11. Stephen J. Hartnett, *Democratic Dissent and the Cultural Fictions of Antebellum America* (Urbana: University of Illinois Press, 2002), 7.

12. Conversations with Ted George helped me to think about the obligations that we all have as caretakers of ideas.

13. Bonnie Dow has argued that rhetorical scholars should "discard the vocabulary of discovery and science" and "embrace the vocabulary of creation and art," in short, "that we think of ourselves not as investigators of rhetoric but as creators of it." "Response: Criticism and Authority in the Artistic Mode," *Western Journal of Communication* 65 (2001): 336–47, 339. Doing so acknowledges both the authority of the critic as the creator of a specific text—in this case I have created a rhetorical history and called it the story of America's founding fictions—and the obligation that the critic has to account for the choices that have been made in the creation of his or her text. Dow rests her argument on three propositions that apply here: first, texts and contexts are created, not discovered; second, there is no such thing as the "actual" audience; and third, the critic gives authority to method, not the reverse. Kathleen Turner has likewise argued that the false claim of objectivity has no place in rhetorical history, for "human beings are not objects but subjects; thus we can only be subjective." Turner, *Doing Rhetorical History,* 8.

14. I was fortunate to conduct archival research at the American Antiquarian Society, the Houghton Library at Harvard University, the Concord Free Public Library, the University of Illinois Rare Books Room, the Phillips Library and Peabody Essex Museum, the Library of Congress, the Newberry Library, the Massachusetts Historical Society, and the Berea Historical Society.

15. Quentin Skinner, "Meaning and Understanding in the History of Ideas," *History and Theory* 8 (1969): 3–53; Quentin Skinner, "On Performing and Explaining Linguistic Actions," *Philosophical Quarterly* 21 (1971): 1–21; Quentin Skinner, "Conventions and the Understanding of Speech Acts," *Philosophical Quarterly* 20 (1970): 118–38; J. G. A. Pocock, "Verbalizing a Political Act: Toward a Politics of Speech," *Political Theory* 1 (1973): 27–45; J. G. A. Pocock, "The Reconstruction of Discourse: Towards the Historiography of Political Thought," *MLN* 96 (1981): 959–80; Peter L. Janssen, "Political Thought as Traditionary Action: The Critical Response to Skinner and Pocock," *History and Theory* 24 (1985): 115–46; Gad Prudovsky, "Can We Ascribe to Past Thinkers Concepts They Had No Linguistic Means to Express?" *History and Theory* 36 (1997): 15–31; John Patrick Diggins, "The Oyster and the Pearl: The Problem of Contexualism in Intellectual History," *History and Theory* 23 (1984): 151–69; John E. Toews, "Intellectual History after the Linguistic Turn: The Autonomy of Meaning and the Irreducibility of Experience," *American Historical Review* 92 (1987): 879–907; Robert W. T. Martin, "Context and Contradiction: Toward a Political Theory of Conceptual Change," *Political Research Quarterly* 50 (1997): 413–36.

16. A great "quick read" of the founding generation is Joseph Ellis, *Founding Brothers: The Revolutionary Generation* (New York: Knopf, 2000). See also David McCullough, *John Adams* (New York: Simon and Schuster, 2001); John Ferling, *Adams vs. Jefferson: The Tumultuous Election of 1800* (Oxford: Oxford University Press, 2004); John C. Miller, *Sam Adams: Pioneer in Propaganda* (Stanford: Stanford University Press, 1936); John P. Kaminski, *George Clinton: Yeoman Politician of the New Republic* (Madison, Wisc.: Madison House, 1993); H. W. Brands, *The First American: The Life and Times of Benjamin Franklin* (New York: Anchor Books, 2000); Walter Isaacson, *Benjamin Franklin: An American Life* (New York: Simon and Schuster, 2003); Broadus Mitchell, *Alexander Hamilton: A Concise Biography* (Oxford: Oxford University Press, 1976); Ron Chernow, *Alexander Hamilton* (New York: Penguin Press, 2004); Moses Coit Tyler, *Patrick Henry* (Colorado Springs: Patrick Henry University Press, 1888/2001); George Pellew, *John Jay* (New York: Chelsea House, 1980); Merrill D. Peterson, *Thomas Jefferson and the New Nation: A Biography* (Oxford: Oxford University Press, 1970); Dumas Malone, *Jefferson and His Time,* 5 vols. (Boston: Little, Brown, 1970); Roger G. Kennedy, *Mr. Jefferson's Lost Cause: Land, Farmers, Slavery, and the Louisiana Purchase* (Oxford: Oxford University Press, 2003); Adrienne Koch and William Peden, eds., *The Life and Selected Writings of Thomas Jefferson* (New York: Modern Library, 1998); Daniel J. Boorstin, *The Lost World of Thomas Jefferson* (Chicago: University of Chicago Press, 1993); Roger G. Kennedy, *Burr, Hamilton, and Jefferson: A Study in Character* (Oxford: Oxford University Press, 1999); Noble E. Cunningham Jr., *In Pursuit of Reason: The Life of Thomas Jefferson* (New York: Ballantine Books, 1987); Merrill D. Peterson, *Adams and Jefferson: A Revolutionary Dialogue* (Oxford: Oxford University Press, 1976); E. M. Halliday, *Understanding Thomas Jefferson* (New York: HarperCollins, 2001); William Maclay, *The Diary of William Maclay and Other Notes on Senate De-*

bates, March 4, 1789–March 3, 1791, ed. Kenneth R. Bowling and Helen E. Veit (Baltimore: Johns Hopkins University Press, 1988); Drew R. McCoy, *The Last of the Fathers: James Madison and the Republican Legacy* (Cambridge: Cambridge University Press, 1989); Ralph Ketcham, *James Madison: A Biography* (Charlottesville: University Press of Virginia, 1990); Harry Ammon, *James Monroe: The Quest for National Identity* (Charlottesville: University of Virginia Press, 1990); Richard Brookhiser, *Gentleman Revolutionary: Gouverneur Morris, the Rake Who Wrote the Constitution* (New York: Free Press, 2003); Harvey J. Kaye, *Thomas Paine and the Promise of America* (New York: Hill and Wang, 2005); Esther Forbes, *Paul Revere and the World He Lived In* (Boston: Mariner Books, 1942/1999); Douglas Southall Freeman, *Washington* (New York: Simon and Schuster, 1968/1992); Bernard Claude Moore Fuess, *Daniel Webster* (Hamden, Conn.: Archon Books, 1963). For the second generation of Americans see Paul C. Nagel, *John Quincy Adams: A Public Life, a Private Life* (Cambridge: Harvard University Press, 1997); Arthur M Schlesinger Jr., *The Age of Jackson* (Boston: Little, Brown, 1945); H. W. Brands, *Andrew Jackson: His Life and Times* (New York: Doubleday, 2005); Robert V. Remini, *Andrew Jackson* (New York: HarperCollins, 1969); John Niven, *Martin Van Buren: The Romantic Age of American Politics* (Newtown, Conn.: American Political Biography Press, 1983/2004); Freeman Cleaves, *Old Tippecanoe: William Henry Harrison and His Times* (Newtown, Conn.: American Political Biography Press, 1939/2000); Oliver Perry Chitwood, *John Tyler: Champion of the Old South* (Newtown, Conn.: American Political Biography Press, 1939/2003); Phillip S. Klein, *President James Buchanan: A Biography* (Newtown, Conn.: American Political Biography Press, 1962/1999). Also useful are Douglass Adair, *Fame and the Founding Fathers* (Indianapolis: Liberty Fund, 1974); Stanley Elkins and Eric McKitrick, *The Age of Federalism: The Early American Republic, 1788–1800* (Oxford: Oxford University Press, 1993); Michael Schudson, *The Good Citizen: A History of American Civic Life* (New York: The Free Press, 1998); Marvin Meyers, *The Jacksonian Persuasion: Politics and Belief* (Stanford: Stanford University Press, 1957); Gary Rosen, *American Compact: James Madison and the Problem of Founding* (Lawrence: University Press of Kansas, 1999); Joanne B. Freeman, *Affairs of Honor: National Politics in the New Republic* (New Haven: Yale University Press, 2001); David P. Szatmary, *Shays' Rebellion: The Making of an Agrarian Insurrection* (Amherst: University of Massachusetts Press, 1980); Bernard Bailyn, *Faces of Revolution: Personalities and Themes in the Struggle for American Independence* (New York: Vintage Books, 1992).

17. "In addition to the historical role of movement studies, 'movement' itself may be a useful notion as a metaphor. Rhetorical behavior of various kinds might be studied productively by examining it through the perspective which this metaphor provides. In this way, we may be able to see the acts in a different light and thereby enhance our critical understanding and appreciation." David Zarefsky, "A Skeptical View of Movement Studies," *Central States Speech Journal* 31 (1980): 245–54, 254. For the work of rhetorical scholars on social movements, see Leland M. Griffin, "The Rhetoric of Historical Movements," *Quarterly Journal of Speech* 38

(1952): 184–88; Franklyn S. Haiman, "The Rhetoric of the Streets: Some Legal and Ethical Considerations," *Quarterly Journal of Speech* 53 (1967): 99–114; Robert L. Scott and Donald K. Smith, "The Rhetoric of Confrontation," *Quarterly Journal of Speech* 55 (1969): 1–8; Herbert W. Simons, "Requirements, Problems, and Strategies: A Theory of Persuasion for Social Movements," *Quarterly Journal of Speech* 56 (1970): 1–11; Ralph R. Smith and Russel Windes, "The Innovational Movement: A Rhetorical Theory," *Speech Monographs* 40 (1973): 123–35; Robert S. Cathcart, "Movements: Confrontation as Rhetorical Form," *Southern Speech Journal* 43 (1978): 233–47; Malcom O. Sillars, "Defining Social Movements Rhetorically: Casting the Widest Net," *Southern Speech Communication Journal* 46 (1980): 17–32; Michael Calvin McGee, "'Social Movement': Phenomenon or Meaning?" *Central States Speech Journal* 31 (1980) 233–44; Stephen E. Lucas, "Coming to Terms with Movement Studies," *Central States Speech Journal* 31 (1980): 255–66; James R. Andrews, "History and Theory in the Study of the Rhetoric of Social Movements," *Central States Speech Journal* 31 (1980): 274–81; Charles J. Stewart, "A Functional Approach to the Rhetoric of Social Movements," *Central States Speech Journal* 31 (1980): 298–305; David Zarefsky, "President Johnson's War on Poverty: The Rhetoric of Three 'Establishment' Movements," *Communication Monographs* 44 (1977): 352–73.

Chapter 1

1. George W. Bush, "President's Radio Address," August 19, 2006, http://www.whitehouse.gov/news/releases/2006/08/20060819.html. Picked at random from a keyword search of "democracy" in President Bush's speeches, messages, and addresses.

2. For recent discussions of the relationship between democracy and terrorism in Bush's war rhetoric see Stephen John Hartnett and Laura Ann Stengrim's *Globalization and Empire: The U.S. Invasion of Iraq, Free Markets, and the Twilight of Democracy* (Tuscaloosa: University of Alabama Press, 2006) and Robert L. Ivie's *Democracy and America's War on Terror* (Tuscaloosa: University of Alabama Press, 2006). According to Stephen J. Hartnett and Jennifer R. Mercieca, "In fact, in a now infamous interview with Ron Suskind, a White House advisor chastised Suskind and his kind for being foolish members of 'the reality-based community.' Whereas most of us believe in some norms of evidence, or at least in fair argument and counterargument, the White House adviser said, "We're an empire now, and when we act, we create our own reality. . . . We're history's actors . . . and you, all of you, will be left to study what we do." Virilio's concern about the "abolition of the appearance of facts" is confirmed here as simply what politics in the empire have become: facts are dead, reality is for losers, we are so soaked in "disinformation by excess information" that we live now in what can only be called an age of make believe." "'A Discovered Dissembler Can Achieve Nothing Great': Or, Four Theses on the Death of Presidential Rhetoric in an Age of Empire," *Presidential Studies Quarterly* 37 (2007): 599–621, 608.

3. "By 'god term' we mean that expression about which all other expressions are ranked as subordinate and serving dominations and powers. Its force imparts to the others their lesser degree of force, and fixes the scale by which degrees of comparison are understood. . . . If one can 'make it stick,' it will validate almost anything. It would be difficult to think of any type of person or of any institution which could not be recommended to the public through the enhancing power of this word." Richard M. Weaver, *The Ethics of Rhetoric* (Davis, Calif.: Hermagoras Press, 1985), 212.

4. "The first phase of separation comprises symbolic behavior signifying the detachment of the individual or group either from an earlier fixed point in the social structure or a set of cultural conditions (a 'state'); during the intervening liminal period, the state of the ritual subject (the 'passenger') is ambiguous; he passes through a realm that has few or none of the attributes of the past or coming state; in the third phase the passage is consummated. The ritual subject, individual or corporate, is in a stable state once more and, by virtue of this, has rights and obligations of a clearly defined and 'structural' type, and is expected to behave in accordance with certain customary norms and ethical standards." Victor W. Turner, *The Forest of Symbols: Aspects of Ndebu Ritual* (Ithaca: Cornell University Press, 1967), 94. See also Charles E. Morris III, "Contextual Twilight/Critical Liminality: J. M. Barrie's Courage at St. Andrews, 1922," *Quarterly Journal of Speech* 82 (1996): 207–28.

5. Fisher Ames, "The Mire of Democracy," *The Boston Athenaeum,* 1805, *Works of Fisher Ames,* vol. 1, ed. Seth Ames (Indianapolis: Liberty Classics, 1983), 3–7. Emphasis in original.

6. Hannah Arendt, for example, premises her view of politics and community on the capacity of the individual to act: "The political realm rises directly out of acting together, the 'sharing of words and deeds.' therefore, action not only has the most intimate relationship to the public part of the world common to us all, but is the one activity which constitutes it." *The Human Condition* (Chicago: University of Chicago Press, 1958), 198.

7. The rhetoric/dialectic/poetic distinction is discussed in John Louis Lucaites and Celeste Michelle Condit, "Re-constructing Narrative Theory: A Functional Perspective," *Journal of Communication* 35 (1985): 90–108.

8. According to Hanna Fenichel Pitkin, "Our cultural arrangements do not just grow naturally, like a tree; they are founded, practiced, and enacted by people. But [Hannah] Arendt thought that we resist acknowledging the degree to which the patterns by which we live are our own doing—if not originally created by us, nevertheless sustained right now by nothing more than ourselves. . . . If our lost treasure had merely been inadvertently misplaced, if our failure to understand action and freedom were simply a matter of ignorance, then teaching about the treasure might suffice to restore it. They would fit one traditional image of political theory's task: to set forth a vision of the shining city on a hill toward which one should strive. But what if what keeps us from that city, from the treasure, is some-

thing about ourselves—something we are doing—then merely extolling and explicating the goal, no matter how eloquently, may not suffice. We may need a better understanding of what is in the way: of how and why we block our own and each others' freedom." *The Attack of the Blob: Hannah Arendt's Concept of the Social* (Chicago: University of Chicago Press, 1998), 2–3.

9. James Arnt Aune, *Selling the Free Market: The Rhetoric of Economic Correctness* (New York: Guilford, 2002), 81; G. Thomas Goodnight, "The Personal, Technical, and Public Spheres of Argument: A Speculative Inquiry into the Art of Public Deliberation," *Journal of the American Forensic Association* 18 (1982): 214–27.

10. Kenneth Burke, *The Philosophy of Literary Form* (Berkeley: University of California Press, 1941), 100–111.

11. See F. R. Ankersmit, *Aesthetic Politics: Political Philosophy beyond Fact and Value* (Palo Alto: Stanford University Press, 1996), for an excellent recent example of an analysis of political theory as poetical, dialectical, and rhetorical language.

12. Michel Foucault, *The Foucault Effect: Studies in Governmentality,* ed. Graham Burchell (Chicago: University of Chicago Press, 1991); Michel Foucault, *The Politics of Truth,* ed. Sylvere Lotringer (New York: Semiotext(e), 1997).

13. "Whereas liberty was the concern of the elites in American society, equality became the concern of the masses." Regina Morantz, "'Democracy' and 'Republic' in American Ideology, 1787–1840" (Ph.D. diss., Columbia University, 1971), 2.

14. Arthur O. Lovejoy, *Great Chain of Being* (Cambridge: Harvard University Press, 1936).

15. Ivie, *Democracy and America's War on Terror,* 50.

16. Ibid., 6.

17. Jacques Rancière, *Hatred of Democracy,* trans. Steve Corcoran (London: Verso, 2007), 2.

18. Ibid., 33.

19. Ibid., 40–43.

20. Robert Dahl, *Democracy and Its Critics* (New Haven: Yale University Press, 1991); Plato, *Republic,* Book VIII, 557a.

21. Aristotle, *Politics:* "Deviations from the constitutions mentioned are tyranny corresponding to kingship, oligarchy to aristocracy, and democracy to constitutional government; for tyranny is monarchy ruling in the interest of the monarch, oligarchy government in the interest of the rich, democracy government in the interest of the poor, and none of these forms governs with regard to the profit of the community" (ed. Ernest Barker [Oxford: Oxford University Press, 1946], 3.1279b).

22. David Held, *Models of Democracy,* 2nd ed. (Palo Alto: Stanford University Press, 1996), 42.

23. Roy N. Lokken, "The Concept of Democracy in Colonial Political Thought," *William and Mary Quarterly* 16 (1959): 568–80, 570; Russell L. Hanson, *The Democratic Imagination in America: Conversations with Our Past* (Princeton: Princeton Uni-

versity Press, 1985), 56; see also George E. Marcus and Russell L. Hanson, *Reconsidering the Democratic Public* (University Park: Pennsylvania State University Press, 1993).

24. "Letters in Answer to the Farmer, Letter VII," *Boston Evening Post* May 15, 1769, 3.

25. James Madison, Federalist 10, *The Federalist Papers,* ed. Charles R. Kesler and Clinton Rossiter (New York: New American Library, 1961), 49.

26. Henry George Liddell and Robert Scott translate *misodemia* as "hatred of democracy" in their *An Intermediate Greek-English Lexicon* (Oxford: Claredon Press, 1889), online at www.perseus.tufts.edu. *Misodemia* can be found in the works of Aeschines (*Speech on the Embassy*), Plutarch (*Lives*), Isocrates (*Antidosis, Areopagiticus*), Plato (*Republic*), Dinarchus (*Against Demosthenes*), Aristophanes (*Wasps*), Andocides (*Against Alcibiades*), Lycurgus (*Against Leocrates*), and Xenophon (*Hellenica*). For example, Andocides argues in *Against Alcibiades,* "ho de pantôn deinotaton esti, toioutos ôn hôs eunous tôi dêmôi tous logous poieitai, kai tous allous oligarchikous kai misodêmous apokalei" (But most monstrous of all is the fact that a man of his character should talk as though he were a friend of the people, and call others oligarchs and foes of the democracy. Yes, although he himself deserves death for behaving as he does, he is chosen by you to proceed against any whose sympathies conflict with yours; and he poses as guardian of the constitution, in spite of the fact that he refuses to be the equal of, or but little superior to, his fellows. So completely, indeed, does he despise you that he spends his time flattering you in a body and insulting you individually). *Minor Attic Orators,* trans. K. J. Maidment (Cambridge: Harvard University Press, 1968), www.perseus.tufts.edu.

27. Cabot to Timothy Pickering, February 14, 1804, in *Documents Relating to New England Federalism, 1800–1815,* ed. John Quincy Adams and Henry Adams (Boston: Little, Brown, 1877), 346–47.

28. "If there have been those who doubted whether a confederated representative democracy were a government competent to the wise and orderly management of the common concerns of a mighty nation, those doubts have been dispelled." John Quincy Adams, Inaugural Address, March 4, 1825, in *Inaugural Addresses of the Presidents of the United States: From George Washington to Barack Obama* (Washington, D.C.: Government Printing Office, 1989), www.bartleby.com/124/pres22.html.

29. On the life of Andrew Jackson, see the following: Arthur M. Schlesinger Jr., *The Age of Jackson* (Boston: Back Bay Books, 1945); John William Ward, *Andrew Jackson: Symbol for an Age* (London: Oxford University Press, 1953); Robert V. Remini, *Andrew Jackson* (New York: HarperCollins, 1969); Marvin Meyers, *The Jacksonian Persuasion: Politics and Belief* (Stanford: Stanford University Press, 1957); H. W. Brands, *Andrew Jackson: His Life and Times* (New York; Doubleday, 2005); Sean Wilentz, *The Rise of American Democracy: Jefferson to Lincoln* (New York: Norton, 2005).

30. Morantz, "'Democracy' and 'Republic' in American Ideology," 222.

31. George Sidney Camp, *Democracy* (New York: Harper and Brothers, Cliff-St., 1841), 3.

32. For example, according to James Wilson's reflections on the debates of the Constitutional Convention, "While a federal republic removed one difficulty, it introduced another, since there existed not any precedent to assist our deliberations; for, though there are many single governments, both ancient and modern, the history and principles of which are faithfully preserved and well understood, a perfect confederation of independent states is a system hitherto unknown." "Speech to the Pennsylvania Ratifying Convention," November 24, 1787, *The Documentary History of the Ratification of the Constitution,* 22 vols. to date (Madison: State Historical Society of Wisconsin, 1976–), 3:342 [hereafter cited as *DHRC*].

33. The work of poststructuralists like Derrida informs this account of word meaning; yet I would hasten to point out that members of the founding generation wrote about the problems of word meaning without the benefit of high theory.

34. Adams to Warren, July 20, 1807, *Correspondence between John Adams and Mercy Otis Warren,* ed. Charles F. Adams (New York: Arno Press, 1972), 338; see also Rosemarie Zagarri, *A Woman's Dilemma: Mercy Otis Warren and the American Revolution* (Wheeling, Ill.: Harlan Davidson, 1995).

35. Linda Kerber, "The Republican Mother: Women and the Enlightenment-An American Perspective," *American Quarterly* 29 (1976): 187–205. For example, Jabez D. Hammond lampooned the wanton use of "republican" as an adjective in his description of Republican efforts to institute banks in New York: "A large majority of the petitioners for the State Bank, claimed to be republicans; they therefore asked for a charter upon party grounds, as a political measure, upon the assumed principle, that the bank, if chartered, was to be a republican bank! How supremely absurd was this pretence! They might as well have talked of republican wheat or corn, of republican air and water, as of republican money or a republican bank." *The History of Political Parties in the State of New York, from the Ratification of the Federal Constitution to December, 1840,* vol. 1 (Buffalo: Phinney, 1850), 194.

36. *American Lyceum, with the Proceedings of the Convention Held in New York, May 4, 1831, to Organize the National Department of the Institution* (Boston: Hiram Tupper, 1831), 3. See also Jennifer Rose Mercieca, "'We the People' and the Rhetorics of Republicanism in America, 1776–1840" (Ph.D. diss, University of Illinois, 2003); Angela Ray, *The Lyceum and Public Culture in the Nineteenth Century United States* (East Lansing: Michigan State University Press, 2005).

37. Mercy Otis Warren, *History of the Rise, Progress, and Termination of the American Revolution,* ed. Lester H. Cohen, 2 vols. (Indianapolis: Liberty Fund, 1994), 2:601.

38. Richard A. Lanham, *A Handlist of Rhetorical Terms,* 2nd ed. (Berkeley: University of California Press, 1991), 141.

39. For a non-elite attempt to define republicanism and expose the elite machinations of power, see William Manning's 1798 *Key of Libberty.* Jennifer R. Mer-

cieca and James Arnt Aune, "A Vernacular Republican Rhetoric: William Manning's *Key of Libberty,*" *Quarterly Journal of Speech* 91 (2005): 119–43.

40. Daniel T. Rodgers, "Keywords: A Reply," *Journal of the History of Ideas* 49 (1988): 669–76, 671; see also Daniel T. Rodgers, *Contested Truths: Keywords in American Politics Since Independence* (Cambridge: Harvard University Press, 1998).

41. Steven Lukes, "A Reply to K. I. Macdonald," *British Journal of Political Science* 7 (1977): 418–19, 418; Steven Lukes, *Power: A Radical View* (London: Macmillan, 1974).

42. Kenneth Burke, *Language as Symbolic Action* (Berkeley: University of California Press, 1966), 50.

43. Thomas Gustafson, *Representative Words: Politics, Literature, and the American Language, 1776–1865* (Cambridge: Cambridge University Press, 1992), 138.

44. Scholars of political theory, following W. B. Gallie, have often noted the "essentially contested" nature of many of the key terms of political life: power, justice, democracy, rights, freedom, etc. "There are concepts, which are essentially contested," writes Gallie, "concepts the proper use of which inevitably involves endless disputes about their proper uses on the part of their users." As Christine Swanton explains, we may properly label a term "essentially contested" when the rhetor recognizes the contestation, when such a contest over proper meaning is inevitable, and when there is no clear method for determining which use of the concept is the correct or the best usage. Gallie, "Essentially Contested Concepts," *Proceedings of the Aristotelian Society* 56 (1955–56): 167–98, 189; Swanton, "On the 'Essential Contestedness' of Political Concepts," *Ethics* 95 (1985): 811–27.

45. Morantz, "'Democracy' and 'Republic' in American Ideology," 8.

46. Bernard Bailyn, *The Ideological Origins of the American Revolution* (Cambridge: Harvard University Press, 1967), 22–23.

47. Ibid., 35.

48. James Madison, Federalist 39, *The Federalist Papers,* 208.

49. W. Paul Adams, "Republicanism in Political Rhetoric before 1776," *Political Science Quarterly* 85 (1970): 397–421; Lance Banning, *The Jeffersonian Persuasion: Evolution of a Party Ideology* (Ithaca: Cornell University Press, 1978), 83.

50. *Journals of Congress,* May 10, 1776, 342.

51. *Records of the Continental Congress,* 1046.

52. *Circular Letter* in 1779 and an August 22, 1781, *Committee Report on the Exposition of the Confederation.*

53. Thomas Jefferson, *The Autobiography,* in *Thomas Jefferson: Writings,* ed. Merrill D. Peterson (New York: Library of America, 1984), 37.

54. *The Federal and State Constitutions Colonial Charters, and Other Organic Laws of the States, Territories, and Colonies Now or Heretofore Forming the United States of America Compiled and Edited Under the Act of Congress of June 30, 1906,* ed. Francis Newton Thorpe (Washington, D.C.: Government Printing Office, 1909).

55. The Preamble of the 1789 Constitution claimed that "we, the People of the United States of America" formed the new government; article 1, section 2, clause

1, granted the people the right to choose their representatives; article 1, section 2, clause 3, fixed the ratio of representatives to constituents (not more than 30,000 to 1); article 4, section 4, guaranteed every state in America a "republican form of government"; article 1, section 9, clauses 8 and 9, respectively, prevented the United States or individual states from granting any "Title of Nobility"; and article 1, section 2, clause 1, article 1, section 3, clause 1, and article 2, section 1, clause 1, each fixed the number of years elected officials could serve before they would have to face reelection (representative, two years; president, four years; senator, six years). All of these features were explicitly republican.

56. For the constitutive role of rhetoric see Maurice Charland, "Constitutive Rhetoric: The Case of the Peuple Québécois," *Quarterly Journal of Speech* 73 (1987): 133–50; James Boyd White, *When Words Lose Their Meaning: Constitutions and Reconstitution of Language, Character, and Community* (Chicago: University of Chicago Press, 1984); James Jasinski, "A Constitutive Framework for Rhetorical Historiography: Toward an Understanding of the Discursive (Re)constitution of 'Constitution' in *The Federalist Papers*," in *Doing Rhetorical History: Concepts and Cases,* ed. Kathleen Turner (Tuscaloosa: University of Alabama Press, 2003), 72–95; Louis Althusser, "Ideology and Ideological State Apparatuses," in *Contemporary Critical Theory,* ed. Dan Latimer (San Diego: Harcourt, 1989), 97.

57. Edmund S. Morgan, *Inventing the People: The Rise of Popular Sovereignty in England and America* (New York: Norton, 1988), 13–15.

58. J. M. Balkin, *Cultural Software: A Theory of Ideology* (New Haven: Yale University Press, 1998), 188.

59. Aristotle, *Poetics,* trans. Gerald F. Else (Ann Arbor: University of Michigan Press, 1967); Paul Ricoeur, *Time and Narrative,* 3 vols. (Chicago: University of Chicago Press, 1984–85); Walter R. Fisher, *Human Communication as Narration: Toward a Philosophy of Reason, Value, and Action* (Columbia: University of South Carolina Press, 1987); Walter R. Fisher, "Narration as Human Communication Paradigm: The Case of Public Moral Argument," *Communication Monographs* 51 (1984): 1–22; Walter R. Fisher, "The Narrative Paradigm: An Elaboration," *Communication Monographs* 52 (1985): 347–67; Walter R. Fisher, "The Narrative Paradigm: In the Beginning," *Journal of Communication* 35 (1985): 74–89; Walter R. Fisher, "The Narrative Paradigm and the Assessment of Historical Texts," *Argumentation and Advocacy* 25 (1988): 49–53; Walter R. Fisher, "Clarifying the Narrative Paradigm," *Communication Monographs* 56 (1989): 55–58; Walter R. Fisher, "Narrative Rationality and the Logic of Scientific Discourse," *Argumentation* 8 (1994): 21–32; Arran Gare, "The Primordial Role of Stories in Human Self-Creation," *Cosmos and History: The Journal of Natural and Social Philosophy* 3 (2007): 93–114; C. Jan Swearington, "Narration of Dialogue and Narration within Dialogue: The Transition from Story to Logic," in *Narrative Thought and Narration within Dialogue,* ed. Bruce K. Britton and Anthony D. Pellegrini (Hillsdale, N.J.: Lawrence Earlbaum, 1990), 173–97.

60. M. M. Bakhtin, *Dialogic Imagination: Four Essays* (Austin: University of Texas Press, 1982), 282. "In point of fact, word is a two-sided act. It is determined equally by whose word it is and for whom it is meant. As word, it is precisely the product of the reciprocal relationship between speaker and listener, addresser and addressee. Each and every word expresses the 'one' in relation to the 'other.' I give myself verbal shape from another's point of view, ultimately, from the point of view of the community to which I belong. A word is a bridge thrown between myself and another. If one end of the bridge depends on me, then the other depends on my addressee. A word is territory shared by both addresser and addressee, by the speaker and his interlocutor." V. N. Volosinov, *Marxism and the Philosophy of Language* (Cambridge: Harvard University Press, 1986), 86.

61. As the founding generation grew into retirement, they squabbled over who should get credit for which extraordinary act of invention. The last surviving signers of the Declaration of Independence—John Adams, Charles Carroll, and Thomas Jefferson—got to have the last word on that document; James Madison got to have the last word on the Constitutional Convention because he retained possession of the convention's *Notes.*

62. Jefferson to Madison, September 6, 1789, *Memoirs, Correspondence, and Private Papers of Thomas Jefferson,* ed. Thomas Jefferson Randolph, 4 vols. (London: Henry Colburn and Richard Bentley, 1829), 3:27–31.

63. Mercieca and Aune, "A Vernacular Republican Rhetoric."

64. John Adams, *Autobiography,* June 2, 1775, *The Spirit of '76,* ed. Henry Steele Commager and Richard B. Morris (New York: Castle Books, 1958), 381.

65. James Madison, *Notes of Debates in the Federal Convention of 1787* (New York: Norton, 1987), 70.

66. This is supported by Robert A. Dahl's "criteria for a democratic process" in *Democracy and Its Critics.* Dahl believes that his four criteria represent the "ideal standards" of a truly democratic process: effective participation, voting equality at the decisive stage, enlightened understanding, and control of the agenda (108–12).

67. Louis Althusser, *Lenin and Philosophy* (New York: New Left Books, 1971), 109–19.

68. For more on the relationship between rhetoric and ideology, see Joshua Gunn and Shaun Treat, "Zombie Trouble: A Propaedeutic on Ideological Subjectification and the Unconscious," *Quarterly Journal of Speech* 91 (2005) 144–74; Mary Frances Hopkins, "The Rhetoric of Heteroglossia in Flannery O'Connor's *Wise Blood,*" *Quarterly Journal of Speech* 75 (1989): 198–212; Martha Solomon, "Ideology as Rhetorical Constraint: The Anarchist Agitation of 'Red Emma' Goldman," *Quarterly Journal of Speech* 74 (1988): 184–201; William R. Brown, "Attention and the Rhetoric of Social Intervention," *Quarterly Journal of Speech* 68 (1982): 17–28; Michael Calvin McGee, "The 'Ideograph': A Link between Rhetoric and Ideology," *Quarterly Journal of Speech* 66 (1980): 1–17; Edwin Black, "The Second Persona," *Quarterly Journal of Speech* 56 (1970): 109–19; Vanessa B. Beasley, "The

Rhetoric of Ideological Consensus in the United States: American Principles and American Prose in Presidential Inaugurals," *Communication Monographs* 68 (2001): 169–84; James Darsey, "Joe McCarthy's Fantastic Moment," *Communication Monographs* 62 (1995): 65–87.

69. Alasdair MacIntyre, *After Virtue: A Study in Moral Theory* (South Bend, Ind.: University of Notre Dame Press, 1981), 207.

70. Charles Taylor, *Modern Social Imaginaries* (Durham, N.C.: Duke University Press, 2004), 23.

71. J. G. A. Pocock, *Politics, Language, and Time: Essays on Political Thought and History* (Chicago: University of Chicago Press, 1989), 22–23.

72. Northrop Frye, *Anatomy of Criticism: Four Essays* (Princeton: Princeton University Press, 1957). As Hayden White argues, while this simple categorization may seem overly reductionistic on its face, "historical 'stories' tend to fall into the categories elaborated by Frye precisely because the historian is inclined to resist construction of the complex peripeteias which are the novelist's and dramatist's stock in trade." Furthermore, as White argues about his analysis of tropes, the claim here is not that these narratives constitute a "law of discourse" but that by "force of convention" narratives tend to fall into these recognizable patterns. In other words, other kinds of narratives are possible and even likely to occur, but historical writing specifically tends to be cast in one of these four modes. Likewise, as Americans struggled to create, define, and implement their republicanism, they told themselves a story about their relationship to their government that tended to fall into two of these four categories. In my analysis of how Americans described republicanism I have not found that they often told a story of republicanism as either comedy or satire—and it makes good sense that they did not draw from these narratives. Comic narratives are premised on a *temporary* resolution to problems, while satirical narratives are premised on the "ultimate inadequacy" of humans to resolve problems; neither of these would have been useful for Americans who hoped to resolve the problem of tyranny and corruption. White, *Metahistory: The Historical Imagination in Nineteenth-Century Europe* (Baltimore: Johns Hopkins University Press, 1973), 8 n. 6.

73. White, *Metahistory,* 8–9.

74. According to Hayden White, "The Organicist attempts to depict the particulars discerned in the historical field as components of synthetic processes . . . individual entities [are portrayed] as components of processes which aggregate into wholes that are greater than, or qualitatively different from, the sum of their parts." Ibid., 15.

75. Ibid., 9.

76. Ankersmit, *Aesthetic Politics,* 227.

77. D. C. Muecke, *Irony and the Ironic* (London: Methuen, 1970), 15.

78. Friedrich von Schlegel, *The Aesthetic and Miscellaneous Works,* trans. E. J. Millington (London: George Bell and Sons, 1900).

79. K. Burke, *Language as Symbolic Action,* 12; see also Wayne C. Booth, *The Rhetoric of Fiction* (Chicago: University of Chicago Press, 1961); Wayne C. Booth, *A Rhetoric of Irony* (Chicago: University of Chicago Press, 1974).

80. In *Inventing the People,* Morgan does not talk about the "monarchical fiction" or the "republican fiction" as such—these are my own interpretations of his ideas of the "fiction of the King" and the "fiction of the people." W. Paul Adams examined the use of the word "republican" and its variations in American political discourse prior to July 4, 1776, and found that when colonials talked about a republican form of government it was always characterized negatively. Always, that is, until the January 1776 publication of Thomas Paine's *Common Sense:* "For the last time in American history, *republic, republican, republicanism,* and *commonwealth* were used in a pejorative sense. Soon after they became totally ineffective in that capacity." W. P. Adams, "Republicanism in Political Rhetoric before 1776," 411–12.

81. See, for example, Isaac Kramnick, "The 'Great National Discussion': The Discourse of Politics in 1787," *William and Mary Quarterly* 45 (1988): 3–32; Cecelia M. Kenyon, "Men of Little Faith: The Anti-Federalists on the Nature of Representative Government," *William and Mary Quarterly* 12 (1955) 3–43.

82. Kurt W. Ritter, "American Political Rhetoric and the Jeremiad Tradition: Presidential Nomination Acceptance Addresses, 1960–1976," *Central States Speech Journal* 31 (1980): 153–71; Sacvan Bercovitch, *The Rites of Assent: Transformations in the Symbolic Construction of America* (New York: Routledge, 1993), 80. See also Barry Brummett, "Premillennial Apocalyptic as a Rhetorical Genre," *Central States Speech Journal* 35 (1984): 84–93; Richard Johannesen, "The Jeremiad and Jenkin Lloyd Jones," *Communication Monographs* 52 (1985): 156–72; Stephen O'Leary, "A Dramatistic Theory of Apocalyptic Rhetoric," *Quarterly Journal of Speech* 79 (1993): 385–426; John Murphy, "'A Time of Shame and Sorrow': Robert F. Kennedy and the American Jeremiad," *Quarterly Journal of Speech* 76 (1990): 401–14; Ronald Reid, "Apocalypticism and Typology: Rhetorical Dimensions of a Symbolic Reality," *Quarterly Journal of Speech* 69 (1983): 229–48; Margaret Zulick, "The Agon of Jeremiah: On the Dialogic Invention of Prophetic Ethos," *Quarterly Journal of Speech* 78 (1992): 125–48.

83. According to Pennsylvania ratification delegate John Smilie on November 28, 1787, "[Quotes from the Declaration of Independence]. Now, sir, if in the proposed plan, the gentleman [James Wilson] can show any similar security for the civil rights of the people, I shall certainly be relieved from a weight of objection to its adoption, and I sincerely hope, that as he has gone so far, he will proceed to communicate some of the reasons (and undoubtedly they must have been powerful ones) which induced the late Federal Convention to omit a bill of rights, so essential in the opinion of many citizens to a perfect form of government." *DHRC,* 2:385–86.

84. According to J. M. Balkin, "Human beings pick up narrative structures easily from watching and observing events. We naturally seem to create narrative

explanations for events or abstract narratives structures from our experiences. We glean narrative structures from life; we impose narrative order on the world." *Cultural Software,* 188.

85. Douglass Adair, *Fame and the Founding Fathers* (Indianapolis: Liberty Fund, 1974), 16–18.

86. Thomas Jefferson to James Madison, September 6, 1789, *Memoirs, Correspondence and Private Papers of Thomas Jefferson,* 3:28–32.

Chapter 2

1. Adams to Jefferson, August 24, 1815, in Lester J. Cappon, ed., *The Adams-Jefferson Letters: The Complete Correspondence between Thomas Jefferson and Abigail and John Adams,* 2 vols. (Chapel Hill: University of North Carolina Press, 1959), 2:454–56, 455. Adams made a similar argument in 1818. See "To Hezekiah Niles," February 13, 1818, in *The Works of John Adams,* ed. Charles F. Adams (Boston, 1856), 10:282–83. Adams dates the change in the minds of colonials to 1760, the year of the accession of King George III.

2. James Otis, "Of the Political and Civil Rights of the British Colonists," *The North-Carolina Magazine; or, Universal Intelligencer,* November 16–23, 1764, 193–97.

3. J. W. Cooke, "Jefferson on Liberty," *Journal of the History of Ideas* 34 (1973): 563–76; Lance Banning, *The Jefferson Persuasion: Evolution of a Party Ideology* (Ithaca: Cornell University Press, 1978); Douglass G. Adair, *The Intellectual Origins of Jeffersonian Democracy: Republicanism, the Class Struggle, and the Virtuous Farmer,* ed. Mark E. Yellin (Lanham, Md.: Lexington Books, 2000); Gary L. McDowell and Sharon L. Noble, eds., *Reason and Republicanism: Thomas Jefferson's Legacy of Liberty* (Lanham, Md.: Rowman and Littlefield, 1997).

4. According to Mary G. Dietz, late-seventeenth-century British Whig oppositional discourse cast the patriot as one who "defends constitutional rights, reveres liberty, agitates for an end to corruption, and struggles against the outrages of centralized power." "Patriotism," in *Political Innovation and Conceptual Change,* ed. Terence Ball, James Farr, and Russell L. Hanson (New York: Cambridge University Press, 1989), 190. David Armitage observes that "the transformation of patriotism into nationalism has become one of the accepted grand narratives of eighteenth-century British history." Armitage, "A Patriot for Whom? The Afterlives of Bolingbroke's Patriot King," *Journal of British Studies* 36 (1997): 397–418, 397. The best analysis of Bolingbroke's pamphlet is by David Eastwood, who observes: "If political language in general is mutable, the language of patriotism is almost chameleonic. More perhaps than most political concepts, the idea of patriotism is constantly reinvented." "Robert Southey and the Meanings of Patriotism," *Journal of British Studies* 31 (1992): 265–87, 266. I have found only one study of Americans' use of Bolingbroke's pamphlet, but it is excellent: William D. Liddle, "'A Patriot King, or None': Lord Bolingbroke and the American Renunciation of George III," *Journal of American History* 65 (1979): 951–70.

5. Liddle describes Bolingbroke's pamphlet as central to the "Country-tradition"; indeed, it was "one of the most infamous yet innocuous publications of the century." As Gordon Wood argues, "Although the Opposition criticism inevitably tended to be Whiggish, many of the critics were not Whigs at all but old fashioned Tories voicing in common terms with Whig radicals their alienation from a corrupted England." Liddle, "A Patriot King, or None," 956–57; Gordon S. Wood, *The Creation of the American Republic, 1776–1787* (Chapel Hill: University of North Carolina Press, 1998), 14.

6. Liddle, "A Patriot King, or None," 956–57.

7. Henry St. John Bolingbroke, *The Idea of a Patriot King,* in *Bolingbroke: Political Writings,* ed. David Armitage (New York: Cambridge University Press), 217–94, 272; Richard Hofstadter, *The Idea of the Party System: The Rise of Legitimate Opposition in the United States, 1780–1840* (Berkeley: University of California Press, 1969), 20.

8. Liddle, "A Patriot King, or None," 968.

9. Stephen Browne also makes this connection between Jefferson and Bolingbroke in *Jefferson's Call for Nationhood: The First Inaugural Address* (College Station: Texas A&M University Press, 2003), 20–26. There is evidence to support the conclusion that Jefferson had actually read and approved of Bolingbroke's *Patriot King;* for example, Jefferson's May 21, 1805, letter to Judge James Sullivan argues that patriotism requires fortitude: "If we suffer ourselves to be frightened from our post by mere lying, surely the enemy will use that weapon; for what one so cheap to those of whose system of politics morality makes no part? The patriot, like the Christian, must learn that to bear revilings and persecutions is a part of his duty; and in proportion as the trial is severe, firmness under it becomes more requisite and praiseworthy. It requires, indeed, self-command." *The Writings of Thomas Jefferson,* vol. 11, ed. Andrew A. Lipscomb (Washington, D.C.: Thomas Jefferson Memorial Foundation, 1905), 73. Jefferson wrote to Francis Eppes about Bolingbroke on January 19, 1821: "He was called indeed a tory; but his writings prove him a stronger advocate for liberty than any of his countrymen, the whigs of the present day. Irritated by his exile, he committed one act unworthy of him, in connecting himself momentarily with a prince [dethroned King James II] rejected by his country. But he redeemed that single act by his establishment of the principles which proved it to be wrong." *The Writings of Thomas Jefferson,* vol. 15, ed. Andrew A. Lipscomb (Washington, D.C.: Thomas Jefferson Memorial Foundation, 1905), 305. This idea of the patriot citizen hero is also consistent with Michel Foucault's description of the *parrhesiastes* in *Fearless Speech,* ed. Josesph Pearson (Los Angeles: Semiotext(e), 2001).

10. The "vernacular republican citizen" was obligated to actively critique the government; such an obligation is consistent with the ideals of the patriotic romantic republican hero. Jennifer R. Mercieca and James Arnt Aune, "A Vernacular Republican Rhetoric: William Manning's *Key of Libberty,*" *Quarterly Journal of Speech* 91 (2005): 119–43.

11. John Ferling, *A Leap in the Dark: The Struggle to Create the American Republic* (Oxford: Oxford University Press, 2003), 30.

12. According to John Ferling, "Early that year [1765] Washington wrote a remarkable letter to his neighbor, George Mason, an influential assemblymen, that indicated he had undergone a political transformation. Two threads ran through Washington's missive. Like a growing number of disillusioned colonists, he had come to see British policy as a deliberate, concerted attack on American liberty. In addition, in strident language Washington expressed disgust with his second-class status as a provincial." Also, "Toward the late 1760s, Colonel Washington had begun to wonder if he would ever turn a profit from his western domain. First, the Proclamation of 1763 had slowed the western advance of Virginia's land-hungry citizenry to a snail's pace. Washington had initially been unconcerned and treated the edict as a temporary inconvenience. But, after five years it no longer appeared to be so temporary." Ibid., 82–83.

13. Mercy Otis Warren, *History of the Rise, Progress, and Termination of the American Revolution,* ed. Lester H. Cohen, 2 vols. (Indianapolis: Liberty Fund, 1994), 1:17.

14. Edmund S. Morgan and Helen M. Morgan, *The Stamp Act Crisis: Prologue to Revolution* (Chapel Hill: University of North Carolina Press, 1995).

15. John Adams, Novanglus III, *The Revolutionary Writings of John Adams,* ed. C. Bradley Thompson (Indianapolis: Liberty Fund Press, 2000), 164; Warren, *History of the Revolution,* 18.

16. Bernard Bailyn, *The Ideological Origins of the American Revolution* (Cambridge: Harvard University Press, 1967), 18. While patriot accounts of Otis are generally encomiums to his honor and virtue, Tories such as Peter Oliver regarded him as "rash, unguarded, foulmouthed, & openly spiteful."

17. All quotations taken from Otis, "Of the Political and Civil Rights of the British Colonists," 193–97.

18. According to Edmund Morgan, "In England the legal fictions that accompanied the everyday workings of the king's government endowed him with all the attributes of divinity. He was, for example, immortal: it could not be admitted that the king ever died. And like God he was perfect: he could do no wrong, so no action at law could ever lie against him. Indeed, like God he was the giver of laws, but also like God he acted according to the laws he gave. Like God he was omnipresent, for in himself he constituted the 'body politic' over which he ruled. But like the son whom God sent to redeem mankind, he was man as well as God; he had a 'body natural' as well as his body politic, and the two were inseparable like the persons of the Trinity." *Inventing the People: The Rise of Popular Sovereignty in England and America* (New York: Norton, 1988), 17.

19. John C. Miller, *Sam Adams: Pioneer in Propaganda* (Stanford: Stanford University Press, 1936), 46.

20. Philip B. Kurland and Ralph Lerner, "Controversy over Petition of Right," *The Founders' Constitution,* vol. 5 (Chicago: University of Chicago Press, 1986), 309.

21. E. Morgan, *Inventing the People,* 19.

22. Warren, *History of the Revolution,* 20.

23. Ferling, *A Leap in the Dark,* 33.

24. John Adams, Novanglus IV, *The Revolutionary Writings of John Adams,* 180.

25. Thomas Jefferson, *The Autobiography,* in *Thomas Jefferson: Writings,* ed. Merrill D. Peterson (New York: Library of America, 1984), 5–6.

26. First, Virginians believed that their original settlers "brought with them and transmitted to their posterity . . . all the liberties, privileges, franchises, and immunities that have at any time been held, enjoyed, and possessed by the people of Great Britain." Second, Virginians' rights as British subjects had been "declared" by "two royal charters." Third, "the distinguishing characteristic of British freedom" was the right of "taxation of the people by themselves, or by persons chosen by themselves to represent them." And fourth, Virginians had never "forfeited" their right "of being governed by such laws, respecting their internal policy of taxation, as are derived from their own consent."

27. Virginia Stamp Act Resolutions, *Journals of Burgesses of Virginia, 1761–1765* (Richmond: State of Virginia, 1907).

28. Warren, *History of the Revolution,* 343.

29. I say "were printed" because it is unclear how northern newspapers got word of the resolutions. On June 24, 1765, the *Newport Mercury* printed a story on the Virginia *Resolutions* that included the news that the House of Burgesses had been dissolved by Virginia's royal governor, Francis Fauquier, after it passed the *Resolutions;* the *Mercury* printed the first four and the last two resolutions. The July 1 and July 29, 1765, *Boston Post Boy* printed two nearly identical versions of the same story; the July 1, 1765, *Boston Gazette, and Country Journal* also printed the exact same story.

30. Quoted in J. C. Miller, *Sam Adams,* 51.

31. The Declaration of Rights of the Stamp Act Congress, October 19, 1765, *Journal of the First Congress of the American Colonies, in Opposition to the Tyrannical Acts of the British Parliament Held at New York, October 7, 1765* (New York, 1845), 27–29; John Adams, Novanglus IV, *The Revolutionary Writings of John Adams,* 180.

32. According to T. H. Breen, "However widespread the popular anger may have been, the Revolution did not in fact occur in 1765. This curious non-event begs explanation. After all, the elements that one assumes were necessary to transform colonial protest into full scale rebellion seem to have been present at that moment: a radical ideology of colonial resistance, organized violence against the established government, and widespread anxiety that new taxes would exacerbate economic hardship. But, instead of provoking a general call to arms, the crisis passed, and we now interpret the protest against the Stamp Act as simply an early chapter in an eleven-year run up to national independence." *The Marketplace of Revolution: How Consumer Politics Shaped American Independence* (New York: Oxford University Press, 2004), 219–20.

33. "At a meeting of the Freeholders and other inhabitants of the Town of

Boston . . . ," Boston, May 16, 1766; "Glorious news. Boston . . ." (Boston: Draper's, Edes & Gill, Green & Russell, and Fleet's, May 16, 1766); "Glorious News. Constitutional liberty revives! New-Haven . . ." (New-Haven: B. Mecom, May 19, 1766); Declaratory Act, quoted in Bailyn, *The Ideological Origins of the American Revolution,* 202.

34. Quoted in H. W. Brands, *The First American: The Life and Times of Benjamin Franklin* (New York: Anchor Books, 2000), 403.

35. John Dickinson to James Otis, December 5, 1767, in Warren, *History of the Revolution,* 348.

36. J. C. Miller, *Sam Adams,* 126.

37. Ferling, *A Leap in the Dark,* 70; Forrest McDonald, introduction to *Empire and Nation* (Englewood Cliffs, N.J.: Prentice-Hall, 1962), xiii.

38. John Dickinson, *Letters from a Farmer,* Letter XI, 73 (*Letters from a Farmer* is contained in McDonald, *Empire and Nation*).

39. Much of Bailyn's analysis in *The Ideological Origins of the American Revolution* centers on the question of conspiracy in pre-revolutionary American political thought: "The colonists believed they saw emerging from the welter of events during the decade after the Stamp Act a pattern whose meaning was unmistakable. They saw in the measures taken by the British government and in the actions of officials in the colonies something for which their peculiar inheritance of thought had prepared them only too well, something they had long conceived to be a possibility in view of the known tendencies of history and of the present state of affairs in England. They saw about them, with increasing clarity, not merely mistaken, or even evil, policies violating the principles upon which freedom rested, but what appeared to be evidence of nothing less than a deliberate assault launch surreptitiously by plotters against liberty both in England and in America. The danger to America, it was believed, was in fact only the small, immediately visible part of the greater whole whose ultimate manifestation would be the destruction of the English constitution, with all the rights and privileges embedded in it" (95).

40. Dickinson, *Letters from a Farmer,* Letter XI, 74–75.

41. Ibid., Letter VII, 43.

42. Ibid., Letter IV, 21.

43. Ibid., Letter VII, 43.

44. Ibid., Letter IX, 50.

45. Further, Dickinson's repeated use of if/then arguments gave his hysterical slippery slope the force of necessity, which as rhetorical scholar Stephen Lucas discussed in a different context, "carried strongly deterministic overtones. To say an act was necessary implied that it was impelled by fate or determined by the operation of inextricable natural laws and was beyond the control of human agents." Lucas, "Justifying America: The Declaration of Independence as a Rhetorical Document," in *American Rhetoric: Context and Criticism,* ed. Thomas W. Benson (Carbondale: Southern Illinois University Press, 1989), 67–130, 75.

46. Dickinson, *Letters from a Farmer,* Letter I, 6.

47. Ibid., Letter XII, 79–80.

48. Ibid., Letter VI, 37.

49. Ibid., Letter VII, 38–39.

50. Breen, *The Marketplace of the Revolution,* 7.

51. J. C. Miller, *Sam Adams,* 125.

52. "American Occurrences. Charles-town," *The American Magazine; or, General Repository,* February 1769, 62–64.

53. I make this argument more fully in Jennifer R. Mercieca, "Choice, Loyalty, and Safety: The Construction of a Distinctly American Imagined Nationalism" (review essay), *Rhetoric and Public Affairs* 9 (2006): 279–302.

54. "The colonial phenomenon . . . involved trust established across space, impersonally, a product of a print culture, and it was absolutely essential for the development of the popular mobilization on which any successful revolutionary action depended. It had to be learned and relearned, nourished, proclaimed, and reaffirmed, for unless firmly grounded in public opinion, trust could not possibly survive rumors of betrayal." Breen, *The Marketplace of the Revolution,* 252.

55. Massachusetts *Circular Letter.*

56. According to John Ferling, "In the spring of 1768, the Pennsylvania assembly refused to assent to the Massachusetts Circular Letter, the only provincial legislature to ignore the pleas of its brethren to act in concert." *A Leap in the Dark,* 78. For example, when Georgia's Commons House of Assembly met on November 7, 1768, Governor James Wright informed it that "his Majesty considers [the *Letter*] to be of a most dangerous and factious tendency, and that I have it in charge to endeavor to prevail on your House not to receive or give any countenance to that letter, and which his Majesty, from the confidence he has in your affections, he expects . . . [if you do, then] it will be my duty to prevent any proceedings thereupon, by immediately putting an end to your sitting." The Georgia Assembly did consider the *Letter,* but they left it until the last business of the session, by which time they considered both the Virginia *Resolutions* and the Massachusetts *Letter.* The House believed that they were not "dangerous and factious," but "only tend to a justifiable union of subjects aggrieved, in lawful and laudable endeavors to obtain redress, by an application founded upon, and expressive of duty and loyalty to the best of Kings." The House was immediately dissolved for cooperating and communicating with its sister colonies on December 24, 1768. "American Occurrences. Savanna," *The American Magazine; or, General Repository;* January 1769, 29–30.

57. Jefferson, *Autobiography,* 6.

58. Breen, *The Marketplace of the Revolution,* 20.

59. *Virginia Non-Importation Resolves,* Payton Randolph, Speaker of the House, May 18, 1769.

60. To be sure, colonials also took conciliatory measures during this period—the separation from Great Britain was not certain by any means. In fact, an equally true alternate reading of the period could chronicle how colonials attempted to

prevent rebellion from 1770 to 1776. My focus on the development of the romantic republican fiction requires that I describe the period with a narrow lens, but I am aware of the limitations of such an orientation.

61. Warren, *History of the Revolution,* 57.

62. J. C. Miller, *Sam Adams,* 241.

63. *Boston Circular Letter,* September 21, 1773.

64. According to Breen, "Sons of Liberty did their best to intimidate newly appointed tea agents . . . [and] patriotic voices sounded the alarm once again, urging the colonists to resist political oppression by refusing to buy imported goods." *The Marketplace of the Revolution,* 300.

65. Jefferson, *Autobiography,* 9. As he continued he remembered that "In this doctrine however I had never been able to get any one to agree with me but Mr. Wythe. He concurred in it from the first dawn of the question What was the political relation between us & England? Our other patriots Randolph, the Lees, Nicholas, Pendleton stopped at the half-way house of John Dickinson who admitted that England had a right to regulate our commerce, and to lay duties on it for the purposes of regulation, but not of raising revenue. But for this ground there was no foundation in compact, in any acknowledged principles of colonization, nor in reason: expatriation being a natural right, and acted on as such, by all nations, in all ages" (9).

66. Stephen E. Lucas, *Portents of Rebellion: Rhetoric and Revolution in Philadelphia, 1765–76* (Philadelphia: Temple University Press, 1976), 88–89.

67. The *Summary View* was published in Williamsburg, Philadelphia, and London.

68. James Arnt Aune and I have written about the importance of vigilant criticism as an indicator of good vernacular republican citizenship in "A Vernacular Republican Rhetoric."

69. Jefferson, *A Summary View,* in *Writings,* 118.

70. *Declaration and Resolves of the First Continental Congress,* October 14, 1774.

71. *Journals of the Continental Congress,* Saturday, October 22, 1774, 103.

72. William H. Hallahan, *The Day the American Revolution Began: 19 April 1775* (New York: Harper, 2000).

73. The committee had previously been composed of John Rutledge, William Livingston, Ben Franklin, John Jay, and Thomas Johnson.

74. Jefferson, *Autobiography,* 12.

75. Resolutions of Congress on Lord North's Conciliatory Proposal, in Jefferson, *Writings,* 331.

76. *Pennsylvania Packet,* November 10, 1775.

77. Proclamation of Rebellion, *Documentary Source Book of American History,* ed. William MacDonald (New York: Burt Franklin, 1943), 189–90.

78. *Journals of the Continental Congress,* December 6, 1775, 412.

79. This power vacuum would prove to be a problem for now-defunct and "traitorous" colonial governments. Petitions poured forth from colonial assemblies

asking for Congress to advise a proper course of action for reestablishing state governments. Congress answered on May 10, 1776, when it recommended that "where no government sufficient to the exigencies of their affairs have hitherto established, to adopt such government as shall, in the opinion of the representatives of the people, best conduce to the happiness and safety of their constituents in particular, and America in general." The representatives of the people were to erect new governments for the people; these governments would promote the people's and America's happiness and safety. John Adams, Edward Rutledge, and Richard Henry Lee were given the task of drafting a preamble to accompany the resolution; Adams wrote the draft and wondered later in life why his document was not considered the true declaration of American independence. He had a point. Adams's preamble declared that it was "absolutely irreconcileable to reason and good Conscience, for the people of these colonies now to take the oaths and affirmations necessary for the support of any government under the crown of Great Britain." Further, Adams argued that "the exercise of every kind of authority under the said crown should be totally suppressed"; that "all the powers of government [should be] exerted under the authority of the people of the colonies"; and that each colony should erect a new government based on the will of the people. These new governments should preserve "internal peace, virtue, and good order" and should defend the "lives, liberties, and properties" of Americans. Yet, while Adams's preamble authorized new governments based on the will of the people, it did not state that Americans irrevocably "broke the political bands which have united them to another," and without this crucial bit of minutia, it cannot be considered the true Declaration of Independence.

80. John Adams to James Warren, April 22, 1776, *Letters of Delegates to Congress,* vol. 3, January 1, 1776–May 15, 1776, ed. Paul H. Smith (Washington, D.C.: Library of Congress, 1976–2000), 570.

81. Ferling, *A Leap in the Dark,* 151.

82. According to Pauline Maier, "much of Paine's case against monarchy had been made in the colonial press or pulpits at one point or another over the previous six years." *American Scripture: Making the Declaration of Independence* (New York: Vintage Books, 1998), 33.

83. Thomas Paine, *Common Sense* (Mineola, N.Y.: Dover, 1997), 18.

84. Ibid., 3.

85. Ibid., 5.

86. Ibid., 13.

87. Ibid., 24–25.

88. Ibid., 30.

89. Ibid., 30–32.

90. John Adams to William Tudor, April 12, 1776, *Letters of Delegates to Congress,* 3:514; John Adams to Thomas Jefferson, June 22, 1819, in Cappon, *Adams-Jefferson Letters,* 2:542. See also John Adams to Mercy Otis Warren, April 16, 1776, *Letters of Delegates to Congress,* 3:538.

91. John Adams to James Warren, May 20, 1776, in *Letters of Members of the Continental Congress,* ed. Edmund C. Burnett, 8 vols. (Washington, D.C.: Carnegie Institution, 1921), 1:460; Washington quoted in Maier, *American Scripture,* 44.

92. Worthington Chauncey Ford, ed., *Journals of the Continental Congress, 1774–1789* (Washington, D.C.: Library of Congress, 1976–79), 5:424–26; Garry Wills, *Inventing America: Jefferson's Declaration of Independence* (Garden City, N.Y.: Doubleday, 1978), 323–33.

93. The fact that Americans celebrate July 4 rather than July 2 as Independence Day is one of those accidents of history—one that annoyed John Adams as much as it has bemused historians such as Carl Becker: "if we were a nation of antiquarians we should no doubt find an incongruity in celebrating the anniversary of our independence on the 4th of July," he wrote in *The Declaration of Independence: A Study in the History of Political Ideas* (New York: Vintage Books, 1958), 3.

94. See "To Hezekiah Niles," February 13, 1818, in *The Works of John Adams,* ed. Charles F. Adams (Boston, 1856), 10, 282–83. Adams dates the change in the minds of colonials to 1760, the year of the accession of King George III.

95. Articles of Confederation and Perpetual Union, July 9, 1778, *The Public Statutes at Large of the United States of America,* vol. 1, ed. Richard Peters (Boston: Little and Brown, 1845), 4.

96. Address of the Mechanicks of New York City to the Delegates to the Congress of New York, June 14, 1776, *The Spirit of '76,* ed. Henry Steele Commager and Richard B. Morris (New York: Castle Books, 1958), 373.

97. For historical and rhetorical analysis of the Declaration of Independence, see Alan P. Grimes, "Conservative Revolution and Liberal Rhetoric: The Declaration of Independence," *Journal of Politics* 38 (1976): 1–19; Pauline Maier, "Why Revolution? Why Democracy?" *Journal of Interdisciplinary History* 6 (1976): 711–32; Pauline Maier, *American Scripture: Making the Declaration of Independence* (New York: Vintage Books, 1998); Phillip F. Detweiler, "The Changing Reputation of the Declaration of Independence: The First Fifty Years," *William and Mary Quarterly* 19 (1962): 557–74; Jay Fliegelman, *Declaring Independence: Jefferson, Natural Language, and the Culture of Performance* (Stanford: Stanford University Press, 1993); Carl Becker, *The Declaration of Independence: A Study in the History of Political Ideas* (New York: Vintage Books, 1958); Lucas, *Portents of Rebellion.*

Chapter 3

1. Gordon S. Wood, *The Creation of the American Republic, 1776–1787* (Chapel Hill: University of North Carolina Press, 1998). Historians and political theorists have long recognized that James Madison's view of government was premised on stability. See, for example, David E. Ingersoll, "Machiavelli and Madison: Perspectives on Political Stability," *Political Science Quarterly* 85 (1970): 259–80; Neal Riemer, "James Madison's Theory of the Self-Destructive Features of Republican

Government," *Ethics* 65 (1954): 34–43; Claude Ake, "A Definition of Political Stability," *Comparative Politics* 7 (1975): 271–83; Donald Burke, "James Madison's Dystopian Vision: The Failure of Equilibrium," *American Journal of Legal History* 43 (1999): 254–79.

2. Benjamin Rush, February 1, 1787, *The Documentary History of the Ratification of the Constitution,* 22 vols. to date (Madison: State Historical Society of Wisconsin, 1976–), 13:46 [hereafter cited as *DHRC*].

3. "Pre-1789, having no power to directly tax the public and receiving insufficient sums from the states, Congress paid no principal or interest on its domestic interest bearing debt and paid no principal on its foreign interest-bearing debt. In effect, the government was in default on most of its interest-bearing debt between 1782 and 1790." Farley Grubb, "The Net Worth of the U.S. Federal Government, 1784–1802," http://www.aeaweb.org/annual_mtg_papers/2007/0105_1015_1001.pdf.

4. Journals of the Continental Congress, March 18, 1780, 260, http://memory.loc.gov/cgi-bin/query/D?hlaw:1:./temp/~ammem_3QAr.

5. James Warren to "a private friend," n.d., in Mercy Otis Warren, *History of the Rise, Progress, and Termination of the American Revolution,* ed. Lester H. Cohen, 2 vols. (Indianapolis: Liberty Fund, 1994), 2:388–89.

6. Letter dated November 30, 1782, submitted to Congress December 12, 1782, *Journals of the Continental Congress,* 23:788.

7. "Perhaps the most telling sign of a failing government was the morale of Congress itself. All too rapidly, the Confederation had sunk into a lassitude bordering on paralysis. By the fall of 1785 attendance at congressional sessions was already embarrassingly low. Throughout the winter and spring of 1786, absences reached crisis proportions, quorums could rarely be met, and the business of Congress—limited though it was—was rapidly coming to a halt. Tired of dealing with problems they could not solve, congressman from every state preferred to stay home." Carol Berkin, *A Brilliant Solution: Inventing the American Constitution* (Orlando: Harcourt, 2002), 21–22. "In 1784, [the Confederated Congress] had broken up in disgust, and the French minister wrote to his master that there was now no general government in the United States, neither congress, president, nor head of any administrative department. Practically this was political chaos, and the next step was anarchy." Jonathan Smith, "The Depression of 1785 and Daniel Shays' Rebellion," *William and Mary Quarterly* 5 (1948): 77–94, 79.

8. J. Smith, "The Depression of 1785," 81.

9. Daggett, "An Oration, Pronounced in the Brick Meeting-House . . . ," *DHRC,* 13:161.

10. *Pennsylvania Gazette,* August 1, 1787, *DHRC,* 13:182.

11. David P. Szatmary, *Shays' Rebellion: The Making of an Agrarian Insurrection* (Amherst: University of Massachusetts Press, 1980), 40; Jeremy Engels, "Reading the Riot Act: Rhetoric, Psychology, and Counter-Revolutionary Discourse in Shays's Rebellion, 1786–1787," *Quarterly Journal of Speech* 91 (2005): 63–88.

12. Charge of the Chief Justice to the Middlesex Grand Jury, *Worcester Magazine,* November 1786, 406.

13. Ibid. Cushing would later preside over the Massachusetts ratifying convention. My thanks to Kathryn Kelly for research assistance.

14. *Worcester Magazine,* August 1786, 218.

15. "To the Citizens of Massachusetts on Conventions," *Worcester Magazine,* August 1786, 262.

16. *Worcester Magazine,* quoted in Szatmary, *Shays' Rebellion,* 47.

17. J. Smith, "The Depression of 1785," 86–87.

18. Despite the people's perception that the legislatures were not doing enough to fix the crisis, George Richards Minot described the Massachusetts's legislature's actions to come to the aid of the people in glowing terms: "Thus, after passing three different laws for easing the burdens of the people, which were, an act for collecting the arrear taxes in specific articles; an act for making real and personal estate tender in discharge of executions and actions commenced in law, and an act for rendering law processes less expensive; after appropriating one third of the proceeds of the impost and excise duties for the exigencies of government; after attempting to enlighten the minds of the citizens, by an instructive address, and to restore peace to the Commonwealth, by providing for the apprehending and trying of dangerous persons; but, at the same time, tendering indemnity to all the insurgents, the General Court rose on the 18th of November, with reasonable expectations, that the people, if yet unsatisfied, would seek further alterations, by the constitutional means of instructing their Representatives, or by a change of officers in the future elections." Minot, *The History of the Insurrection in Massachusetts in the Year 1786 and the Rebellion Consequent Thereon* (Worcester, Mass.: Isaiah Thomas, 1788), 70.

19. *DHRC,* 13:92.

20. Szatmary, *Shays' Rebellion,* 124–26.

21. Ibid., 106.

22. "By contributing to a change in the outlook of some localists, rural outbursts in New England and throughout the country may have made a general convention in Philadelphia possible. Backcountry violence did not cause the May 1787 meeting—in fact, the assembly had been planned before the most extreme Shaysite activity had occurred—but domestic unrest helped to ensure in certain quarters a favorable reaction toward the meeting. Developing at a critical juncture in time, the rebellion convinced the elites of sovereign states that the proposed gathering at Philadelphia must take place." Ibid., 127.

23. Knox to Washington, October 23, 1786, *DHRC,* 4:xxxix.

24. Washington to Lee, October 31, 1786, *The Writings of George Washington,* ed. Worthington Chauncey Ford, 11 vols. (New York: Putnam, 1891), 76–79.

25. Madison to Pendleton, February 24, 1787, *James Madison: Writings* (New York: Library of America, 1999), 63.

26. James Madison, *Notes of Debates in the Federal Convention of 1787* (New York: Norton, 1987), 145.

27. Ibid., 30.

28. Ibid., 143.

29. Ibid., 15.

30. Ibid., 75–77.

31. Ibid., 222.

32. *Baltimore Gazette,* May 22, 1787, *DHRC,* 13:112.

33. States that enacted debtor relief were as much a part of the problem as the rebels, especially states like Vermont that allowed the rebels into their state and refused to return them to Massachusetts for prosecution (because the people would not let them). Rhode Island ("rogue island") complied with all of the rebels' requests while refusing to comply with the confederacy and refusing to send delegates to the Constitutional Convention. As Gordon Wood argues, "The Federalists were not as much opposed to the governmental power of the states as to the character of the people who were wielding it. The constitutions of most of the states were not really at fault. Massachusetts after all possessed a nearly perfect constitution. What actually bothered the Federalists was the sort of people who had been able to gain positions of authority in the state governments, particularly in the state legislatures. Much of the quarrel with the viciousness, instability, and injustice of the various state governments was at bottom social." *The Creation of the American Republic,* 507.

34. Madison, *Notes,* 175. Those outside the convention also expressed this view: "Is it not time, my dear sir, for politicians to begin to consider mankind *as they are* and not *what they ought to be*? If I mistake not, this is the rock upon which many of our best writers on government have split. . . . Let no one suppose that I am an enemy to freedom—I am a friend to liberty, and to secure it inviolate to the people, would wish to banish licentiousness. But let them know, that without a sacred regard to the laws—a reverential submission to authority—an impartial and sometimes a severe administration of justice—this invaluable jewel, this boasted liberty will be inevitable lost. For when the laws are vague—when the administration of justice becomes feeble and irregular—when political empires, ever courting popularity, give to a distempered multitude whatever their depraved appetites may crave—when the people are wallowing in the superfluity of liberty—then, unless their eyes were darkened, would they see tyranny in his horrid form, brandishing the bloody scourge and entering the door—then, unless they were deafer than adders, would they hear the chain of slavery clanging in their ears." Extract of a letter from a gentleman in Washington County to his friend in Albany, *New York Daily Advertiser,* June 28, 1787, 141–44.

35. Madison, *Notes,* 78. According to Gordon Wood, "In short, through the artificial contrivance of the Constitution overlying an expanded society, the Federalists meant to restore and to prolong the traditional kind of elitist influence in politics

that social developments, especially since the Revolution, were undermining. . . . The Constitution was intrinsically an aristocratic document designed to check the democratic tendencies of the period, and as such it dictated the character of the Antifederalist response." *The Creation of the American Republic,* 513.

36. Madison, *Notes,* 42.

37. Ibid., 75–77.

38. Ibid., 86.

39. Ibid., 402–3.

40. Ibid., 167.

41. Ibid., 39, 73–74.

42. Ibid., 405.

43. Ibid., 39.

44. Ibid., 402–3.

45. Ibid., 75–77. On the question of debtors and creditors, the perspective of Georgia's "Tullius" was very different from Madison's: "Nothing can be more obvious if we consider it [payment of debts by installments] as an act of necessary justice. Those of the citizens of this state [Georgia] who were attached to the cause of their country, when it fell into the hands of the enemy, were obliged to fly from the rage of the conquerors. They could take only a small part of their property with them; the rest was considered as captured and was either destroyed or carried away by the enemy when they were driven from the country. While they were in a state of exile, they were compelled to contract new debts for their subsistence. Upon the restoration of peace, when they returned to their country, they found their lands so impoverished and out of order as to have lost nearly half their value, and they had been deprived of the means of improving and rendering them productive. Their old debts were accumulating, and they must contract new ones before they could proceed to plant. Since the peace, there has been an almost universal failure in crops, which has thrown the balance of trade against us in favor of Great Britain, that commercial usurer, who has drained us of all our money and left us not the means to pay our debts. This is the true state of the matter, and now is the time to consider whether some relief is not necessary." *Gazette of the State of Georgia,* June 5, 1788, 301.

46. Madison, *Notes,* 193–95.

47. Ibid., 74.

48. Ibid., 40–41.

49. Ibid., 187.

50. Ibid., 73.

51. Ibid., 405–6.

52. Ibid., 107. The debates of the convention were kept strictly secret—Madison would not allow his *Notes* to be published until after his death for fear that they would be used against delegates—and thus it is safe to assume that Madison was correct that no delegate could accurately gauge precisely what the opinions of his constituents were.

53. Ibid., 70.
54. Ibid.
55. Ibid., 349.
56. Ibid., 404.
57. Ibid., 348–53.
58. Edmund Pendleton to James Madison, *DHRC,* 13:354.
59. *Carlisle Gazette,* November 14, 1787, *DHRC,* 2:258.
60. *Boston Gazette,* October 29, 1787, *DHRC,* 4:165.
61. Melancton Smith, "Speech at the New York Ratifying Convention, June 23, 1788," *The Anti-Federalist Papers,* ed. Ralph Ketcham (New York: Mentor, 1986), 347.
62. Ratification went as follows: Delaware, December 7, 1787 (30 to 0); Pennsylvania, December 12, 1787 (46 to 23); New Jersey, December 18, 1787 (38 to 0); Georgia, December 31, 1787 (26 to 0); Connecticut, January 9, 1788 (128 to 40); Massachusetts, February 6, 1788 (187 to 168); Maryland, April 26, 1788 (63 to 11); South Carolina, May 23, 1788 (149 to 73); New Hampshire, June 21, 1788 (57 to 47); Virginia, June 25, 1788 (89 to 79); New York, July 26, 1788 (30 to 27); North Carolina, November 21, 1789 (194 to 77); and finally, Rhode Island, May 29, 1790 (34 to 32).
63. In states like Massachusetts and Connecticut, each town's freeholders sent delegates to their state convention, while the freeholders in states like Virginia, Pennsylvania, and New York were only represented by county delegates.
64. For example, Virginia voters who were eligible to elect representatives to the legislature were qualified to vote for convention delegates in March 1788. Voters elected 170 delegates: two from each of the state's 84 counties and one each from Williamsburg and Norfolk borough (*DHRC,* 9:561). Virginia allowed those who were already appointed elsewhere to serve as delegates, and there were no residence requirements for candidates—meaning that a candidate could run in another county if his prospects did not look good in his home county. Five of the seven Constitutional Convention delegates were elected; George Washington and James McClurg did not run (*DHRC,* 9:596). Virginians generally knew the candidate's opinions before the election, some made speeches, some counties clearly listed which party they were in. The April 9, 1788, *Virginia Centinel* printed a list of which counties were Federalist and which were Anti-Federalist (*DHRC,* 9:627–28). In Massachusetts, selectmen convened the inhabitants of their towns qualified to vote for members of the state House of Representatives (adult males, one-year resident of the town, possessed of a freehold estate of the value of sixty pounds). There were no qualifications for delegates. The number of delegates a town could elect depended on how many taxpayers were in the town and was equal to their number of representatives in the Massachusetts House. Some towns voted on separate ballots, some voted seriatim. One hundred more delegates attended the state convention than attended the House. "Most towns neither instructed delegates nor commented on the Constitution. A few voted whether or not to instruct delegates. Sometimes, towns voted immediately on instructions, which were read and

voted on later in the day or at a later date to which the meeting had adjourned. The propriety of instructions was an issue before, during, and after the Convention" (*DHRC,* 5:890). Most of the instructions were Anti-Federalist. Many towns copied Northampton's instructions, which gave their delegate discretionary power. Some of the delegates instructed to vote Anti-Federalist did not—some got permission from their towns to change their vote. Many towns (Belchertown and Bellingham, for example) appointed a special committee to consider and draw up instructions for their representative (*DHRC,* 5:901). In Pennsylvania at midnight on election night a mob attacked the houses of several Philadelphia Anti-Federalist leaders and Major Alexander Boyd's boardinghouse, where western assemblymen and councilors were lodged. They were never prosecuted (*DHRC,* 2:224–25). It appears that Pennsylvania voted by county and only freeholders were allowed to cast ballots. Some counties, like Northampton, made the candidates swear that they would vote to approve the constitution before they voted for any of them (*DHRC,* 2:229). In Delaware there were lots of threats of violence, which kept people away from the pools; there were also lots of voting irregularities, and fewer than seven hundred people voted total. The state's two main parties—Whigs and Tories—were both supposed to be Federalist (*DHRC,* 3:92). Delaware also voted by county and only allowed freeholders to cast ballots. New Jersey freeholders voted by county, and the same qualifications were used as for voting for members of the General Assembly: adults worth 50 proclamation money who were residents of the county for a year. Only thirty-nine delegates met in convention; the constitution was unanimously ratified. Georgia voted by county, each sending three delegates. Thirty-three delegates voted unanimously to ratify after examining the constitution paragraph by paragraph for a mere four days (December 28–31). In Connecticut only freeholders twenty-one years of age could vote; citizens had to petition to get the right to vote, had to be approved by the selectman of their town, had to own a freehold estate worth forty shillings annually or personal property worth forty pounds, and had to be "of a quiet and peaceable behavior, and civil conversation" (*DHRC,* 3:315).

65. *Massachusetts Centinel,* April 14, 1787, *DHRC,* 13:80.

66. *Pennsylvania Packet,* June 25, 1787, *DHRC,* 13:145.

67. *New Haven Gazette,* September 20, *DHRC,* 3:349.

68. *Pennsylvania Packet,* September 25, 1787, *DHRC,* 3:52; Petition of the Grand Jurors, Newcastle, Delaware, October 7, 1787, *DHRC,* 3:53; A Jerseyman: To the Citizens of New Jersey, *Trenton Mercury,* November 6, 1787, *DHRC,* 3:150.

69. "Freeman of Pennsylvania, consider the character and services of the men who made this government. Behold the venerable FRANKLIN, in the 70th year of his age, cooped up in the cabin of a small vessel, and exposing himself to the dangers of a passage on the ocean, crouded with British cruisers, in a winter month, in order to solicit from the court with France that aid, which finally enabled America to close the war with so much success and glory—and then say, it is possible that this man would set his hand to a constitution that would endanger your liberties?—From this aged servant of the public, turn your eyes to the illus-

trious American hero, whose name has ennobled human nature—I mean your beloved WASHINGTON. Behold him, in the year 1775, taking leave of his happy family and peaceful retreat, and flying to the relief of a distant, and at that time an unknown part of the American continent. See him uniting and cementing an army, composed of the citizens of thirteen states, into a band of brothers. Follow him into the field of battle, and behold him the first in danger, and the last out of it. Follow him into his winter quarters, and see him sharing in the hunger, cold, and fatigues of every soldier in his army. Behold his fortitude in adversity, his moderation in victory, and his tenderness and respect upon all occasions for the civil power of his country. But above all, turn your eyes to that illustrious scene he exhibited at Annapolis in 1782 [1783], when he resigned his commission, and laid his sword at the feet of Congress, and afterwards resumed the toils of an American farmer on the banks of Potowmack. Survey, my countrymen, these illustrious exploits of patriotism and virtue and then say, is it possible that the deliverer of our country would have recommended an unsafe form of government for that liberty, for which he had for eight long years contended with such unexampled firmness, constancy and magnanimity?" *Pennsylvania Gazette,* October 10, 1787, *DHRC,* 13:364.

70. *Virginia Journal,* November 22, 1787, *DHRC,* 14:152. "A Landholder IV" and "A Landholder V" responded to Elbridge Gerry's October 18, 1787, letter to the Massachusetts General Court. *DHRC,* 14:476–84.

71. Constitutional Convention delegates who later attended their state conventions were Bassett, Bedford, Few, McHenry, Gorhman, Strong, Langdon, Bearly, Hamilton, Lansing, Yates, Davie, Wilson, Madison, Wythe, Johnson, Sherman, Ellsworth, King, Mason, Randolph, Mercer, Martin, Spaight, Williamson, Rutledge, Cotesworth Pinckney, Pinckney, and Gilman. Mason, Mercer, Martin, Lansing, and Yates were the only Constitutional Convention delegates to vote against the Constitution in their home states.

72. Gary Wills, *Cincinnatus: George Washington and the Enlightenment* (New York: Doubleday, 1984).

73. Massachusetts Convention, January 25, 1788, *DHRC,* 6:1345–46.

74. For more on the controversy over the accessibility of the press see *DHRC,* 13:312–23; for more on "The Controversy Over the Post Office and the Circulation of Newspapers," see *DHRC,* 16:540–96; for the letters between George Bryan and John Ralston, see *DHRC,* 16:485–93.

75. *New York Journal,* November 8, 1787, *DHRC,* 14:4.

76. A. Craig Baird, *American Public Addresses, 1740–1952* (New York: McGraw-Hill, 1956), 32.

77. Patrick Henry, "Speech at the Virginia Ratifying Convention June 5, 1788," *DHRC,* 9:951.

78. Ibid., 955.

79. Ibid., 953.

80. James Madison, "Speech at the Virginia Ratifying Convention June 6,

1788," *DHRC,* 9:989; see also Terence S. Morrow, "Representation and Political Deliberation in the Massachusetts Constitutional Ratification Debate," *Rhetoric and Public Affairs* 3, no. 4 (2000); 529–53.

81. Madison, "Speech at the Virginia Ratifying Convention," 989–90.

82. See note 1 for this chapter for more on the role of stability in Madison's political theory.

83. Madison, "Speech at the Virginia Ratifying Convention," 990.

84. William H. Riker, "The Heresthetics of Constitution-Making: The Presidency in 1787, with Comments on Determinism and Rational Choice," *American Political Science Review* 78 (March 1984): 1–16; William H. Riker, *The Strategy of Rhetoric: Campaigning for the American Constitution* (New Haven: Yale University Press, 1996), 253–54.

85. Federalists charged Anti-Federalists with not having a clear critique of the proposed constitution, but I believe this is not true. Anti-Federalists uniformly critiqued the constitution on several points: lack of trial by juries, consolidated government versus confederated government, standing armies, power of taxation, unlimited presidential terms, freedoms protected in the state Bills of Rights, and representation.

86. Madison, *Notes,* 655.

87. The *DHRC* reports that while sixteen essays signed by "Brutus" were published in the *New York Journal* between October 18, 1787, and April 10, 1788, they were not widely reprinted. Despite only appearing in the newspapers of five towns, the essays were known to have circulated more widely and were directly criticized in at least three newspapers in which the essays did not appear. The identity of "Brutus" remains a mystery: Abraham Yates, Richard Henry Lee, John Jay, George Clinton, Thomas Treadwell, Robert Yates, and Melancton Smith have all been believed to be Brutus at some point since 1787 (*DHRC,* 19:103).

88. For more on the difference between mirroring and filtering constituents' will, see James A. Morone, *The Democratic Wish: Popular Participation and the Limits of American Government,* 2nd ed. (New Haven: Yale University Press, 1998), 33–73.

89. Saul Cornell, *The Other Founders: Anti-Federalism and the Dissenting Tradition in America, 1788–1828* (Chapel Hill: University of North Carolina Press, 1999).

90. Emery G. Lee III, "Representation, Virtue, and Political Jealousy in the Brutus-Publius Dialogue," *Journal of Politics* 59 (1997): 1073–95.

91. Brutus, *Anti-Federalist Papers,* 276–77.

92. *Journal of the House of Representatives of the United States, 1789–1793,* Tuesday, July 21, 64.

93. The Senate also debated the amendments before sending them back to the House and then to the states for ratification. Unfortunately, the Senate did not record what that body said. Historians usually turn to the diary of Senator William Maclay for information on the Senate from 1789 to 1791, but Maclay had a knee injury when the Senate debated the amendments, so we do not have his witty perspective on these debates. Therefore, due to the lack of information on the Senate proceedings, I have focused my discussion on the House.

94. *Annals of Congress,* 1st Cong., 1st sess., 748.

95. Ibid., 750.

96. The amendment that would have become the first amendment to the Constitution if it had been ratified by the states would have fixed the ratio of representation such that there would be "one Representative for every thirty thousand, until the number shall amount to one hundred, after which . . . there shall be not less than one hundred Representatives, nor less than one Representative for every forty thousand persons, until the number of Representative shall amount to two hundred, after which the proportion shall be so regulated by Congress, that there shall not be less than two hundred Representatives, nor more than one Representative for every fifty thousand persons." Only New Hampshire, New York, Maryland, South Carolina, North Carolina, Rhode Island, New Jersey, and Virginia agreed to this proposition. *DHRC,* 2:321–24.

97. *Annals of Congress,* 1st Cong., 1st sess., 759.

98. Ibid., 760.

99. Ibid., 761–62.

100. Ibid., 762–63.

101. The quote in its entirety reads: "The right of freedom of speech is secured; the liberty of the press is expressly declared to be beyond the reach of this Government; the people may therefore publicly address their representatives, may privately advise them, or declare their sentiments by petition to the whole body; in all these ways they may communicate their will. If gentlemen mean to go further, and to say that the people have a right to instruct their representatives in such a sense as that the delegates are obliged to conform to those instructions, the declaration is not true." Ibid., 766–67.

102. Ibid., 769.

103. Ibid., 767–68.

104. Ibid., 771.

105. Ibid., 772.

106. Benjamin Rush, February 1, 1787, American Museum, *DHRC,* 13:49.

107. Comte de Moustier to Comte de Montmorin, August 2, 1788, *DHRC,* 18:308.

108. *Annals of Congress,* 1st Cong., 1st sess., 766–67.

109. Jefferson to Madison, December 20, 1787, *The Writings of Thomas Jefferson,* ed. Paul Leicester Ford, vol. 4 (New York: Putnam, 1894), 476.

Chapter 4

1. William Maclay, *The Diary of William Maclay and Other Notes on Senate Debates, March 4, 1789–March 3, 1791,* ed. Kenneth R. Bowling and Helen E. Veit (Baltimore: Johns Hopkins University Press, 1988).

2. Jefferson to Lafayette, June 16, 1792, and Jefferson to Paine, June 19, 1792, *Thomas Jefferson: Writings,* ed. Merrill D. Peterson (New York: Library of America, 1984), 990–91, 991–92.

3. According to historian Bruce Miroff, "the charge was half true; Adams wanted a political aristocracy, but feared an aristocracy based upon wealth. He advocated balanced institutions to check depredations upon the public good, but also called for political actors who would actively promote that good." "John Adams: Merit, Fame, and Political Leadership," *Journal of Politics* 48 (1986): 116–32, 118; see also Stanley Elkins and Eric McKitrick, *The Age of Federalism: The Early American Republic, 1788–1800* (New York: Oxford University Press, 1993), 531–79.

4. John Adams, *Defence of the Constitutions of Government of the United States of America,* (London, 1787), Letter LV, Conclusion, 372.

5. John Adams, *Discourses on Davila: A Series of Papers on Political History Written in the Year 1790 and Then Published in the Gazette of the United States* (Boston: Russell and Cutler, 1805), 90.

6. Richard N. Rosenfeld, *American Aurora: A Democratic-Republic Returns* (New York: St. Martins Press, 1997).

7. Jefferson to Jonathan B. Smith, April 26, 1791, *Papers of Thomas Jefferson,* ed. Julien P. Boyd, 36 vols. to date (Princeton: Princeton University Press, 1950–), 20:290.

8. John Quincy Adams, "Publicola I," *Columbian Centinel,* June 8, 1791.

9. Jefferson's letter to John Adams in which he attempted to explain away the offensive comment is excruciatingly awkward: "The importance which you still seem to allow to my note, and the effect you suppose it to have had, though unintentional in me, induces me to show you that it really had no effect. Paine's pamphlet, with my note, was published here (Philadelphia) about the second week in May. Not a word ever appeared in the public papers here on the subject for more than a month; and I am certain not a word on the subject would ever have been said, had not a writer, under the name of Publicola, at length undertaken to attack Mr. Paine's principles, which were the principles of the citizens of the United States. Instantly a host of writers attacked Publicola in support of those principles. He had thought proper to misconstrue a figurative expression in my note; and these writers so far noticed me as to place the expression in its true light. But this was only an incidental skirmish preliminary to the general engagement, and they would not have thought me worth naming, had not he thought proper to bring me on the scene. His antagonists, very criminally, in my opinion, presumed you to be Publicola, and on that presumption hazarded a personal attack on you. No person saw with more uneasiness than I did, this unjustifiable assault; and the more so, when I saw it continued after the printer had declared you were not the author. But you will perceive from all this, my dear Sir, that my note contributed nothing to the production of these disagreeable pieces. As long as Paine's pamphlet stood on its own feet and on my note, it was unnoticed. As soon as Publicola attacked Paine, swarms appeared in his defence. To Publicola, then, and not in the least degree to my note, this whole contest is to be ascribed and all its consequences. You speak of the execrable paragraph in the Connecticut papers. This, it is true, appeared before Publicola; but it had no more relation to Paine's pamphlet and my note, than to the Alcoran. I am satisfied the writer of it had never seen either;

for when I passed through Connecticut about the middle of June not a copy had ever been seen by anybody, either in Hartford or New Haven, nor probably in the whole State; and that paragraph was so notoriously the reverse of the disinterestedness of character which you are known to possess by everybody who knows your name, that I never heard a person speak of the paragraph, but with an indignation in your behalf which did you entire justice. This paragraph, then, certainly did not flow from my note, any more than the publications which Publicola produced. Indeed it was impossible that my note should occasion your name to be brought into question; for so far from naming you, I had not even in view any writing which I might suppose to be yours, and the opinions I alluded to were principally those I had heard in common conversation from a sect aiming at the subversion of the present government to bring in their favorite form of a king, lords, and commons. Thus I hope, my dear Sir, that you will see me to have been as ignorant in effect as I was in intention. I was brought before the public without my own consent, and from the first moment of seeing the effect of the real aggression in this business to keep me before the public, I determined that nothing should induce me to put pen to paper in the controversy. The business is now over, and I hope its effects are over, and that our friendship will never be suffered to be committed, whatever use others may think proper to make of our names." Jefferson to Adams, August 30, 1791, *The Writings of Thomas Jefferson,* vol. 7, ed. Albert Ellery Bergh (Washington, D.C.: Jefferson Memorial Association, 1907), 242–45.

10. Monroe to Jefferson, June 17, 1791, *The Writings of James Monroe,* vol. 1, ed. Stanislaus Murray Hamilton (New York: Putnam, 1898), 223.

11. According to Jefferson, "In truth, I did not know myself under the pens either of my friends or foes. It is unfortunate for our peace, that unmerited abuse wounds, while unmerited praise has not the power to heal. These are hard wages for the services of all the active and healthy years of one's life. I had retired after five and twenty years of constant occupation in public affairs, and total abandonment of my own. I retired much poorer than when I entered the public service, and desired nothing but rest and oblivion. My name, however, was again brought forward, without concert or expectation on my part (on my salvation I declare it)." Jefferson to Edward Rutledge, December 27, 1796, *The Writings of Thomas Jefferson,* ed. Paul Leicester Ford, vol. 7 (New York: Putnam, 1896), 93–94.

12. Stephen J. Hartnett and Jennifer R. Mercieca, "'Has Your Courage Rusted?' National Security and the Contested Rhetorical Norms of Republicanism in Post-Revolutionary America, 1798–1801," *Rhetoric and Public Affairs* 9 (2006): 79–112; James Jasinski and Jennifer R. Mercieca, "The Constitutive Approach to Effect and the Alien and Sedition Acts," in *Rhetoric and Public Address in the Twenty-first Century: A Handbook,* ed. Shawn J. Parry-Giles and J. Michael Hogan (Hoboken, N.J.: Wiley–Blackwell Press, forthcoming).

13. See Lester J. Cappon, ed., *The Adams-Jefferson Letters: The Complete Correspondence between Thomas Jefferson and Abigail and John Adams,* 2 vols. (Chapel Hill: University of North Carolina Press, 1959).

14. Rush to John Adams, October 16, 1809, *Pennsylvania Magazine of History and*

Biography 70 (1946): 109–10, 109; Joseph Ellis, *Founding Brothers: The Revolutionary Generation* (New York: Knopf, 2000), 220.

15. Benjamin Rush to John Adams, October 16, 1809, ibid., 110.

16. John Adams to Rush, October 25, 1809, *Old Family Letters Copied from the Originals for Alexander Biddle,* Series A (Philadelphia: Lippincott, 1892), 244–47, 246.

17. Cappon, *Adams-Jefferson Letters,* 1:xlvi.

18. Jefferson to John Adams, 28 October 1813, ibid., 2:389.

19. John Adams to Jefferson, 14 August 1813, ibid., 365.

20. John Adams to Jefferson, September 2, 1813, ibid., 371.

21. Douglass Adair, *Fame and the Founding Fathers* (Indianapolis: Liberty Fund, 1998).

22. Jefferson to John Adams, October 28, 1813, in Cappon, *Adams-Jefferson Letters,* 2:388.

23. John Adams to Jefferson, November 15, 1813, ibid., 401.

24. Regina Morantz, "'Democracy' and 'Republic' in American Ideology, 1787–1840" (Ph.D. diss. Columbia University, 1971).

25. Jefferson to William Short, January 8, 1825, *Letters and Addresses of Thomas Jefferson,* ed. William B. Parker and Jonas Viles (New York: Unit Book Publishing, 1905), 283; Jefferson to Martin Van Buren, June 29, 1824, *The Writings of Thomas Jefferson,* vol. 15, ed. Albert Ellery Bergh (Washington, D.C.: Thomas Jefferson Memorial Association, 1907), 52–69.

26. James A. Bear Jr., "The Last Few Days in the Life of Thomas Jefferson," *Magazine of Albemarle County History* 32 (1974), quoted in Andrew Burstein, *America's Jubilee: How in 1826 a Generation Remembered Fifty Year of Independence* (New York: Knopf, 2001), 263.

27. I heartily agree with Stephen Browne's description of Jefferson's rhetorical style as "felicitous republicanism." See his *Jefferson's Call for Nationhood: The First Inaugural Address* (College Station: Texas A&M University Press, 2003), 88–131. For an excellent history of how Americans have appropriated Jefferson for their own purposes, see Merrill D. Peterson, *The Jefferson Image in the American Mind* (Charlottesville: University Press of Virginia, 1998). For example, in 1852 Oliver B. Bunce asked Americans to "see into the hearts" of the heroes of the Revolution, for the stories of their heroism would be "the surest preservers of a people's patriotism, and the most certain link between the present and former ages." *The Romance of the Revolution, Being a History of the Personal Adventures, Heroic Exploits, and Romantic Incidents as Enacted in the War of Independence* (New York: Bunce and Brother, 1852), xii.

28. Thomas Jefferson, "Mr. Jefferson's Last Letter," June 24, 1826, An American Time Capsule: Three Centuries of Broadsides and other Printed Ephemera, Portfolio 153, Folder 1, Library of Congress.

29. According to Carl Becker, "This title [The Declaration of Independence] is not, strictly speaking, the official title of the document in question. The document never knew itself, in any of its various forms, by that name. Jefferson, in making the first draft, gave it the following title: *A Declaration by the Representatives of*

the United States of American, in General Congress assembled. This title was retained in all the copies of the Declaration, except the engrossed parchment copy. On the 19 of July, 1776, Congress voted that the Declaration be engrossed on parchment, 'with the title and stile of *The unanimous Declaration of the thirteen united States of America.*' It is true, the Declaration, in the form adopted by Congress, incorporates in its final paragraph the resolution of July 2; and so the Declaration may be said to be a declaration of independence, inasmuch as in it Congress once more declared what it had already declared two days before. Nevertheless, the primary purpose of the Declaration was not to declare independence, but to proclaim to the world the reasons for declaring independence. It was intended as a formal justification of an act already accomplished." *The Declaration of Independence: A Study in the History of Political Ideas* (New York: Vintage Books, 1958), 4–5. For more on this question see Pauline Maier, *American Scripture: Making the Declaration of Independence* (New York: Vintage Books, 1998); Garry Wills, *Inventing America: Jefferson's Declaration of Independence* (Garden City, N.Y.: Doubleday, 1978); and Stephen E. Lucas, "The Rhetorical Ancestry of the Declaration of Independence," *Rhetoric and Public Affairs* 1 (1998): 143–84.

30. Jefferson, "Last Letter," 1; Douglass Adair, "Rumbold's Dying Speech, 1685, and Jefferson's Last Words on Democracy, 1826," *William and Mary Quarterly* 9 (1952): 521–31. According to Adair, "On the scaffold, Colonel Rumbold, as was the custom, made a speech justifying his actions. One of the most striking statements in it was that 'there was no man born marked by God above another; for none comes into the world with a saddle on his back, neither any booted and spurr'd to ride him'" (525).

31. George Campbell, *The Philosophy of Rhetoric* (New York: Harper and Brothers, 1849), 97; Giambattista Vico, *The New Science,* trans. Thomas Goddard Bergin and Max Harold Fish (Ithaca: Cornell University Press, 1744/1968), 129.

32. See, for example, Chilton Williamson, *American Suffrage: From Property to Democracy, 1760–1860* (Princeton: Princeton University Press, 1960); M. D. Naar, *The Law of Suffrage and Elections* (Trenton: Naar, Day and Naar, 1880); Kirk H. Porter, *A History of Suffrage in the United States* (New York: Greenwood Press, 1918); Dudley O. McGovney, *The American Suffrage Medley: The Need for a National Uniform Suffrage* (Chicago: University of Chicago Press, 1949); and Alexander Keyssar, *The Right to Vote: The Contested History of Democracy in the United States* (New York: Basic Books, 2000).

33. Arthur M. Schlesinger Jr., *The Age of Jackson* (Boston: Little, Brown, 1945), 30.

34. Charles Sellers, *The Market Revolution: Jacksonian America, 1815–1846* (New York: Oxford University Press, 1991), 239.

35. "Nearly" bankrupt is a charitable description of Jefferson's financial status. The newspapers from 1825 to after his death are full of embarrassing articles about Jefferson's desperate financial situation.

36. Bear, "The Last Few Days in the Life of Thomas Jefferson," quoted in Burstein, *America's Jubilee,* 263.

37. David McCullough, *John Adams* (New York: Simon and Schuster, 2001), 649.

38. As Douglass Adair has observed, Jefferson's choice of epitaphs was a "final reminder of how seriously he took [Francis] Bacon's hierarchy of fame set forth in the *Advancement of Learning* and its promise of immortality to scientist-legislators." *Fame and the Founding Fathers,* 27.

39. McCullough, *John Adams,* 649. Details of Adams's last days were taken from McCullough and Burstein, although neither described exactly the same scene.

40. John Adams to Jefferson, July 3, 1813, Cappon, *Adams-Jefferson Letters,* 2:349.

41. John Adams to Rush, March 23, 1809, *The Spur of Fame: Dialogues of John Adams and Benjamin Rush, 1805–1813,* ed. John A. Schultz and Douglass Adair (San Marino, Calif.: Huntington Library, 1966), 139.

42. "On the Deaths of Presidents Jefferson and Adams," *Georgetown Metropolitan-Extra,* July 12, 1826.

43. Clay to John Quincy Adams, July 25, 1826, *The Papers of Henry Clay,* 10 vols. (Lexington: University of Kentucky Press, 1959–92), 5:567–68. On the importance of personal honor to the revolutionary generation see Joanne B. Freeman, *Affairs of Honor: National Politics in the New Republic* (New Haven: Yale University Press, 2002).

44. "Another Coincidence," *New Hampshire Gazette,* July 25, 1826, 2; *Georgetown Metropolitan,* July 10, 1826.

45. Sacvan Bercovitch, *The Rites of Assent: Transformations in the Symbolic Construction of America* (New York: Routledge, 1993), 80; Kurt W. Ritter, "American Political Rhetoric and the Jeremiad Tradition: Presidential Nomination Acceptance Addresses, 1960–1976," *Central States Speech Journal* 31 (1980): 153–71.

46. "Miscellany," *Vermont Gazette,* July 25, 1826, 2.

47. *Philadelphia National Gazette,* July 8, 1826.

48. "Death of John Adams," *Charleston Courier,* July 17, 1826, 2.

49. *New York American,* July 8, 1826.

50. "Funeral Procession and Eulogium," *Charleston Courier,* July 19, 1826, 2.

51. *Maryland Gazette,* July 13, 1826, 2.

52. Elizabeth Wirt to William Wirt, July 6, 1828, William Wirt Papers, Massachusetts Historical Society, quoted in Burstein, *America's Jubilee,* 274.

53. Charles Warren, "Fourth of July Myths," *William and Mary Quarterly* 2 (1945): 251.

54. "Adams and Jefferson," *The Masonic Mirror and Mechanic's Intelligencer,* July 15, 1826, 230. According to Andrew Burstein, newspapers like the July 15, 1826, edition of the *Niles Weekly Register* published similar accounts: "It was, Niles asserted, concurring with the *United States Gazette,* 'nearly if not precisely' the hour of Jefferson's death when the Declaration was approved, and 'nearly, if not precisely' the same hour that Adams died when the Declaration was 'first proclaimed' in the state-house yard in Philadelphia." *America's Jubilee,* 275.

55. According to James M. Farrell, the eulogy was considered "a masterwork of American eloquence" almost immediately after it was delivered. "The Speech Within: Trope and Performance in Daniel Webster's Eulogy to Adams and Jeffer-

son," in *Rhetoric and Political Culture in Nineteenth Century America,* ed. Thomas W. Benson (East Lansing: Michigan State University Press, 1997), 17; see also Stephen H. Browne, "Webster's Eulogy and the Tropes of Public Memory," in *Rhetoric and Political Culture in Nineteenth Century America,* ed. Thomas W. Benson (East Lansing: Michigan State University Press, 1997), 39–45.

56. Daniel Webster, *A Discourse in Commemoration of the Lives and Services of John Adams and Thomas Jefferson, Delivered in Faneuil Hall, Boston, August 2, 1826* (Boston: Cummings, Hilliard, 1826), 6, 8, 59, 60. For a sampling of eulogies delivered around the nation see *A Selection of Eulogies, Pronounced in the Several States, in Honor of those Illustrious Patriots and Statesmen, John Adams and Thomas Jefferson* (Hartford: D. F. Robinson and Norton and Russell, 1826).

57. John Quincy Adams, Inaugural Address, *Journal of the Executive Proceedings of the Senate of the United States of America, 1789–1873* (Washington, D.C.: Printed by order of the Senate of the United States), March 4, 1825.

58. Joyce Appleby, *Inheriting the Revolution: The First Generation of Americans* (Cambridge: Belknap Press, 2001), 265.

59. George B. Forgie, *Patricide in the House Divided: A Psychological Interpretation of Lincoln and His Age* (New York: Norton, 1979), 6.

60. Peterson, *The Jefferson Image in the American Mind,* 5.

61. Burstein, *America's Jubilee,* 6.

62. Hannah Arendt, *The Human Condition* (Chicago: University of Chicago Press, 1958), 186. Stephen H. Browne, "Remembering Crispus Attucks: Race, Rhetoric, and the Politics of Commemoration," *Quarterly Journal of Speech* 85 (1999): 169–87, 169. For more on public memory see Kendall R. Phillips, ed., *Framing Public Memory* (Tuscaloosa: University of Alabama Press, 2004); Kathleen J. Turner, ed., *Doing Rhetorical History: Concepts and Cases* (Tuscaloosa: University of Alabama Press, 1998); Stephen H. Browne, "Review Essay: Reading, Rhetoric, and the Texture of Public Memory," *Quarterly Journal of Speech* 81 (1995): 237–65.

63. Celeste Condit, "The Functions of Epideictic: The Boston Massacre Orations as Exemplar," *Communication Quarterly* 33 (1985): 284–98.

64. Seymour Lipset, *American Exceptionalism: A Double-Edged Sword* (New York: Norton and Norton, 1996).

65. Jim Cullen, *The American Dream: A Short History of an Idea That Shaped a Nation* (New York: Oxford University Press 2003).

66. I am indebted to Stirling Newberry for this observation. See note 82 in chapter 1 for more on jeremiadic rhetoric.

67. A Democrat, "Miscellany from the New Hampshire Patriot," *New Hampshire Gazette,* September 12, 1826.

68. Richard Hofstadter, *The Idea of the Party System: The Rise of Legitimate Opposition in the United States, 1780–1840* (Berkley: University of California Press, 1969), 248.

69. Sean Wilentz, *The Rise of American Democracy: Jefferson to Lincoln* (New York: Norton, 2005), 182.

Chapter 5

1. Noah Webster to William Stone, August 29, 1837, *Letters of Noah Webster,* ed. Harry R. Warfel (New York: Library Publishers, 1953), 504–6.

2. According to Regina Morantz, "As the word democracy became acceptable, its meaning began to change. It was now understood in it very general sense, as connoting a large degree of popular sovereignty." "'Democracy' and 'Republic' in American Ideology, 1787–1840" (Ph.D. thesis, Columbia University, 1971), 153.

3. James Madison, "Parties," *National Gazette,* January 23, 1792.

4. George Washington, Farewell Address, September 19, 1796, *American Daily Advertiser.*

5. Thomas Jefferson, First Inaugural Address, *Thomas Jefferson: Writings,* ed. Merrill D. Peterson (New York: Library of America, 1984), 493; James M. Banner Jr., *To the Hartford Convention: The Federalists and the Origins of Party Politics in Massachusetts, 1789–1815* (New York: Knopf, 1970).

6. *Columbian Centinel,* July 12, 1817, 2.

7. C. Edward Skeen, *1816: America Rising* (Lexington: University Press of Kentucky, 2003), 13.

8. *Annals of Congress,* 14th Cong., 1st sess., 1127.

9. Ibid., 1130.

10. Ibid., 1160.

11. Ibid., 1161.

12. Ibid.

13. Ibid., 1168.

14. Ibid., 185, 203–4.

15. *Examiner: Containing Political Essays on the Most Important Events of the Time,* March 25, 1816, 233–34.

16. "Compensation Bill, OR Fifteen Hundred Dollars for a Member of Congress," *Federal Republican,* June 17, 1816, 34.

17. "From the Republican Constellation: Compensation Bill," *Western American,* August 3, 1816, 1.

18. "Double Pay of Congress," *Pittsfield (Mass.) Sun,* July 4, 1816, 3.

19. *The People's Advocate,* November 20, 1816, 3.

20. "The Compensation Bill," *Niles Weekly Register,* July 20, 1816, 339.

21. "Compensation Law," *Columbian,* August 16, 1816, 2.

22. "Rising the Tempest," *Richmond Enquirer,* September 6, 1816, 1.

23. *Washington City Weekly Gazette,* August 17, 1816, 2.

24. *Columbian,* April 29, 1816, 297.

25. John C. Calhoun to Alexander J. Dallas, June 15, 1816, *The Papers of John C. Calhoun,* vol. 1, *1801–1817,* ed. Robert L. Meriwether (Columbia: University of South Carolina Press, 1959), 361–62.

26. "The Compensation Bill," *Niles Weekly Register,* July 20, 1816, 340.

27. *Country Courier,* July 11, 1816, 156.

28. *Weekly Messenger,* November 14, 1816, 76.

29. "The Compensation Bill," *Niles Weekly Register,* July 20, 1816, 340.

30. Kenneth C. Martis, *The Historical Atlas of Political Parties in the United States Congress* (New York: Macmillan, 1989).

31. "Compensation Bill," *National Register,* July 6, 1816, 290.

32. *Western Monitor,* July 12, 1816, 1.

33. *People's Advocate,* October 29, 1816, 4; "The Compensation Bill," *Niles Weekly Register,* July 20, 1816, 340.

34. "The Compensation Law," *Essex Register,* July 20, 1816, 1.

35. *New York Evening Post,* July 23, 1816, 2.

36. *Albany Advertiser,* December 19, 1816, 3.

37. "The Compensation Law," *Daily National Intelligencer,* August 9, 1816, 2; "Political," *Albany Advertiser,* November 16, 1816, 2.

38. Henry Adams, *The History of the United States of America during the Second Administration of James Madison,* vol. 3 (New York: Scribner, 1904), 138, 144.

39. *Annals of Congress,* 14th Cong., 2nd sess., 625.

40. Ibid., 517.

41. Ibid., 543.

42. Ibid., 237.

43. Ibid., 498.

44. Ibid., 512.

45. Ibid., 553.

46. Ibid., 627.

47. Ibid., 664.

48. See Robert L. Ivie's analysis of the "distemper of democracy" for an extended discussion of elite distrust of the people's ability to withstand demagoguery in his *Democracy and America's War on Terror* (Tuscaloosa: University of Alabama Press, 2006).

49. *Annals of Congress,* 14th Cong., 2nd sess., 544.

50. Ibid., 1st Cong., 1 sess., 760.

51. Ibid., 766–67.

52. Ibid., 14th Cong., 2nd sess., 490.

53. Ibid., 545.

54. Ibid., 650.

55. Ibid., 674–75.

56. Ibid., 648.

57. Ibid., 625–27.

58. Ibid., 666.

59. Ibid., 577.

60. Ibid., 549.

61. Ibid., 321.

62. Ibid., 597.

63. Ibid., 616.

64. Ibid., 518.
65. Ibid., 629–30.
66. Ibid., 628.
67. Ibid., 651.
68. Ibid., 627.
69. Ibid., 499.
70. Ibid., 708.
71. Ibid., 548.
72. Ibid., 530.
73. Ibid., 549.
74. Ibid., 604.
75. Ibid., 690.
76. Ibid., 486.
77. Alexander Keyssar, *The Right to Vote: The Contested History of Democracy in the United States* (New York: Basic Books, 2000), 328–35. See also Chilton Williamson, *American Suffrage: From Property to Democracy, 1760–1860* (Princeton: Princeton University Press, 1960); M. D. Naar, *The Law of Suffrage and Elections* (Trenton: Naar, Day and Naar, 1880); Kirk H. Porter, *A History of Suffrage in the United States* (New York: Greenwood Press, 1918); and Dudley O. McGovney, *The American Suffrage Medley: The Need for a National Uniform Suffrage* (Chicago: University of Chicago Press, 1949).
78. *Baltimore Patriot and Evening Advertiser,* May 30, 1815, 5, 126, p. 2.
79. Richard Hofstadter, *The Idea of a Party System: The Rise of Legitimate Opposition in the United States, 1780–1840* (Berkley: University of California Press, 1969).
80. John Quincy Adams to Alexander Everett, March 1818, quoted in Paul C. Nagel, *John Quincy Adams: A Public Life, and Private Life* (Cambridge: Harvard University Press, 1997), 246.
81. See Jackson to Andrew J. Donelson, January 21, 1824, and Jackson to John Donelson, February 9, 1824, *Correspondence of Andrew Jackson,* ed. John Spencer Bassett, 7 vols. (Washington, D.C.: Carnegie Institution, 1926–35), 3:224–25, 226–27.
82. Clay to Blair, January 8, 1825, *The Papers of Henry Clay,* 10 vols. (Lexington: University of Kentucky Press, 1959–92), 4:9.
83. Clay to Gales and Seaton, January 30, 1825, ibid., 48.
84. Jackson to Swartout, March 5, 1825, *Correspondence of Andrew Jackson,* 3:280.
85. Nathan Sargent, *Public Men and Events from the Commencement of Mr. Monroe's Administration, in 1817, to the Close of Mr. Filmore's Administration, in 1853,* vol. 1 (Philadelphia: Lippincott, 1875), 84.
86. Jackson to William B. Lewis, February 14, 1825, *Correspondence of Andrew Jackson,* 3:276.
87. Jackson to Lee, October 7, 1825, ibid., 291–92.
88. H. W. Brands, *Andrew Jackson: His Life and Times* (New York: Doubleday, 2005), 389.
89. "Mr. Adams, is an open candid man, he has at my Table Publickly answered

Mr Clay that he was in favour of a Judicious Tariff—every person that knows him knows this. Now it is the greatest peace of Hypocrisy, to say that because I voted as every body who knew me, had read my words for years, knew I would—would make this objection. I love a candid open enemy, but a hypocritical friend, who professing friendship acts the hidden enemy, I despise. It is such that injure most. I have good feeling toward Mr Adams, and there is no conduct of Hypocritical friends that can alter this feeling. I wish you so soon as the meeting is over to give me the names of those apostate hypocritical friends that I may know them. They can do me no harm. I never have, or will ask any favour of them." Jackson to William S. Fulton, July 4, 1824, *Correspondence of Andrew Jackson,* 3:261.

90. John Quincy Adams, Inaugural Address, March 4, 1825, in *Inaugural Addresses of the Presidents of the United States: From George Washington to Barack Obama* (Washington, D.C.: Government Printing Office, 1989), www.bartleby.com/124/pres22.html. I am indebted to Jim Aune for this fact.

91. John Quincy Adams, First Annual Message, *The American Presidency Project,* ed. John Woolley and Gerhard Peters, http://www.presidency.ucsb.edu/ws/?pid=29467.

92. Sargent, *Public Men and Events,* 35–36.

93. Clay to George William Featherstonhaugh, January 21, 1825, *Papers of Henry Clay,* 4:34.

94. Henry Clay, "Address to the People of the Congressional District," March 26, 1825, ibid., 143–66; Jackson to Samuel Swartwout, May 16, 1825, *Correspondence of Andrew Jackson,* 3:284.

95. "The whole object of the coalition is to calumniate me, cart loads of coffin hand-bills, forgeries, and pamphlets of the most base calumnies are circulated by the franking privileges of Members of Congress, and Mr. Clay, even, Mrs. J. is not spared, and my pious Mother, nearly fifty years in the tomb, and who, from her cradle to her death, had not a speck upon her character, has been dragged forth by Hammond and held to public scorn as a prostitute who intermarried with a Negro, and my eldest brother sold as a slave in Carolina." Jackson to Brigadier General Richard K. Call, August 16, 1828, *Correspondence of Andrew Jackson,* 3:426.

96. For more on the culture of honor, see Jennifer R. Mercieca, "The Culture of Honor: How Slaveholders Responded to the Abolitionist Mail Crisis of 1835," *Rhetoric and Public Affairs* 10 (2007): 51–76.

97. Jackson to Call, August 16, 1828, *Correspondence of Andrew Jackson,* 3:426.

98. Ibid., 426–27.

99. Jackson to Houston, December 15, 1826, ibid., 325.

100. Hofstadter, *The Idea of a Party System,* 246–47.

101. Martin Van Buren to Thomas Ritchie, January 13, 1827, Van Buren Papers, Library of Congress. "Van Buren the first man in that State is *zealously cordially* and *entirely* with us. He travels to the South with me after the adjournment to spend his Spring in Carolina and Georgia, and next Summer I shall join him at the North, and pass it with *our friends.*" James Hamilton Jr. to Jackson, February 16, 1827, *Correspondence of Andrew Jackson,* 3:344.

102. Hofstadter, *The Idea of the Party System,* 246.

103. Marvin Meyers, *The Jacksonian Persuasion: Politics and Belief* (Stanford: Stanford University Press, 1957), 7.

104. Campbell to Jackson, February 4, 1827, and Hamilton to Jackson, February 16, 1827, *Correspondence of Andrew Jackson,* 3:333, 344.

105. Robert V. Remini, *Andrew Jackson* (New York: HarperCollins, 1969), 110. South Carolina senator Robert Y. Hayne wrote Jackson on June 5, 1827, advising him that since "Mr. Clay *will use every effort to draw you into some public controversy,* whether on the question of *the Tariff,* or *his intrigues,* or any other matter, is to him not very material. . . . In relation to the two great questions of the Tariff and internal improvements, your opinions can need no elucidation." *Correspondence of Andrew Jackson,* 3:358–59.

106. Jackson to George W. Campbell, February 14, 1828, *Correspondence of Andrew Jackson,* 3:390–91.

107. Jackson to Sam Houston, December 15, 1826, ibid., 325.

108. From "Obediah Penn" to the United States Telegraph, July 7, 1827, *Papers of Henry Clay,* 6:697.

109. *Boston Masonic Mirror,* May 28, 1831, 382.

110. Samuel D. Ingham, "An Exposition of the Political Character and Principles of John Quincy Adams Showing by Historical Documents and Incontestible Facts that he was educated a Monarchist: has always been hostile to Popular Government, and particularly to its great bulwark, the Right of Suffrage: and that he affected to become a Republican only to attain the power to pervert and degrade the Democratic Party; and to pave the way for such a change of the Constitution as would establish the United States, and Aristocratical and Hereditary Government" (Washington, D.C.: Duff Green, 1827), 1.

111. For example, Old Hillsborough used arguments from Ingham's "Exposition" in his August 18, 1828, *New Hampshire Patriot and State Gazette* attack on Adams.

112. Ingham, "Exposition," 7.

113. Ibid., 9. "Can any one read Mr. Adams' defence of the American constitutions without seeing that he was a monarchist? And J. Q. Adams, the son, was more explicit than the father, in his answer to Paine's rights of man. So much for leaders. Their followers were divided." Thomas Jefferson to William Short, January 8, 1825, *The Writings of Thomas Jefferson,* vol. 7, ed. H. A. Washington (New York: Derby and Jackson, 1859), 390.

114. Ingham, "Exposition," 10.

115. Ibid., 20.

116. "[The Federalist Party] was thereby broken down, by Jefferson and Samuel Adams, and men like them, succeeded in satisfying them of their error in respect to the outlines of the Constitution, and Madison procured the adoption of amendments that obviated their other objections and, as I have said before, a cordial and enduring union was formed between them and the Republicans, under the latter name. Since that period the party has undergone no change, either in its organiza-

tion, its principles, or the general political dispositions of the individuals of which it has been composed. Its name has been changed from Republican to Democratic, in consequence of the increasing popular development of its course and principles, and in some degree by the circumstance that its old opponent had assumed the name of Federal Republican and by a natural desire to keep the line of demarcation between them as broad and as well defined as possible." Martin Van Buren, *An Inquiry in the Origin and Course of Political Parties in the United States,* ed. Smith T. Van Buren (New York: Hurd and Houghton, 1867), 270.

117. Henry Louis Gates, *The Signifying Monkey: A Theory of African-American Literary Criticism* (New York: Oxford University Press, 1989), 44–45.

118. Jackson to Swartwout, February 22, 1825, *Correspondence of Andrew Jackson,* 3:278–80.

119. James Porton, *Life of Andrew Jackson,* vol. 1 (New York: Mason Brothers, 1860), 297–304.

120. *Connecticut Journal,* March 4, 1817, 2; *Boston Gazette,* March 27, 1817, 2; *Connecticut Journal,* April 1, 1817, 2; *Newburyport Herald,* April 1, 1817, 1; *Rhode Island American,* April 1, 1817, 2; *Boston Commercial Gazette,* November 4, 1822, 2; "Divide and Conquer," *Newbury Herald,* April 1, 1823, 2; *New Hampshire Patriot,* May 5, 1823, 1; *Watch Tower,* May 4, 1823, 1; *Eastern Argus,* May 6, 1823, 2; *Portsmouth Journal of Literature and Politics,* May 17, 1823, 1; *New-Hampshire Patriot and State Gazette,* January 23, 1826, 1; *New-Hampshire Gazette,* May 13, 1828, 2; *Eastern Argus,* November 21, 1828, 2.

121. James Boyd White, *When Words Lose Their Meaning: Constitutions and Reconstitution of Language, Character, and Community* (Chicago: University of Chicago Press, 1984), 3. For more on the idea of the "empty signifier" and its application to political discourse see Ernesto Laclau, *Emancipation(s)* (London: Verso, 1996), 36–47.

122. *Pittsfield Sun,* April 1, 1830; *Salem Gazette,* April 2, 1830.

123. Jackson to Coffee, December 11, 1828, *Correspondence of Andrew Jackson,* 3:452.

124. Esther Singleton, *The Story of the White House* (New York: McClure, 1907), 195–96.

125. Daniel Webster to Ezekiel Webster, February 23, 1829, and Daniel Webster, "Memorandum," February 1829, *The Letters of Daniel Webster from Documents Owned Principally by the New Hampshire Historical Society,* ed. C. H. Van Tyne (New York: McClure, Phillips, 1902), 142.

126. Daniel Webster to Ezekiel Webster, February 5, 1829, ibid., 144.

127. Lyn Ragsdale, *Vital Statistics on the Presidency* (Washington, D.C.: Congressional Quarterly Press, 1998), 132–38.

128. Martin Van Buren, *The Autobiography of Martin Van Buren,* ed. John C. Fitzpatrick (Washington, D.C.: Government Printing Office, 1920), 275.

129. Ibid., 276.

130. Ibid., 284, 288.

131. Ibid., 295.

132. Amy F. Sturgis, *The Trail of Tears and Indian Removal* (Westport, Conn.: Greenwood Press, 2006), 2.

133. Andrew Jackson, First Annual Message, December 8, 1829, The American Presidency Project, www.presidency.ucsb.edu/ws/index.php?pid=29471.

134. *Baltimore Patriot,* January 6, 1830, 3.

135. *New York Daily Advertiser,* January 20, 1830, 2.

136. Mary Hershberger, "Mobilizing Women, Anticipating Abolition: The Struggle against Indian Removal in the 1830s," *Journal of American History* 86 (1999): 15–40, 25, 15; Susan Zaeske, *Signatures of Citizenship: Petitioning, Antislavery, and Women's Political Identity* (Chapel Hill: University of North Carolina Press, 2003), 23; Alisse Portnoy, *Their Right to Speak: Women's Activism in the Indian Removal and Abolition Campaigns* (Cambridge: Harvard University Press, 2005).

137. *Pittsfield Sun,* January 27, 1831, 3.

138. *Register of Debates in Congress,* 21st Cong., 1st sess., vol. 6 (Washington, D.C.: Gales and Seaton, 1825–37), 506.

139. Ibid., 506–11.

140. The Senate voted in favor of removal 28 to 19 on April 24, and the House voted in favor of removal 102 to 97 on May 26.

141. I say "reportedly" because according to Charles Warren it is likely a fabrication of Horace Greely. *The Supreme Court in United States History* (Boston: Little, Brown, 1922), 2:219.

142. Jackson to Lewis, August 25, 1830, *Correspondence of Andrew Jackson,* 4:177–78.

143. William W. Freehling, *The Road to Disunion: Secessionists at Bay, 1776–1854* (Oxford: Oxford University Press, 1990); Lyon Rathbun, "The Debate over Annexing Texas and the Emergence of Manifest Destiny," *Rhetoric and Public Affairs* 4 (2001): 459–93; Susan Zaeske, "Signatures of Citizenship: The Rhetoric of Women's Antislavery Petitions," *Quarterly Journal of Speech* 88 (2002): 147–68; Zaeske, *Signatures of Citizenship;* Cal M. Logue, "Transcending Coercion: The Communicative Strategies of Black Slaves on Antebellum Plantations," *Quarterly Journal of Speech* 67 (1981): 31–46; Michael William Pfau, "Time, Tropes, and Textuality: Reading Republicanism in Charles Sumner's 'Crime against Kansas,'" *Rhetoric and Public Affairs* 6 (2003): 385–414; Gary S. Selby, "Mocking the Sacred: Fredrick Douglass's 'Slaveholder's Sermon' and the Antebellum Debate over Religion and Slavery," *Quarterly Journal of Speech* 88 (2002): 326–41; William E. Wiethoff, "The Nature and Limits of Slave Insolence in the American South," *Quarterly Journal of Speech* 87 (2001): 197–207; David Zarefsky, "Rhetorical Interpretations of the American Civil War," *Quarterly Journal of Speech* 81 (1995): 108–38; David Zarefsky, "The Continuing Fascination with Lincoln," *Rhetoric and Public Affairs* 6 (2003): 337–70; Stephen Browne, "'Like Gory Spectres': Representing Evil in Theodore Weld's American Slavery As It Is," *Quarterly Journal of Speech* 80 (1994): 277–92; E. Culpepper Clark, "Pitchfork Ben Tillman and the Emergence of Southern

Demagoguery," *Quarterly Journal of Speech* 69 (1983): 423–33; Donald K. Enholm, David Curtis Skaggs, and W. Jeffrey Welsh, "Origins of the Southern Mind: The Parochial Sermons of Thomas Cradock of Maryland, 1744–1770," *Quarterly Journal of Speech* 73 (1987): 200–218; V. William Balthrop, "Culture, Myth, and Ideology as Public Argument: An Interpretation of the Ascent and Demise of 'Southern Culture'," *Communication Monographs* 51 (1984): 339–52; Kirt H. Wilson, "The Racial Politics of Imitation in the Nineteenth Century," *Quarterly Journal of Speech* 89 (2003): 89–108; Mercieca, "The Culture of Honor."

144. See "Detestable Villainy" from the *National Intelligencer* and the *Southern Patriot,* both of July 29, 1835.

145. Andrew Jackson, Annual Message, *Congressional Globe,* Senate, 24th Cong., 1st sess., December 8, 1835, 10.

146. *Register of Debates,* 24th Cong., 1st sess., 1961.

147. William Lee Miller, *Arguing about Slavery: John Quincy Adams and the Great Battle in the United States Congress* (New York: Vintage, 1998), 111.

148. Ibid., 28.

149. *Register of Debates,* 1961.

150. Ibid., 1966.

151. Ibid.

152. William Cost Johnson, January 28, 1840, *Congressional Globe,* 150. Rule 21 read: "No petition, memorial, resolution, or other paper praying the abolition of slavery in the District of Columbia, or any State of Territory, or the slave trade between the States or Territories of the United States, in which it now exists, shall be received by the House, or entertained in any way whatever."

153. Andrew Jackson, President Jackson's Veto Message Regarding the Bank of the United States, July 10, 1832, in *A Compilation of the Messages and Papers of the Presidents,* ed. James D. Richardson, 11 vols. (New York: Bureau of National Literature and Art, 1789–1908), 2:576–606.

154. Jackson, First Annual Message.

155. "It may be, sir, that the politicians of the State of New York are not so fastidious as some gentleman are, as to disclosing the principles on which they act. They boldly preach what they practice. When they are contending for victory they avow their intention of enjoying the fruits of it. If they are defeated, they expect to retire from office. If they are successful, they claim, as a matter of right, the advantages of success. They see nothing wrong in the rule, that to the victor belong the spoils of the enemy." William L. Marcy, Speech in the Senate on the Confirmation of Martin Van Buren to Minister to England, January 25, 1832, in Sargent, *Public Men and Events,* 200; "We know not what line of policy General Jackson will adopt. We take it for granted, however, that HE WILL REWARD HIS FRIENDS AND PUNISH HIS ENEMIES." *United States Telegraph,* November 2, 1828.

156. David Crockett, *The Life of Martin Van Buren, Heir Apparent to the "Government," and the Appointed Successor of General Andrew Jackson Containing Every Authentic*

Particular by Which His Extraordinary Character Has Been Formed With A Concise History of the Events That Have Occasioned His Unparalleled Elevation; Together With a Review of His Policy as a Statesman (New York: Nafis and Cornish, 1845).

157. Andrew Jackson, Farewell Address, March 4, 1837, in Richardson, *Compilation of the Messages and Papers of the Presidents,* 3:292–308, 307.

158. Ibid., 293.

159. Noah Webster to William Stone, August 29, 1837, *Letters of Noah Webster,* 504–6.

160. Jackson, Farewell Address, 295.

161. Freehling, *The Road to Disunion;* Keyssar, *The Right to Vote.*

162. See note 143 in this chapter for the work of rhetorical scholars on slavery and southern culture.

163. Freehling, *The Road to Disunion,* 450.

164. John Quincy Adams, *Parties in the United States,* ed. Charles True Adams (New York: Greenburg, 1941), 10.

165. Robert Gray Gunderson, *The Log-Cabin Campaign* (Lexington: University of Kentucky Press, 1957).

166. "Position of Parties," *The American Review: A Whig Journal of Politics, Literature, Art and Science* 1 (1845): 17–18.

167. "There are usually several motives involved in any particular act. But where there is such 'conjunct action of motives,' the speaker may represent the lot by selecting one motive as significant and neglecting the others. Such a procedure is inevitable, since any decision usually sums up a complexity of motives. Rhetorically, this fact invites to censorial appellatives since, if the speaker is identifying an act of his own, or of an ally, he can gain an easy advantage by picking out the most favorable motives and presenting it as either predominant or exclusive (or as the one that sets the tone for the lot). And conversely, he can select the least favorable to name the essence of an enemy's motives. But, sometimes 'no such sufficiently respected motive can be found'—and then, Bentham observes, instead of the actual motive, a speaker may select some other which 'shall, by the nearness of its connexion with the actual one, have been rendered most difficultly distinguishable from it.' He calls such changes 'substituted' or 'covering' motives." Kenneth Burke, *Rhetoric of Motives* (Berkley: University of California Press, 1969), 99.

168. George Sidney Camp, *Democracy* (New York: Harper and Brothers, Cliff-St., 1841), 11.

169. "Position of Parties," 17–18.

170. Crockett, *The Life of Martin Van Buren,* 3.

171. William L. Marcy, Speech in the Senate on the Confirmation of Martin Van Buren to Minister to England, January 25, 1832, in Sargent, *Public Men and Events,* 200.

172. *United States Telegraph,* December 2, 1828.

173. Quoted in Hofstadter, *The Idea of a Party System,* 244.

174. John Niven, *Martin Van Buren: The Romantic Age of American Politics* (Newtown, Conn.: American Political Biography Press, 2004), 63–64.

175. Joel H. Silbey, *Martin Van Buren and the Emergence of American Popular Politics* (Lanham, Md.: Rowman and Littlefield, 2002), 25.

176. "Party, or rather faction, is every thing. The people at elections move as armies do, under command. The mind that directs is not that of the people, or of any great part of them, but of men who are called leaders—an oligarchy to all intents and purposes. Their leaders were, in general, aware that Van Buren had no principles whatever—that he had professed every thing, or anything, and had been on any and every side—but they endorsed his orthodoxy, because he suited their purposes, and he succeeded." William L. Mackenzie, *The Life and Times of Martin Van Buren: The Correspondence of His Friends, Family and Pupils Together with Brief Notices, Sketches, and Anecdotes, Illustrative of the Public Career of . . .* (Boston: Cooke, 1846), 31.

Conclusion

1. Michael C. McGee, "'Not Men, but Measures': The Origins and Import of an Ideological Principle," *Quarterly Journal of Speech* 64 (1978): 141–54, 142.

2. Regina Morantz, "'Democracy' and 'Republic' in American Ideology, 1787–1840" (Ph.D. thesis, Columbia University, 1971); Russell L. Hanson, *The Democratic Imagination in America: Conversations with Our Past* (Princeton: Princeton University Press, 1985); Arthur M. Schlesinger Jr., *The Age of Jackson* (Boston: Little, Brown, 1945); Sean Wilentz, *The Rise of American Democracy: Jefferson to Lincoln* (New York: Norton, 2005). "It is our common belief that our government is distinguished in principle from other governments, is radically different. If a man were seriously to propose for our adoption monarchical or aristocratical institutions, he would be overwhelmed with public obloquy. We should feel, not as if he were indulging a mere harmless error of the understanding, not as if he had erred simply on a question of expediency, but as if he had been guilty of a moral delinquency on a moral question; and, should he actually attempt to carry his plans into execution, he would be execrated as a public traitor having designs upon our liberties; no party, and no individual, but would shun the contamination of his alliance." George Sidney Camp, *Democracy* (New York: Harper and Brothers, Cliff-St., 1841) 12.

3. Alexis de Tocqueville, *Democracy in America* (New York: Signet Classics, 2001), 57.

4. Matthew J. Mancini, *Alexis de Tocqueville and American Intellectuals: From His Times to Ours* (Lanham, Md.: Rowman and Littlefield, 2006).

5. International Institute for Democracy and Electoral Assistance (International IDEA) Strömsborg, SE-103 34 Stockholm, Sweden, 2008, available at http://www.idea.int/vt/survey/voter_turnout_pop2-2.cfm.

6. Michael Shudson, *The Good Citizen: A History of American Civic Life* (New

York: The Free Press, 1998); Rogers M. Smith, *Civic Ideals: Conflicting Visions of Citizenship in U.S. History* (New Haven: Yale University Press, 1997).

7. Robert L. Ivie, *Democracy and America's War on Terror* (Tuscaloosa: University of Alabama Press, 2006), 63.

8. Jacques Rancière, *Hatred of Democracy,* trans. Steve Corcoran (London: Verso, 2007), 36.

9. Ivie, *Democracy and America's War on Terror,* 74, 78.

10. Michael Hardt and Antonio Negri, *Multitude: War and Democracy in an Age of Empire* (New York: Penguin Press, 2004), 99–100.

11. Benjamin R. Barber, *Consumed: How Markets Corrupt Children, Infantilize Adults, and Swallow Citizens Whole* (New York: Norton, 2007); Robert Asen, "A Discourse Theory of Citizenship," *Quarterly Journal of Speech* 90 (2004): 189–211.

12. Thomas Jefferson to James Madison, January 30, 1787, *The Writings of Thomas Jefferson,* vol. 5, ed. Albert Ellery Bergh (Washington, D.C.: Thomas Jefferson Memorial Association, 1907), 63–73, 65.

Index